To M.H.Holten with best wishes
and kind regards

Marihuana—

Deceptive Weed

Gabriel G. Nahas, O.B.E., M.D., Ph.D.

Professor of Anesthesiology
College of Physicians & Surgeons of Columbia University
New York, N.Y.

Foreword by W. D. M. Paton, C.B.E., F.R.S., D.M.
University of Oxford

Raven Press, Publishers • New York

Made in the United States of America

International Standard Book Number 0–911216–39–1
Library of Congress Catalog Card Number 72–76743

To

Michele
Anthony
Christiane

and all their young friends
so that they may build a
better world.

Homo sum; nil humani a me alienum est, puto.
Plautus, 100 A.D.

Foreword

This book fills an important gap. The literature on *Cannabis* is unusual and awkward for those seeking to learn about it. There is a mass of older material, often interesting and amusing, illuminating about the attitudes and problems of the time, but of limited relevance to the decisions taken today, with vastly changed medical and social conditions. The more recent material includes, of course, many research papers in scientific journals and symposia, and very valuable are the recent summary reports from the U.S. Department of Health, Education and Welfare and the World Health Organization. But if one seeks a single, reasonably comprehensive, general account with a general medical background, there has been none published. Psychiatry, law, sociology, pharmacology, and journalism have produced their authors, but this is the first book to come from an author experienced in pharmacology as well as medicine. It is its realistic, medically responsible approach that gives this book such a freshness of outlook in a controversial field.

Dr. Nahas has come to the conclusion, which I share, that the innocuousness of *Cannabis* is being overstated, and its dangers underestimated. The term "deceptive weed" is very apt, and reflects the unusual nature of the drug and its actions. But the particular opinions of authors are less important than the evidence and the argument. Here the reader will find, not only a general account of the plant and of the history of its use, but also the scientific and medical evidence so often neglected or discounted. In discussing *Cannabis* and social policy, a major effort of the imagination is needed. If legislation is introduced which facilitates its use, one must try to assess how, in subsequent decades, the pattern of use would change, particularly in frequency, quantity and potency; and then one must try to assess the medical and social consequences for our own society. In this extrapolation, rarely attempted in considering drug use although familiar enough in the fields of *external* pollution or population problems, all the information one can gather, whether in animals or in man, whether with marihuana or with preparations richer in the active resin, is important. It is by weighing such possibilities that this book provides the best general account yet available.

W.D.M. Paton, C.B.E., F.R.S., D.M.
Professor of Pharmacology
University of Oxford, and
Fellow of Balliol College, Oxford

Acknowledgments

I first should mention my mentors in medicine, the late Dr. Selim Nahas, Dr. Albert Nahas, Prof. Louis Bugnard, the late Prof. J. Ducuing, Prof. Yves Laporte, the late Prof. W. O. Fenn, the late Dr. Albert Schweitzer, Prof. A. Cournand, Prof. H. Rahn, Dr. J. Armstrong, Prof. E. H. Wood, Prof. L. Kuhn, and Prof. D. V. Habif. They may not have agreed with my treatment of some aspects of this subject, but they firmly and kindly guided my first and later steps in the field of clinical and experimental medicine, for which I am grateful.

My colleagues and friends, Drs. W. M. Manger, M. Bessis, R. E. Esser, K. E. Shaefer, G. Vourc'h, Vic-DuPont, G. Hyman, J. M. Converse, C. Escoffier-Lambiotte, J. Cassagneau, and D. Zagury, have encouraged me in the course of this study with their pertinent comments and criticisms. Dr. Albert Greenwood was very helpful in discussing many of the broad issues raised by this subject. M. Pierre Philippe supported an important part of this investigation. Mr. and Mrs. D. Van Alstyne extended to me the most gracious hospitality, and Mr. and Mrs. H. Doll were most generous.

Prof. Granier-Doyeux, Vice-Chairman of the International Narcotics Control Board of the United Nations, and Prof. Chrusciel of the Drug Dependence Unit of the World Health Organization in Geneva were most helpful in providing me with information related to *Cannabis* intoxication throughout the world. Dr. O. J. Braenden, chief of the Scientific and Technical Sections of the Division of Narcotic Drugs, United Nations, Geneva, made available to me his excellent documentation center. Dr. A. Lande, the former Deputy Executive Secretary of the United Nations Conference for the Adoption of a Single Convention on Narcotic Drugs, kindly discussed with me the history of the International Conferences called since 1914, to establish worldwide control of *Cannabis* and other stupefying drugs. Professor M. J. Soueif of Cairo University gave me the main results of the major study of hashish consumption in Egypt, conducted at the National Center for Social and Criminological Research in Cairo since November 1957. Colonel Daoud Eweis and Miss Christine Ambre were most helpful in organizing my trip through upper and lower Egypt. Dr. Joseph Jacob and Dr. J. Mabileau, members of the World Health Organization (W.H.O.) Expert Committee on Drug Dependence, kept me informed of the work of that committee. Mr. El Kettani, attorney general of Casablanca, was most helpful in discussing the legal problems of kif usage in Morocco. Dr. M. Teste, Psychiatrist-in-Chief of the Ibn Nafis Psychiatric Hospital in Marrakech, gave me the benefit of his 20 years of study of *Cannabis* intoxication in North Africa.

Dr. W. M. Paton of Oxford University shared with me his pharmacological insight. Dr. Monique Braude of the National Institute of Mental Health was exceedingly helpful and courteous in answering all of my many inquiries.

I wish to thank Dr. Doorenbos for making available to me his manuscript describing the botanical aspects of *Cannabis* and Drs. Lemberger, MacIsaac, Paton, Isbell, Soueif, Renault, Petrzilka, Stearn, Haney, Agurell, Hardman, and Truitt for allowing me to reproduce illustrations from some of their studies.

The studies performed in my laboratory and reported here were supported in part by a grant from the National Institutes of Health (GM–09069–10).

The curator of the Medical Library of the University of Paris was kind enough to loan me one of the few available copies of J. Moreau's book "Du Hachisch et de l'Aliénation Mentale." This loan enabled me to translate from this the excerpts which make the main section of Chapter VI, "Cannabis Intoxication and Mental Illness."

I am grateful to Miss M. Verosky and Mrs. I. Schwartz for their assistance in the preparation of the manuscript, to Mrs. J. Ouchi for her very fine secretarial help, to Mrs. J. Gaston, Miss Kathy Haynes, and Miss Jane Stuart for typing parts of the manuscript.

Special illustrations were elegantly drawn by Zena Lupjan and finely reproduced by A. T. Lamme.

The legal advice of Edmund Nahas and the close support of Robert Nahas were invaluable.

I thank my wife for her gentle guiding light and my sister, Prof. Hélène Peters, for her lucid council. Finally, the example of my mother, with her unfailing courage and inquisitive mind, was a constant source of inspiration.

Preface

Intoxication with *Cannabis,* one of the oldest drugs known to man, is now widespread all over the world, including Western countries where it had never been observed before. As a result, pharmacologists are asked to study the properties of the derivatives of *Cannabis* and to reevaluate their effects on man. It should be emphasized that such a task goes beyond classical pharmacology, which is based on animal experimentation. There are, as yet, no precise methods to measure the psychosociological behavior of laboratory animals. The study of "psychotropic" drugs requires, therefore, a joint effort among pharmacologists, physicians, psychologists, psychiatrists, and sociologists, studying either volunteers or chronic users. It is presumptuous to claim that scientists working in the United States or elsewhere will be able to determine whether or not marihuana is harmful to man within a few years merely by performing pharmacological or behavioral studies on man or laboratory animals. If the acute effect of a single dose of *Cannabis* can be evaluated in a relatively short lapse of time (provided investigators use active material), it is not possible to assess in less than a generation the effects resulting from its chronic use on the health, social, and cultural activities of Western man. A general appraisal of the effects of *Cannabis* must take into account, in addition to pharmacological data, historical and ethical factors as well as the perspective of a humanistic society in which man could preserve "a healthy mind in a healthy body" in order to develop fully his creative potential and to face the challenge of an uncertain future. This monograph is an attempt to consider the problem of *Cannabis* intoxication in a historical perspective within as well as beyond the continental limits of the United States.

Contents

1

From Bhang to Delta-9-THC: Four Thousand Years of History

ORIGINS: CHINA, INDIA—BHANG AND GANJA

The first recorded use of *Cannabis* as a remedy occurred in China nearly 4000 years ago. A mythical Chinese emperor and pharmacist, Shen Nung, advocated its use as a sedative and as an all-purpose medication. But *Cannabis* was never used extensively in China as a psychoactive substance. From China the use of *Cannabis* spread, several centuries before Christ, to India and the surrounding Asian countries.

On the Indian subcontinent *Cannabis* was regarded as a holy plant and played an important religious role. It is referred to in the Sanskrit literature as "food of the gods," "glory," and "victory." Around 2000 B.C., "Banghu" was mentioned as a sacred grass in the religious book *Atharva Veda*. *Cannabis* was associated with the god Shiva, as shivbooty or Shiva's plant, and was used during the performance of religious rituals in temples. In these old texts *Cannabis* is also referred to as "unconquered," "hero-leaved," "joy," "rejoicer," "desired in three worlds," all adjectives that clearly refer to its mind-altering and euphoric properties.

It was not for its textile properties that hemp was first used in India; in fact, at the beginning of the Christian era the use of its fiber was still unknown there. It was through the Iranian tribes that the priestly class in India, the only educated one at that time, learned of the properties of *Cannabis* at a period difficult to determine accurately. While it is easy to show that the priestly classes knew and used the properties of hemp for the performance of religious rites, it is difficult to establish where and how its use as an inebriant was learned by the common people. In Hindustan, when the secret of the priests was revealed or betrayed, hemp was used solely for the preparation of beverages. But the Brahmans tried to control the use of *Cannabis* potions, which were authorized only for religious celebrations. The generalized use of

Cannabis by the common people of India apparently appeared when the custom of smoking hemp arose and became socially acceptable. This practice has more rapid effects and may be better titrated than when the drug is ingested. It is becoming the prevalent method of *Cannabis* intoxication throughout the world.

Among the Muslim Indians, *Cannabis* (bhang or ganja) was associated with the prophet Elijah, the patron saint of water, and was referred to as "joy-giver," "sky-flyer," "heavenly guide," "soother of grief," and "poor man's heaven." The drug had the property of promoting union with the divinity. "We drank bhang and the mystery that 'I am God' grew plain—so grand a result, so tiny a sin," writes a Persian poet.

The ancient Hindus also hailed the medicinal properties of the plant, which was credited with curing leprosy, catarrh, and fever, as well as with "creating vital energy and stimulating the mind." It was used as a sedative, an anesthetic, an antitussive agent, to relieve constipation, and to decrease appetite (in cases of obesity). In the Muslim system of medicine in India (Unami), *Cannabis* extracts were prescribed to cure asthma, urinary infections, loss of appetite, dandruff, piles, and inflammation. The use of *Cannabis* derivatives through the ages in India may have contributed to the introspective, meditative aspect of the yogi culture. A number of holy men, writes a Christian missionary, "live in a state of perpetual intoxication and call this stupefaction which arises from smoking intoxicating herbs, fixing the mind on God" (Campbell, 1903).

From India, the use of *Cannabis* spread to Persia, Assyria, and the Middle East. The Assyrians were familiar with *Cannabis* in the eighth century B.C. and called it "quanabu," a derivation of the Persian "kanabas." Herodotus (Historiae III) reports that the barbarian Scythians of the Caspian and Aral Seas intoxicated themselves with vapors from burning hemp. *Cannabis* was unknown to the ancient Egyptians and the Hebrews; there is no mention of it either in hieroglyphic texts or paintings of the Pharaonic era or in the Scriptures of the Old Testament; no cloth made of hemp has been found in the ancient Egyptian tombs. The Greeks and the Romans did not use *Cannabis* as a pleasure-inducing drug as they did alcoholic beverages. For unknown reasons these ancient civilizations did not accept in their culture the use of hemp drugs in spite of the many contacts they had with Assyria and Asia Minor.

HASHISH IN THE MIDDLE EAST: TENTH TO FIFTEENTH CENTURY

The next widespread use of *Cannabis* after India occurred in the Middle East. It started in the wake of the rise of Islam and met little cultural opposition, since the Muslim religion forbids the use of alcohol and wine but not explicitly the derivatives of *Cannabis*. The Arabic name for the *Cannabis* extract used in the Middle East is hashish, which means "grass." In Hebrew the name is "shesha." Many tales in Arabian literature are associated with its early use. There is the story of the monk Sheraz, of the order of Haider, who lived in the mountains of Rama around 500 A.D. and discovered the divine properties of a plant which appeased hunger and thirst while giving joy. He told his disciples, "Almighty God has bestowed upon you by a special favor the virtues of this plant, which will dissipate the shadows which cloud your souls and brighten your spirits." Haider recommended that his followers conceal from the people the divine properties of this precious herb. But such secrets cannot be kept for centuries, and soon the poets extolled the wonderful qualities of the "magic" plant; "abandon wine, take the cup of Haider, this cup which has the fragrance of amber and sparkles like a green emerald."

Many have heard the story of Hassan, the old man of the mountain who snared young men and fed them hashish in the splendid gardens of his fortress, the Alamut. In this earthly paradise their main activity was to make love with sensuous women. Hassan was able to keep his young followers under his spell and send them on dangerous missions to assassinate his opponents. He promised them, "Upon your return, my angels shall bear you into paradise." It might be that the word "assassin" derives from "Hassan"; it is much more unlikely that it derives from "hashish," a word which antedates Hassan's reign.

The Arab invasions of the ninth through twelfth centuries introduced *Cannabis* preparations into all of North Africa from Egypt to Tunisia, Algeria, and Morocco. Spain was the only conquered land where the habit was never established, perhaps because of its reconquest by Isabella the Catholic and the firm grip taken by the Roman church over the Iberian peninsula.

The Tales of the Thousand and One Nights, written from 1000 to 1500 A.D., refer often to the marvelous properties of bhang and hashish. The author of the "flying carpet" might have himself experienced the feeling of levitation and flying which results from *Cannabis* intoxication. And the use of hashish spread on the wings of poetry through the Moslem world and became an inherent part of its culture. In the sixteenth century, the historian Aldunis noted that in Egypt, the common people, following the lead of the wealthy class, sought intoxication by smoking or ingesting *Cannabis* extracts. From then on, *Cannabis* was considered in Egypt "the grass of the poor" (hashichat-oul-fouquar'a).

According to the Arab historian Maqrizy, hashish was introduced into Egypt in the thirteenth century. The widespread use of hashish in Egypt coincided with the start of a lengthy period of economic, social, and cultural decadence under the Mamelouk dynasties (1250–1517). This somber period of Egyptian history was followed by the ruthless domination of the Ottoman Empire, which lasted until 1805.

For centuries a privileged and dissolute Circassian or Turkish ruling class alien to Egypt exploited the laborers of the indigenous agrarian population. Hashish consumption was common to oppressor and oppressed alike. The rulers took it to enhance their pleasure (see Moreau, 1845) and the peasants as a means to escape the dreariness of their daily lives.

The hashish habit was probably accompanied by unfavorable social consequences, since some sultans and emirs of Persia, Turkey, and Egypt tried belatedly (after the thirteenth century) to reverse the trend toward *Cannabis* abuse among their people. In Egypt in the fourteenth century, Emir Soudouni Schekhouni ordered that all plants be uprooted and destroyed, and condemned all consumers of *Cannabis* to have their teeth extracted (De Sacy, 1826). Other offenders were jailed. But the habit was too ingrained, and when Napoleon conquered Egypt in 1800, he was shocked by the extent of *Cannabis* use among the people. He related the general stagnation observed among the Egyptian people to their indulgence in *Cannabis* and decreed, "The use of the strong liquor made by some Moslems with a certain weed called hashish, as well as the smoking of the flowering tops of hemp are forbidden in all of Egypt" (De Sacy, 1826). This interdiction failed, as did many others before and after, to stop *Cannabis* abuse in the Moslem world. And to this day, *Cannabis* is still widely abused among the Moslem populations of the Middle East, in spite of all the efforts exerted by their leaders.

Although many commercial and cultural contacts occurred after the thirteenth century (as a result of the Crusades) between the Arab world and the European nations lining the Mediterranean Sea, the use of *Cannabis* as a pleasure-seeking, mind-altering drug did not spread to Western Europe until the second part of the twentieth century.

In a poem quoted by the Arab historian Maqrizy (1892), the rejection of hashish by the Christian ritual is clearly described:

"Never has the minister of the Christian rite mixed the liquor of hashish in his profane chalice; the blasphemous priest who preaches a deceitful religion has never drawn from this liquor the substances of his sacrilegious offering."

Early Venetian traders and explorers brought back spices and incense, but not *Cannabis,* from Turkish-dominated ports. This still held true when the major European powers of the seventeenth and eighteenth centuries, France and England, entered the colonial era and exerted direct control over large portions of Eastern, Middle Eastern, and African countries where *Cannabis* intoxication was prevalent. There seemed to be a cultural cleavage which prevented the Europeans from adopting this Oriental habit. The representatives of the colonial powers kept on using their own traditional pleasure-inducing substances. The British imported with them whiskey and sherry. The French brought along wine or planted vineyards, as they did in Algeria after the 1831 conquest.

HASHISH CROSSES THE MEDITERRANEAN SEA

It was only toward the middle of the nineteenth century that a small group of initiates finally described the hashish experience to Western man. The first use of the drug was reported by Moreau (1845), who may be regarded as the father of clinical psychopharmacology. After ingesting hashish he described the mental effects of *Cannabis* intoxication. In addition to euphoria, he experienced definite hallucinations, as well as derealization, flight of ideas, and incoherence, which he likened to the mental processes likely to occur in mental patients. He also was careful to note that the environmental and social setting, as well as the psychological and emotional condition of the user, profoundly influenced the nature and development of *Cannabis* intoxication with its waxing and waning. His classical description of the hashish experience will be described in detail in Chapter 6. Indeed, for Moreau the hashish experience was a way to gain insight into mental disease. He advised some of his pupils and friends to share in this extraordinary psychological and emotional experience. One of them was a writer of considerable talent, Théophile Gautier, a member of the Romantic iconoclastic côterie which also included Charles Baudelaire and Alexandre Dumas, which became "Le Club des Hachischins" or "The Club of the Hashish Eaters." Gautier (1846) described his experience at the Hotel Pimodan when, in the company of his literary friends, he absorbed during a lavish meal a potent hashish extract so that he could "taste the joys of Mohammed's heaven." Gautier reveled in the ensuing intoxication, which he describes in great detail and with some poetic license in an article written for *La Revue des Deux Mondes*.

> "Hallucination, that strange guest, had set up its dwelling place in me. It seemed that my body had dissolved and become transparent. I saw inside me the hashish I had eaten in the form of an emerald which radiated millions of tiny sparks. All around me I heard the shattering and crumbling of multicolored jewels. I still saw my comrades at times but as disfigured half plants half men. I writhed in my corner with laughter. One of the guests addressed me in Italian which hashish in its omnipotence made me hear in Spanish."

Transposition of tongues, though it is referred to in the Bible, is a sign of profound mental disorganization, reported during LSD intoxication. As the hashish intoxication continued, Gautier experienced the waning and waxing of his hallucinations.

> "For several minutes I found myself with all my composure, and quite amazed at what had happened. Then I fell again under the power of hashish. Millions of butterflies, with wings beating like fans, continuously swarmed in a faintly luminous atmosphere. I heard the sounds of colors: green, red, blue and yellow sounds in successive waves. An overturned glass echoed through me like thunder. My voice appeared so powerful that I dared not speak for fear of breaking the walls and bursting like a bomb. I became entirely disengaged from myself, absent from my body, that odious witness which accompanies you wherever you are. I experienced the particular discontinuous effect of hashish which takes you and leaves you —you mount to heaven and you fall back to earth without transition, as insanity has its moments of lucidity."

Charles Baudelaire (1858), another member of Le Club des Hachischins, also wrote of his experiences with the drug in *Les Paradis Artificiels*. He was fascinated by the sensory effects of hashish and described, as Gautier did, the interchange of sensory modalities: "Sounds have colors and colors are musical. The eyes pierce infinity and the ears perceive the most imperceptible sound in the midst of the sharpest noises." He experienced halluciations: "External objects take on monstrous appearances and reveal themselves in forms hitherto unknown." Baudelaire also describes the more esoteric aspects of the hashish experience. He depicts "the oriental kif where tumultuous and whirling sensations are replaced by a calm and motionless beatitude, a glorious resignation." And finally comes the ultimate religious experience, the glorious merging of oneself with the cosmos: "You are a king unrecognized," says a voice inside him, "and have become the center of the universe. Everything on earth has been created for me, for me. I have become God." Soon this storm of pride changes to restful beatitude and the universality of man is announced colorfully in a yellow dawn. However, Baudelaire became disenchanted about hashish and gave it up, claiming that, "like all solitary pleasures, it makes the individual useless to men and the society superfluous for the individual. Hashish never reveals to the individual more than he is himself. Moreover, there is a fatal danger in such habits. One who has recourse to poison in order to think, will soon be unable to think without taking poison."

The admonition of Baudelaire seems to have been followed by his contemporaries, and *Cannabis* intoxication has never spread to the French intellectual elite.

CANNABIS IN ENGLAND: THE MIRACLE DRUG

In the nineteenth century, *Cannabis* was introduced into England from India as an all-purpose medication by O'Shaugnessy, an Irish physician who had spent several years in India. He used the drug to treat many afflictions but found it most effective in relieving pain, muscle spasms, and convulsions occurring in tetanus, rabies, rheumatism, and epilepsy. In the prescientific era of medicine, when patent medicines were numerous, the claims of O'Shaugnessy (1842) were amplified by his European and American colleagues, who were eagerly seeking novel medications. *Cannabis indica* (imported from India) became a wonder drug used to treat a wide variety of ailments, from menstrual cramps and excessive menstrual bleeding to inflamed tonsils and migraine headaches. It is remarkable that this medication alleviated so many ailments in spite of its relatively low potency—1 to 6 gr (65 to 400 mg) were administered by mouth to obtain the desired effects, which were not accompanied by any of the signs of hashish intoxication. At least the numerous British medical reports which noted the therapeutic effects of the drug failed to mention its typical intoxicating properties.

The wise physicians of the nineteenth century apparently gave their patients enough *Cannabis* to produce a placebo effect, as many medications do even today. However, the difficulty of obtaining reproducible effects with the drug and the extreme variability in potency of different lots of *Cannabis* extracts discouraged many nineteenth century physicians; one of them even declared that *"Cannabis* is hardly worthy of a place in our list of remedial agents."

When more specific medication of known potency such as aspirin, barbiturates, and anesthetic agents became available, hemp preparations fell rapidly into disrepute. In 1932 hemp drugs were deleted from the British pharmacopeia because of their variable potency and unexplained variations in response to their use in man.

HASHISH COMES TO POUGHKEEPSIE, NEW YORK

Hemp plants were widely cultivated in the United States as a fiber crop by early American settlers. George Washington grew *Cannabis* on his own farm, not to smoke but to use in making ropes.   Marihuana and hashish were unknown as pleasure-inducing drugs.   The vigorous and industrious endeavors of the young Puritan American Republic seemed to be incompatible with a habit of inner contemplation and departure from reality.

Cannabis extracts were first utilized by American physicians in the nineteenth century as an all-purpose medication.   The preparation used was Tilden's Extract of Cannabis Indica, an olive-brown paste of the consistency of pitch and with a decided aromatic odor.   It was dispensed for a large variety of ailments, from lockjaw to phtysis.

These preparations, which had to travel to America from East Bengal, lost a great deal of their original potency and were given in small doses, usually from 1 to 5 gr.   This explains why there is no record in nineteenth century American literature of the intoxicating properties of Tilden's Extract, except for the isolated report of Fitz Hugh Ludlow (1857), *The Hasheesh Eater.* Ludlow, the son of a minister, was a bright young scholar who lived and taught in the charming town of Poughkeepsie, N.Y., located in the Hudson River Valley.   An early amateur psychopharmacologist, he lounged in the local pharmacy of his friend Anderson, the apothecary.   He liked to smell all of the drugs which altered consciousness, such as incense, or chloroform which sent him "careening on the wings of an exciting life."   He became intensely interested in hashish after reading one of the best-sellers of 1855, *The Land of the Saracens,* by Bayard Taylor.   This American explorer recalls, in a chapter of his book, *The Arabian Night,* his encounter with hashish, the first such account by an English writer.

It is therefore important to recall Taylor's experience, which inspired Ludlow's own use of *Cannabis* a few years later.   Bayard Taylor ate hashish preparations several times during his voyage through Egypt and Syria.   His first attempts had little effect; his last one, in Damascus, where he took a teaspoonful of a mixture "distinctly bitter and repulsive," had impressive results. For several days he traveled from "the raptures of Paradise into the fiercest Hell."   At first he had pleasant visual and auditory hallucinations: He inhaled the most pleasant perfumes, saw thousand-layer rainbows of colors like gems, listened to music such as Beethoven may have heard but never wrote. "My journey was that of a conqueror, not of a conqueror who subdues— either by Love or by Will, for I forgot that man existed—but one victorious over the grandest and subtlest forces of nature.   Light, color, odor, sound and motion were my slaves."   At the same time he was enjoying his visions, he was also aware of his immediate surroundings.   But unpleasant visions next occurred; he felt transformed into a mass of jelly and states, "I tortured and contorted myself for some time to force my loose substance into a mould. I felt I was in the grasp of some giant force and grew earnestly alarmed." Blood was rushing through his body at a distressingly high rate.   "It was projected into my eyes until I could no longer see; it beat quickly in my ears, and so throbbed in my heart that I feared the ribs would give way." This might have been the tachycardia associated with *Cannabis* intoxication, but never systematically observed until 100 years later by the investigators of the La Guardia Report. When taking his pulse he felt two different heart rates, one beating at 1000 times a minute, the other with a slow rhythm. Taylor was in the throes of a "sensation of distress which was far more severe than pain itself," and suffered what would probably be called today, acute anxiety. It took Taylor 2 or 3 days to recover from "involuntary fits of absence" and reunite his "divided perceptions." He did not repeat his experience, for it revealed to him the "depth of rapture and suffering which my natural faculties never could have sounded" and nobly concludes, "it had taught me the majesty of human reason and will, and the awful perils of tampering with that which assails their integrity." Taylor also expressed the hope that the account of his experience would discourage others from trying hashish; but if they were curious enough to use the drug, he cautioned them against taking too large a dose.

Ludlow did not benefit from Taylor's advice, as he recalls in his own book, *The Hasheesh Eater*. Without leaving Poughkeepsie, and thanks to his friend Anderson the apothecary, he was able to experience the wavelike spell-binding effects of hashish. Not long after reading *The Arabian Night* of Bayard Taylor, whose account moved him to curiosity and admiration, Ludlow saw on the shelf of his friend's pharmacy what he was now longing for: a vial of Tilden's Extract of Cannabis Indica.

Over the next few days he helped himself to successive doses of extracts until he had ingested 55 gr or 3.3 g, a hefty dose. He found himself in the power of hashish. He oscillated between deep beatitude and uncontrollable terror—he was transported to Venice, the Alps, the Nile Valley amidst Ethiopians, and even once ended up in Paradise. His soul changed to a vegetable essence. His heart was beating so loudly and so fast that he went to consult the local physician. Ludlow's tumultuous recollections might have been colored by those he had read in Taylor's book, and they seem somewhat repetitious. Like Taylor, he had numerous hallucinations, both pleasant and frightful. He experienced the sensation of double consciousness. His rational self was preserved enough to realize the insanity of his visions. But Ludlow, unlike Taylor, was seeking the mystical union of mind and matter which occurs during *Cannabis* intoxication. He repeated the hashish experience many times, always using Tilden's Extract and trying not to exceed 15 gr a day, and seemed to have become quite dependent on the drug. His life was a prolonged state of hashish exaltation; many of his hallucinations had a religious content, including appearances of God and Christ. He finally gave up this enslaving habit with the help of a good physician, but not without ex-

periencing considerable suffering. He became subsequently a successful jour-
nalist and critic and a friend of Mark Twain. He died prematurely at 34
years of age, probably of tuberculosis.

Ludlow's example was not followed by his contemporaries. In spite of the
easy availability of Tilden's Extract of Cannabis Indica, young Americans of
the last century seemed to have had little inclination to escape into the fantasies and vagaries of a chemically induced religious experience.

One hundred years later the cult of expanded consciousness through the
use of *Cannabis* and other hallucinogens was revived by Dr. Timothy Leary
(1966) and the poet Allen Ginsberg (1966), who wrote and lectured widely
about their drug experiences. They found an eager audience of young Americans who had become blasé from the effects of a consumer society where
acquisition of goods seemed to have become the ultimate goal of life. Many
American students listened and followed the self-appointed prophets of a new
age, who were in reality bringing to the expectant minds of their audiences the
most ancient recipes of escape into heaven without the painful awakenings
experienced by Taylor and Ludlow.

From the descriptions given by French and American experimenters of the
nineteenth century, it is clear that *Cannabis* extracts produce in Western man
inner experiences very similar to those reported by the Oriental poets and
writers of India, Persia, and Arabia many centuries before. Euphoria and
uncontrollable laughter, exacerbation and alterations of all sensory precep-
tions affecting time, space, vision, and hearing; interchange of sensory perceptions, which the Arab poets hailed long ago in their sensuous songs and
which our present-day psychologist call "synesthesia" ("I hear yellow and I
see music"). The nineteenth century's hashish eaters of the Western world
also experienced "depersonalization," the feeling of becoming separated from
the body and merged with the cosmos. So did many Hindu holy men who,
centuries before, used the hallowed bhang for the same purpose. As Chopra
(1969) reminds us, even today, "In holy places, yogis take deep drinks of
Bhang so that they may center their thoughts on the Eternal." The similarity
of the effects of hashish on Oriental and Western man is somewhat comforting
to the pharmacologist or the physiologist who tends to consider all men, irre-
spective of their geographical location, as belonging to the same stabilized
species, *homo sapiens*.

THE REPORT OF THE INDIAN HEMP DRUG COMMISSION

The report of the Indian Hemp Drug Commission (1893–1894) was the
first attempt to evaluate the physical, mental, and moral effects of *Cannabis*

intoxication on the population of India. The four commissioners, including one physician, relied strictly on the testimonials of 1193 witnesses, of whom a minority (335) were physicians, and who were given seven questions to answer. The written or oral answers constituted the "evidence" before the Commission.

The testimony of the medical witnesses concerning the physical effects of chronic *Cannabis* intoxication were conflicting and illustrate the confusion and limited knowledge of the profession at that time. "A large number of medical witnesses of all classes ascribe dysentery, bronchitis, and asthma to the moderate use of the drugs. An equally representative number gave a diametrically opposite opinion." No wonder: The use of hemp drugs was recognized at that time as a remedial agent against asthma, bronchitis, and dysentery!

Some of the consumers maintained, others denied, that evil effects were produced by the drug. One lonely physician said, "I have not seen any evil results mentioned when taken moderately, but it is very difficult to keep to moderation." The Commission concluded, "In regard to the physical effects, the moderate use of hemp drugs is practically attended by no evil results at all. . . . The excessive use does cause injury by weakening the constitution and rendering the consumer more susceptible to disease." The Commission also stated that excessive use of hemp drugs does not cause asthma, that it may indirectly cause dysentery by weakening the constitution, but not by direct effect of the drug on the intestine, and that it may cause bronchitis. The Commission did not define what it meant by "moderate use" or "excessive use." No medical witnesses described the most commonly observed physical effects of *Cannabis* intoxication, namely, conjunctival injection, acceleration of pulse, hand unsteadiness, and ataxia.

With respect to the alleged mental effects of the drug, the Commission did not trust the unfavorable reports they received linking hemp to mental illness. The commissioners made their own inquiry among the 2344 patients admitted during the year 1842 to Indian asylums. It concluded that some cases might have been caused by hemp drugs alone, but went on to state that even in such cases the evidence was not convincing.

In regard to the moral effects of the drug, the Commission was of the opinion that moderate use produces no moral injury whatever, while excessive consumption indicates and intensifies moral weakness or depravity.

The undertaking of the Indian Hemp Drug Commission was a laudable one. It was, however, doomed from the beginning to report ambiguous results because of the deceptive nature of the topic under consideration. As the commissioners themselves pointed out, it was impossible to obtain proper records, accurate statistics, or reliable information, since many of the subjects under investigation were illiterate peasants. It was impossible to dissociate the effects of hemp drugs per se from those of all the other "vices in which a dissipated man indulges." It was a "can of worms." But instead of acknowledging the impossibility, under such muddled circumstances, of establishing a cause–effect relationship between hemp drugs and physical or mental effects, they gave *Cannabis* the benefit of the doubt, and for all practical purposes threw the case against *Cannabis* out of court. In taking such an attitude, the commissioners assumed the role of impartial judges and lawyers and not of physicians and scientists, who would be unwilling to draw any conclusions from such poor evidence.

They acknowledged that excessive use of hemp was harmful but that moderate use was not. However, they failed to define what they meant by moderate and excessive, both in terms of quantity of material used and of frequency of use. A similar failure in defining these terms is apparent in those who today, like Grinspoon (1971) and Kaplan (1971), take a view similar to that of the Indian Hemp Drug Commission.

Cannabis derivatives at the time of the Indian Hemp Drug Commission inquiry were still among the most popular remedies in India, where they had been used for centuries as wonder drugs in the treatment of a wide variety of ailments. Hemp was also considered by many to be a holy plant, employed for the performance of certain rituals in temples. *Cannabis* derivatives did have a definite place within the social and cultural fabric of India, and the Indian Hemp Drug Commission, as asked by the Secretary of State to Her Majesty, weighed all of these factors against the untoward effects of *Cannabis*. The Commission was warned that prohibition might represent an "unjustifiable interference and that repressive laws might be impossible to enforce." The conclusions of the Commission, based as they were on contradictory testimonials and uncontrollable evidence more than on scientific studies, could not be construed as general ones applicable to other countries with different cultures and histories. The Indian Hemp Drug Commission was committed to respect the cultural traditions of India and did not have to answer the following question: Does the apparent lack of untoward physical and mental effects of hemp drugs on the Indian population justify their use in England and Europe? The Commission did not recommend the extension of the use of these drugs to other countries. The conclusions of the Indian Hemp Drug Commission might have been somewhat tainted by the colonial Victorian conviction of the nineteenth century that the use of the hemp drugs was good enough for the natives of India. The commissioners were not social reformers and did not care to see the people of India rival Western man. For all of these reasons, the conclusions drawn by the Indian Hemp Drug Commission could not be applied to a people with a totally different culture, living in another age. Still, many contemporary American writers abundantly quote the scientifically unsubstantiated conclusions of the Indian Hemp Drug Commission to justify their claim that *Cannabis* is a mild intoxicant. They hail the "impartial" findings of the Commission as being most authoritative and as if they were still relevant to the use of marihuana in the United States today.

CANNABIS INTOXICATION IN THE TWENTIETH CENTURY

The use of *Cannabis* became worldwide in the second half of the twentieth century. The 1968 United Nations multilingual list of stupefying drugs under international control gives 267 names for *Cannabis* and *Cannabis* preparations used throughout the world. A few of these are listed in Table 1. While *Cannabis* intoxication tended to stabilize or to decrease in countries where it had prevailed for centuries, it increased significantly in Western countries, especially the United States, as the first generation after World War II was coming of age (Fig. 1).

Table 1

Names and Compositions of *Cannabis* Preparations in Various Countries

Country	Name	Composition
Indian subcontinent	Bhang	Dried mature leaves
Indian subcontinent	Sawi (green-leaved)	Dried mature leaves
Indian subcontinent	Ganja	Flowering tops
Indian subcontinent	Charas	Resinous material
Arabia, Iran, Middle East	Kannabis and cannabis	Entire plant
Arabia, Iran, Middle East	Banji	Entire plant, mostly leaves
Arabia, Iran, Middle East	Hashish	Resinous material and flowering tops
Israel	Shesha	Entire plant
Turkey and Iran	Esrar	Resinous material with flowering tops
U.S.S.R. (southern)	Anascha	Resinous material and flowering tops mixed with leaves
Egypt	Hashish	Resinous material and flowering tops
Morocco and North African coast	Kif	Resinous material mixed with leaves and flowers
West coast of Africa	Dimba	Entire plant
Congo, Central Africa	Suma, dacha	Entire plant
South and Southwest Africa	Dagga	Entire plant, mostly leaves and flowering tops
Zulu, Swazi	Lebake	Entire plant
East Africa	Njemu	Entire plant
Madagascar	Vongony	Entire plant
United States, Canada, Mexico	Marihuana	Leaves and flowering tops
Brazil	Machona	Entire plant with leaves

THE INDIAN SUBCONTINENT—THE CHOPRA STUDIES

The use of *Cannabis* for religious and medical purposes over many centuries ingrained this habit among the peoples of the Indian subcontinent.

In 1969, Chopra, the Indian pharmacologist and physician, who with other members of his family extensively studied *Cannabis* intoxication in his country, reported that the habitual use of *Cannabis* still prevails in many parts of India, Pakistan, Nepal, and Bhutan. Chopra's study on "Man and Marihuana" (1969) is the latest in a series on hemp addiction in India, published over the past three decades with his father and brothers. All of the Chopra reports are fraught with uncertain methodology and are difficult for the factual-minded scientist to evaluate, since the scientist tends to discard as folklore any observations not statistically treated to indicate "significance." If one adopts, however, a less rigorously scientific outlook, some insight may be acquired into the physical, mental, and social effects of chronic *Cannabis* abuse in a land where this habit has been socially acceptable for centuries. Viewed in this perspective the studies of Chopra are quite informative and will therefore now be summarized.

Hemp is still cultivated for use as a psychoactive agent, under government control, in selected areas of northern and eastern India. In addition, *Cannabis* grows wild on extensive tracts in northern Pakistan and India, from the slopes of the Himalayas to the plains. From the cultivated or wild plants, three intoxicating preparations are made by local villagers, bhang, ganja, and charas in their order of potency. Bhang, a concoction of *Cannabis* leaves, is regarded as a drug of inferior quality and is consumed as a beverage. Ganja is prepared from the flowering tops of cultivated female plants and has a pungent odor very much appreciated by habitual users; it is crushed or rolled in the hands in the process of preparation and consists of flower clusters coalesced with resin. There are three varieties, flat, round, and chur ganja, in the form of a coarse, yellowish powder which is usually consumed where it is manufactured. Charas is the resinous material, and its manufacture and use are banned throughout India. Ganja and bhang are still used, and originate from limited areas where *Cannabis* is specially cultivated to provide psychoactive preparations. The plants which grow wild in large areas of northern India and Pakistan are also illegally harvested and used. The incidence of *Cannabis* abuse, according to Chopra, is high in the religious, industrial, and urban centers, and it is the most extensively employed drug in the poorer sections of the population. Chopra insists that *Cannabis* preparations are consumed today by the lower strata of Indian society, while the middle and upper classes shun the use of hemp drugs in spite of the fact that "this practice was once held in great esteem in ancient India" in various religious cere-

Fig. 1. (*See next page.*) The spread of *Cannabis* intoxication (1970) throughout the world. This spread follows an epidemio-logic pattern.

Endemic areas: Those where *Cannabis* intoxication is part of the local culture and has been accepted socially for centuries by the whole population.

Epidemic areas: Those with a recent propagation of *Cannabis* intoxication in the adolescent culture. However, the drug is not yet socially accepted. In most endemic as well as in all epidemic areas the use of marihuana is illegal. In the rest of the world the laws banning marihuana are strictly enforced.

Inset: In the Middle East, Israel is the only country where *Cannabis* is not used or accepted socially, as it is in neighboring states.

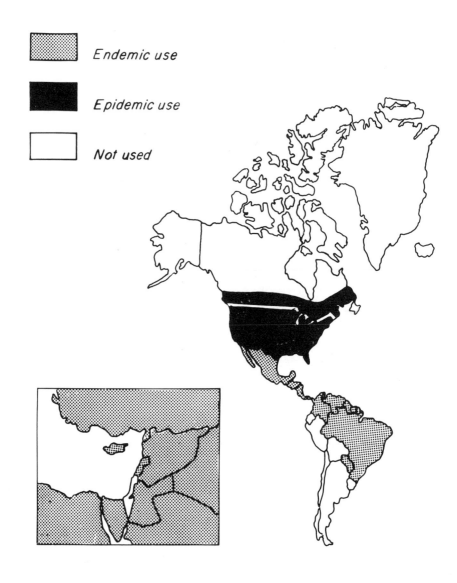

monies where it seemed to contribute to the practice of meditation. In addition to religious tradition, Chopra attributes the continued hemp habit in India to "personality problems, a low standard of living, economic and social factors in the life of the individual." It therefore provides an escape from all things which constitute unpleasantness for the user. "For regular consumers the use of this drug often becomes a psychological crutch for a weak personality. In addition to the physical need to prevent discomfort, deterioration may result from intense mental and physical reactions accompanying larger doses. Indeed, for hemp users, the desire for the mental fantasies far exceeds that of any physical well-being. Even after an effective withdrawal from hemp, this subjective, mental desire may cause a rehabituation."

It is not possible to evaluate the number of consumers of hemp in India since there is no registration system. Chopra (1969) gives the figure of 257,000 kg of *Cannabis* officially consumed in 1 year, except for five states "where the incidence of hemp use is higher"; the illicit consumption should also be added to these figures. On the basis of such fragmentary information it is not possible to determine the extent of *Cannabis* use in India today. In any event, it would appear that the consumption of *Cannabis* preparations has decreased since India assumed its independence from the British crown.

By empirical assessment, Chopra estimates the potency of bhang as twice that of American-grown marihuana, while ganja is twice and charas four to five times as strong as bhang. The average dose taken by users averages from 0.25 to 5 g per day according to the different preparations. The experiments performed by Chopra on nonhabituated individuals given ganja to smoke indicate that this preparation is quite strong.

> "Immediately after taking a pull on a ganja charged pipe, there was intense irritation of the throat and the act of smoking had sometimes to be abandoned half finished. After a few pulls there was a dryness of the throat, sweating, and dizziness in the head. There were hallucinations of sight and hearing and of general sensibility. The ideas of time and space became somewhat hazy. The appetite decreased and sleep was disturbed."

Such symptoms contrast significantly with the rather mild reactions reported in the La Guardia Report or the more recent studies performed in the United States on subjects who smoked several marihuana cigarettes (Crancer, 1969; Weil et al., 1968).

The acute mental effects reported by habitual smokers were reminiscent of the experience of the French and American hashish eaters of the nineteenth century: "In favorable circumstances, life becomes a wonderful dream in which the bonds of time and space are broken, delirious joy results in inexhaustable laughter and nothing seems impossible to accomplish." There is an exacerbation of all sensory perceptions, mostly visual and auditory, which are combined with hallucinations, the subject claiming to see "fireworks, rockets and colored stars flying from his head." Sometimes unpleasant sensations of fear and anxiety supersede the intense feeling of well-being; the subject has the illusion of being raised into the air or experiences the unpleasant sensation of being suspended over an abyss. In the end, sleep supersedes. All of these reactions have been reported by those who have experienced *Cannabis* intoxication.

Many of the users of hemp in India attribute their original use of *Cannabis* to the belief that it would increase their sexual powers, a belief widely held in the Orient. Chopra finds little evidence to justify such a contention. The chronic physical effects of *Cannabis* are mentioned briefly: "Typical ganja abusers are thin, emaciated persons with a sallow look. There is a lowering of general vitality which renders the user more prone to intercurrent diseases. Excessive smoking of the drug produces bronchial irritation and chronic catarrhal laryngitis. Most chronic hemp smokers show congestion of conjunctival vessels." He also mentions that, "when taken occasionally and in moderation, the drug does not affect physical health." But Chopra does not define what is moderate and occasional use of *Cannabis,* or what is a "typical ganja abuser."

As for adverse mental effects, Chopra states: "The risk of transient psychosis attends the use of hemp. This may sometimes occur even in stable persons. *Cannabis* may precipitate psychic disorder in an unstable, disorganized personality. . . . Hemp does not usually produce a psychosis in healthy, stable persons. In unstable users, personality factors and the mood preceding the ingestion of the drug determine the syndrome and type of psychosis that may result."

Chopra believes that the abuse of *Cannabis* does not lead to violent crime, but rather to mental and physical deterioration, with resulting social effects. He points out the lack of physical dependence except in chronic cases where some withdrawal symptoms occur. However, repetitive use leads to psychological dependence. The treatment advocated for chronic, habitual intoxication is radical, similar to that for chronic alcoholism. "To avoid mental and physical ruin, the only solution is total, sudden and complete abstinence from the use of drugs."

Chopra also points out the different aspects of *Cannabis* intoxication in Eastern and Western countries. In the East, extreme poverty, ignorance, old religious beliefs, and social acceptance lead the destitute Oriental to the use of hemp drugs. In the West, affluence, education, revolt against established values, and rebellion against social regulation entice the wealthly student to the *Cannabis* experience.   Despite the differences, says Chopra, the use of hemp is a dangerous practice which should be carefully studied and controlled.

NEIGHBORING INDIAN STATES AND SOUTHEAST ASIA

In the Himalayan states of Nepal, Bhutan, and Sikkim, *Cannabis* grows wild and yields a great deal of resinous material.   Hemp is freely available and many of the people smoke the drug, which is also smuggled in from the adjoining states of India.   In Ceylon, ganja smuggled from India is used by a significant segment of the population.   For two decades local authorities have been taking severe repressive measures against smugglers and users.

The smoking of *Cannabis* is widespread throughout Southeast Asia: Burma, Malaysia, Thailand, Cambodia, Laos, and South Vietnam.   The People's Republic of North Vietnam claims to have been successful in stopping *Cannabis* intoxication throughout the territory they control.   Their partisans and soldiers are under strict orders not to use the drug.   Except for a few remote areas on the southeastern border of China, the ban on *Cannabis* derivatives is strictly enforced in that People's Republic.   *Cannabis* intoxication has always been, and still is, alien to Japanese culture.

MOSLEM LANDS OF THE MIDDLE EAST, ASIA MINOR, AND CENTRAL ASIA

In all of the Moslem countries, *Cannabis* preparations are still widely used in spite of restrictive legislation.   But it is difficult, if not impossible, to obtain valid statistics describing the extent of habituation, occasional or chronic.

In the Middle East there are currently three different kinds of stock preparations deriving from *Cannabis sativa:* (1) the flowering tops, (2) the resinous materials secreted by the tops, which look like solid carpenter glue, and (3) a complex mixture in which *Cannabis* or its resins are associated with spices, aromatic substances, and excipients.   Each tribe has its own technology for collecting the resin and treating it according to processes developed empirically over the centuries and transmitted from one generation to the next.   The resin is the part of the plant which is most carefully collected and prepared. The best grade of resin is collected from fresh, uncut plants by rubbing the flowering tops with either leather aprons (North Africa) or a thick carpet (Iran).   It is then scraped off with a knife, dirt and impurities are removed, and it is rolled by hand with a little water into flat lumps or tapering sticks, which are left to dry.   Today, sealed plastic bags have replaced the paper and cloth containers in which the resin was formerly wrapped for final distribution and sale. From the stock material innumerable preparations are concocted by local merchants and traders or by the consumers themselves for three main uses: smoking mixtures; beverages and elixirs for drinking; pastries, candies, and sweetmeats for eating. All of the products are prepared locally when required for consumption. The mixtures keep for only a short time, and the tastes of the consumers vary from one location to the next. Whether smoked, drunk, or eaten, all of these preparations often contain other pharmacological agents. Preparations used for smoking may contain different tobacco mixtures. In Middle Eastern countries and other poor countries where cigarette paper is not readily available, *Cannabis* is smoked mostly in various types of pipes. The pipe smoker will smoke alone or in a group, passing the pipe around the circle while holding the smoke in his lungs. If he smokes alone, he may extinguish the *Cannabis* while he is holding his breath, and rekindle the dried herb after each exhalation. Many of the beverages contain sweet alcohol or wines. Recipes for pastries, candies, and sweetmeats are innumerable.

The potencies of all of these different preparations vary considerably, depending on the concentration of active ingredient (delta-9-THC)—which is maximal in the bracts and leaves close to the flowering tops—and on the possible presence of other psychoactive agents such as cantharide, datura, or belladonna.

Since delta-9-THC is inactivated by humidity and exposure to air and light, *Cannabis* preparations tend to lose their potency with time and after exposure to the many atmospheric and other hazards associated with shipment to areas far from their place of origin.

Syria and Lebanon are major providers of hashish for neighboring countries; they offer four varieties, colored from brown to yellow. The plant is cultivated in special areas such as the Alauite territory in Lebanon and around Homs and Aleppo in Syria, where certain tribes have specialized in the preparation of hashish for centuries. The Lebanese population is about equally divided between Moslem and Christian communities. The use of *Cannabis* prevails primarily among the Moslems of the poorer agrarian class. The Christians of Lebanon, who over the centuries have adopted the language and many of the other cultural and culinary traits of their Moslem neighbors, have to this day refrained from using *Cannabis* preparations. In Syria, *Cannabis* abuse is more prevalent than it is in Lebanon. A similar situation is observed in Jordan, Saudi Arabia, and Iraq, where *Cannabis* preparations are available in the local markets and souks, and are freely used, mostly by the poor agrarian or nomadic male population, as they have been for centuries. By contrast, members of the educated class claim that they do not indulge in smoking or eating hashish. This claim is, however, open to question.

The use of hashish is also widespread among the peasants and small traders of Turkey and Iran and among the semi-autonomous Uzbek and Tartar tribes. In Turkey, *Cannabis* is considered the opium of the poor. Proceeding to the south and northeast, *Cannabis* habituation is also found in adjoining areas of the U.S.S.R., Chinese Turkistan, Afghanistan, and Balushistan. In recent years the Shah of Iran has ordered very harsh measures, including the death penalty, against all drug users and dealers; in the land where the drinking of bhang was once hailed for its redeeming properties, *Cannabis* has become scarce. In the past, similar measures were unsuccessful in uprooting the use of *Cannabis* from Oriental cultures, so deeply is it ingrained among the people. However, many centuries ago these countries were not destitute and barren and hopeless as they seem today. Six hundred years before Columbus landed in the Caribbean, at a time when North America was covered by forests and plains and populated by wild animals and a few thousand Indians, the Arab world was one of the centers of civilization in the world. In fabulous cities, such as Persepolis, Bagdad, and Damascus, an industrious population of traders and craftsmen were thriving. They built elegant mosques and palaces, and financed famous universities, where the best scientists and scholars of the time could be found. Their shrewd and effective leaders swept through North Africa into the South of Europe, to be stopped finally in Poitiers by the French. The decline of this brilliant Moslem civilization can certainly not be attributed to a single cause but to many of the interacting factors which tend to erode man's creative energy and blunt the full exercise of his power. Among these, abuse of *Cannabis,* the deceptive weed, with its promise of instant heaven on earth, cannot be excluded. This possibility might be one of the reasons why concerned physicians and responsible leaders from Arab countries have fought, during the past 50 years, to eradicate the use of hashish from a land once known as "the fertile crescent," which is now stagnant and destitute. It has been until now the ever-losing battle of a few courageous men attempting to turn an overwhelming tide.

ISRAEL AND THE DISCOVERY OF DELTA-9-THC

Among all of the countries of the Middle East, Israel, which occupies by far the smallest area, is the only one where *Cannabis* is not abused to any extent (Fig. 1). The number who indulge in hashish smoking was estimated at 10,000 in 1966, only a small fraction (0.5%) of its entire population. "Though neither a producer nor a large consumer," write Mechoulam et al. (1970), "Israel is a crossroad for smugglers, mostly Arab bedouin who get

Lebanese hashish from Jordan through the Negev and Sinai deserts to Egypt. Hence, the police vaults are full of material waiting for the chemists."

The users of *Cannabis* preparations in Israel are found mostly among the Moslem minority groups and the Sephardic immigrants from the Oriental communities. The State vigorously applies repressive measures against dealers and supports educational and rehabilitation programs for users, in contrast with the more lenient attitudes of its immediate neighbors. But Israeli scientists have contributed in a major way to the knowledge of the chemical structure of the different constituents of *Cannabis* or cannabinoids. Mechoulam and Gaoni (1965), working in the Laboratory of the National Products of Hebrew University in Jerusalem, were the first to isolate and synthesize the psychoactive substance of *Cannabis sativa,* delta-9-*trans*-tetrahydrocannabinol (delta-9-THC). This brilliant discovery paved the way for all of the extensive research performed in the life sciences in the past 5 years to clarify the physiological and psychological mechanisms of *Cannabis* intoxication.

THE AFRICAN CONTINENT

Cannabis intoxication prevails all over the African continent, and *Cannabis* preparations are widely used in all the countries of North, South, West, and East Africa. *Cannabis* extracts are smoked or used to make beverages, pastries, and delicacies adapted to local tastes.

Egypt

In Egypt, the abuse of *Cannabis* drugs has continued for nearly a millennium, in spite of repeated attempts to stop this popular habit. Even when the cultivation of hemp was finally discontinued in the 1920's, hashish smuggled from Syria and Lebanon rapidly became available. After assuming power in 1954, the government of Nasser, intent upon giving a new impetus to the country, ordered strict enforcement of the laws banning the use of *Cannabis.* In 1958, 18.6 tons and in 1961, 5 tons of smuggled hashish were seized. Most of the material was smuggled from Syria and Lebanon, and the relations between Egypt and these countries became quite strained. The number of users of hashish has declined in the past years, and would include, according to some optimistic estimates, 4 to 5% of the male Egyptian population between 20 and 40 years old. But, according to Galal (1968), General Director of the Research Control Center of the Egyptian Organization for Pharmaceuticals, "dependence on hashish has represented and still represents the main challenge in the control of dangerous drugs in Egypt. Dependence resulting from its continuous use has obvious social and medical aftereffects." Chopra (1969) notes that "while the number of hashish users has fallen considerably in Egypt, the number of dealers does not record a corresponding decrease, because a large number of people are tempted into trafficking in the drug because of large profits. This would indicate that the damage done to society is not limited to the addicts but extends to the corruption of society as a whole." The latest appraisal by Sami-Ali (1971) indicates that "the habit of taking hashish which prevails in all the strata of the population raises a problem of national dimension." According to this author, hashish intoxication is not associated in Egypt with an increase in crime or severe mental illness but rather with a general stagnation and decrease in productivity of the people.

In 1954 President Nasser directed a committee of scholars to perform an in-depth study of the effects of hashish consumption on the Egyptian population. This "psycho-social" study has been conducted since 1957 by the National Center for Social and Criminological Research in Cairo. Reports presenting the findings of this study have been published regularly since 1962. A summary of these findings has also been published in the *Bulletin of Narcotics* (Soueif, 1967, 1971). This is the first study of chronic *Cannabis* users conducted by specially trained psychologists using standardized methods of sampling, interviewing and analysis. The reliability of the schedule was confirmed by the retake method. Items of low reliability were dropped from the study. The group of hashish users was matched with a control group of nonusers. A large number of psychomotor and cognitive tests were utilized. According to these studies, hashish usage prevails in Egypt among a significant fraction of the young male population; they start the habit when they are 16 to 18 years old under the influence of a male relative or of peer group pressure. Hashish users are more neglected by their fathers and families and are more "anxious" than controls. They develop a marked psychic dependence on the drug; they have great difficulty in stopping, especially if they are daily users and started the habit at an early age. Under drug effect, they present memory impairment for recent events, flight of ideas, and difficulty in concentration. *Cannabis* users have a lower criminal record than controls. Under conditions of being drugged and of craving for the drug, the work capacity of the hashish users is significantly impaired as to quality and quantity. This impairment could be correlated with the deterioration of psychomotor performance induced by hashish. Some of the findings of a study comparing 850 *Cannabis* users to 839 controls should be carefully studied: A positive relationship was established between duration of hashish use and opium taking; *Cannabis* takers crave for agents acting on the central nervous system more than non-takers do. *Cannabis* users are slow learners compared with non-takers; controls scored significantly better than hashish takers on most of the objective tests. This comprehensive study on hashish consumption in Egypt is by far the most thorough investigation of chronic *Cannabis* intoxication ever made. It should not have been ignored by all of the surveys performed at great expense of public funds in the United States (Report to Congress on Marihuana and Health, 1971, 1972; President's Commission Report on Marihuana, 1972).

Tunisia, Algeria, and Morocco

Moving westward along the path followed by the Arab conquerors of the ninth and tenth centuries, one finds, in spite of the vigorous efforts of past and present governments, widespread *Cannabis* use in Tunisia, Algeria, and Morocco. The plant grows wild in the sunny and sheltered spots of the mountains of the Rif and Atlas regions and is also cultivated by the peasants as a cash crop. In Morocco, some observers estimate that 30 to 35% of the adult male population uses *Cannabis* to some degree. Several studies on *Cannabis* addiction have been made in North Africa, by Bouquet (1944, 1950, 1951) in Tunisia and by Benabud (1957) and Christozov (1965) in Morocco. These studies are clinical, fragmentary observations, fraught with the same methodological uncertainties as those of Chopra; they contain very few relevant figures or statistics, and no laboratory tests. But they all conclude, as did Chopra, that chronic *Cannabis* use leads to physical and mental deterioration as well as social stagnation. Benabud emphasizes the "progressive degeneration which affects the chronic *Cannabis* user who presents an over-all deterioration of the faculties. This affects his occupational capacity, idleness being the first consequence, and breakdown in family relations following next. Physically, inveterate smokers suffer from precocious senescence which occurs sometimes in the forties."

Benabud devotes most of his study to the history of patients admitted to the Berrechid Psychiatric Hospital for *"Cannabis-*induced psychosis." The occurrence of psychosis among chronic users of kif has been questioned by many who have raised objections similar to those of the Indian Hemp Drug Commission and who point out the lack of specific symptomatology and the many other factors contributing to the development of insanity. However, the specific role of *Cannabis* intoxication in the development of "toxic psychosis" in Morocco has been corroborated by other European and French psychiatrists stationed at the Berrechid Psychiatric Hospital in the past decade (Rolland and Teste, 1957; Christozov, 1965). These psychoses are more frequent among the uprooted neoproletariat of the new urban centers, such as Casablanca and Rabat, than among the villagers living in more stable conditions.

Common Traits of *Cannabis* Intoxication in North Africa

In North Africa the use of hashish is an ingrained habit of the people. *Cannabis* extracts are used by the poor peasants or craftsmen to help them in performing their daily routine tasks. Hashish intoxication may provide them with the only available means of escaping from a dreary reality into a more pleasant world. Hashish consumers or kif smokers also report that they use the drug to enhance and prolong their sexual power. *Cannabis* preparations are also consumed by the wealthy, in a more covert and discriminate way, for their own enjoyment and pleasure.

Such wide social acceptance of *Cannabis* for reasons which seem perfectly valid to the users is associated with dormant, stratified societies. With the help of hashish, the poor are more likely to accept their marginal existence, while the wealthy enjoy one more pleasure.

West, Central, South, and East Africa

Smoking of *Cannabis* also prevails in nearly all other parts of Africa—in Gabon, Mozambique, Liberia, and the Congo, local tribes smoke "dimba" or "dumo" in "calabash" pipes made out of clay, or in water pipes. The custom of smoking hemp is based on religious beliefs and follows rituals which differ from one sect to another. In Central Africa, from Rhodesia to Zambia all along the trail of Arab traders of past centuries, *Cannabis* is widely used. In some tribes the plant is still considered sacred, as it was in ancient times. The Blacks of Kalamba regard *Cannabis* extracts as magic drugs which confer universal protection against all injury to life and as symbols of peace and friendship.

The earliest European explorers observed the smoking of hemp or "dagga" by all the racial groups which populated South Africa: Bushmen, Hottentots, and Bantus. *Cannabis* is still widely abused among the poor Black apartheid or destitute native Hindus of South Africa. This habit was not adopted by the white settlers until a decade ago, when young affluent students followed the example of their European and American counterparts.

Cannabis is also utilized all along the East Coast of Africa, from Mozambique to Tanzania and Somaliland.

CANNABIS INTOXICATION IN EUROPE

Hemp plants have been grown in continental Europe and in England since the beginning of the Christian era for their fiber, from which ropes and clothing were made. But Europeans never cultivated or used *Cannabis* for its psychoactive or medicinal properties until the middle of the twentieth century.

In 1949, the United Nations report of the Commission on Stupefying Drugs stated that "the use of Indian Hemp in Europe is confined chiefly to Greece and Turkey." Very shortly after this conclusion was made, the situation changed dramatically (Fig. 1).

Marihuana and Hashish in England

Cannabis sativa was first used as a mind-altering drug by significant segments of the European population in the 1950's, when the economic recovery of the postwar years created a demand for industrial and construction workers. With the influx of West Indians, Africans, and Turkish Cypriots, the use of *Cannabis* in the forms specific to each of these cultures became part of the British scene for the first time in the history of Great Britain. But the use of *Cannabis* rapidly extended from these migrant workers to the new "swinging" generation which was coming of age in Britain. The erosion of traditional religious values, the breakdown of a life centered around the family, the Church of England, and the monarchy, and the general permissive attitude adopted by many educators, are general factors difficult to evaluate but which did contribute to the adoption of *Cannabis* intoxication as part of a new life style. Marihuana and hashish use are also inextricably linked among the young with the appearance of popular "rock" music, all-night clubs, coffee bars, Beatnik and Hippie culture.

Another factor in the rapid spread of *Cannabis* use might be the rapid dissemination by modern mass communications media, mostly television, newspapers, and magazines, of many of the manifestations of this new life style.

Cannabis was first smuggled to England by migrant workers from the West Indies or Cyprus. But now criminal elements have taken over what has become a lucrative trade. Private planes are used to smuggle *Cannabis* extracts from the Middle East and parachute the material at different prearranged spots before landing in Britain. *Cannabis* is now available in all large British cities at a cost of $10 to $12 an ounce for hashish and $1 for two marihuana cigarettes. Its use, most prevalent among high school and university students, is now spreading into the recreational activities of early adult life. Many students from the British Isles take advantage of travel facilities to go to the Middle East and Africa, where they learn about kif in Morocco, golden grain in Lebanon, or dagga in Africa.

In May of 1971, *The Observer* reported that *"Cannabis* smoking is an established part of British university life, increasingly accepted by both academics and the police. But anxieties remain." Therefore, within a decade, a significant segment of the youth of England has come to believe that marihuana smoking is not a dangerous or criminal form of behavior. It is a normal form of pleasure-seeking, preferable to drinking alcohol. It is not considered dangerous to health or addictive.

Most young people in the United States and Canada share the same view. The use of *Cannabis* in England falls under the Dangerous Drug Act of 1965, which states that individuals may not import preparations of *Cannabis* without a license, possess or distribute *Cannabis,* or permit their premises to be used for the smoking of *Cannabis.* Through this legislation, England followed the recommendations of the U.N. Single Convention on Stupefying Drugs (Geneva, 1961), which proposes national control of the use of *Cannabis* as a pleasure-giving drug. The amount of hashish and of marihuana seized by British authorities has increased annually over the past 20 years, as has the number of offenses associated with possession or supply of *Cannabis* preparations (from 4 in 1945 to 2393 in 1967). On July 22, 1967, a petition was published in *The Times* of London which advocated reform of the law regulating the possession and use of *Cannabis.* This petition, signed by prominent persons from the worlds of literature, arts, and science, declared that *Cannabis* was used by ordinary persons to increase their sensory perception and to find solace and pleasure. The controversy created by this petition was fanned by the Wooton Report, published a year later. This extensive review of the *Cannabis* literature by a commission of the British House of Lords very closely duplicated the conclusions of the Indian Hemp Drug Commission. It concluded "that no reliable observation of a syndrome of mental deterioration due to *Cannabis* has been made in the Western world, and from the Eastern reports available to us it is not possible to form a judgement on whether such behavior is directly attributable to *Cannabis* taking." The report also mentioned that English physicians were still prescribing extracts and tincture of *Cannabis.* The commission also concludes that, on the basis of convictions alone, *Cannabis* use is widespread in Great Britain and cuts across class and color lines.

The British government has ordered further investigations into the physical, mental, and social effects of *Cannabis* use, but it is not ready to lift the legal prohibition of the drug in England.

After 1960, the use of *Cannabis* extracts also spread among the young people of college age dwelling in the large cities of Western Europe. Sweden and Denmark were primarily affected, but the use of *Cannabis* was much less popular than the use of amphetamines, which reached epidemic proportions until the liberal dispensing policies were revised in 1965. Amsterdam became the European capital of *Cannabis* smoking, which was tolerated by the city authorities. Many vagrant, idle youth congregated in the large squares of this northern city to smoke away their ennui. However, the use of *Cannabis* in France, Germany, Italy, and Spain is relatively rare and until recently does not appear to have gone beyond a passing youthful fad. This is particularly the case in France, in spite of the presence in that country of half a million North African workers who use hashish and make it available around them.

Present lack of interest in marihuana in some countries of Western Europe, such as France, may be attributed to different factors: wine and alcohol, allied with fine cuisine, are still used preferentially in small amounts sufficient to bring about some measure of euphoria; some *joie de vivre* is still present; an interest in politics with a polarization towards the extremes with its call for action is not compatible with the "integration of the ego in the universe" brought about by *Cannabis* intoxication.

However, the U.S. scene still remains the focal point as well as the dynamic example for a large portion of the new European generation. What happens in America to the development of *Cannabis* intoxication is certain to have an impact in Western Europe.

Cannabis Intoxication in the U.S.S.R. and Its Allied Countries

Bejerot (1970) quotes circumstantial evidence indicating that "there is obviously a problem with *Cannabis* preparations in the Soviet Union." The contrary would be surprising. In a society where social and individual programming leaves very little place for personal initiative and adventure, there would be a natural tendency to seek an escape into the nirvana of *Cannabis* intoxication. But the Soviet State considers drug abuse and dependence as a crime against the State, the greatest crime of all in a socialist regime which exerts a very repressive policy against abusers of drugs. This policy has prevented the problem of *Cannabis* intoxication from surfacing in communist-dominated societies (Fig. 1).

CANNABIS INTOXICATION IN THE AMERICAS

Cannabis in Latin America

Cannabis sativa was brought to the New World by Spanish conquistadors when they conquered Mexico and Central and South America. *Cannabis* was then adopted by the local indigenous population, which was already accustomed to other intoxicants. The Negro slaves who were later imported to

South America were familiar with hemp preparations in their native lands. Hemp now grows in a wild state in most of South America and is generally smoked in the form of cigarettes and cigars or in pipes.

In Brazil, "maconha" is smoked or added to certain beverages which are taken at various religious ceremonies. From the countryside, the tenant farmers and sharecroppers of African and Indian origin of the northeastern coastal plains emigrated to find industrial occupation in the growing cities of southern Brazil, São Paulo and Rio de Janeiro. *Cannabis* preparations, first used exclusively by these impoverished workers, are now also consumed by the younger members of the ruling classes.

A similar trend is observable in other countries of South America adjoining Brazil to the north and west such as Venezuela, Peru, Bolivia, and Ecuador. In Chile, Argentina, and Uruguay *Cannabis* intoxication is much less prevalent. In Central America and Mexico the use of *Cannabis* has long been common among the rural and urban poor.

In the Caribbean, especially in Jamaica, "ganja" is still used by the descendants of the African slaves who populated the islands. Some groups center its use around religious rituals and many of their daily living habits. Ganja is mixed with food or drinks and smoked in large pipes. The drug is also used as a remedy for many ailments. Chronic *Cannabis* intoxication is not uncommon among members of the poorer rural and urban classes of Jamaica. In addition, in those islands, as well as in all of Latin America, *Cannabis* is also used today by the affluent youth of the upper and middle classes.

Marihuana Comes to the United States: The Marihuana Tax Act

Marihuana, as a pleasure-inducing drug which could be smoked, came to the United States from Mexico around 1910, when Mexican farmers started to smuggle it into Texas. After the impact of World War I and the beginning of widespread cigarette smoking, marihuana became widely used among the poor Black and Mexican workers in Texas and Louisiana. New Orleans became the main port of entry for *Cannabis* smuggled from Mexico, Cuba, and South America. The drug was shipped up the Mississippi to river ports and from there to large cities. By 1930, marihuana was available in most major American cities. But the users of the drug were generally found among Black minority groups and jazz musicians.

In Louisiana, marihuana was used widely enough to cause public concern, especially after a series of articles published in 1926 in the *New Orleans Morning Tribune* denouncing the "Marihuana Menace." Many of the crimes committed in New Orleans were attributed, rightly or wrongly, to marihuana users. At that time the majority of the people in the United States were not very concerned about the problem of *Cannabis* use, which was still alien to "the American way of life."

The Federal Bureau of Narcotics, however, led by Harry Anslinger, was convinced of the harm that *Cannabis* intoxication might bring to the individual and society. There was no serious opposition when he proposed to Congress that it pass the Marihuana Tax Act which, in fact, banned cultivation, possession, and distribution of hemp plants, except for the mature stalk from which twine and light cordage can be manufactured. Only the birdseed industry, which used 2 million tons of *Cannabis* seed every year, protested, and sterilized seed, incapable of germination, escaped the general prohibition spelled out by the Marihuana Tax Act of 1937.

In turn the states, following the lead of the federal government, voted legislation somewhat excessively repressive, aiming at banning the use of *Cannabis* on their territories. It should be mentioned here that the representatives of the Federal Bureau of Narcotics were working in liaison with other organizations throughout the world to control the use of the "stupefying drugs" which were already being consumed at an alarmingly growing rate. If the United States and Western Europe were concerned primarily with stopping the extension of the white drugs (opium derivatives), the underdeveloped nations were concerned by the abuse of the black drugs (*Cannabis* derivatives). In 1925, at the International Opium Conference, Egypt, which had been plagued for centuries by *Cannabis* intoxication, proposed that *Cannabis* be placed in the same category as the opiates and that rigid controls should prohibit its use as an intoxicant. The United States was merely fulfilling its obligation to this 1925 convention with the passage of the Marihuana Tax Act, which brought *Cannabis* under federal control and declared that importation, possession, or sale was a criminal offense.

Passage of the Act met with some criticism from a number of physicians and scientists who thought, not without good reason, that the dangers of *Cannabis* to health and social structure had been exaggerated in America. They also believed that the possible medical applications of *Cannabis* derivatives should be further investigated. Some of the arguments of the spokesmen from the Federal Bureau of Narcotics concerning the "killer weed" were designed to frighten the general public, not to educate them. At that time, most of the marihuana smoked in the United States was of local or Mexican origin, as it still is, and had limited potency. With such material, *Cannabis* intoxication similar to that observed in the East could not be achieved. By fighting the spread of marihuana, the Federal Bureau of Narcotics wanted to stop the eventual usage of the stronger *Cannabis* preparations which in the Orient were associated with many individually and socially undesirable effects. If one accepts marihuana, how can one outlaw hashish? This point was never made clear in America.

The strong tactics used by the Federal Bureau of Narcotics in denouncing the harmful effects of marihuana in the United States antagonized a number of independent-minded American scientists and physicians. This was the start of a controversy which has increased yearly ever since except for a short interlude following World War II. There are those who believe that marihuana is a mild intoxicant, constitutes a minor danger to public health, and that its ban is a piece of unfair, repressive legislation. There are others who think that *Cannabis* is a dangerous, toxic substance which throughout history has done great harm to man and society.

This controversy was further compounded by the conclusions of the La Guardia Report.

The La Guardia Report

Following the passage of the Marihuana Tax Act and because of a significant incidence of marihuana use in New York City, mostly in Harlem, Mayor Fiorello La Guardia asked the New York Academy of Medicine in 1938 to conduct a scientific and sociological investigation on "The Marihuana Problem in the City of New York."

Conducted from 1940 to 1941, this was the first systematic investigation of acute *Cannabis* intoxication performed on volunteers receiving *Cannabis* extracts from plants commonly used in the New York area. Prison inmates were the subjects of the study, with users and nonusers in different experimental groups. Measured quantities of crude plant, provided from material seized by the Federal Bureau of Narcotics, or alcoholic extracts were smoked or ingested by the prisoners. The concentration of the psychoactive ingredients of the raw material could not be measured at the time, but the average reactions of the subjects indicate that the preparations used were far less potent than the hashish ingested by the American and French experimenters a century before. Twenty to fifty grains (1.2 to 3 g) of Tilden's Extract of *Cannabis indica* taken by Ludlow in 1851 produced profound hallucinations, not comparable to any of the symptoms reported by the subjects in the La Guardia study, including those who developed "psychoses." The subjects of the La Guardia study absorbed from 2 to 22 ml of the alcoholic extract and from 1 to 11 cigarettes. A large spectrum of subjective symptoms was observed, from euphoria to dysphoria and floating sensations, hallucinations, and psychotic episodes. Tachycardia and congestion of the conjunctivae were observed for the first time. Selected tests showed impairment of mental and motor performance. Former users of *Cannabis* showed some tolerance to some of the measurable effects of the drug. It was also noted that smoked *Cannabis* produced its effect more rapidly than the ingested material and required smaller quantities of the drug. But at that time, the nature of the psychoactive constituents of *Cannabis* was unknown, and there was no way of assaying the potency of *Cannabis* preparations. In their conclusions, the authors of the La Guardia study took a relatively benign view of marihuana intoxication, which in 1940–1943 had not yet become a serious problem in the New York City school population.

One of the main shortcomings of the La Guardia Report is the lack of dose-response curves relating quantity of drug to physical and psychological response. Furthermore, some of the critics of the report pointed out that while contradictory statements are to be expected in any study which does not yield clear-cut results, some of those contained in the report are truly misleading. For instance, in the chapter "Addiction and Tolerance," the author first states his clinical observations: *"Tolerance develops during the period when the drug is being taken and accounts for the necessity of increasing the dosage to bring about the desired effects."* However, the author has a sudden change of heart following personal interviews with 48 users who revealed to him that "the smoking of 1 or 2 cigarettes is sufficient to bring on the high, at which time the smoker will stop for fear of becoming too high. When the desired effects have passed off and the smoker has 'come down,' smoking a cigarette brings the high effect again. This could not be the case had a steadily increasing tolerance developed." And the author concludes that "no increase in dosage is required to repeat the desired effect in users, [justifying] the conclusion that tolerance is not found in marihuana users." In the final conclusion of the Report, the chairman of the committee takes a similar stand and concludes, "no evidence was found of an acquired tolerance for the drug." This is an example where a personal testimony carries more weight than actual, observed fact. The final sentence of the conclusion dealing with "Addiction and Tolerance" is pure conjecture when it states: "The continuation and the frequency of usage of marihuana as in the case of many other habit-forming substances depend on the easily controlled desire for its pleasurable effects."

The conclusions of the report, in spite of their contradictions and conjectures, apply only and specifically to the effects of the relatively inactive marihuana used in 1940 in New York City. It is obvious that this preparation was quite mild, since it allowed the "confirmed user to smoke 6 to 10 cigarettes a day." We are told that those who had been smoking marihuana for a period of years showed "no mental or physical deterioration which could be attributed to the drug." We are also informed that "if the subject reaches 'too high' a state, the taking of beverages such as beer or sweet soda pop, or a cold bath are considered effective counter measures." It seems doubtful that such methods would be effective treatment of untoward effects of *Cannabis* intoxication ranging from hallucinations to panic reactions; as reported by others. Therefore, it seems questionable to generalize the conclusion of the La Guardia Report and claim that marihuana is a mild intoxicant which should be made available to the general public as cigarettes and alcohol are, or that the moderate "social use" of marihuana, corresponding to the American habit of social drinking, is unlikely to have grave harmful consequences. To claim, as Grinspoon (1971) did, that the La Guardia Report is "the most thorough and detailed collection of factual finding in the whole body of scientific literature on marihuana" is to ignore the older studies of Moreau (1845) and the more recent ones by Williams (1946), Isbell (1971), Hollister (1969), and Forney (1971), as well as the comprehensive study of hashish consumption in Egypt (Soueif, 1967, 1971).

The Post-World War II Marihuana Epidemic

The controversy surrounding the release of the conclusions of the La Guardia Report did not develop into a national debate because World War II was providing more vital issues for the American people to discuss. The marihuana debate was postponed until years after the postwar period, which was marked by the remarkable growth of the United States as one of the greatest powers in the modern world.

When the war and postwar generation entered high school and college, the marihuana debate reopened, louder than ever, on a nationwide scale. This new generation was affluent and articulate and eager to experiment. It was disenchanted and rebellious. Church, country, and family did not motivate the young people, who rebelled against those "irrelevant vestiges of the past." Freedom and liberation were the order of the day; anything which entailed regulation was interpreted as being repressive. There was outrage at the Vietnam war, the consumer society, and social inequities. Marihuana smoking became at the same time a pleasurable pastime, a sign of independent behavior, and an expression of rebellion against a rigid, uninspiring society. The popular singers of the rock festivals openly used the drug and were followed by their enthusiastic audiences. The youth were left without guidelines and at times had to face the rigors of repressive legislation.

And little was known about marihuana except that it was forbidden by law and that it usually came from Mexico. In this general confusion many educators, caught by more violent manifestations of student revolt, tended to be permissive on the question of *Cannabis* intoxication. Some, with little fundamental knowledge about the subject, even claimed that "marihuana did not have any harmful physical effects, that it was less dangerous than alcohol and cigarettes and that it should be legalized and sold to anyone over the age of 16" (Mead, 1969). This view was widely held by the American student population, who by that time had started to experiment extensively with marihuana, as indicated by a 1969 survey (Mizner et al., 1970) conducted on nine campuses in the western United States and which is summarized in Table 2. The high incidence of marihuana smoking among medical students is another indication of the widespread belief in the innocuity of this drug. A survey conducted in 1970–1971 among high school students by the Columbia University School of Public Health indicated that 15% of young Americans

Table 2

Marihuana Use in Nine Western Colleges (1969)[a]

Institution	Percent
Medical center	20
Large private university	16
Large state university	16
State commuter college	12
University commuter branch	11
Nursing school	11
Small male technical college	7
Small denominational women's college	7
Small denominational men's college	7

[a] From Mizner et al., 1970.

from 12 to 17 years of age, 17% of the boys and 14% of the girls, had smoked marihuana. In the meantime, numerous books and publications have appeared in the United States claiming that marihuana is a mild intoxicant, that it should be legalized, and that "the health sciences have the obligation to guide our society in the judicious use of marihuana" (Lesse, 1971).

The federal government responded to this situation by sponsoring a comprehensive program on the health consequences of marihuana use, directed and administered by the National Institute of Mental Health (N.I.M.H.). Delta-9-THC was made available to qualified investigators, and within the past 2 years more has been learned of the effects and mechanism of action of this psychoactive component of *Cannabis* than in the previous 4000 years. The first Report to Congress on Marihuana and Health, released in 1971, did not include many of these more recent studies and its conclusions were rather ambiguous—reminiscent of those of the La Guardia Report and the Indian Hemp Drug Commission, which were generously quoted.

By contrast, very little attention was given to the conclusions of the 1961

U.N. Geneva Conference of 78 nations which assembled to adopt "a single convention on stupefying drugs." The convention recommended that the national legislation of its member countries consider the possession of *Cannabis* as an offense to be penalized. This convention was signed by the President of the United States and approved by the Senate in 1967. It is the law of the land. It seems that some attention should be given to the reasons which led to the adoption of the Geneva Convention, after 50 years of studies by the representatives of all the major countries of the world.

THE INTERNATIONAL REGULATION OF *CANNABIS* AND OTHER DANGEROUS DRUGS

The First and Second Opium Conferences of The Hague (1912) and Geneva (1924)

At the turn of the century, with the development of intercontinental communications, it became apparent to the nations of the world that the control of substances dangerous to man's health and to society, primarily opium at that time, had to be controlled on a global basis. Representatives of sovereign nations held conferences to formulate regulations for the international control of opium and dangerous drugs. Hemp, as *Cannabis* was called, was considered at the first "Opium Conference" at The Hague in 1912. The preamble to the text of this conference spells out its general goals.

> "The Emperor of all Russias, The King of England and Emperor of India, The Kaiser of Germany, The President of the French Republic, The President of the United States of America, . . . desirous of advancing a step further on the road opened by the International Commission of Shanghai of 1909; determined to bring about the gradual suppression of the abuse of opium, morphine and cocaine and also of the drugs prepared or derived from these substances which give rise or might give rise to similar abuses; taking into consideration the necessity and the mutual advantage of an international agreement on this point; convinced that in this humanitarian endeavor they will meet with the unanimous adherence of all States concerned; have decided to conclude a convention with this object."

While *Cannabis* was not mentioned in the text of the conference, an "Indian Hemp resolution" was included: "The Conference considers it desirable to study the question of Indian Hemp from the statistical and scientific point of view with the object of regulating its abuses, should the necessity be felt, by internal regulation or by international agreement."

At the Second Opium Conference (1924), held under the auspices of the League of Nations in Geneva, Dr. El Guindy, the delegate from Egypt, proposed that *Cannabis* be added to the list of dangerous substances to be controlled by international legislation.

> "There is, however, another product, which is at least as harmful as opium, if not more so, and which my government would be glad to see in the same category as the other narcotics already mentioned. I refer to hashish, the product of *Cannabis sativa*. This substance and its derivatives work such havoc that the Egyptian government has for a long time past prohibited their introduction into the country. I cannot emphasize sufficiently the importance of including this product in the list of narcotics, the use of which is to be regulated by this Conference.
>
> "It should be an accepted principle that all narcotic substances which are already known and although not classed as stupefying drugs may be regarded as such together with all other stupefying drugs which may be discovered or produced in the future should fall automatically within the scope of the measures of the convention which we hope to conclude."

Dr. El Guindy claimed that while the growing of *Cannabis* had been forbidden in Egypt since 1884, large amounts were still smuggled from neighboring countries. This illicit use of hashish was the principal cause of insanity in Egypt, varying from 30 to 60% of the total number of cases reported. These were due to hashish intoxication, with a threefold greater incidence of insanity among men than among women, because only men use the drug.

> "Taken occasionally and in small doses, hashish perhaps does not offer much danger, but there is always the risk that once a person begins to take it, he will continue. He acquires the habit and becomes addicted to the drug and once this happens it is very difficult to escape."

The greatest hazards of *Cannabis* intoxication mentioned by Dr. El Guindy were "acute hashishism," marked by crises of delirium and insanity, and "chronic hashishism," marked by physical and mental deterioration.

The Egyptian proposal was supported by the delegates from South Africa, Brazil, Turkey, and Greece, where *Cannabis* use was widespread. The representatives from Japan, Poland, China, and the United States, where *Cannabis* use was not prevalent, also favored, as a matter of principle, the inclusion of *Cannabis* among the dangerous drugs to be regulated. The delegates from the British Empire and France (who were speaking for one-third of the world) were willing to accept the regulations for *Cannabis* in England and continental France, where hashish intoxication was practically unknown. However, they were reluctant to impose such regulations on the countries in Africa or Asia which they administered and where the use of *Cannabis* preparations was "endemic." But Dr. El Guindy managed to convince a majority of his colleagues, and the control of Indian Hemp was included in the convention. Indian Hemp was defined as "the dried flowering or fruiting tops of the pistillate plant *Cannabis sativa* from which the resin has not been extracted, under whatever name they may be designated in commerce."

All the representatives at this Conference signed a document which was to be implemented by the legislative and governing bodies of their respective countries.

By approving the Marihuana Tax Act of 1937, the U.S. Congress was merely fulfilling its obligation as a signatory member of the Second International Opium Conference of 1925.

The U.N. Single Convention (1961)

After World War II the United Nations, in succeeding the League of Nations, inherited the duty of enforcing a highly complex international legislation on narcotics and dangerous drugs which involved more than a half dozen international treaties. The U.N. Department of Economic and Social Affairs organized a Division of Narcotic Drugs to undertake preparatory work, with a view to establishing a single convention to replace the existing eight international instruments and to strengthen and simplify the international control machinery. The Division of Narcotic Drugs of the United Nations also publishes, since 1949, a very informative *Bulletin on Narcotics*.

In 1948, the World Health Organization (W.H.O.) came into being. Through this organization, the public health and medical professions of more than 120 countries are able to exchange their knowledge and experience. W.H.O. has appointed an expert Committee on Drug Dependence which serves as an advisory committee to the U.N. Commission on Narcotics on technical and scientific matters. The members of such expert groups are selected primarily on the basis of their ability and technical experience and serve without remuneration in a personal capacity and not as representatives of government or of other bodies. In 1954, this W.H.O. Expert Committee on Drug Dependence advised the U.N. Commission on Narcotics that *Can-*

nabis had no medical value and that use of the drug was dangerous from every point of view, whether physical, mental, or social. In 1960, the W.H.O. Committee on Drug Dependence advised the U.N. Commission on Narcotics that *"Cannabis* preparations are practically obsolete and there is no justification for their medical use." If *Cannabis* is as harmless as claimed by many scientists and scholars, the Western world has been the victim of the greatest and most prolonged hoax ever perpetrated by the East. There is also the possibility that these scholars may have been deceived by the subtle toxicity of this deceptive weed.

It was primarily on the basis of the successive reports of the W.H.O. Expert Committee on Drug Dependence issued over the last decade that the U.N. Commission on Narcotics recommended that *Cannabis* derivatives be included in the 1961 Single Convention for the control of narcotics and stupefying drugs. After years of preparatory work through the U.N. Commission on Narcotics, the U.N. Conference of member nations assembled to draft this Single Convention. Five hundred delegates from 74 nations worked from January 24 to March 25, 1961, in New York. Some of the best toxicologists and pharmacologists were present among the national delegations. Advisors to the U.S. delegation included Drs. N. B. Eddy and H. Isbell, pharmacologists of international reputation specializing in the study of psychotropic drugs.

In addition there were present Dr. Mabileau from France, Dr. D. L. Goldberg from Sweden, Prof. Kaymackalam from Turkey, and Prof. Joachimoglu from Greece.

The Single Convention on Narcotic Drugs, the Convention to which the United States is a party, obligates the parties to "limit exclusively to medical and scientific purposes, the production, manufacture, export, import, distribution of, trade in, use and possession of drugs covered by the Convention" [Art. 4(C)]. These drugs include, in addition to opium, coca leaves, and all of their known derivatives, "the flowering or fruiting tops of the *Cannabis* plant (excluding the seeds and leaves when not accompanied by the tops) from which the resin has not been extracted, by whatever name they may be designated" [Art. 1–1(b)]. The leaves of the plant were excluded from the convention as a compromise gesture to the delegates from India and Pakistan, where bhang, a concoction made of *Cannabis* leaves, was still widely used.

However, in order to limit the use of *Cannabis* leaves, the following article was added: "The parties shall adopt such measures as may be necessary to prevent the misuse of, and illicit traffic in, the leaves of the *Cannabis* plant" [Art. 28(3)]. Finally, the Convention recognized the need for transitional reservations in countries where *Cannabis* preparations had been used for centuries. "The use of *Cannabis* for other than medical and scientific purposes must be discontinued as soon as possible but in any case within twenty-five

years from the coming into force of this Convention" [Art. 49.2 (f)]. However, countries where *Cannabis* had never been cultivated for its intoxicating
properties were requested to make a special pledge: "Whenever the prevailing conditions in the country or a territory of a Party render the prohibition
of the cultivation of opium poppy, the coca bush or the *Cannabis* plant, the
most suitable measure in its opinion, for protecting the public health and welfare and preventing the diversion of drugs into the illicit traffic, the Party concerned shall prohibit cultivation."

The Single Convention was hailed by most countries as a landmark for the
control of dangerous drugs throughout the world. It was also hailed as a
model of the international cooperation the United Nations can achieve. In
the ensuing years, the Convention was ratified by most of the participating
nations, and by the United States in 1967. It certainly gives better tools to
the governments to stem the ever-increasing usage of stupefying drugs
throughout the world.

However, there were dissenting voices, because the Convention had included *Cannabis* among the drugs to be banned from use and this inclusion
was felt to be the fault of Mr. Harry Anslinger. The American delegation to
the Convention was led by Harry Anslinger, a career diplomat who had become Commissioner of Narcotics and who was known in the United States
primarily for his strong stand in support of the Marihuana Tax Act. Because
of this stand Anslinger became the *bête noire* of the pot culture and of their
American or English sympathizers. Schofield (1971), for instance, claims
that "the inclusion of *Cannabis* into an international agreement mainly concerned with opiates and cocaine was due to the efforts of one determined
man, Harry Anslinger," and John Kaplan (1971) writes: "The section on
marihuana was proposed by the United States delegation headed by H. Anslinger." Dr. Adolf Lande, who was Deputy Executive Secretary of the Convention, and who participated in all of the preparatory work leading to it,
emphatically rejected such statements as incorrect and incompatible with the
scientific, historical, and political facts which dominated this Conference.

It would seem that Kaplan and Schofield are opposing a worldwide movement of the twentieth century to propound a parochial viewpoint involving
the sudden growth of a *Cannabis* drug culture in the United States and England. Unfortunately, in the process, they are unfairly using a scapegoat to
strengthen their viewpoint. Anyone reading the two volumes of documents
related to the Single Convention will immediately realize that it was not the
work of one man, but the result of a historical humanitarian movement which
started at the turn of the century. Anslinger did not in any way participate in
starting this movement. *Cannabis* was included in the 1961 Single Convention for the following reasons: (1) All of the available expert advice from

W.H.O. indicated that *Cannabis* did constitute a danger to health and a hazard to society; (2) the purpose of this Convention was to embody in a single treaty all of the previous international agreements and protocols for the control of all dangerous and stupefying drugs presenting a large potential for abuse among the people of the world. These included the Second Opium Conference of Geneva of 1924, which requested the control of *Cannabis*. By including *Cannabis* in the 1961 Convention, the representatives of sovereign nations were following the purpose set in 1912 at the First Hague Conference on Opium, which was to "bring about the gradual suppression of drugs which give rise to abuse." Therefore, in reading the debates of the *United Nations Conference for the Adoption of a Single Convention on Narcotic Drugs* (1961), it seems clear that the delegates, after carefully listening to the reports of the expert committee, were attempting to control and eliminate as much as possible, throughout the world, the use of dangerous psychotropic drugs including *Cannabis*.

In such a context one is at a loss to understand Kaplan's statement that "anyone reading the Single Convention on Narcotic Drugs might well conclude that a major purpose of the entire treaty was to make sure that the federal (U.S.) marihuana laws were not relaxed."

In any event, the U.N. Single Convention of 1961 is not the last in the series of conferences held since the turn of the century to limit and control the use of dangerous drugs. New agreements have been called for by the W.H.O. Committee on Drug Dependence on such "nonnarcotic opiate drugs" as hallucinogens, central nervous depressants (barbiturates), and stimulants (amphetamines). A new conference held in Vienna in 1971 resulted in an international agreement to control the use of many of the newer psychotropic drugs. Delta-9-THC and its derivatives were also included in this new agreement, which will be followed by a New Single Convention to be held in 1973. Such a tendency to legislate against the use of dangerous drugs runs counter to a position assumed by many distinguished American scholars, who believe that such legislation infringes upon individual freedom, and that repressive laws actually foster the spread of drug abuse.

The First Report of the National Commission on Marihuana (1972)

The drug control act of 1970, passed by the United States Congress, authorized the appointment of a National Commission on Marihuana and Drug Abuse made up of two members of the Senate, two members of the House of Representatives, and nine members appointed by the President. Its assignment was to study and investigate the causes of drug abuse and their significance; for the first year the primary emphasis was to be placed on all aspects of marihuana use and especially on the following: (1) the extent of use of marihuana in the United States, to include its various sources, the number of users, number of arrests, number of convictions, amount of marihuana seized, type of user, and nature of use; (2) an evaluation of the efficacy of existing marihuana laws; (3) a study of the pharmacology of marihuana and its immediate and long-term effects, both physiological and psychological; (4) the relationship of marihuana use to aggressive behavior and crime; (5) the relationship between marihuana and the use of other drugs; and (6) the international control of marihuana. Within a year after its formation, the Commission was to submit to the President and Congress a comprehensive report on its study, which would include its recommendations and such proposals for legislation and administrative action as would be necessary to carry out its recommendation.

To carry out its work, in addition to its 13 members, the Commission had a 55-member staff which included 16 "youth consultants" and 18 "student researchers." The 38 contributors and contractors listed in the Report included lawyers (14), psychiatrists and psychologists (10), and sociologists (5). Three of the sociologists are known for their strong views favoring the legalization of marihuana. Similarly, of the 46 consultants listed, psychiatrists or psychologists (16) outnumbered all other specialists. This strong representation in the social and behavioral sciences might account for the general content of the Report which emphasizes primarily the psychosocial aspects of marihuana usage within the continental United States during the past decade.

The Report is divided into five sections; four of these are devoted to the sociological aspects of marihuana usage in the United States.

Marihuana and the problem of marihuana

In this section the Commission considers the marihuana problem in very general philosophical and sociological terms, summarized as follows by its Vice-President, Dr. Farnsworth:

> "Although certain marginal groups in this country have used marihuana as an intoxicant for 75 years, neither the drug nor the practice of using it was defined as a national problem until the mid-1960's. . . ." The following factors probably fostered its emergence as a defined problem: "(1) the high visibility of an illegal behavior, marihuana use, among a fairly large group of persons within the mainstream of American society; (2) the threats which many people felt that marihuana posed not only to the health and morality of the individual,

but to the public safety, public health and dominant social order. . . ."

". . . The threat which marihuana is thought to present to the dominant social order is a major undercurrent of the marihuana problem; use of the drug is frequently linked with idleness, lack of motivation, hedonism, sexual promiscuity, conflict with moral precepts, 'dropping out' and rejection of the established value system. In this context, marihuana has become more than a drug; it has become 'a symbol of the rejection of cherished values.' Past myth and misconceptions, present symbolism and apprehension concerning what is to come have all combined to give marihuana many meanings, and it is these which constitute the marihuana problem."

"Marihuana use and its effects"

Prevalence of Cannabis usage in the United States

A survey made by the Commission indicated that contemporary use of marihuana involves all segments of the population. About 24 million Americans over the age of 11 (15% of the adults 18 and over, and 14% of the 12 to 17 year-olds) have used marihuana at least once, with 8.3 million still using it.

The largest group comprises the experimenters (50% of adults and 60% of youth) who have discontinued use after one trial or who use marihuana once a month or less. Intermittent users (12% of adults, 19% of youth) use the drug from twice a month to once a week. Six percent of adults and 5% of youth are "moderate" users (several times a day to once a week). "About 2% of those who have ever used marihuana, or 500,000 people, now use the drug heavily (several times a day). Marihuana plays an important role in their lives. . . . These heavy marihuana users constitute the greatest 'at risk population' in the United States." Only a minute number of Americans are very heavy users (in a state of chronic, constant intoxication with potent *Cannabis* preparations), an observation which "places the United States at the present time in a fortunate position."

The psychological and physiological effects of marihuana usage

This section reports ambiguous and conflicting results in a rather disorganized fashion, dispensed amidst sociological rhetoric and many qualifications. This holds true for the only new data compiled by the Commission, which describes two studies of chronic *Cannabis* smokers performed in Boston and Jamaica. In the Boston study, 20 American "intermittent" (eight cigarettes a month) or moderate to heavy users (average 33 cigarettes monthly) were allowed to smoke for 21 days as much marihuana as they wished (delta-9-THC content not mentioned, but presumably 10 mg per cigarette). These young adults averaged five years (range 2 to 17 years) of daily use of marihuana. The mean age of these subjects was 23. Based on I.Q. testing, they were superior intellectually, although they had completed, on the average, only 2½ years of college. Their job histories were rather erratic, characteristic of a pattern of "itinerant living." Under conditions of free availability of marihuana, all of the subjects increased their consumption of the drug from 6 to 12 times; "intermittent users" (up to 10 times a month) became heavy users (three times daily), and heavy users (one to two a day) became very heavy smokers (3½ to 8 cigarettes a day). A similar significant increase in marihuana consumption when the drug was freely available was observed in the La Guardia study, and in the study by Williams, Himmelsbach, and Wikler (1946). In both these studies, increased marihuana consumption was attributed primarily to the development of tolerance. Not so by this Report, which prefers to incriminate such an indefinite social factor as "the confined condition of the study." The Report even states, "In the intermittent use pattern and even moderate use (one cigarette a day), little evidence exists to indicate the development of tolerance to the desired high." However, in the Commission's own study, daily users of marihuana when the drug was freely available increased their consumption from three- to sixfold! Such a fact has major health and social implications since heavy usage, as concluded by the Commission itself, represents a high risk for the individual and society.

The Commission is satisfied to conclude that the heavy marihuana usage of the subjects studied was accompanied by few observable untoward effects. "During this free access study, no harmful effects were observed on general body functions, motor functions, mental functions, personal or social behavior or work performance." But how should one reconcile this categorical statement of overall lack of physical and mental and social effects of marihuana with the following three observations in the same Report?

> "Many of the subjects were in fair to poor physical condition, as judged by exercise tolerance."

> "The performance of one-fifth of the subjects in a battery of tests sensitive to brain function was poorer on at least one index than would have been predicted on the basis of their I.Q. scores and education."

> "The social adjustment of the daily users, when judged from

a traditional psychiatric standpoint, was impaired. Individuals tended to be more withdrawn and to interact less with each other than the intermittent users, regardless of the type of activity or state of intoxication."

However, these pronouncements, which might be construed as indicating that chronic marihuana use might have some deleterious effects on mental function and social behavior, are again qualified by the following contradictory statements: "A definite relationship between the poor test scores and prior marihuana or hallucinogen usage could not be proven," and "However, the daily users did appear to accommodate themselves better than the intermittent users to the effects of the intoxication on social interaction." Another example of this "balancing" act performed by the Commission follows: "Despite a relatively high level of scholastic attainment and superior intelligence, many of the subjects were performing well below their intellectual capacity, usually working at menial, mechanical or artisan tasks. They were not oriented toward achieving the traditional goals of the large society." However, this "dropping out" attitude of marihuana smokers is qualified by the following statement: "Nonetheless, the subjects could not be characterized as displaying a general lassitude and indifference, carelessness in personal hygiene or lack of productive activity, all supposed to be characteristic of very heavy use. Even during the period of heaviest marihuana smoking, they maintained a high level of interest and participation in a variety of personal activities such as writing, reading, keeping up with current world events, and participating in athletic and esthetic endeavors."

A similar ambiguity does not prevail in the section of the Report summarizing a study on long-time users of ganja in Jamaica, performed on 30 smokers who had used this strong *Cannabis* preparation daily for at least 10 years. The report states:

> "No significant physical or mental abnormalities could be attributed to marihuana use (concentration not specified) according to an evaluation of tests. Pulmonary function tests were impaired but this could not be attributed to marihuana alone since the subjects also smoked tobacco. These subjects did not show any evidence of deterioration of mental or social functioning which could be attributed solely to heavy long-term *Cannabis* use. They were alert and realistic, with average intelligence based on their education. Most functioned normally in their communities, with stable families, homes, jobs, and friends. They seemed to have survived heavy long-term *Cannabis* use without major physical or behavioral defects."

This sweeping conclusion is difficult to reconcile with one of the best documented results of the Jamaican study. The authors of this study, Rubin and Comitas (1972), report that, under the influence of ganja, the Jamaican farmers present a significant decrease in efficiency of work performance, as measured by videotape recordings and metabolic techniques: "Most smokers, immediately after drug use, enact more movements per minute, often with greater variation, and expend more kilocalories per unit of space cultivated."

These observations of Rubin and Comitas are in agreement with those of Soueif (1971) who reported in Egypt a significant fall in productivity of the workers under the influence of hashish.

In the summary of the section on chronic marihuana use, the Report concludes with statements which take into account other studies of chronic users, and its conclusions are more qualified:

> "The heavy user shows strong psychological dependence on the drug. Organ injury, especially diminution of pulmonary function, is possible. Specific behavioral changes are detectable."

Such a conclusion might be indicative of the fact that the Commission is unwilling at this time to state that chronic, heavy use of marihuana does not produce any physical or mental abnormalities, as the Jamaican study of 30 chronic users would imply. And, in the end, ambiguity prevails about the effects of chronic marihuana usage.

In order to maintain such an ambiguous stand on this subject, the Commission had to ignore the results of the three-year study performed by the United States Army on heavy chronic American users of hashish in Germany (Tennant and Groesbeck, 1972). This study clearly indicates that daily heavy use of *Cannabis* for three to twelve months by 110 soldiers stationed in Germany was accompanied by significant physical and mental deterioration as well as decreased work performance (see Chapter 6).

The social impact of marihuana use

The report first notes, as did many others before, that marihuana use does not lead to violent crime. On the contrary, it inhibits the expression of aggressive impulses. Most of the subsequent part of this section is written in the same ambiguous way as the preceding one. For instance, the report states:

> "Recent research has not yet proven that marihuana use significantly impairs driving ability or performance. The Commission believes nonetheless that driving while under the

influence of any psychoactive drug is a serious risk to public safety; the acute effects of marihuana intoxication, spatial and time distortion, and slowed reflexes may impair driving performance . . ."

"Marihuana use at the present in the United States does not constitute a major threat to public health. However, this statement should not lead to complacency. Marihuana is not an innocuous drug . . ."

"No evidence exists that marihuana causes or leads to the use of other drugs. There is, however, a correlation between use of marihuana and use of other drugs."

Such ambiguity concerning one of the most potentially harmful effects of marihuana, escalation to other drugs, is not warranted because of the rapid development of tolerance to marihuana which tends to lead the user to experiment with more potent drugs. Indeed, the overwhelming evidence gathered in the United States and abroad indicates that chronic use of marihuana is clearly associated with use of stronger psychotropic drugs, legal or illegal.

The Report also tends to minimize the potential harmful effects of marihuana.

For instance, on the subject of tolerance, the report states:

"By definition the development of tolerance is neither beneficial nor detrimental. In the intermittent use pattern and even in the moderate use pattern (up to once a day) little evidence exists to indicate the development of tolerance to the desired 'high' . . . although the high may persist for a shorter period."

This conclusion is at variance with that of Jones (1971) who showed in double-blind studies that daily smokers of marihuana did develop a tolerance to the euphoriant effects of marihuana.

On the subject of psychological dependence, the Report says:

. . ."although evidence indicates that heavy, long-term *Cannabis* users may develop psychological dependence, even then the level of psychological dependence is no different from the syndrome of anxiety and restlessness seen when an American stops smoking tobacco cigarettes."

On the overall effects of marihuana, the Report states:

"No outstanding abnormalities in psychological tests, psychiatric interviews or coping patterns have been conclusively

documented in studies of *Cannabis* users in other countries of
the world . . ."

This statement does not entirely agree with the following:

"Clinical reports describing transient psychosis, other psychiatric difficulties and impairment of cognitive function after use
of marihuana do not prove causability but cannot be ignored."

One wonders if the clinical report alluded to by the Commission may not
be the one by Soueif (1971) who, after studying 850 chronic hashish users,
concludes: "Under conditions of being drugged and/or craving for the drug,
the work capacity of the hashish users is significantly impaired as to quantity
and quality. This impairment could be correlated with the deterioration of
psychomotor performance induced by hashish."

The Commission, however, sounds a note of caution: "We must state
that a significant increase in the at-risk population (now including 2% of
marihuana users in the U.S.) could convert what is now a minor public
health concern to one of major proportions."

The report deals at great length with "marihuana and the social dominant
order," indicating that in the United States (as in any ordered society) the
use of drugs is seen as a threat to social order. The young marihuana user,
rather than the adult who just smokes for his enjoyment, is seen as the
greatest threat because of his apparent rejection of social, political, and legal
responsibilities. "Young people who use marihuana also seem to reject often
values upon which American society was founded. Parents are concerned
about marihuana use leading to idleness, dropping out, underachieving,
abandonment of work ethics, and radical politics." However, the Commission finds little basis for such fears, and takes a rather optimistic view of the
social impact of marihuana use:

"Most users, young or old, demonstrate an average or above
average degree of social functioning, academic achievement
and job performance. Based upon present evidence, it is unlikely that marihuana users will become less socially responsible
as a result of their marihuana use or that their patterns of
behavior and values will change significantly. The use of
marihuana by the nation's youth must be seen as a relatively
minor change in social pattern."

It seems highly debatable to qualify as "minor change in social pattern"
the acceptance of *Cannabis* intoxication, a habit which has been alien to
Western Society since its inception more than 2,000 years ago. The Commission is even unwilling to interpret marihuana usage as a symptom of social

forcement authorities to concentrate on the prosecution of more serious offenses.

Therefore, the Commission recommends that the present Federal law be changed to read:

> "Possession of marihuana for personal use would no longer be an offense but marihuana possessed in public would remain contraband subject to summary seizure and forfeiture. Casual distribution of small amounts for no or insignificant remuneration not involving profit would no longer be an offense."

The discouragement policy: the practical implemention.

If the Commission claims to have formulated recommendations which would allow a legal implementation of their "discouragement" policy of marihuana usage, it fails to detail the practical, educational measures which should be taken to discourage people from using *Cannabis*.

It is certainly not on the basis of the material released in the Report that educators will be able to formulate a policy of discouragement of marihuana use among the young. Educators or parents will find little reason to advise against the "moderate use" of marihuana (up to once weekly) which, according to the surveys performed by the Commission, is accompanied by little or no untoward effects.

Youth wants to know if smoking marihuana is harmful. The Report of the Commission does not answer this basic question. How can the Commission advocate a discouragement policy of marihuana usage when its own Report (*page 85*) states: "The effects of marihuana (when smoked occasionally or up to once a day) on the individual organs or bodily functions are of little importance. . . . By and large the immediate effects of marihuana intoxication have little or no permanent effect upon the individual."

Why should one advise high school students not to smoke marihuana if, as noted in the Report (*page 99*), "No conclusive evidence was found demonstrating that marihuana *by itself* is responsible for academic or vocational failure or 'dropping down' (although it could be one of many contributing reasons). Many studies reported that the majority of young people who have used marihuana received average or above-average grades in school."

As we have previously noted, all of these statements in the Report are qualified by others indicating that heavy or very heavy use of marihuana (not occurring in the United States) may be harmful. However, the overall impression of the reader of the Report is that marihuana is a mild intoxicant and that its usage causes little risk to the individual. This was the interpretation given to this Report by science writers of the American and foreign press, through whom the general public is informed. *U.S. News and World Report* of April 3, 1972, presented the findings of the Commission under the headline: "Evils of Marihuana, More Fantasy than Fact."

The recommendations of the Commission and the Single Convention

Removing all penalties (including a fine for simple possession for personal use) would make marihuana smoking more socially acceptable, since it would suppress the stigma attached to an unlawful act; the fear of breaking the law presently deters a number of young people. The Commission claims that its recommendation eliminating penalties for possession is compatible with the United States obligation under the Single Convention of 1961 and will not contravene any of the following articles:

Article 4 requires "parties to limit exclusively to medical and scientific purposes the production, manufacture, export, import, distribution of, trade in, use and possession of drugs." The Commission states that this article does not include penal sanctions.

Article 33 provides that "the parties shall not permit the possession of drugs except under legal authority." To comply with this article, the Commission advocates seizure and forfeiture of any amount found in public.

Article 36 states that "cultivation, production, manufacture, extractions, possession, offering, offering for sale, distribution, purchase, sale, delivery on any terms whatsoever, brokerage dispatch, dispatch in transit, and transport shall be punishable offenses when committed intentionally." The Commission claims that Article 36 refers not to possession for *personal use* as a punishable offense but to possession as a link in illicit trafficking.

Many lawyers will disagree with the Commission's interpretation of the Single Convention, which applies equally to *Cannabis sativa* (except the leaves), coca leaves, and opium derivatives. Because of this major departure from the intent of the Single Convention, perhaps the International Court of Justice of the Hague should be asked to state its opinion. By eliminating penalties for possession for use, the Commission is indeed suggesting a new interpretation of the laws formulated for the international control of stupefying drugs, including opiates.

It might, therefore, seem premature to sponsor legislation which could conflict with the international agreements of the United States. However, such legislation has already been introduced in both Houses of Congress. In the Senate, the sponsors of the Bill are the two senators who are members of the Commission. This proposed legislation even extends beyond the Commission's recommendations by eliminating its contraband proposition and by making it legal to transfer and possess in public "reasonable amounts" (three ounces). Such proposed legislation seems to be definitely in contradiction with Article 36 of the Single Convention.

The lack of potency distinction of different marihuana preparations

A great deal of confusion could have been avoided if the Commission had elected to give a precise, scientific definition of marihuana rather than using loosely this undefined deceptive word. Marihuana is not a single simple substance like alcohol. Everyone agrees that delta-9-THC is a toxic substance and that the amount of delta-9-THC contained in marihuana constitutes the only reliable index of its psychotoxicity and its potential harmfulness. This amount, which may vary 500-fold (from 0.01 to 5%) according to plant preparations, can be readily measured, and should become the criterion used by the legislator. It is obviously unfair to punish an individual for possession of what may amount to lawn grass or powdered rope. The substitution of "delta-9-THC" for "marihuana" in the present international and national legislation would help to dissipate the confusion created by those who have failed to distinguish between the fiber and drug types of the marihuana plant.

However, the Commission elected not to take into consideration potency distinction because of "the prevailing American pattern of marihuana usage." The Commission also stated that "analytical considerations [and] legal technicalities made it impractical to emphasize a scale of THC content in legislation," and claimed "whatever the potency of the drug used, individuals tend to use only the amount necessary to achieve the desired drug effect." As if this were not true for all the drugs used by man! It is equally true that self-medication is bad medication.

No meaningful educational program concerning marihuana can be undertaken without discussing the fundamental cause of marihuana psychotoxicity, which is its delta-9-THC content. As long as a clear and meaningful definition of *Cannabis* toxicity in terms of its delta-9-THC content is not given, any resulting essay on marihuana becomes a "signal of misunderstanding" or, to put it more simply, an exercise in ambiguity.

Verdict of the President

The Commission was given a monumental task and only 1 year in which to perform it. It is impossible, for instance, to perform within such a period of time a meaningful study of the "long-term effects of chronic marihuana use" in endemic areas. (The study of chronic hashish consumption in Egypt took more than a decade to perform, but it is not discussed or even mentioned in the Report.) It is, therefore, not surprising that the Report of the Commission, in my opinion, falls short of achieving its assigned goals, although it modestly deems "to present the most significant information gathered to date about the drug and its users, and recommendations concerning the most appropriate public response to marihuana usage in our society."

In reality, the Report reads most of the time as if it were written by two persons who had conflicting views or interpretations of observed data, and who were writing their opinions in sequence without transition on the same ream of paper.

In view of the foregoing, the President of the United States had little choice but to reject the ambiguous recommendations of the Commission with the subtle distinction implied in its "partial prohibition" policy which would make *private* use and possession legal but *public* use and possession illegal. "I oppose," said President Nixon, "the legalization of marihuana, and that includes its sale, possession and its use. I do not believe you can have effective criminal justice based on the philosophy that something is half legal and half illegal."

CONCLUSION

There are, therefore, two irreconcilable attitudes toward *Cannabis* use today. The first, which until recently prevailed throughout the world, considers *Cannabis* to be a stupefying drug which should fall under national and international legislation aimed at eliminating its use. The second, which developed in England and the United States in the past decade, is claiming a repeal of all marihuana laws in order to make a mild intoxicant freely available to those who wish to enjoy it.

In the following chapters, the basis of these two attitudes towards *Cannabis* will be carefully scrutinized.

SUMMARY

1. *Cannabis sativa* was first mentioned for its medicinal properties by Chinese texts more than 4000 years ago.

2. The plant was first used for its intoxicating properties by Iranian and Hindu priests, in the performance of religious rites, more than 3000 years ago. The generalized use of *Cannabis* by the common people of India began when the custom of smoking hemp became socially acceptable several centuries before our era. This habit has prevailed ever since, especially among the poorest people of the Indian subcontinent.

3. *Cannabis* intoxication spread next to the Arabian peninsula and, with the Arab invasions of the tenth to twelfth centuries, to the Middle East, Egypt,

and North Africa. All of the repressive measures taken since the fifteenth century by the successive rulers of these countries to curb this habit have not been successful.

4. Although many commercial and cultural contacts occurred after the thirteenth century between the Arab world and the European nations lining the Mediterranean Sea, the use of *Cannabis* as a pleasure-seeking, mind-altering drug did not spread to Western Europe until the second part of the twentieth century.

5. *Cannabis* extracts were used in England and the United States during the nineteenth century as an all-purpose medication and a miracle drug. At that time a few French writers experimented with the intoxicating properties of hashish.

6. The Indian Hemp Drug Commission (1893–1894) Report was the first attempt to evaluate the physical, mental, and moral effects of *Cannabis* intoxication on the population of India. It was based on written or oral testimonies and concluded that "excessive use of hemp was harmful but moderate use was not." It failed to define what was meant by "moderate" or "excessive" use both in terms of quantity of material used and of frequency of use. The findings of this Commission cannot be applied to a people living in a totally different culture.

7. Presently, the use of *Cannabis* is widespread among the poor populations of the Indian subcontinent, the Far East and Middle East, Africa, and Latin America, but the more affluent classes tend to avoid its usage.

8. Israel is the only country of the Middle East where *Cannabis* use is not prevalent. Israeli scientists isolated in 1965 the biologically active constituent of the plant: delta-9-THC.

9. The habit of smoking marihuana as a pleasure-inducing drug came to the United States from Mexico around 1910 and spread to Black minority groups and jazz musicians. In 1937 the Marihuana Tax Act brought *Cannabis* under federal control and declared that importation, possession, or sale was a criminal offense.

10. The La Guardia Report (1944) was the first systematic investigation of acute *Cannabis* intoxication performed on volunteers. The *Cannabis* extracts used in this study could not be assayed for potency and appeared to be relatively low in psychoactive material. Dose-response curves could not be established. One of the conclusions of the Report states that no evidence was found of an acquired tolerance for the drug, in direct contradiction to the actual observed findings.

11. *Cannabis* intoxication has always been and still remains alien to the strongly structured Eastern societies of Japan and China. The ban against its use appears to be enforced throughout the Soviet Union and its allies.

12. By contrast, an "epidemic" of marihuana smoking has occurred among British, Scandinavian, and American youth since 1960, along with other toxicomania. As a result, many American and British educators and writers are calling for a repeal of all marihuana laws in order to make a "mild intoxicant" freely available to those who wish to enjoy it.

13. The United States is a signatory of the U.N. Single Convention on Narcotic Drugs (1961), which obligates the parties to "limit exclusively to medical and scientific purposes the production, use and possession of *Cannabis*." The United States also approved the 1971 Vienna Convention, which added delta-9-THC to the list of dangerous drugs to be banned from common use.

14. The first Report of the National Commission on Marihuana (1972) does not contain any novel information concerning *Cannabis* intoxication. It merely describes the prevalence of the usage of a mild form of marihuana in the United States during the past decade. Its recommendations, which would make private use and possession legal but public use and possession illegal, are difficult to reconcile with its policy of "discouragement" of marihuana usage. These recommendations were rejected by the President of the United States.

REFERENCES

Anonymous (1962). The cannabis problem: A note on the problem and the history of international action. *Bull. Narcotics,* 14:27–31.

Asuni, T. (1964). Socio-psychiatric problems of cannabis in Nigeria. *Bull. Narcotics,* 16:17–28.

Baudelaire, C. (1858). De l'ideal artificiel. *La Revue Contemporaine,* Paris.

Bejerot, N. (1970). *Addiction and Society.* Charles C. Thomas, Springfield, Ill.

Benabud, A. (1957). Psycho-pathological aspects of the cannabis situation in Morocco: Statistical data for 1956. *Bull. Narcotics,* 9:1–16.

Berg, D. (1970). *Illicit Use of Dangerous Drugs in the United States.* Bureau of Narcotics and Dangerous Drugs, Washington, D.C.

Bouquet, J. R. (1944). Marihuana intoxication. *J. Amer. Med. Ass.,* 124:1010–1011.

Bouquet, J. R. (1950). Cannabis, parts I and II. *Bull. Narcotics,* 2:14–30.

Bouquet, J. R. (1951). Cannabis, part III–V. *Bull. Narcotics,* 3:22–43.

Bryan, H. D., Denny, J. J., Schiff, L. P., and Walter, C. W. (1970). *Annotated Bibliography of Marihuana (Cannabis sativa L.) 1964–1969.* Research Institute of Pharmaceutical Sciences, University of Mississippi.

Campbell, O. J. (1903). *The Mystic Ascetics and Saints of India.* T. F. Unwin, London.

Canadian Commission on Inquiry into the Non-Medical Use of Drugs: Interim Report (1970). Queen's Printer for Canada, Ottawa.

Cannabis (1969). Report by the Advisory Committee on Drug Dependence, London.

Carstairs, G. M. (1954). Daru and bhang: Cultural factors in choice of intoxicant. *Quart. J. Studies Alcohol,* 15:220–237.

Chopra, G. S. (1969). Man and marihuana. *Int. J. Addictions,* 4:215–247.

Chopra, G. S., and Chopra, P. S. (1965). Studies of 300 Indian drug addicts with special reference to psychol-sociological aspects, etiology and treatment. *Bull. Narcotics,* 17:1–9.

Chopra, R. N. (1935). Drug addiction in India and its treatment. *Indian Med. Gaz.,* 70:121–132.

Chopra, R. N. (1940). Use of hemp drugs in India. *Indian Med. Gaz.,* 75:356–367.

Chopra, R. N., and Chopra, G. S. (1939). The present position of hemp-drug addiction in India. *Indian J. Med. Res. Memoirs,* 31:1–119.

Chopra, R. N., Chopra, G. S., and Chopra, I. C. (1942). *Cannabis sativa* in relation to mental diseases and crime in India. *Indian J. Med. Res.,* 30:155–171.

Christozov, C. (1965). L'aspect Marocain de l'intoxication cannabique d'après des études sur des malades mentaux chroniques: 1ère partie et 2ème partie. *Maroc. Med.,* 44:630–642; 866–899.

Crancer, A. (1951). Dagga. *S. Afr. Med. J.,* 25:284–286.

Crancer, A. (1969). Marihuana and simulated driving. *Science,* 166:640.

de Felice, P. (1936). *Poisons Sacres Ivresses Divines.* Editions Albin Michel, Paris.

De Sacy, S. (1826). *Chrestomathie Arabe.* Paris.

Drug Dependency and Drug Abuse in New Zealand (1970). Board of Health, Report Series No. 14. A. R. Shearer, Wellington, New Zealand.

Dwarakanath, C. (1965). The use of opium and cannabis in the traditional systems of medicine in India. *Bull. Narcotics,* 17:15–19.

Edes, R. T. (1893). Cannabis indica. *Boston Med. Surg. J.,* 129–273.

El Hadka, A. A. (1965). Forty years of the campaign against narcotic drugs in the United Arab Republic. *Bull. Narcotics,* 17:1–12.

Farnsworth, D. L. (1972). Marihuana: A signal of misunderstanding. *Psychiatric Annals,* 2:7–26.

Forney, R. B. (1971). Toxicology of marihuana. *Pharmacol. Rev.,* 23:279–284.

Freedman, I., and Peer, I. (1968). Drug addiction among pimps and prostitutes in Israel. *J. Addictions,* 3:271–300.

Galal, E. (1968). The changing pattern and control of dangerous drugs in the United Arab Republic. In *Adolescent Drug Dependence,* C. Wilson (ed.). Pergamon Press, Oxford.

Gautier, E. F. (1931). *Moeurs et Coutumes des Musulmans.* Payot, Paris.

Gautier, T. (1846). Le club des hachischins. In *La Revue des Deux Mondes,* Paris.

Ginsberg, A. (1966). The first manifesto to end the bring down. In *The Marijuana Papers,* D. Solomon (ed.). Bobbs-Merrill, Indianapolis, Ind., pp. 183–200.

Grinspoon, L. (1971). *Marihuana Reconsidered.* Harvard University Press, Cambridge, Mass.

H.E.W. Report to Congress (1971). *Marihuana and Health.* U.S. Government Printing Office, Washington, D.C.

Hollister, L. E. (1951). The illicit traffic in narcotics throughout the world. *Bull. Narcotics,* 3:1–15.

Hollister, L. E. (1969). Criminal laws and the control of drugs of abuse: An historical view of the law (or, it's the lawyer's fault). *J. Clin. Pharmacol.,* 9:345–348.

Indian Hemp Drug Commission (1969). *Report on Marihuana of the Indian Hemp Drug Commission, 1893–1894.* Thomas Jefferson Publishing Co., Silver Springs, Md.

Isbell, H. (1971). Clinical pharmacology. *Pharmacol. Rev.,* 23:337–338.

Jones, R. T. (1971). Marihuana-induced "high": Influence of expectation, setting and previous drug experience. *Pharmacol. Rev.,* 23:359–370.

Kaplan, J. (1971). *Marihuana—The New Prohibition.* World Press, New York.

Lambo, T. A. (1965). Medical and social problems of drug addiction in West Africa. *Bull. Narcotics,* 17:3–14.

Leary, T. (1966). The politics, ethics and meaning of marijuana. In *The Marijuana Papers,* D. Solomon (ed.). Bobbs-Merrill, Indianapolis, Ind., pp. 82–89.

Lesse, S. (1971): Surprise doctor! Pot is here to stay! Where were you when the grass was cut? *Amer. J. Psychotherapy,* 25:1–3.

Lewin, L. (1930). *Phantastica Narcotic and Stimulating Drugs,* Kegan Paul, Trench and Co., London.

Ludlow, F. H. (1857). *The Hasheesh Eater: Being Passages from the Life of a Pythagorean.* Harper and Row, New York.

McGlothin, W. H. (1964). *Hallucinogenic Drugs: A Perspective with Special Reference to Peyote and Cannabis.* Rand Corp., New York.

Maqrizy, T. E. (1892). *Al-Khiftate (Chronicle) Cairo,* 1270 (of Hegira era).

Marihuana: A signal of misunderstanding (1972): First Report of the National Commission on Marihuana and Drug Abuse. U.S. Government Printing Office, Washington, D.C., pp. 1–184.

Mayor's Committee on Marihuana (1944): *The Marihuana Problem in the City of New York—Sociological, Medical, Psychological and Pharmacological Studies.* Cattell Press, Lancaster, Pa.

Mead, M. (1969). Competitive problems in the drug industry. *U.S. Senate Subcommittee on Monopoly Proc.,* 13:5455–5477.

Mechoulam, R., and Gaoni, Y. (1965). A total synthesis of *dl*-delta-1-tetrahydrocannabinol, the active constituent of hashish. *J. Amer. Chem. Soc.,* 87:3273–3275.

Mechoulam, R., Shani, A., Yagnitinsky, R., Ben-Zvi, Z., Braun, P., and Gaoni, Y. (1970). Some aspects of cannabinoid chemistry. In *The Botany and Chemistry of Cannabis,* C. R. B. Joyce and S. H. Curry (eds.). J. & A. Churchill, London, pp. 93–117.

Mikuriya, T. H. (1968). Mental and moral effects of marihuana, the Indian Hemp Drug Commission Report. *Int. J. Addictions,* 3:253–270.

Mizner, G. L., Barter, J. T., and Werme, P. H. (1970). Patterns of drug use among college students: Preliminary report. *Amer. J. Psychiat.,* 127:15–24.

Moreau, J. J. (1845). *Du Hachish et de L'Alienation Mentale: Etudes Psychologiques 34.* Libraire de Fortin, Masson, Paris.

Multi-Lingual List of Narcotic Drugs Under International Control (1968). United Nations, New York.

Murphy, H. B. M. (1963). The cannabis habit—A review of recent psychiatric literature. *Bull. Narcotics,* 15:15–23.

O'Shaughnessy, W. B. (1842). Case of tetanus, cured by a preparation of hemp. *Trans. Med. Psychiat. Soc. Calif.,* 8:462–469.

Parreiras, D. (1949). Cannabismo on maconhismo: Estudios brasileiros. *Impresna Medica,* 430:34–64.

Rennie, S. J. (1886). On the therapeutic value of tincture cannabis indica in the treatment of dysentery: More particularly in its sub-acute chronic forms. *Indian Med. Gaz.,* 21:353–354.

Report of the Advisory Committee on Drug Dependence (1969). *Cannabis.* (Wootten Report). Her Majesty's Stationery Office, London.

Robinson, V. (1925). *An Essay on Hasheesh.* Dingwall-Rock, Ltd., New York.

Robinson, V. (1946). Concerning cannabis indica. *Ciba Symposia,* 8:378.

Rolland, J. L., and Teste, M. (1957). Le cannabisme au maroc. *Maroc. Med.,* 387:694–703.

Rubin, V., and Comitas, L. (1972): Effects of chronic smoking of cannabis in Jamaica. Research Institute for the Study of Man, New York and the Center for Studies of Narcotic and Drug Abuse, National Institute of

Mental Health, Contract No. HSM–42–70–97.

Sami-Ali (1971). *Le Haschisch en Egypte.* Payot, Paris.

Schofield, M. (1971): *The Strange Case of Pot.* Penguin Books, Middlesex, England.

Sigg, B. W. (1963). Le cannabisme chronique, fruit du sous-development et du capitalisme: Etude socio-economique et psycho-pathologique. Thesis, University of Algiers Medical School.

Siler, J. F., Sheep, W. L., Bates, L. B., Clark, G., Cook, G. W., and Smith, W. A. (1933). Marihuana smoking in Panama. *Milit. Surg.,* 73:269–280.

Silver, A. (1923). On the value of Indian hemp in menorrhagia and dysmenorrhea. *Med. Times Gaz.,* 2:59–61.

Soueif, M. I. (1967). Hashish consumption in Egypt with special reference to psychological aspects. *Bull. Narcotics,* 19:1–12.

Soueif, M. I. (1971): The use of cannabis in Egypt: A behavioural study. *Bull. Narcotics,* 33 (4):17–28.

Suckling, C. W. (1891). On the therapeutic value of Indian hemp. *Brit. Med. J.,* 11:12.

Taylor, B. (1855). *The Land of the Saracens; or Pictures of Palestine, Asia Minor, Sicily, and Spain.* G. P. Putnam and Sons, New York.

Taylor, N. (1949). *Flight from Reality.* Duell, Sloan and Pearce, New York.

Tylden, E. (1967). A case for cannabis? *Brit. Med. J.,* 3:556.

United Nations Conference for the Adoption of a Single Convention on Narcotic Drugs (1961). United Nations, New York.

Waller, C. W., and Scigliano, J. A. (1970). The national marihuana program. *Report to the Commission on Problems of Drug Dependence, National Academy of Science,* 4:28–32.

Walton, R. P. (1938). *Marihuana, America's New Drug Problem.* Lippincott, New York.

Watt, J. M. (1961). Dagga in South Africa. *Bull. Narcotics,* 13:9–14.

Watt, J. M., and Breyer-Brandwijk, M. B. (1936). The forensic and sociological aspects of the dagga problem in South Africa. *S. Afr. Med. J.,* 10:573–579.

Weil, A. T., Zinberg, N. E., and Nelsen, J. M. (1968). Clinical and psychological effects of marihuana in man. *Science,* 162:1234–1242.

Williams, E. G., Himmelsbach, C. K., and Wikler, A. (1946): Studies of marihuana and pyrahexyl compounds. *Public Health Report,* 61:1059–1083.

Winick, C. (1960). The use of drugs by jazz musicians. *Social Problems,* 7:240–253.

Wood, T. B., Spivey, W. T. N., and Easterfield, T. H. (1896). Charas, the resin of Indian hemp. *J. Chem. Soc.,* 69:539–544.

2

Botany:
The Unstabilized Species

Cannabis sativa is a plant widely distributed throughout the temperate and tropical zones of the world. It is considered by most botanists to be a single, nonstabilized species, with as many as 100 varieties or races described.

In Latin, the word *Cannabis* means hemp, and denotes the genus of the hemp family of plants. *Sativa,* the species name, means planted or sown, and indicates the nature of the plant's growth. The adjective "indica" or "Americana" identifies the varieties of the single species which are grown in various geographical locations. *Cannabis sativa indica* is the plant which grows in India. However, these adjectives do not describe any of the basic characteristics of the plant. The many variations observed in the different plants are due to a certain genetic plasticity, to environmental influences, and to human manipulation, but not specifically to the country of origin.

Cannabis sativa has been cultivated for centuries for the hemp in its stem, the oil in its seed, and the biologically active substance in its flowering tops. Its oil is used in the composition of paint and varnish, its fiber is made into rope, twine, and bags, and the biologically active ingredients are used mostly as intoxicants.

TAXONOMY

Cannabis is closely allied to *Humulus,* the genus of the hop plant. *Cannabis* and *Humulus* are the only two genera of the *Cannabacea.* They each lack the milky juice characteristic of the family *Moracea* (mulberry family) and have quite different fruits.

BOTANICAL FEATURES

In spite of many variations among individual plants of *Cannabis sativa,* the species is so distinct from all others that it can be identified at all stages of growth by its botanical characteristics.

It is an "herbacious" annual plant, that is, like many other kinds of grass, it grows from a seed for a season and dies down; it grows up again the following spring from its own hardy seed. The seeds need just be covered by a thin layer of soil or leaves to weather the winter and be ready for a new growth. In France, 500 years ago, as Rabelais observed, "it is sown at the first coming of the swallows and pulled out of the ground when the cicadies begin to get hoarse." *Cannabis sativa* will spread like a wild weed—just as thistle, milkweed, or dandelion. It thrives in barren as well as fertile soils, and grows especially well in alluvial soils or flooded plains low in clay.

The plants cultivated for hemp may reach 15 to 20 ft in height (4 to 6 m), growing at a speed of 3½ in. (10 cm) per day. The stalk of the plant, which may be 3 to 4 in. thick, is hollow and square; it has ridges running along its length and well-carved nodes circling its stem at regular intervals. It is covered with tiny hairs curved upwards. Similar hairs cover most parts of the plant and are formed by one cell which contains a cystolith at its base.

The plant is solidly anchored to the soil by a long tap root which divides. *Cannabis sativa* tends to branch out, and its branching depends upon its mode of cultivation. In dense rows, branching is reduced, but in the wild with no crowding, extensive branching is observed.

The morphological characteristics of this ornamental plant are distinct enough to make it easily identifiable (Figs. 2 and 3). Its palmated leaves are supported by a slender stalk 5 to 7 cm long, with a narrow groove along the upper side. Each leaf presents 5 to 11 dark green leaflets radiating from the top of the stalk. The soft-textured leaflets, which may be as long as 10 in. (25 cm), are narrow and shaped like a lance finely sharpened to a narrow point; the edges of the leaflets are regularly dentated like the blade of a saw, with deep ridges running diagonally from the center to the periphery. The upper side of the leaf is dark green, contrasting with the lighter color of its underside.

The leaflets of a given leaf are unequal in size, the larger and longer ones located in the center of the palm. Their upper and lower surfaces are covered by hairs which are more profuse and longer on the lower side. The leaves of *Cannabis,* unlike those of tobacco, retain their grassy green color long after they have been cut. In the dried form, they resemble hay and have an odor reminiscent of alfalfa. They burn with a very distinctive sweet scent which lingers long after the smoke has dissipated.

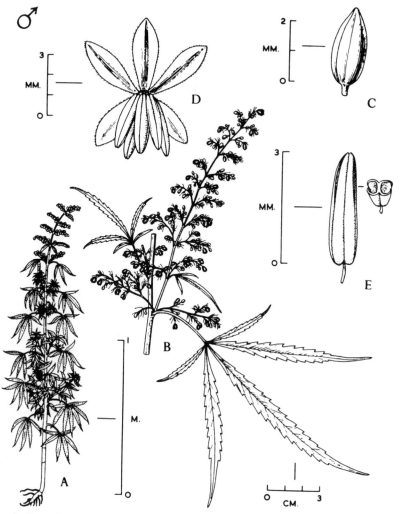

Fig. 2. *Cannabis sativa:* Male plant, primary specimen—W. T. Dress. No. 1135 in British Museum of Natural History, London. A. Grown plant. B. Male inflorescence with individual flowering branches standing out of the leaves. C. Closed flower. D. Open flower with sepals and pendulous stamina. E. Anthers containing pollen. Drawn by D. Eramus. Reproduced courtesy of W. T. Stearn and J. A. Churchill, London.

Cannabis is a dioecious plant, producing in a single sowing an equal proportion of female pistillate flowers and male staminate ones. Monoecious plants with both male and female flowers also occur, but seldom and under unfavorable conditions. *Cannabis sativa* also has the ability, rarely observed

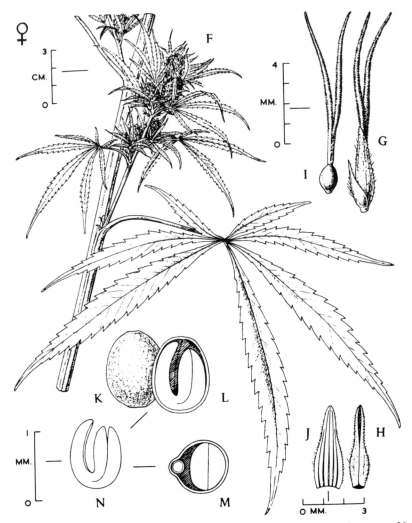

Fig. 3. *Cannabis sativa:* Female plant, primary specimen—Mary F. Spencer. No. 887—fruit from Virgin Is. H. Chase No. 13005 in British Museum of Natural History, London. F. Female inflorescence with flower not projecting beyond the leaves. G. Female flower. H., J. Bract or calyx which enwraps the ovary. I. Pollen-catching stigmas. K., L. Fruit (achene). M., N. Embryo with cotyledons.

in nature, to reverse its sex after being transplanted. Pistillate plants cannot be distinguished until they are mature and flower buds are well developed.

Female plants have a heavy foliage up to the top, while the leaves of the male plants are sparse. Male plants wither earlier than female plants and are harvested and weeded out sooner when a better yield of resin from the female plant is sought (see Fig. 3).

The male flower clusters, with their pollen-laden stamina standing out from the leaves on individual flowering branches, are covered with bristly hair. The flowers consist of five whitish or greenish hairy petals 3 mm long and five pendulous stamens which open lengthwise to release the pollen (Fig. 2).

The female flower clusters, with their pistils awaiting pollination, are larger, appear in more densely packed clusters, and do not project beyond the leaves. Each flower presents a green organ, the bract, a tubular sheath which surrounds the ovary and out of which projects two long pollen-catching stigmas. The bract is covered with hairs and stalkless circular glands which secrete drops of resin, mostly in hot weather. The female flower is pollinated by the wind, and not by flying or crawling insects.

After pollination the stigmas fall off, but the bract increases in size and produces the fruit, which is an achene: a hard shell containing a single seed. This achene is small (3 × 5 mm), elliptical, flat, smooth, and of greyish or brown color. The embryo in the seed is made of two cotyledons (seed leaves), the radicle (potential root), and some endosperm (food supply). The seed yields significant amounts of oil.

The male plant, which is taller, is short-lived, dying after the pollen is shed and the reproduction cycle has been initiated. The female plant survives until killed by frost or until the seeds have matured.

Cannabis is a very resistant plant which tolerates weather changes well, except for heavy frost. It is attacked by only a very few pests or insects. Its seeds grow in many different soils and climates and require very little care once it has sunk its root in the ground. *Cannabis* has a distinctive odor and smells like fresh hemp rope. Particularly in the female plant at the time of flowering, "its odor is strong and none too pleasant for delicate nostrils," as Rabelais declares. The flowering tops of the female plant secrete a clear, shiny, sticky resin called "charas" in India. In the hot dry climate of North Africa, so much resin may be produced that even under the noon sun the plant appears to be covered with dew. The resin is formed from the time the flowers first appear until the seeds reach maturity. The resin production might be an adaptive reaction of the plant to shield its maturing seed against heat and low moisture content in the air. Under this protective coating, the fertilized ovules may mature and develop into seeds. The resin of *Cannabis* was thought to contain the most concentrated psychoactive ingredients, but this claim has not been substantiated.

ORIGINS

Cannabis sativa represents one of man's oldest cultivated plants, and according to Schultes (1970), one of the oldest plants not grown specifically for its food content. It is an Old World plant, unknown to the Western Hemisphere until the sixteenth century.

Cannabis sativa seems to have originated in the plains of Central Asia, north of the Himalayas. It was known in China nearly 5000 years ago, where it was cultivated for its fiber and its medicinal properties. The exact area where *Cannabis* originated in Asia is not precisely known. The French author De Candolle (1855), who was the first to study the origin of cultivated plants, states that "the species has been found wild, to the south of the Caspian Sea, near the Irtysch, in the desert of Kirghiz, beyond Baikal in Dahuria. . . . Authors mention it throughout southern and central Russia and to the south of the Caucasus, but its wild nature is here less certain. . . . The antiquity of the cultivation of hemp in China leads me to believe that its area extends further to the east, although this has not yet been proven by botanists."

This opinion is also that of Vavilov (1926), a Russian botanist. Furthermore, the exact locations where *Cannabis sativa* was first grown as a crop plant for its fiber or its medicinal properties or oil is not known. It might be very difficult to establish such locations because the cultivated plants, or cultigens, disperse readily to neighboring soils and revert to wild types. New varieties emerge from these wild plants, and some of them are in turn selected for stronger fiber, superior oil yield, or more potent drug content. This type of cultivation of naturally selected wild plants has contributed to the emergence of the many varieties of *Cannabis sativa* which either grow in the wild or are cultivated. *Cannabis sativa* spread to Southeast Asia and India, where its intoxicating features were appreciated some 1000 years B.C.

Archeological evidence indicates that the plant was brought into Western Europe from Asia by the Scythian invaders about 1500 B.C. It reached the Mediterranean area at a later date. Writing in 450 A.D., Herodotus states that "hemp grows in Scythia; it is very like flax, only that it is a much taller and coarser plant. Some grows wild about the country; some is produced by cultivation. . . . The Scythians take some of this hemp seed, and, creeping under felt coverings, throw it upon the red-hot stones; immediately it smokes and gives out such a vapour as no Grecian bath can excel" (Book III).

Cannabis sativa did not come into Europe through the Mediterranean countries, where it remained unknown until the Christian era. It was not cultivated as a plant crop in Western Europe until about 500 A.D., but from then on it was grown and used extensively for its fiber only.

There is no mention of the intoxicating properties of *Cannabis* in the description given by Rabelais of what he called the herb "Pantagruelion." He refers to its seeds loved by birds and its fibers feared by robbers. If this truculent and inquisitive scholar had any inkling of the mind-altering properties of *Cannabis,* he would probably have written an entire book about them.

Cannabis sativa was introduced into the Americas by the Spanish Conquistadors and the English colonists. In South and Central America, the plant was first used for its fiber. Its intoxicating properties were discovered before the end of the nineteenth century by the Indian agrarian population. In the United States, *Cannabis* was used until the twentieth century for its hemp, in the manufacture of rope and cloth. Its widespread use as an intoxicant is of very recent vintage.

CULTIVATION

When *Cannabis sativa* is cultivated for its textile properties, the fibers of its stem may reach 1 to 4 ms; they are strong and durable and make sturdy ropes. Its seed contains 35% of a greenish yellow oil, which has an unpleasant smell and is used as a varnish, like linseed oil. It is also used as a cattle feed and in manufacturing soap. The seeds may also be roasted and consumed by man. The flowering tops of a special variant will contain biologically active substances which have been used for medicinal and intoxicating purposes.

Cannabis sativa was probably first used for its fiber, as indicated from archeological evidence and the widespread geographical cultivation of hemp for this purpose. Next appeared its use for its psychoactive effects, as a result of its ingestion by man. The discovery by early man of the intoxicating properties of *Cannabis* conferred on the plant a major religious role. Finally came its cultivation and use for the oil in its seed.

There was most certainly a gradual transition from the collection of wild plants to the planting of cultivated ones. *Cannabis* is presently found in many parts of the world, in both the cultivated and wild forms. Wild hemp grows from cultivated plants and the reverse also takes place, accounting for the wide variety of plants. The main purpose for cultivation of *Cannabis sativa* throughout the Western world has been to obtain its fiber and its oil, but not to use its intoxicating properties as did the people of Southeast Asia, India, and the Middle East.

Cannabis grows best in fertile ground containing nitrogen. It is a heavy feeder and a soil-depleting crop, requiring a great deal of organic fertilizer such as barnyard manure. The plant grows very poorly in soil rich in clay. It may develop in sandy soils, reaching a height of only 1 m, but still producing flowers and seeds.

After it is well established, *Cannabis* efficiently controls competing weeds, as a result of shading, but also because it produces volatile oils such as terpenes, which inhibit growth and germination (Pratt and Youngken, 1951).

The growth of the seedlings of *Cannabis* are inhibited by competing weeds.

Only a few fungus diseases kill hemp (Dewey, 1914) or its seedlings (Robinson, 1943b). Few animals are reported to browse in *Cannabis,* and few insects attack the plant. Only one, the broom rape, a root parasite, is known to attack the cultivated hemp. It might provide a method of controlling the growth of *Cannabis,* provided it does not attack other useful plants.

Wild *Cannabis* is different from the cultivated plant; it is deciduous and has smaller seeds, which are scattered and present delayed germination. Under cultivation, *Cannabis* has large nondeciduous seeds which germinate spontaneously, and is prone to mutation. Man has been the major disseminator of *Cannabis* seeds for plant cultivation. After such implantation, birds are great feeders on hemp seeds and important in the wild spread of the plant (Haney and Bazzaz, 1970).

Cultivation of *Cannabis* took place in different areas at different times, as indicated by the great diversity of "cultivars," a term describing the geographical and morphological types among cultivated plants.

As noted by Schultes (1970), "the germ plasm represented by these numerous types must have been very ample to have permitted in subsequent times the extraordinary morphological plasticity that is now seen in *Cannabis,* and its almost unique geographical and climatic adaptability over a great part of the world."

These ubiquitous plants continue to spread spontaneously from the areas of the tropical and temperate zones of the world where they were once grown or are still cultivated. *Cannabis* is today the most widely disseminated plant which contains biologically active substances.

CANNABIS SATIVA IN THE UNITED STATES

In the United States, *Cannabis* was extensively cultivated for its fiber until the end of the nineteenth century. During World War II the need for rope fiber led to renewed cultivation. However, in recent years the industrial production of strong synthetic fibers has for all practical purposes eliminated the use of natural hemp fiber. At present, *Cannabis* is widely disseminated and grows in the wild throughout the central plains of the United States, in and near the areas where it was once cultivated as a fiber crop. *Cannabis* has spread rapidly throughout the Midwest, following the course of the major riverways where alluvial soils are deposited when flooding occurs (Fig. 4). The plant also grows in all major cities except those in the South. States where hemp has been collected show a steady spread of *Cannabis* with no indication of an adjustment phase. The plant is also common in the East but is of much smaller size than in the Midwest (Iowa, Illinois, and Missouri). *Cannabis* is not at all common in the dry mountainous regions of the West. All of these wild plants have escaped from crop plants cultivated for fiber or oil, varieties imported from the temperate areas of Europe or Asia. This wild variety has not spread to the South, but it grows well when cultivated under optimal conditions (Doorenbos et al., 1971). The variety present in the United States derives from the fiber-type plant and usually has a low content

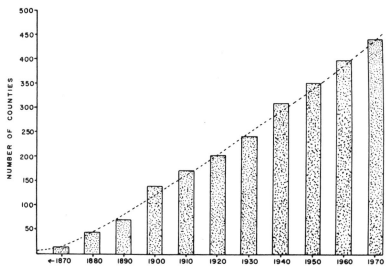

Fig. 4. Number of counties in the United States from which marihuana was collected by the date indicated (number for 1970 extrapolated). This data indicates a rapid spread of the escaped variant of the plant cultivated for fiber. There is no indication that the asymptote of the growth course has been reached. (From Haney and Bazzaz, 1970.)

of psychoactive material (Table 3). However, it may be noted that one specimen from Illinois contained 1% delta-9-THC, which represents, when present in a 1-g cigarette, a psychoactive dose (10 mg).

Commenting on the spread of *Cannabis sativa* (fiber type) in the United States, Haney and Bazzaz (1970) write:

> "Spread is most rapid in the Midwest on alluvial soils and soils relatively low in clay; however, the species can and does invade sites less suited. It shows a tremendous ecological amplitude in this respect and has been collected in nearly every conceivable site from lake shores to cracks in concrete walls and upland pine plantations. Although most of the marijuana

used in the United States at present results from imported material, as that source is controlled the naturalized variety will probably be used much more. Controlling the collection of a weed that occurs in thousands of vacant lots across the country will be a problem of tremendous magnitude."

It is apparent that the fiber variety of *Cannabis sativa* in its wild form was already spreading at an increasing rate throughout the United States before the occurrence of the present epidemic of marihuana smoking. Home-grown

Table 3

Cannabinoid Content of Native U.S. Marihuana

Origin	% cannabidiol	Delta-9-THC cigarette[a]			Phenotype ratio	Pheno-type
		%	Content/mg	% cannabinol		
Minnesota, 1968 (1)	0.77	0.07	0.7	0.028	0.13	II
Minnesota, 1968 (2)	1.2	0.07	0.7	0.016	0.075	II
Minnesota, 1969	0.71	0.05	0.5	0.0095	0.089	II
Minnesota, female bracts	1.3	0.05	0.5	0.0033	0.044	II
Minnesota, female leaves	1.0	0.04	0.4	t^b	0.043	II
Iowa, 1968 (1)	0.95	0.06	0.6	0.026	0.092	II
Iowa, 1968 (2)	1.2	0.07	0.7	0.010	0.068	II
Illinois male, 1968[c]	0.26	1.10	11.0	0.085	4.6	I
Laboratory grown	2.1	0.19	1.9	t^b	0.091	II

[a] Assuming a 1000-mg cigarette. Amount of delta-9-THC absorbed is 20 to 50% of dose contained in cigarette.

[b] t = trace.

[c] Only the plant from Illinois possesses any psychoactive property.

Table 4

Cannabinoid Content of Marihuana Variants Grown in Different Places

Variant	Place Grown	Year	% cannabidiol	Delta-9-THC cigarette[a]		
				%	Content/mg	% cannabinol
Thailand	Thailand	1969	0.14	4.8	48.0	0.12
	Mississippi	1970	0.17	3.4	34.0	0.11
Minnesota	Minnesota	1968	1.70	0.038	0.4	0.15
	Mississippi	1969	1.60	0.077	0.8	0.14
Panama	Panama	1969	0.29	3.2	32.0	0.80
	New Hampshire	1970	0.38	4.0	40.0	0.01

[a] Assuming a 1000-mg cigarette. The genetic factor responsible for the drug concentration is dominant over a 1-year period.

Cannabis is now widely collected and used in spite of its low content of psychoactive substance. However, it must be noted that seeds of the drug-type variety from Thailand or Panama have been grown in Mississippi and New Hampshire and have yielded delta-9-THC concentrations (3 to 4%) similar to that of the plants grown in their original locations (Table 4). The possibility is quite real that these drug variants of *Cannabis sativa* may also be grown throughout large portions of the United States from only a few imported seeds.

VARIATIONS: CULTIVARS AND CHEMOVARS

It is recognized that *Cannabis sativa* presents a high degree of genetic plasticity which results in extreme polymorphism in its different varieties. The plasticity of *Cannabis* was noted by Darwin (1868), who wrote that "plants long cultivated can generally endure with undiminished fertility, various and great changes, and may be so much affected that the nature of their chemical ingredients are modified."

Many factors, such as climate, altitude, soil fertility, rainfall, sun exposure, and temperature, influence the growth of the different *Cannabis* cultigens and the production of its cultivars for hemp material or its chemovars for biologically active constituents or cannabinoids. It has been reported, for instance, that *Cannabis* cultivated for hemp fiber is grown in cold or temperate regions where there is abundant rainfall and where the soil is moist, friable, and high in nitrogen (Dewey, 1914). To limit branching, the cultigens are also grown close to each other. Grown in such a fashion, the plants are soft and fibrous. Human manipulation has allowed man, over several centuries, to select empirically different cultigens of *Cannabis sativa* for maximal yield of fibers. Through appropriate methods, the fiber content has been increased from 100 to 200% in some strains. Similar selection has been applied to increase the yield of psychoactive constituents in the plant. There are at least 20 varieties of *Cannabis* cultivated for fiber. The hemp first grown in the United States was of European origin. The type basic to modern American fiber production, known as Kentucky, came originally from China. A more recent selection has resulted in a cultivar known as Kymington. In Europe, there are five or six outstanding varieties. Morphological characteristics define the different cultivars. The tallest form of cultigens yielding fiber are produced in Japan and China, where the plants have slender, sparsely branched internodes 25 cm apart. European cultigens have shorter, more rigid stems and mature 2 weeks earlier than the Asiatic variants. When grown in uncrowded conditions, in a hot, dry, and sunny climate, the cultigens supposedly contain a greater concentration of active cannabinoids. However, the exact effect of temperature, moisture content of the soil, nutrient level, and cultivation methods on the growth of cultigens which yield elevated concentrations of psychoactive ingredients has not been documented except in a recent study (Doorenbos et al., 1971).

Chopra and Chopra (1957) state that "even the plant grown under different climatic conditions in the vast Indo-Pakistan subcontinent shows remarkable variations in appearance. These variations at first may give the impression of different species."

The plasticity of *Cannabis* was shown by Bouquet (1951). Plants grown in England and France from seeds imported from India were after several

Table 5

Cannabinoid Content of Three Successive Generations of Mexican and Turkish
Cannabis sativa Grown in Mississippi[a]

Variant	% cannabidiol	Delta-9-THC cigarette[b]		
		%	Content/mg	
Mexican (first year)	0.31	3.7	37.0	0.11
Mexican (second year)	0.19	3.9	39.0	0.17
Mexican (third year)	0.18	3.7	37.0	0.22
Turkish (first year)	3.1	0.16	1.6	0.12
Turkish (second year)	2.1	0.06	0.6	0.05
Turkish (third year)	1.9	0.62	6.2	0.37

[a] From Doorenbos et al. (1971).
[b] Assuming a 1000-mg cigarette. The genetic factor responsible for the drug concentration is dominant over a 1-year period.

generations indistinguishable from the cultigens acclimatized to European conditions. Conversely, European cultigens planted in dry, warm areas of Egypt to supply fiber for rope making tend to produce, after several generations, plants with high psychoactive ingredients and very little fiber. Hamilton (1915) showed conclusively that American-grown hemp did contain active psychoactive ingredients. It seems, therefore, that *Cannabis sativa's* botanical and chemical characteristics change markedly but not permanently as a result of environmental factors and human manipulation. Adams (1940) states, "the morphological characteristics are modified easily by change in climatic conditions."

Doorenbos cultivated in Mississippi a Mexican and a Turkish variant of *Cannabis sativa* for three successive generations. During that period, the delta-9-THC content did not change in the Mexican variant, but it increased in the third year in the Turkish variant (Table 5). Doorenbos attributed this increase to cross pollination from the drug plant. But it might also result from genetic plasticity and the reversal of the "fiber type" plant to the "drug type" because of the warm Mississippi climate, where the Mexican variant of the drug type appears to grow with unchanged chemical characteristics.

The mechanisms by which such external factors modify the characteristics and morphology of the plant are not known. They are of great interest to the botanist who wishes to elucidate the secrets of the age-old interactions between nature and nurture.

BIOLOGICALLY ACTIVE CONSTITUENTS OF *CANNABIS* VARIANTS

The concentration of cannabinoids in the plant is a function of genetic and environmental factors. The genetic factor appears to be predominant under stable environmental conditions. Other factors must also be considered, including methods of preparation and extraction from the different parts of the plant, conditions of storage such as exposure to heat, and time elapsed since maturation.

The exact composition and concentration of the cannabinoids contained in different variants of *Cannabis sativa* have only been recently defined (Fetterman et al., 1970; Agurell, 1970; Doorenbos et al., 1971).

The cannabinoids principally present in *Cannabis* cultigens are delta-9- and delta-8-THC (tetrahydrocannabinol), which are the active psychotoxic substances, cannabinol (CBN), and cannabidiol (CBD). The contents of these substances is the same in male and female flowering tops. Chromatographic analyses have shown that CBD content is high, while delta-9- and delta-8-THC content is low, in the hemp cultigen which is grown for its fiber. The opposite occurs in plants grown for their intoxicating properties. It therefore appears that there are two "types" of *Cannabis* or marihuana: the drug type, with a high percentage of delta-8- and mostly delta-9-THC (1 to 7%); and the fiber type, with a high percentage of CBD.

Most analyses were performed on plant material from variants which had been cut at the stem beneath the lowest leaves and air dried. Seeds, bracts, flowers, leaves, and small stems were then stripped from the plant. Most of the small stems were removed by a 10-mesh screen, and the seeds were eliminated with a mechanical seed separator. This preparation of marihuana contains less seed and stem than most of the illicit material available in the United States.

Cannabinoids were extracted from the plant material and analyzed by standard techniques. Waller and Scigliano (1970) have suggested a method of classifying variants according to the following ratio of the identified cannabinoids (Fetterman et al., 1971).

$$\text{Phenotype ratio} = \frac{\%\ \text{delta-9-THC} + \%\ \text{CBN}}{\%\ \text{CBD}}$$

It has been noted (Levine, 1944) that the loss of potency of *Cannabis* preparations is accompanied by conversion of delta-9-THC to CBN. This observation suggests that delta-9-THC + CBN might approximate the delta-9-THC content of a sample when it was freshly harvested. *Cannabis* prepara-

Table 6

Cannabinoid Content of Marihuana Seized in Different Parts of the United States

| Origin | % CBD | Delta-9-THC cigarette[a] | | | Phenotype ratio | Phenotype |
		%	Content/mg	% CBN		
California	0.88	0.084	0.8	t[b]	0.095	II
California	0.71	0.077	0.8	t[b]	0.11	II
Kentucky	1.08	0.15	1.5	0.049	0.18	II
Kentucky	0.48	0.51	5.1	0.100	1.30	I
N.I.M.H.	0.095	0.58	5.8	0.370	10.00	I
N.I.M.H.	1.0	0.52	5.2	0.020	0.072	II
Unknown	0.19	0.025	0.3	0.018	0.23	II

[a] Assuming a 1000-mg cigarette. Amount of delta-9-THC absorbed is 20 to 50% of dose contained in cigarette. Only three samples of seven contain enough delta-9-THC to possess any psychoactive properties.
[b] t = trace.

tions with ratios greater than 1.0 are classified as the "drug phenotypes" and those with ratios smaller than 1.0 as the "fiber phenotypes." Since no evidence concerning fiber content of the plant used in these experiments was given, it might be safer to classify the two phenotypes as "biologically active" and "nonbiologically active," or more precisely as the delta-9-THC phenotype (I) and the cannabidiol phenotype (II). In any case, most samples analyzed in Mississippi by Fetterman and Doorenbos presented phenotype ratios smaller than 0.2 or larger than 1.0 (Tables 3 and 6).

It should also be noted that the terminology used by Fetterman et al. is somewhat misleading, especially in view of their contention that "environmental factors, including climate, are not as important as heredity in determining the cannabinoid content of cultigens." In this case, one should not use the word phenotype (which is a type distinguished by visible characteristics rather than by genetic traits). Genotype would be more appropriate (a type distinguished by its genetic trait).

Figure 5 is an illustration of the gas chromotograms obtained from preparations of the Mexican variant (delta-9-THC type) and of the Turkish variant (CBD type).

Analysis of the wild marihuana plants grown in the midwestern United States has shown that they belong to the "fiber" type and contain mostly CBD and little delta-9-THC. By contrast, the cultigens grown in Mississippi (Table

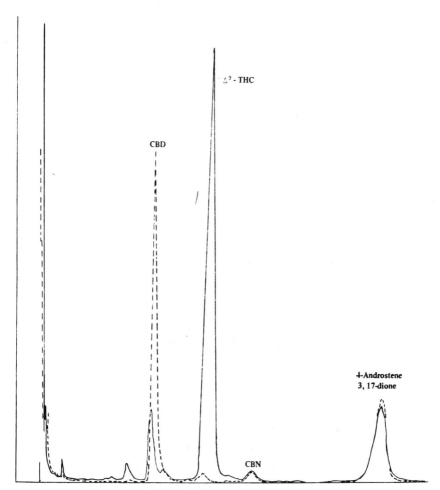

Fig. 5. Gas chromatogram of the two main genotypes of *Cannabis sativa*. The hemp type (from a Turkish cultigen) with low delta-9-THC and high CBD concentration, and the drug type (from a Mexican cultigen) with high delta-9-THC and low CBD concentration. Both contain similar amounts of cannabinol and steroids. (From Waller, 1971.)

4) from seeds of Mexican and Thailand or Panama plants have high THC content (3.4 to 4.8%). Cannabinoid content of different variants of *Cannabis* grown in Mississippi varied widely (Table 7), although environmental factors were the same. This indicates the importance of the genetic factor during this time period of 1 year.

A comparison of the cannabinoid content of different variants grown at widely different latitudes from Panama to New Hampshire indicates that

Table 7

Cannabinoid Contents of Some Marihuana Produced
at the University of Mississippi—1970

Variant	Sex	% CBD	Delta-9-THC Cigarette[a]	
			%	Content/mg
India (I)	Male	2.10	0.81	8.0
	Female	0.89	1.30	13.0
India (II)	Male	0.15	2.20	22.0
	Female	0.12	1.20	12.0
Mexico	Male	0.86	3.70	37.0
	Female	0.46	3.70	37.0
Thailand (I)	Male	0.35	2.10	21.0
	Monoecious	0.31	2.50	25.0
Thailand (II)	Male	0.15	2.40	24.0
	Female	0.41	2.50	25.0
Thailand (III)	Male	0.08	3.20	32.0
	Female	0.42	3.20	32.0
Korea	Male	0.16	1.20	12.0
	Female	0.13	0.94	9.0
Iowa	Female	2.70	0.07	0.7
Russia	Female	2.40	0.16	1.6
Lebanon	Female	2.00	1.00	10.0

[a] Assuming a 1-g cigarette. Smoking a cigarette containing 15 mg of delta-9-THC or more is psychotomimetic.

heredity more than climate over this one year time span is a determining factor in producing cannabinoid content.

Individual plants within a given variant may differ considerably in cannabinoid content. *Cannabis* preparations from male and female plants of a Mexican variant ranged from 1.7 to 7.2% and 1.5 to 4.8%, respectively (Doorenbos et al., 1971).

Delta-9-THC and CBD are present in the fresh material mostly in the form of their respective acids (95%), suggesting that the acids are products of biosynthesis and the nonacids are decarboxylation products. The acid content of a 1-year-old *Cannabis* preparation was found to have dropped to 50% or less.

Krejci (1970) also notes that in dried material stored for a long time, the amount of cannabidiolic acid decreases as a result of decarboxylation and changes to cannabidiol.

CANNABINOID IN THE PLANT AND PLANT GROWTH

Some of the information reported in the literature will have to be revised following the chemical analysis for cannabinoid content of *Cannabis* made by Doorenbos et al. (1971) and Agurell (1970). For instance, cannabinoid content of plants is not determined by the sex expression of the cultigens. Equivalent amounts of delta-9-THC have been found in material prepared from male and female plants alike. The generally held belief that the content of active cannabinoid is highest in the resinous exudate of the female unfertilized flower might have to be revised. Bracts with delta-9-THC contents of 11.4% have been analyzed.

Cannabinoid content varies in different parts of the plant, decreasing progressively from bracts to flower to leaves to small stems, and being very low in seeds and roots. The presence of trace amounts of delta-9-THC in the seeds suggest that cannabinoids are naturally occurring metabolic constituents not requiring photosynthesis.

Successive daily analysis of cultigens grown in Mississippi from Mexican seed have shown that the cannabinoid content of the seedling and of the foliage of the growing plant increases slowly, reaching a plateau at midseason. Appearance of the first flower buds produces an increased synthesis and accumulation of cannabinoid in the green apical and floral parts of the plant. The concentration of CBD appears to cycle during the growth period, with THC content inversely proportional to CBD: THC is high on the day that CBD is low and vice versa (Philipps et al., 1970). Such a cycling in cannabinoids suggests that CBD is a precursor of THC in the plant (Mechoulam, 1970).

Krejci (1970) also observed that cannabidiolic acid appears at early stages of development, with increasing amounts found as maturation of the plant progresses to full ripeness. Cannabidiolic acid is known to have antibiotic activity, which may account for the parallel between the appearance of cannabidiolic acid and that of antibiotic activity which occurs at the eighth week of development.

The selective distribution of the cannabinoids in different parts of the cultigen, as well as the marked variability in concentration of these active ingredients depending on genetic and environmental factors, easily accounts for the extreme range of potency of different preparations. This range may be as large as 120-fold from the lowest to the highest concentration of active ingredients reported in different samples (from 0.04 to 4.80% (Tables 3 and 4).

It is difficult to reconcile this botanical data with the generalization by Snyder (1971) that "hashish is the only *Cannabis* derivative that has the capacity to produce hallucinogenic and psychotomimetic effects with any regularity," or "hashish is about ten times as powerful as marihuana." A 1-g cigarette made with the marihuana prepared from the drug-type plant contains 34 to 48 mg of delta-9-THC. Such an amount has produced a psychotomimetic episode in a healthy person (see Chapters 5 and 6). Snyder, like many American authors when speaking of marihuana, refers to the fiber-type plant or to some drug-type plant which has been generously cut with oregano or lawn grass. More potent and less expensive material might become rapidly available. Doorenbos et al. (1971) report that a plant allegedly grown in a closet with a tungsten light bulb contained 6.8% delta-9-THC, 0.26% CBD, and 0.28% CBN. Such a concentration of THC is within the range of that of hashish.

THE MARIHUANA SMOKED IN THE UNITED STATES

The recent North American experience of *Cannabis* intoxication appears to be to a great extent limited to the casual use of the home-grown fiber-type marihuana with little psychoactive material, or to mixtures of imported weeds in which cannabinoid content varies widely. In fiscal year 1970, analysis of all the marihuana seized in the United States by the Federal Bureau of Narcotics and Dangerous Drugs indicates that 12.2% of the samples did not contain any intoxicating material. In addition, there were seasonal variations; 14% of the specimens analyzed in the first quarter were negative for cannabinoid content, 16% in the second quarter, 7% in the third, and 12% in the fourth. In Ontario, Canada, similar observations were made: 33% of the samples of "marihuana" collected from smokers did not contain any cannabinoid. "Some of it appeared literally to be grass lawn clippings; some of it looked like hay and smelled like hay."

By contrast, all of the hashish, or plant extract, which was seized contained some psychoactive material.

It is quite clear that a large amount of the "marihuana" sold on the streets of America is generously cut with oregano or other plentiful and inexpensive material, making the trade in this drug a profitable one.

OTHER CHEMICALS ISOLATED FROM CANNABIS

Several other cannabinoids have been isolated from *Cannabis* (Table 8): cannabigenol, cannabicyclol, cannabichromene, cannabidivarin, cannabivarin, tetrahydrocannabivarin. The last two of these are psychoactive (Merkus, 1971).

Alkaloids have been isolated from leaves and stems and flowering tops of fresh plants in very small amounts (0.003%). They are cannabamine A, B,

Table 8

Cannabis Constituents Isolated from the Plant

	Psychotoxicity
Cannabinoids	
Delta-9-tetrahydrocannabinol	+
Delta-8-tetrahydrocannabinol	+
Cannabidiol	−
Cannabinol	−
Cannabigenol	−
Cannabicyclol	−
Cannabichromene	−
Cannabidivarin	−
Cannabivarin	+
Tetrahydrocannabivarin	+
Alkaloids	
Cannabamine A, B, C, D	+
Steroids	
β-Sitosterol	Carcinogenic
Campestrol	Carcinogenic
Triterpenes	
Friedelin	Carcinogenic
Epifriedelanol	Carcinogenic

C, D which have shown pharmacological activity in mice (Klein et al., 1971).

Steroids, β-sitosterol, and campestrol, as well as triterpenes, have been isolated from *Cannabis*. These substances can be converted into carcinogens.

CONCLUSION

Cannabis sativa, or marihuana, is not a single uniform plant like many of those encountered in nature, but a rather deceptive weed with several hundred variants. The intoxicating substances prepared from *Cannabis* vary considerably in potency according to the nature of the plant (fiber or drug type), according to the varying mixtures of different parts of the plant, and according to the techniques of fabrication. As a result, the psychoactive properties of *Cannabis* cover a very wide range of activity, from nonexistent for the fiber type, to hallucinogenic for the well-prepared, non-extracted drug type. Such a basic botanical fact has been overlooked by physicians and educators, who have spoken and written about marihuana as if it were a simple, single substance, "a mild intoxicant," similar to beer or coffee, which uniformly yield a low concentration of psychotoxic substances. Such a view is at variance with all of the experimental data that we have just reviewed.

All of the botanical features of *Cannabis* show the unusually wide variability of this plant. In addition to changes due to its own genetic plasticity, it has been modified throughout the ages by environmental factors and human manipulations, and is not yet a stabilized species. All of these factors underline the inherent pitfalls of any study devoted to the biologically active constituents of marihuana when their exact concentration is not defined.

SUMMARY

This plant presents the following botanical features:

1. *Cannabis sativa* or marihuana is one of the oldest plants grown by man. From Central Asia, where it originated and was cultivated 5000 years ago, it has spread all over the temperate and tropical zones of the globe.

2. *Cannabis sativa* is used for the fiber in its stem, the oil in its seeds, and the intoxicating substances in its flowering tops.

3. *Cannabis sativa* is a single "unstabilized species," with many variants due to genetic plasticity, environmental influences, and human manipulations.

4. Two main types of *Cannabis* plants have been defined according to the concentration of biologically active substance (delta-9-THC) contained in their flowering tops. The fiber-type plant has a low delta-9-THC content (less than 0.2%), and the drug-type plant has a high delta-9-THC concentration (3.4 to 4.8%).

5. A 1-g marihuana cigarette prepared from such drug-type plants contains 34 to 48 mg of delta-9-THC. This amount has produced hallucinations and other psychotomimetic symptoms in a healthy person.

6. Concentration of delta-9-THC in the plant is a function of genetic and environmental factors. The genetic factors appear to be predominant under stable environmental conditions for one to three years.

7. The fiber-type marihuana is widely disseminated and grows in the wild throughout the central plains of the United States next to areas where it had been cultivated as a fiber crop. Drug-type marihuana with 3.4 to 4.8%

delta-9-THC has been cultivated successfully from Mississippi to New Hampshire.

8. Controlling the collection of such plants, which may grow in thousands of vacant lots across the land, may be a problem of tremendous magnitude.

REFERENCES

Adams, R. (1940). Marihuana. *Science,* 92:115–119.

Agurell, S. (1970). Constituents of male and female cannabis. In *The Botany and Chemistry of Cannabis,* C. R. B. Joyce and S. H. Curry (eds.). J. A. Churchill, London, pp. 1–217.

Ames, O. (1939). *Economic Annuals and Human Cultures.* Botanical Museum of Harvard University, Cambridge, Mass.

Arnoux, M. (1966a). Influence des facteurs du millieu sur l'expression de la sexualité du chanvre monoique (*Cannabis sativa* L.). *Ann. Amélior Plantes,* 16:259–262.

Arnoux, M. (1966b). Influence des facteurs du millieu sur l'expression de la sexualité du chanvre monoique (*Cannabis sativa* L.): II. Action de la nutrition azotée. *Ann. Amélior Plantes,* 16:123–134.

Asahina, H. (1957). Studies in cannabis obtained from hemp plants grown in Japan. *Bull. Narcotics,* 9:17–20.

Baily, L. H. (1949). *Manual of Cultivated Plants* (2nd ed.). Macmillan Company, New York.

Benson, L. (1957). *Plant Classifications.* D. C. Heath and Co., Lexington, Mass.

Black, C. A., and Vessel, A. J. (1945). The response of hemp to fertilizers in Iowa. *Soil Sci. Soc. Amer. Proc.,* 9:178–184.

Bois, D. (1893). *Dictionnaire d'Horticulture. pt. 1 246.* Librairie des Sciences Naturelles, Paul Klincksieck, Paris.

Bouquet, R. J. (1951). *Cannabis. Bull. Narcotics,* 3:14–30.

Boyce, S. S. (1900). *A Practical Treatise on the Culture of Hemp (Cannabis sativa) For Seed and Fibre, with a Sketch of the History and Nature of the Plant.* Orange Judd and Co., New York.

Boyce, S. S. (1912). *Hemp (Cannabis sativa).* Orange Judd and Co., New York.

Bureau of Narcotics and Dangerous Drugs, Lab. Op. Div. (1970). Private communication.

Camp, W. H. (1936). The antiquity of hemp as an economic plant. *J. N.Y. Bot. Gard.,* 37:110–114.

Charen, S. (1945). Facts about marihuana: A survey of the literature. *Amer. J. Pharm.*, 117:422–430.

Cheek, F. E., Newell, S., and Joffe, M. (1970). Deceptions in the illicit drug market. *Science,* 167:1276.

Cheuvart, C. (1954). Studies on the development of *Cannabis sativa* L. at constant temperature and under different photoperiods (sexuality and foliage pigments). *Bull. Acad. Roy. Med. Belg.: C. Science,* 40:1152–1168.

Chopra, I. C., and Chopra, R. N. (1957). The use of cannabis drugs in India. *Bull. Narcotics,* 9:4–29.

Cone, E. L. (1955). *Plant Taxonomy.* Prentice-Hall, Inc., Englewood Cliffs, N.J.

Cook, O. F. (1914). Sexual inequality in hemp. *J. Hered.,* 5:203–206.

Darwin, C. (1868). *The Variation of Animals and Plants Under Domestication.* Orange Judd and Co., New York.

De Candolle, A. (1855). *Geographie Botanique Raisonee.* Librairie de Victor Masson, Geneva.

De Candolle, A. (1884). *Origin of Cultivated Plants.* Kegan Paul, Trench & Co., London.

Dewey, L. H. (1914). Hemp. *U.S.D.A. Yearbook,* 1913:283–346.

Dewey, L. H. (1928). Hemp varieties of improved type are result of selection. *U.S.D.A. Yearbook,* 1927:358–361.

Doorenbos, N. J., Fetterman, P. S., Quimby, M. W., and Turner, C. E. (1971). Cultivation, extraction and analysis of *Cannabis sativa* L. *Ann. N.Y. Acad. Sci.,* 191:3–15.

Duquenois, P. (1950). Chemical and physiological identification of Indian hemp. *Bull. Narcotics,* 2:30–33.

Eckler, C. R., and Miller, F. A. (1912). A study of American grown *Cannabis* in comparison with samples from various other sources. *Amer. J. Pharm.,* 84:488–495.

Farnsworth, N. R. (1968). Hallucinogenic plants. *Science,* 162:1086–1092.

Fetterman, P. S., Doorenbos, N. J., Keith, E. S., and Quimby, M. W. (1971). A simple gas liquid chromatography procedure for determination of cannabinoidic acids in *Cannabis sativa* L. *Experientia,* 27:988–989.

Fetterman, P. S., Keith, E. S., Waller, C. W., Guerrero, O., Dorrenbos, N. J., and Quimby, M. W. (1970). Mississippi grown *Cannabis sativa* L.—A preliminary observation on the chemical definition of phenotype and variations in the content versus age, sex and plant park. *J. Pharm. Sci.,* 60:1246–1249.

Godwin, H. (1967). Pollen analytic evidence for the cultivation of *Cannabis* in England. *Rev. Palaeobot. Palynol.,* 4:71–80.

Goode, Erich (1970). *The Marihuana Smokers.* Basic Books, New York.

Grinspoon, L. (1971). *Marihuana Reconsidered.* Harvard University Press, Cambridge, Mass.

Hamilton, H. C. (1912). The pharmacopoeial requirements for *Cannabis sativa. J. Amer. Pharm. Ass.,* 1:200–203.

Hamilton, H. C. (1915). *Cannabis sativa;* Is the medicinal value found only in the Indian grown drug? *J. Amer. Pharm. Ass.,* 4:448–451.

Haney, A., and Bazzaz, F. A. (1970). Some ecological implications of the distribution of hemp (*Cannabis sativa* L.) in the United States of America. In *The Botany and Chemistry of Cannabis,* C. R. B. Joyce and S. H. Curry (eds.). J. & A. Churchill, London, pp. 38–48.

Hanson, H. C., and Kossack, C. W. (1963). The mourning dove in Illinois. *Ill. Dept. Agr. Exp. Sta.,* Cir. No. 547.

Heslop-Harrison, J. (1957). The experimental modification of sex expression in flowering plants. *Biol. Rev.,* 32:1–51.

Heuser, O. (1927). Die Hanfpflanze. In *Technologie der Textilfasern 5, pt. 2, Hanf und Hartfasern,* R. O. Herzog (ed.). Julius Springer, Berlin.

H.E.W. Report to Congress (1971). *Marihuana and Health.* U.S. Government Printing Office, Washington, D.C.

Houghton, E. M., and Hamilton, H. C. (1908). A pharmacological study of *Cannabis americana (Cannabis sativa). Amer. J. Pharm.,* 80:16–20.

Jordan, H. V., Lang, A. L., and Enfield, G. H. (1946). Effects of fertilizers on yields and breaking strengths of American hemp, *Cannabis sativa. J. Amer. Soc. Agron.,* 38:551–563.

Joyce, C. R. B., and Curry, S. H. (eds.) (1970). *The Botany and Chemistry of Cannabis.* J. & A. Churchill, London.

Kabelik, J., Krejci, Z., and Santavy, F. (1960). Cannabis as a medicament. *Bull. Narcotics,* 12:5–23.

Kaplan, J. (1971). *Marihuana—The New Prohibition.* World Press, New York.

Kechatov, E. A. (1959). Chemical and biological evaluation of the hemp grown for seed in the central districts of the European part of the USSR. *Bull. Narcotics,* 11:5–9.

Klein, F. K., Rapoport, W., and Elliott, H. W. (1971). Cannabis alkaloids. *Nature,* 232:258–259.

Koehler, B. (1946). Hemp seed treatments in relation to different dosages and conditions of storage. *Phytopath.* 36:937–942.

Korte, F., and Sieper, H. (1965). Recent results in hashish analysis. In *Hashish: Its Chemistry and Pharmacology,* G. E. W. Wolstenholme and J. Knight (eds.). Little, Brown and Company, Boston.

Krejci, Z. (1970). Changes with maturation in the amounts of biologically interesting substances of *Cannabis*. In *The Botany and Chemistry of Cannabis*, C. R. B. Joyce and S. H. Curry (eds.). J. & A. Churchill, London, pp. 49–55.

Laskowska, R. (1961). Influence of the age of pollen and stigmas on sex determination in hemp. *Nature,* 192:147–148.

Lerner, P. (1969). The precise determination of tetrahydrocannabinol in marijuana and hashish. *Bull. Narcotics,* 21:39–43.

Levine, J. (1944). Origin of cannabinol. *J. Amer. Chem. Soc.,* 66:1868–1870.

McPhee, H. C. (1924a). Meiotic cytokinesis of *Cannabis, Bot. Gaz.,* 78:335–338.

McPhee, H. C. (1924b). The influence of environment on sex in hemp, *Cannabis sativa* L. *J. Agric. Res.,* 28:1067–1080.

Malinovskij, S. M. (1927). Stimulation of hemp seed (*Cannabis sativa* L.). *Mem. Inst. Agron. a'Lenin,* 4:289–348.

Mechoulam, R. (1970). Marihuana chemistry. *Science,* 168:1159–1166.

Merkus, F. W. H. M. (1971). Cannabivarin and tetrahydrocannabivarin, two new constituents of hashish. *Nature,* 232:579–580.

Metcalfe, C. R., and Chalk, L. (1950). *Anatomy of the Dicotyledons,* Vol. 2. Clarendon Press, Oxford.

Miller, N. G. (1970). The genera of cannabaceae in the south-eastern United States. *J. Arnold Arb.,* 51:185–203.

Nakamura, G. R. (1969). Forensic aspects of cystolith hairs of cannabis and other plants. *J. Ass. Offic. Anal. Chem.,* 52:5–16.

Nordal, A. (1970). Microscopic detection of cannabis in the pure state and in semi-combusted residues. In *The Botany and Chemistry of Cannabis,* C. R. B. Joyce and S. H. Curry (eds.). J & A Churchill, London, pp. 61–68.

Phillips, R., Turk, R., Manno, J., Naresh, J., and Forney, R. (1970). Seasonal variations in cannabinolic content of Indiana marihuana. *J. Forensic Sci.,* 15:191–200.

Prain, D. (1893). *Report on the Cultivation and Use of Ganja.* Bengal Secretariat Press, Calcutta.

Pratt, R., and Youngken, H. W. (1951). *Pharmacognosy.* J. B. Lippincott Co., Philadelphia.

Rabelais (1944). *The Five Books of Gargantua and Pantagruel,* Jacques Le Clercq (transl.). The Modern Library, Random House, Inc., New York. Book III, Chapters 49–51, pp. 470–482.

Ram, H. Y., and Nath, R. (1964). The morphology and embryology of *Cannabis sativa* L. *Phytomorph.,* 14:414–429.

Robinson, B. B. (1943a). Greenhouse seed treatment studies on hemp. *J. Amer. Soc. Agron.,* 35:910–916.

Robinson, B. B. (1943b). Hemp. *Farmers' Bull.,* No. 1935, U.S.D.A., U.S. Government Printing Office, Washington, D.C.

Sabalitschka, T. (1925). Uber *Cannabis indica,* insbesondere uber eine Gewinnung hochwertiger Herba *Cannabis indica* durch kulter in Deutschland. *Heil-und Gewurz-Pflanzen,* 8:73–82.

Schaffner, J. H. (1923). The influence of relative length of daylight on the reversal of sex in hemp. *Ecology,* 4:323–334.

Schaffner, J. H. (1931). The functional curve of sex-reversal in staminate hemp plants induced by photoperiodicity. *Amer. J. Bot.,* 18:424–430.

Schreiber, A. (1958). Cannabis. In *Illustrierte Flora von Mittle-Europa,* G. Hegi (ed.). Carl Hanser, Munich, pp. 290–295.

Schultes, R. E. (1969). Hallucinogens of plant origin. *Science,* 163:245–254.

Schultes, R. E. (1970). Random thoughts and queries on the botany of cannabis. In *The Botany and Chemisty of Cannabis,* C. R. B. Joyce and S. H. Curry (eds.). J. & A. Churchill, London, pp. 11–38.

Schwanitz, F. (1966). *The Origin of Cultivated Plants.* Harvard University Press, Cambridge, Mass.

Slatkin, D. N., Doorenbos, N. J., Harris, L. S., Masoud, A. N., Quimby, M. W., and Schiff, P. L., Jr. (1971). Chemical constituents of *Cannabis sativa* L. root. *J. Pharm. Sci.,* in press.

Snyder, S. H. (1971). *Uses of Marijuana.* Oxford University Press, New York.

Stearn, W. T. (1970). The *Cannabis* plant: Botanical characteristics. In *The Botany and Chemistry of Cannabis,* C. R. B. Joyce and S. H. Curry (eds.). J. & A. Churchill, London, pp. 1–10.

Stephan, J. (1928). Stimulationversuche mit *Cannabis sativa. Faser frosch,* 7:292–298.

Talley, P. J. (1934). Carbohydrate–nitrogen ratios with respect to the sexual expression of hemp. *Plant Physiol.,* 9:731–748.

U.S. Treasury Department (1938). *Marihuana—Its Identification.* U.S. Government Printing Office, Washington, D.C.

Valle, J. R., Lapa, A. J., and Barros, G. G. (1968). Pharmacological activity of *Cannabis* according to the sex of the plant. *J. Pharm. Pharmacol.,* 20:798–799.

Vavilov, N. I. (1926). Studies on the origin of cultivated plants. *Institute de Botanique et Appliquié et d'Amélioration des Plants,* Leningrad.

Waller, C. W. (1971). Chemistry of marihuana. *Pharmacol. Rev.,* 23:265–271.

Waller, C. W., and Scigliano, J. A. (1970). The national marihuana program. *Report to the Commission on Problems of Drug Dependence,* Nat. Acad. Sci., N.R.C. 4:28–32.

Walter, H. (1935). Cannabis. In *Lebensgeschichte der Blutenpflanzen Mitteleuropas,* O. von Kirchner (ed.). Eugen Ulmer, Stuttgart, pp. 875–909.

Watt, G. (1908). *The Commercial Products of India.* John Murray, London.

Watt, J. M., and Breyer-Brandwijk, M. G. (1962). *Medicinal and Poisonous Plants of Southern and Eastern Africa.* E. and S. Livingston, Edinburgh.

Wilsie, C. R., Black, C. A., and Aandahl, A. R. (1944). Hemp production experiments; Cultural practices and soil requirements. *Iowa Agr. Exp. Sta. and Iowa Sta. Col. Agr. Ext. Serv. Comp. Bull.,* p. 63.

Wilsie, C. R., and Reddy, C. S. (1946). Seed treatment experiments with hemp. *J. Amer. Soc. Agron.,* 38:693–701.

Wisset, R. (1808). *A Treatise on Hemp.* J. Harding, London.

Wollner, H. J., Matchett, J. R., Levine, J., and Valaer, P. (1938). Report of the marihuana investigation. *J. Amer. Pharm. Ass.,* 27:29–36.

Zhukovskii, P. M. (1962). *Cultivated Plants and Their Wild Relatives,* P. S. Hudson (transl.). Commonwealth Agricultural Bureau, Farnham Royal, Bucks, England.

3

Chemistry: The Elusive Delta-9-THC and Its Active Metabolites

CHEMICAL CHARACTERIZATION OF MARIHUANA CONSTITUENTS

Until 1965, the intoxicating effects of marihuana could not be related to a specific chemical compound. This was not the case for the two other most commonly used natural intoxicating substances, opium and coca leaves; the chemical nature of the active ingredients or alkaloids, morphine and cocaine, which they contain has been known for nearly a century, and their effects could be accurately and quantitatively related to the dose administered.

Modern developments in chemistry have only recently made it possible to isolate, identify, and synthesize the specific plant constituents of *Cannabis sativa.* Waxes, resins, fixed and volatile oils, alkaloids, steroids, sugars, and fatty acids have been isolated from *Cannabis,* but the cannabinoids are the constituents unique to this plant. The wide variations in psychoactive potency among extracts from different plants was well known but could not be explained until the relationship between the structure and the biological activity of the cannabinoids was finally elucidated in 1965.

EARLY MARIHUANA CHEMISTRY

Before 1965, the major active component had not been isolated in a pure form, and its exact structure was not determined. Numerous "cannabinoids" were known to be present in the flowering tops and resins of the plant, but only one, cannabinol, which is not psychoactive, had been isolated (Adams et al., 1940; Todd, 1942). Numerous synthetic derivatives were also made by Adams and his group for animal and clinical experimentation. Some of these derivatives produced behavioral effects similar to those observed after smoking or ingesting *Cannabis* extracts.

Since the active substance in *Cannabis* was not identified, all of the extracts of plants and resin, the isomeric compounds, and the synthetic substances used were reported to be "tetrahydrocannabinol."

Many investigators assumed that the psychoactive constituents of *Cannabis* were unidentified mixtures of isomers of these tetrahydrocannabinols. For

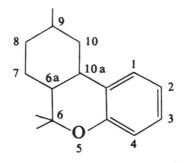

**Dibenzopyran
numbering**

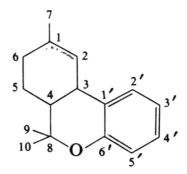

**Monoterpenoid
numbering**

Fig. 6. The two most common numbering systems used to describe the structure of the cannabinoids.

this reason, most of the experiments carried out until 1965 with these mixtures of cannabinoid compounds of dissimilar biological activity cannot be compared.

NOMENCLATURE

Two numbering systems are in use to describe the tetrahydrocannabinols. In the first, used by Chemical Abstracts, the formal rules for numbering the pyran-type compounds are utilized. In the second, the cannabinoids are regarded as substitute monoterpenoids. Mechoulam (1970) prefers the second classification, because it has a biogenetic basis and can be used for all cannabinoids, having the advantage that a carbon atom in the molecule retains the same number in all chemical transformations. In this classification, the active cannabinoids are designated as delta-1- and delta-1(6)-THC. The dibenzopyran classification will be utilized in this book (Fig. 6). In this classification, the active constituents of cannabis are designated as delta-8- and delta-9-THC. The abbreviation THC refers only to tetrahydrocannabinol and implies the presence of a double band which is specifically designated by the delta prefix: Delta-9-THC is delta-9-trans-tetrahydrocannabinol.

SEPARATION AND EXTRACTION OF CANNABINOIDS

There is no simple direct method for separating and identifying the natural cannabinoids, which boil within the same temperature range. Separation of the active constituents to form the red oil of *Cannabis* extract by fractional distillation is difficult, unless a constituent of the plant is present in high concentration (Mechoulam and Gaoni, 1967a). Modern chromatographic techniques preceded by extraction of the nearly insoluble oil with petroleum ether are required. Most natural cannabinoids are soluble in petroleum ether. By repeated extraction with this solvent, all the active material in the crude plant preparation can be dissolved. The remaining material contains phenolic polymers and other unidentified compounds. The petroleum ether is separated into acidic and neutral fractions, which yield the numerous cannabinoids by column chromatography.

STRUCTURAL CHARACTERIZATION OF THE NATURAL CANNABINOIDS

It is only in the past few years that the complex chemistry of marihuana has been clarified, and that intensive investigations have led to characterization of the cannabinoids. These include all the C_{21} compounds present in *Cannabis sativa,* their carboxylic acid analogs, and their transformation products. All of these compounds have been isolated, and methods for their detection and quantitation have been developed. The chemical structures of the cannabinoids could only be determined by extensive use of the most sophisticated modern physical techniques such as mass spectrometry, nuclear magnetic resonance spectroscopy, and proton magnetic resonance.

THE TETRAHYDROCANNABINOLS

Gaoni and Mechoulam (1964) first isolated the major biologically active constituent of *Cannabis sativa,* delta-9-THC. They showed that the double bond in the synthetic compound described by Adams in 1940 was in a different position in the natural psychoactive THC compound. Hively et al. (1966) isolated the natural second psychoactive constituent of *Cannabis sativa,* delta-8-THC. The major biologically active constituent of *Cannabis sativa* is delta-9-THC, which duplicates fully the effects of crude *Cannabis* in animals and in man. The isomer delta-8-THC also produces these same biological effects. The total delta-8- and delta-9-THC content of different *Cannabis* preparations varies widely. The delta-8 form, when present, occurs in low amounts.

A gas chromatographic technique has been described (Lerner and Zeffert, 1968) which allows for separation and identification of delta-8- and delta-9-THC from *Cannabis* extracts. With this technique, a mixture of leaves, stems, and seeds of 14 samples of *Cannabis sativa* Mexicana was analyzed and shown to contain 1.2% THC by weight, of which 0.4% was the delta-8-THC isomer. Analyses of Lebanese hashish over a 5-year period indicated that delta-8-THC did not exceed 0.5 to 1% of the amount of delta-9-THC. Delta-8- and delta-9-THC are unstable, oily, viscous liquids, insoluble in water, and readily transformed into inactive compounds after exposure to light or air or following temperature changes.

Delta-9-THC is rapidly isomerized to delta-8-THC under acid conditions, and oxidation converts both compounds to cannabinol, which is not psychoactive. The lack of solubility of delta-THC in water creates a difficulty for the investigator who wants to study its pharmacological effect by intravenous administration to animals or man. Attempts so far to solubilize delta-9-THC in ethanol, polyethyleneglycol dimethylsulfoxide, Triton × 100, and the tweens have not been satisfactory. In addition, such emulsions cannot be properly used for enzymatic studies *in vitro*. There is a great need for water-soluble derivatives of delta-9-THC such as the diethylaminobutyric ester, which has been reported in preliminary tests to have a similar pharmacological profile (Howes, 1970).

OTHER NEUTRAL NATURAL CANNABINOIDS

In addition to cannabinol and cannabidiol, which are present in the plant, a number of related chemical compounds such as cannabigerol, cannabicyclol, cannabichromene, and cannabidivarin have also been isolated from resinous mixtures and extracts of the plant. But one cannot state with certainty whether some of these specific compounds are natural products or are formed during extraction and isolation (Fig. 7).

All of these cannabinoids are not psychoactive. It is not known to what extent they interact with the active THC. Cannabidiol potentiates barbiturates (Loewe, 1950). Cannabidiol and cannabigerol are antibiotic *in vitro* (Kabelik et al., 1960). Cannabidiol is the only cannabinoid which occurs in crystalline form.

NATURAL CANNABINOID ACIDS

The natural cannabinoid acids which have been isolated in *Cannabis sativa* differ from the neutral cannabinoids by the presence of an additional carboxylic group. These acid cannabinoids are not psychoactive. Two THC acids, A and B, have been isolated according to the position of the carboxylic group in the benzene ring. After storage and heating, these acids can be decarboxylated to the respective neutral cannabinoids. According to Mechoulam (1970), when the inactive THC acids (A or B) are smoked, they give active delta-9-THC, which is one of the reasons for the higher activity of marihuana following smoking than after ingestion. Cannabidiolic acid is the predominant natural cannabinoid. In the fiber-type hemp, it is the only major constituent. It presents antibiotic activity for gram-positive bacteria *in vitro*.

It is not yet established whether the neutral cannabinoids are natural products or are formed by decarboxylation of their respective cannabinoid acids. As we have seen in the preceding chapter, the amounts of cannabinoids vary considerably from one type of *Cannabis* cultigen to the next.

SYNTHESIS OF NATURAL CANNABINOIDS

Extracting the principal psychoactive substance delta-9-THC from *Cannabis* extracts is difficult and relatively low in yield. The first synthetic

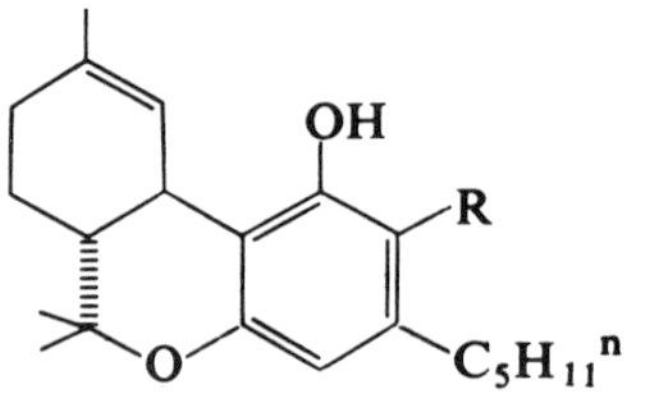

R = H: Δ^1-Tetrahydrocannabinol (Δ^1-THC)   , or
    Δ^9-Tetrahydrocannabinol (Δ^9-THC)
R = CO_2H: Δ^1-Tetrahydrocannabinolic acid (Δ^L-THCA), or
    Δ^9-Tetrahydrocannabinolic acid (Δ^9-THCA).

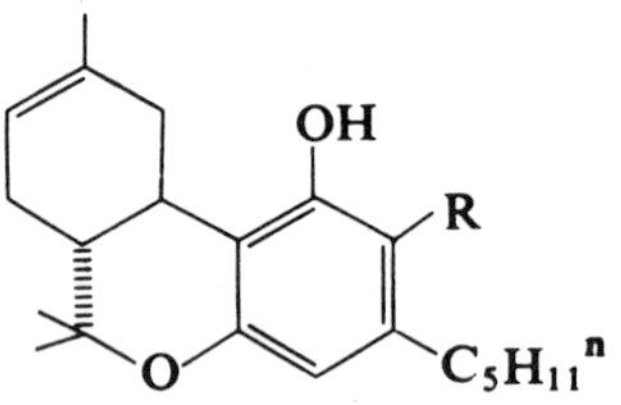

R = H: $\Delta^{1,(6)}$-Tetrahydrocannabinol ($\Delta^{1,(6)}$-THC)   , or
    $\Delta^{6,1}$-Tetrahydrocannabinol ($\Delta^{6,1}$-THC), or
    Δ^8-Tetrahydrocannabinol (Δ^8-THC)
R = CO_2H: $\Delta^{1,(6)}$-Tetrahydrocannabinolic acid ($\Delta^{1,(6)}$-THCA), or
    $\Delta^{6,1}$-Tetrahydrocannabinolic acid ($\Delta^{6,1}$-THCA), or
    Δ^8-Tetrahydrocannabinolic acid (Δ^8-THCA).

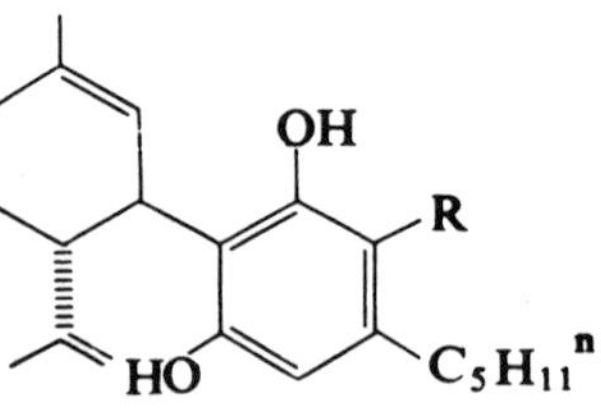

R = H: Cannabidiol
R = CO_2H: Cannabidiolic acid

Fig. 7. Some important cannabinoids isolated from *Cannabis* extracts—delta-8- and delta-9-THC, cannabidiol, and their acids.

method, proposed by Mechoulam and Gaoni (1965), was long and expensive. Petrzilka and Sikemeier (1967) published an original and simple method to synthesize delta-8- and delta-9-THC by condensation of olivetol with (+)*cis*-menthadienol. This method was further developed in the United States for large-scale production of quantities of delta-9- and delta-8-THC sufficient to satisfy the current research program supported by the National Institutes of Health. Synthetic delta-9-THC is 95% pure and free of nonvolatile material, but it is unstable when exposed to air, light, or temperature above 10°C. Delta-8-THC is more stable and can be produced in a 98% pure form. The limited amounts of other cannabinoids have also been synthesized under National Institute of Mental Health (N.I.M.H.) contract and made available for research and use as analytical standards.

SYNTHESIS OF TETRAHYDROCANNABINOL DERIVATIVES

A large number of synthetic cannabinoid derivatives have been made and tested for their biological activity in animals and man.

Adams and his group (1940) were the first to synthesize such active derivatives. Synhexyl or pyrahexyl with a double bond in position 6a, between two of the rings and having a hexyl rather than an amyl side chain, were tested by many investigators. Hollister (1971) showed that synhexyl had, in man, the same psychoactive potency as its homolog D^{6a}-THC (which has an amyl instead of a hexyl side chain). Both compounds are one-third to one-sixth less potent than delta-9-THC (Fig. 8). Other derivatives synthesized by Adams were dimethylheptylpyran (DMHP), methyloctylpyran (MOP), and *n*-amyl-pyran (NAP) (as represented in Fig. 8). These compounds were extensively studied in animals for their pharmacological properties by Hardman, Seevers, and Domino (1971) under contract with the Army Chemical Center at Edgewood Arsenal, Maryland. The most potent was found to be DMHP, which was 10 to 62 times more active than delta-9-THC.

Pars and Razdan (1971) have synthesized water-soluble ester derivatives as well as nitrogen analogs which were all pharmacologically active in the animal.

STRUCTURE-ACTIVITY RELATIONSHIP

Edery et al. (1971) have completed a definitive study of the structure-activity-relationship of the main cannabinoid, natural and synthetic derivatives in the adult rhesus monkey. They showed that changes in the side chain of

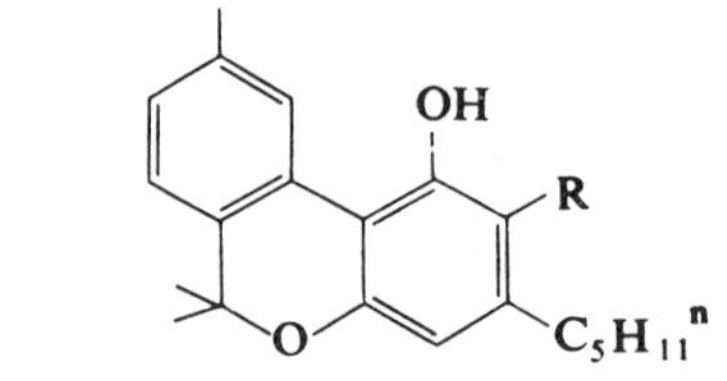

R = H: Cannabinol
R = CO_2H: Cannabinolic acid

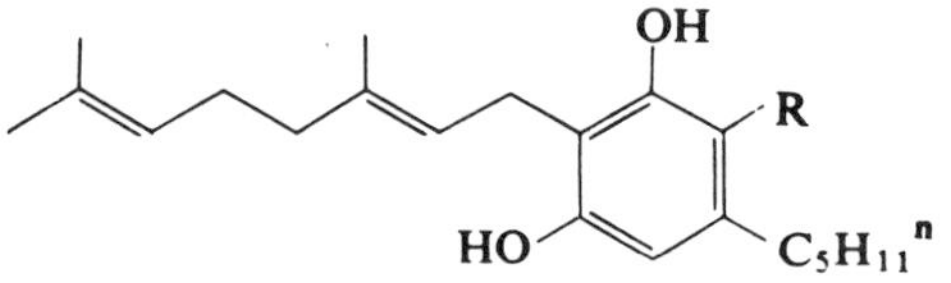

R = H: Cannabigerol (CG)
R = CO_2H: Cannabigerolic acid

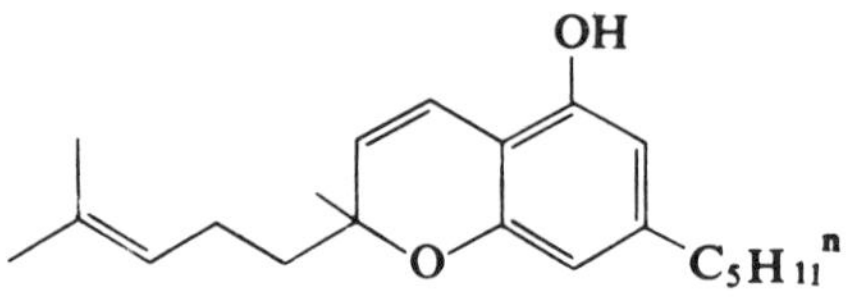

Cannabichromene

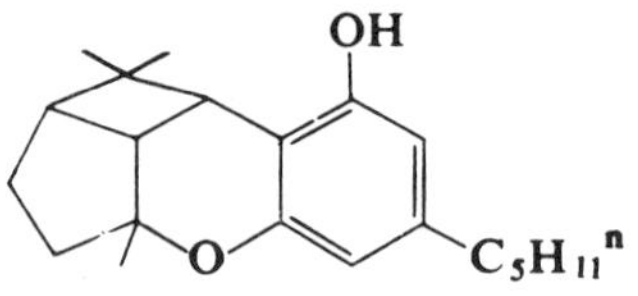

Cannabicyclol

Fig. 8. Other cannabinoids extracted from *Cannabis sativa*.

the aromatic moiety increased or prolonged activity of the compounds. The most active was the delta-9-THC in which the side chain was a dimethylheptyl group. Its activity lasted 48 hours, and it was five times more active than delta-9-THC. Petrzilka (1970) attempted "to correlate structure and hallucinogenic activity of the known hallucinogens: delta-9-THC, LSD, and psilocybin." All showed structural similarities (Fig. 9). Even "with some imagination," mescaline may be fitted into this scheme.

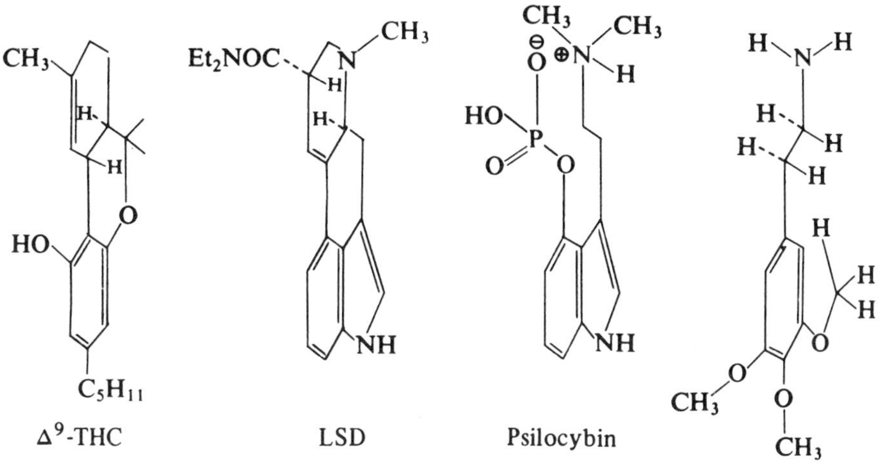

Fig. 9. Delta-9-THC, LSD, psilocybin, and mescaline drawn to demonstrate structural similarities. (From Petrzilka, 1970.)

ANALYTICAL METHODS OF DETECTION

Differential detection of *Cannabis sativa* is possible by colorimetric and chromatographic methods.

The most widely used color test was described by Beam (1911). Five percent ethanolic potassium hydroxide gives a purple color in the presence of cannabidiol and cannabigerol, which are oxidized to hydroquinines. The Duquenois–Levine reaction with vanillin, acetaldehyde, and ethanol in hydrochloric acid is more sensitive than the Beam test. These chemical tests, in combination with a botanical identification of the characteristic cystolith hair of *Cannabis,* were used as the standard procedure by the Federal Bureau of Narcotics and Dangerous Drugs to identify marihuana. However, it is not specific enough to determine the potency of a sample or its delta-9-THC concentration.

The measurement of delta-9-THC, cannabinol, and cannabidiol in different variants of *Cannabis* was performed by Fetterman et al. (1970) on many variants with gas chromatographic techniques. More sophisticated techniques combining thin-layer chromatography on a silver-impregnated silica gel in conjunction with color reactions are required to detect cannabinoids in body fluids. One of these, developed by Turk (1969), identifies natural cannabinol, THC, and cannabidiol, and is sensitive to concentrations of 0.05 mg. These methods were sensitive enough to detect cannabinol in the urine of man after a massive, lethal intoxication (as reported by Heyndrickx et al., 1970). However, such methods, as well as the one of Bullock et al. (1970), are not accurate enough to detect the metabolites of marihuana in body fluids of habitual users, especially in plasma, where they are present in extremely low concentrations. Further refinements and developments of micro methods for the identification of the active psychoactive cannabinoids and their metabolites in body fluids are to be expected in the near future.

STANDARDIZATION OF ACTIVE MATERIAL IN *CANNABIS* PREPARATION

Total THC content of a *Cannabis* product was used as a standard of potency by investigators until pure delta-9- and delta-8-THC became available and were selected as THC reference standards. Total THC content is an unreliable index of the biological potency of a preparation. Only the pure compounds now available from the National Institutes of Health can allow for standardization of dosage for comparative studies.

Since delta-9-THC oxidizes rapidly in the presence of room air, above 10°C, or when exposed to light, it should be always kept in sealed ampules, under nitrogen, protected from light, and refrigerated to 4°C. The same precautions should be taken with the crude unextracted material.

Many of the early experiments with *Cannabis* (Weil et al, 1968; Crancer et al., 1969) were performed with material which had not been properly assayed for active ingredients or which had not been stored under optimal conditions.

TOTAL PLANT EXTRACT

It is presently believed that delta-9-THC and its isomer delta-8-THC are the main psychoactive constituents in *Cannabis*. However, the chemical identity as well as the pharmacological nonpsychoactive properties of other plant constituents must be clarified. There are still unidentified alkaloids in *Cannabis* which must be isolated and tested (Braenden, 1970). The pharmacological effect of the total plant extract is probably different from the effects of each of the individual constituents which have been isolated from *Cannabis*. For this reason, the National Institute of Mental Health has prepared a marihuana extract distillate (MED) containing 15% delta-9-THC. Extraction procedures are known to alter the concentration as well as the nature of the different plant constituents and must therefore be strictly standardized.

BIOTRANSFORMATION AND ACTIVE METABOLITES

Although delta-9- and delta-8-THC duplicate the psychoactive effects of *Cannabis* extracts, it is not known with certainty whether these effects are due to the compounds themselves or to some of their metabolites (e.g., products of transformation by body process), or to both THC and their active metabolites. The active biological compound might be the 11-hydroxy-THC (11-hydroxy-*trans*-delta-8-THC or -delta-9-THC). These metabolites were isolated in the liver of rats and rabbits administered intraperitoneally ^{14}C-labeled delta-9-THC or delta-8-THC (Wall et al., 1970). They were also found in

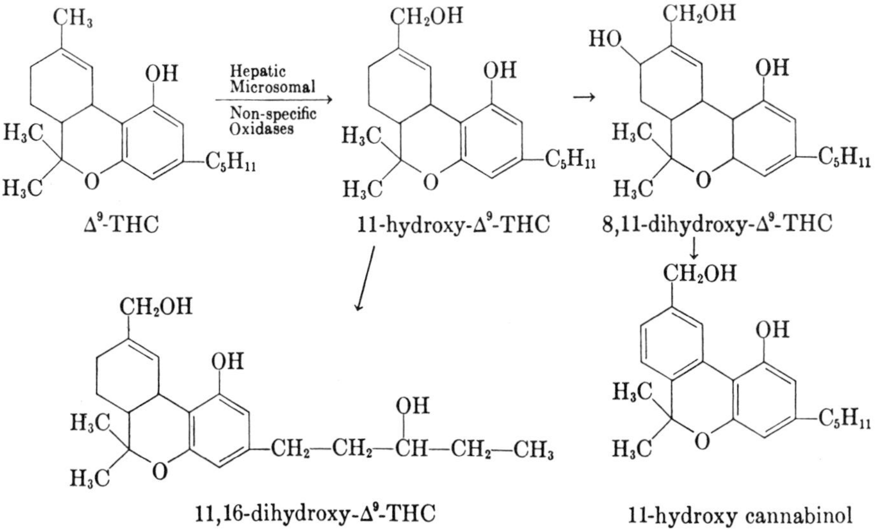

Fig. 10. Biotransformation of delta-9-THC into hydroxylated active metabolites by nonspecific liver oxydases.

homogenates of rabbit livers incubated with ^{14}C-labeled delta-8-THC (Truitt, 1970). These metabolites, which are pharmacologically active in mice and monkeys (Ben-Zvi et al., 1970), would be formed by the action of a liver enzyme on delta-8- or delta-9-THC. They are converted to inactive cannabinol by the same dehydration procedure used by Burstein et al. (1970). On the basis of these results, some workers have speculated that a metabolite and not delta-9-THC is the active compound which triggers the biological effects of *Cannabis* intoxication at the molecular level (Fig. 10).

Wall et al. (1970) and Ben-Zvi et al. (1971) have observed that other active metabolites of delta-9-THC are also formed by side-chain oxidation at the beta position.

It is reported that marihuana has little effect when smoked for the first time. Such a fact, if clearly established, could be due to the induction in the liver or lung of a hydroxylation enzyme which would be triggered by an initial dose of delta-9-THC. Subsequent administration of this compound would lead to a more rapid formation of the active metabolite hydroxy-THC.

Ben-Zvi et al., (1971) sum up the complexity of *Cannabis* action as follows:

> "It is generally assumed that the non-identical psychological reactions produced by *Cannabis* are due to the different personalities of the users and the varying environmental conditions. While these factors are probably of considerable importance, one has now to take into account the possibility that several compounds (in varying ratios and with presumably different biochemical profiles) contribute to the overall effects."

CHEMICAL ANALYSIS OF MARIHUANA SMOKE

Since *Cannabis* preparations are often smoked, studies have been performed to determine the chemical nature of the composition of *Cannabis* smoke and the possible conversion of the constituents of the plant into active or inactive substances.

The relationship between the active constituents of different *Cannabis* preparations and the chemical by-products resulting from the process of burning (pyrolysis) depend on a great number of variables, including moisture content of the preparation, current of air passed through, and temperature of combustion.

To analyze *Cannabis* smoke it is necessary to use the techniques developed for the study of tobacco smoke. These methods allow one to control the effects of important variables such as the nature of the cigarette paper, the amount of air drawn through the cigarette, and the rate of puffing.

Miras et al. (1964) have compared the sublimate obtained from a smoking machine to an extract of the natural plant using chromatographic techniques. THC was unchanged in both sublimate and extract, but cannabidiol, present in the natural product, was missing in the sublimate.

The same authors carried out other studies with labeled cannabinoids isolated from plants cultivated in an atmosphere of $^{11}CO_2$ (Coutselinis and Miras, 1971). It was observed that the smoking process destroys THC to a lesser degree in the hashish extract or in a mixture with other pure cannabinoids, and to a greater extent if the THC is pure and alone in the cigarette. The opposite was observed with cannabidiolic acid.

In a study made according to the procedures recommended for the analysis of tobacco cigarettes by the U.S. Federal Trade Commission, *Cannabis* cigarettes were prepared: They contained 1 gr of *Cannabis* leaves of 8 to 25 mesh size and with 1.4% delta-9-THC content and 12% moisture; they were wrapped in 14-second paper 68 mm long. The cigarette was consumed on a smoking machine in a series of 35-ml puffs of 2-sec duration every 60 sec. All of the side-stream smoke (produced during static burning) and the mainstream smoke (from the puffing) were collected separately and passed through a standard Cambridge fiberglass filter, which collects particles of 3 μ or larger. Equal amounts (21%) of delta-9-THC (analyzed by gas chromatography) were received in the side-stream and mainstream smoke, while 52% was found in the 20 mm of cigarette end remaining unsmoked. Therefore it appears from this study that about 10% of the delta-9-THC is pyrolyzed. This figure is considerably lower than the one reported by Claussen and Korte (1967), who observed a 90% destruction of the biologically active constituents of *Cannabis*. The temperature of combustion and technique utilized might have accounted for their results.

Manno et al. (1970) and Truitt (1970), using a calibrated smoking machine, reported that 50% of the total THC dose in a cigarette is delivered in the resulting smoke, provided the cigarette is entirely consumed. In the study of Truitt's group, a smoking machine was programmed to reproduce the puff interval, rate, and volume characteristics of chronic young American smokers. The ratios of cannabinoids in smoke were similar to those found in the plant. (The major exception is that the heat of combustion converts all the delta-9-THC acid precursors to delta-9-THC.) There was little conversion of cannabidiol to THC as suggested by Miras, and minimal isomerization of delta-9- to delta-8-THC.

The figure of 50% active material delivered from an American marihuana cigarette completely consumed according to the technique prevalent in the United States is the one presently accepted in clinical studies. However, such a percentage of delivery could not be applied to other *Cannabis* mixtures smoked in different containers and in a different way.

Indeed, one should keep in mind the following remarks by Miras (1971):

> "If one considers the great differences in the quantity and the quality of the active cannabinoids (and isomers, etc.) which are contained in the various *Cannabis* preparations produced according to miscellaneous techniques (time of maturation, variety of plants) all over the world, in addition to the problems in connection with the smoking process, the great conflict about the action of *Cannabis* on human smokers can easily be understood."

CONCLUSION

It has taken all of the refinements of modern technology to isolate and define the elusive psychoactive substance which has led man to use *Cannabis* as an intoxicant. Now that this substance is available, the pharmacologist and biochemist will be able to assess quantitatively its mechanism of action, and some advances in understanding basic biological processes are to be expected.

However, the chemical identification of delta-9-THC will not solve in any way the social problem of *Cannabis* use or abuse by man. Indeed, the history of the past 100 years indicates that when morphine and heroin were isolated from the poppy and cocaine from coca leaves, these alkaloids were rapidly abused in preference to the less potent natural substances from which they were derived. The same holds true for the Mexican peyote cactus and its alkaloid, mescaline. If there is any continuity in history, one might therefore expect delta-9-THC to be increasingly used by man as a euphoriant and mind-altering drug in preference to the deceptive *Cannabis* of fluctuating potency. Furthermore, it is very simple to synthesize delta-9-THC from olivetol, a basic chemical available commercially in the United States.

The use of delta-9-THC would greatly simplify the problems of production, distribution, and quality control required by the legalization of marihuana advocated by an increasing number of American intellectuals. It is probably for this reason that the Vienna 1971 Convention of the U.N. Committee on Drug Dependence added delta-9-THC to its growing list of psychoactive substances to be banned from general use. The pharmacology of delta-9-THC, summarized in the following chapter, might explain this decision.

SUMMARY

1. The major psychoactive substance contained in *Cannabis sativa* is delta-9-THC, a unique chemical not found anywhere else in nature.

2. Like other synthetic delta-tetrahydrocannabinols, it is an oily substance insoluble in water but soluble in alcohol.

3. It is rapidly inactivated by exposure to oxygen, light, humidity, and elevated temperatures.

4. Its molecular structure has been correlated with that of other hallucinogens, such as LSD and psilocybin, although it does not contain a nitrogen atom.

5. The amount of delta-9-THC or of its acid precursor contained in a crude extract which will be transferred to an individual will differ according to the route of administration (inhalation or ingestion).

6. The amount of delta-9-THC or of its acid precursor contained in a crude extract which is transferred in the process of smoking is difficult to ascertain, but is quite variable.

7. Delta-9-THC undergoes complex biotransformation in the body, producing both psychoactive and nonpsychoactive metabolites.

8. The psychoactive properties of delta-9-THC appear to be mediated in part through active metabolites.

9. The possible biological effects of other cannabinoids or other chemicals contained in *Cannabis* (alkaloids, terpenes, steroids) have not yet been ascertained.

REFERENCES

Adams, R. (1942*a*). Marihuana. *Bull. N.Y. Acad. Med.,* 18:705–730.

Adams, R. (1942*b*). Marihuana. *Harvey Lec.,* 37:168–197.

Adams, R., Pease, D. C., Clark, T. H. (1940). The structure of cannabinol. III. Synthesis of cannabinol. *J. Amer. Chem. Soc.,* 62:2204–2207.

Agurell, S. (1970). Chemical and pharmacological studies of cannabis. In *The Botany and Chemistry of Cannabis,* C. R. B. Joyce and S. H. Curry (eds.). J. & A. Churchill, London, pp. 175–191.

Agurell, S., Nilsson, I. M., Olsson, A., and Sandberg, F. (1969). Elimination of tritium-labeled cannabinols in the rat with special reference to the development of tests for the identification of cannabis users. *Biochem. Pharmacol.,* 18:1195–1201.

Archer, R. A., Boyd, D. B., DeMarco, P. V., Tyminski, I. J., and Allinger, N. L. (1970). Structural studies of cannabinoids—A theoretical and proton magnetic resonance analysis. *J. Amer. Chem. Soc.,* 92:5200–5206.

Beam, W. (1911). Fourth Report, Wellcome Tropical Research Lab. Chem. Sect. Khartoum, No. 25.

Ben-Zvi, Z., Mechoulam, R., and Burstein, S. H. (1970). Identification through synthesis of an active delta-1,6-tetrahydrocannabinol metabolite. *J. Amer. Chem. Soc.,* 92:3468.

Ben-Zvi, Z., Mechoulam, R., Edery, H., and Porath, G. (1971). 6β-hydroxy-Δ^1-tetrahydrocannabinol synthesis and biological activity. *Science,* 174:951–952.

Braenden, O. (1970). Discussion. In *The Botany and Chemistry of Cannabis,* C. R. B. Joyce and S. H. Curry (eds.). J. & A. Churchill, London, p. 156.

Bullock, F. J., Bruni, R. J., and Werner, E. A. (1970). Fluorescent assay of submicrogram amounts of cannabis constituents in biological fluids. *Abstr. 160th Nat. Mtg. Amer. Chem. Soc.* 077:14–18.

Bureau of Narcotics and Dangerous Drugs, Lab. Op. Div. (1970). Private communication.

Burstein, S. H., Menezes, F., Williamson, E., and Mechoulam, R. (1970). Metabolism of delta-1-(6)-tetrahydrocannabinol, an active marihuana constituent. *Nature,* 225:87–88.

Caddy, B., and Fish, F. (1967). A screening technique for Indian hemp (*Cannabis sativa* L.) *Chromatogr.,* 31:584–587.

Claussen, U., and Korte, F. (1967). Hashish. XIII. Behavior of constituents of *Cannabis sativa* during smoking (in German). *Tetrahedron Lett.,* 22:207.

Coutselinis, A., and Miras, C. (1971). The effects of the smoking process on cannabinols. *J. Forensic Med.,* 18:108–113.

Crancer, A., Dille, J. M., Delay, J. C., Wallace, J. E., and Haykin, M. D. (1969). Comparison of the effects of marihuana and alcohol on simulated driving performance. *Science,* 164:851–854.

da Silva, J. B. (1957). Chromatographic determination of cannabinol in the blood, urine and saliva of subjects addicted to *Cannabis sativa. Rev. Fac. Farm. Biogurm.,* 5:205–214.

Edery, H., Grunfeld, Y., Ben-Zvi, Z., and Mechoulam, R. (1971). Structural requirements for cannabinoid activity. *Ann. N.Y. Acad. Sci.,* 191:40–53.

Farnsworth, N. R. (1969). Pharmacognosy and chemisty of *Cannabis sativa. J. Amer. Med. Ass.,* 9:410–414.

Fetterman, P. S., Keith, E. S., Waller, C. W., Gurrero, O., Doorenbos, N. J., and Quimby, M. W. (1970). Mississippi grown *Cannabis sativa* L.

—A preliminary observation on the chemical definition of phenotype and variations in the content versus age, sex and plant part. *J. Pharm. Sci.,* 60:1246–1249.

Foltz, R. L., Fentimena, A. F., Jr., Leighty, E. G., Walter, J. L., Drewes, H. R., Schwartz, W. E., Page, T. F., Jr., and Truitt, E. B., Jr. (1970). Metabolite of (−) *trans* delta 8 tetrahydrocannabinol: Identification and synthesis. *Science,* 168:844–845.

Gaoni, Y., and Mechoulam, R. (1964). Isolation, structure and partial synthesis of an active component of hashish. *J. Amer. Chem. Soc.,* 86:1646–1647.

Hardman, H. F., Domino, E. F., and Seevers, M. H. (1971). General pharmacological actions of some synthetic tetrahydrocannabinol derivatives. *Pharmacol. Rev.,* 23:295–315.

Harris, L. S., Razdan, R. K., Dewey, W. L., and Pars, H. G. (1967). The pharmacology of some new tetrahydrocannabinol analogs. *Chim. Ther.,* 2:167.

Heyndrickx, A., Scheiris, C., and Schepens, P. (1970). Toxicological study of a fatal intoxication in man due to cannabis smoking. *J. Pharm. Belg.,* 24:371–376.

Hively, R. L., Mosher, W. A., and Hoffman, F. W. (1966). Isolation of *trans*-delta-9-tetrahydrocannabinol from marihuana. *J. Amer. Chem. Soc.,* 88:1832–1833.

Hollister, L. E. (1971). Actions of various marihuana derivatives in man. *Pharmacol. Rev.,* 23:349–357.

Howes, J. F. (1970). A study of two water soluble derivatives of delta-9-tetrahydrocannabinol. *Pharmacologist,* 12:258.

Kabelik, J., Krejci, Z., and Santavy, F. (1960). Cannabis as a medicament. *Bull. Narcotics,* 12:5–23.

Klein, F. K., Rapoport, W., and Elliott, H. W. (1971). Cannabis alkaloids. *Nature,* 232:258.

Korte, F., and Sieper, H. (1965). Recent results of hashish analysis. In *Hashish: Its Chemistry and Pharmacology,* G. E. W. Wolstenholme and J. Knight (eds.). Little, Brown and Company, Boston.

Lerner, M., and Zeffert, J. T. (1968). Determination of tetrahydrocannabinol isomers in marihuana and hashish. *Bull. Narcotics,* 20:53–54.

Loewe, S. (1950). *Cannabis.* Wikstoffe und Pharmacologie der Cannabinole. *Arch. Exp. Pathol. Pharmak.,* 211:175–189.

Manno, J. E., Kiplinger, G. F., Scholz, N. E., and Forney, R. B. (1970). The influence of alcohol and marihuana on motor and mental performance of volunteer subjects. *Clin. Pharmacol. Ther.,* 12:202–211.

Mechoulam, R. (1970). Marihuana chemistry. *Science,* 168:1159–1166.

Mechoulam, R., Ben-Zvi, Z., Yagnitinksi, B., and Shani, A. (1969). A new tetrahydrocannabinolic acid. *Tetrahedron Lett.,* 28:2339–2341.

Mechoulam, R., and Gaoni, Y. (1965). A total synthesis of *dl*-delta-1-tetrahydrocannabinol, the active constituent of hashish. *J. Amer. Chem. Soc.,* 87:3273–3275.

Mechoulam, R., and Gaoni, Y. (1967a). The absolute configuration of delta-1-tetrahydrocannabinol, the major active constituent of hashish. *Tetrahedron Lett.,* 12:1109–1111.

Mechoulam, R., and Gaoni, Y. (1967b). Recent advances in the chemistry of hashish. *Fortschr. Chem. Organ. Naturst.,* 25:175–213.

Mechoulam, R., Shani, A., Edery, H., and Grunfeld, Y. (1970). Chemical basis of hashish activity. *Science,* 169:611–612.

Merkus, F. W. H. M. (1971). Cannabivarin and tetrahydrocannabivarin, two new constituents of hashish. *Nature,* 232:579–580.

Miras, C. (1971). Distribution of THC in man. *Med. Sci. Law,* 11:197–199.

Miras, C., Simon, S., and Kiburis, J. (1964). Comparative assay of the constituents from the sublimate of smoked cannabis with that from ordinary cannabis. *Bull. Narcotics,* 16:13–15.

Nilsson, I. M., Agurell, S., Nilsson, J. L. G., Ohlsson, A., Sandberg, F., and Wahlquist, M. (1970). Delta-1-tetrahydrocannabinol: Structure of a major metabolite. *Science,* 168:1228–1229.

Pars, H. G., and Razdan, R. K. (1971). Tetrahydrocannabinols and synthetic analogs. *Ann. N.Y. Acad. Sci.,* 191:15–22.

Petrzilka, T. (1970). Synthesis of (−)-tetrahydrocannabinol and analogous compounds. In *The Botany and Chemistry of Cannabis,* C. R. B. Joyce and S. H. Curry (eds.). J. & A. Churchill, London, pp. 79–92.

Petrzilka, T., and Sikemeier, C. (1967). Components of hashish. II. Synthesis of (−)-delta-6, 1–3, 4 *trans*-tetrahydrocannabinol and (+)-delta-6, 1–3, 4 *trans*-tetrahydrocannabinol. *Helv. Chim. Acta.,* 50:2111–2113.

Phillips, R., Turk, R., Manno, J., Naresh, J., and Forney, R. (1970). Seasonal variation in cannabinolic content of Indiana marihuana. *J. Forensic Sci.,* 15:191–200.

Song, C. H., Kanter, S. L., and Hollister, L. E. (1970). Extraction and gas chromatographic quantification of tetrahydrocannabinol from marihuana. *Res. Commun. Chem. Pathol. Pharmacol.,* 1:375–382.

Taylor, E. C., Lenard, K., and Shvo, Y. (1967). Active constituents of marihuana. Synthesis of delta 6-3, 4-*trans*-tetrahydrocannabinol. *J. Amer. Chem. Soc.,* 88:367–369.

Todd, A. R. (1942). The chemistry of hashish. *Sci. Roy. Coll. Sci.,* 12:37–45.

Truitt, E. B., Jr., (1970). Pharmacological activity in a metabolite of (1)-*trans* delta 8 tetrahydrocannabinol. *Fed. Proc.,* 29:619.

Turk, R. F., Dharir, H. I., and Forney, R. B. (1969). A simple chemical method to identify marihuana. *J. Forensic Sci.,* 14:389–392.

Vieira, F., Aguiar, M., Alencar, J. W., Seabra, A. P., Tursch, B. M., and Leclerq, J. (1967). Effects of the organic layer of hashish smoke extract and preliminary results of its chemical analysis. *Psychopharmacologia,* 10:361–362.

Wall, M. E., Brine, D. R., Brine, G. A., Pitt, C. G., Freudenthal, R. I., and Christensen, H. D. (1970). Isolation, structure and biological activity of several metabolites of delta-9-tetrahydrocannabinol. *J. Amer. Chem. Soc.,* 92:3466–3468.

Weil, A. T., and Zinberg, N. E. (1969). Acute effects of marihuana on speech. *Nature,* 222:434–437.

Widman, M., Nilsson, I. M., Nilsson, J. L. G., Agurell, S., and Leander, K. (1971). Metabolism of cannabis IX. Cannabinol: Structure of a major metabolite formed in the liver. *Life Sci. Pt. II,* 10:157–162.

4

Toxicology and Pharmacology

Classical texts describing the pharmacological and toxicological actions of *Cannabis* and its derivatives are difficult to interpret and even misleading. Indeed, the experimenters had no way to assess the nature of the preparations they used, since they did not have at their disposal any pure reference compounds of a known potency. Consequently, the reports of toxicological and pharmacological effects of crude extracts or synthetic derivatives of *Cannabis* published before 1968 lack precision and uniformity and preclude any quantitative correlation between physiological effects and chemical composition.

The recent availability of delta-9- and delta-8-THC has allowed pharmacologists and toxicologists to establish dose-response curves relating physiopathological effects to dose administered. These quantitative experiments do replicate to a great extent the qualitative results obtained with *Cannabis* extracts.

However, one cannot draw a complete parallel between the pharmacological or other effects produced by delta-9-THC and those engendered by *Cannabis* extracts. *Cannabis* extracts contain, in addition to delta-9- and delta-8-THC, many other cannabinoids and chemical compounds, such as esters and alkaloids, the effects of which will have to be evaluated separately and in combination. Furthermore, pharmacological and toxicological studies are performed on animals with compounds administered intravenously, by mouth, or intraperitoneally. Results observed in such studies cannot be strictly compared with those produced by smoking *Cannabis* extracts. Indeed, smoking will release plant constituents such as tars, carbon monoxide, acids, aldehydes, and particulate irritant substances. In addition to the delta-9-THC content of smoke, therefore, all of these by-products of smoking should also be considered in toxicity studies, especially those on chronic use.

ADMINISTRATION AND ABSORPTION OF DELTA-9-THC

Few animal experiments are performed with smoked material, which is a rapid and efficient method of absorption but difficult to quantify. The lack of water solubility of delta-9-THC makes its administration and absorption a difficult problem for the pharmacologist.

Many different methods for suspending, solubilizing, or emulsifying delta-9-THC have been suggested (Rosenkrantz et el., 1972). These include the use of surfactants (Tween 80, Triton X-110, Pluronic), solvents (ethanol, propylene glycol, dimethylsulfoxide, olive oil), and suspending agents (resin, albumin, dextrans), as well as ultrasonic emulsifiers. None of these methods is entirely satisfactory, because they all influence the rate of absorption as well as pharmacological activity. The fact that all of these methods have been used by various investigators makes quantitative comparisons difficult.

The insolubility of delta-9-THC in water also makes it very difficult to study delta-9-THC in isolated tissue preparations suspended or incubated in the standard electrolyte solutions (such as Krebs Ringer), and to obtain dose-response curves of enzyme activity or functional parameters. Intraperitoneal administration is slow and limited. It may also be accompanied by chemical peritonitis. The intravenous route is satisfactory for acute studies, but it is too dissimilar to the human use. The oral method would appear to be the most satisfactory, although the amount of active material absorbed by this route is unknown. This author uses an emulsion of delta-9-THC in Tween 80 and cornstarch, or in sesame oil, which is fed by stomach tube.

TOXICITY OF *CANNABIS* AND DELTA-9-THC

Acute Toxicity

The acute oral toxicity of the *Cannabis* derivatives used as intoxicants (marihuana, kif, hashish) is low.

O'Shaughnessy (1842) and Moreau (1845) administered large amounts of hashish extracts to mice, rabbits, and rats without producing any lethal effects. Moreau observed, in some pigeons and two rabbits given very strong doses of pure extract to swallow, a "slight excitement followed by an apparent somnolence of short duration."

According to Loewe (1946), the LD_{50} (a dose sufficient to be lethal to 50% of the animals given the toxic) of *Cannabis* extracts administered to mice orally, subcutaneously, and intravenously were 21.6, 11.0, and 0.18 g/kg, respectively. Joachimoglu (1965) reported an LD_{50} of 1.5 g/kg for natural hashish extract administered intraperitoneally. The figures reported by Gill et al. (1970) for this same animal are within the same range.

However, the acute toxicity of delta-9-THC, especially when administered intravenously, is much greater. It was established by Phillips et al. (1971) in rodents (Table 9). The intravenous LD_{50} in rats and mice is in the vicinity of 30 to 40 mg/kg, respectively, with death occurring in 15 min. The LD_{50} by intraperitoneal and oral routes requires a dosage 10 to 20 times greater, with death occurring 10 to 36 hours after administration. These results in-

Table 9

Acute Toxicity of Delta-9-THC in rats and mice[a]

	Route of administration[b]	No. of animals in group	Observation time (days)	LD_{50} (mg/kg)
Rats	i.v.	6	7	29 (27–30)[c]
	i.p.	6	7	373 (305–454)
	i.g.	6	7	666 (604–734)
Mice	i.v.	6	7	43 (37–49)
	i.p.	10	7	455 (419–493)
	i.g.	10	7	482 (451–515)

[a] Vehicle: 10% Tween 80.
[b] Administration was intravenous (i.p.), intraperitoneal (i.v.), or intra-gastric (i.e.).
[c] Confidence interval 95%.

dicate that delta-9-THC is slowly absorbed by the gut, or through the peritoneal route. In addition, by these two routes it might be more rapidly metabolized into inactive compounds. Toxic signs preceding death in both species were ataxia, hyperexcitability, depression, loss of righting reflex and dyspnea progressing to respiratory arrest. Diarrhea in mice and rats, and, additionally, tremor and lacrimation in rats were observed after intraperitoneal or intragastric administration. Immediate postmortem examination showed edema and congestion of the lungs in all animals. All toxic signs disappeared within 24 hours in the surviving animals. By the oral route, LD_{50} is greater in female than in male rats. There is also evidence of variation in toxicity between rat species. With the same compound Scheckel et al. (1968) observed a 50% mortality in the squirrel monkey after a dosage varying from

36 to 64 mg/kg administered intraperitoneally. The acute toxicities of delta-9- and delta-8-THC are low relative to the pharmacologically active doses.

In man it is unlikely that delta-9-THC plasma concentrations elevated enough to produce such acute toxic effects could be reached after ingestion of *Cannabis* preparations. Cannabinoids are poorly and irregularly absorbed by the gut. Only two cases of fatalities due to ingestion of very large amounts of charas are recorded in the Indian literature.

Since no serious impairment of vital functions has ever been reported in the United States following inhalation or ingestion of *Cannabis* preparations (which have in general low—1% or less—content of delta-9-THC), it has been commonly stated that *Cannabis* is an innocuous drug, safer than alcohol or cigarettes. Such a contention should be made with caution in view of two recent case reports of severe acute *Cannabis* intoxication.

The first case is "a toxicological study of a fatal intoxication in man due to *Cannabis* smoking" reported by Heyndrickx et al. (1970). This fatality allegedly due to *Cannabis* is somewhat better documented than the three others reported in the Indian literature at the end of the last century: A 23-year-old student was found dead in his room, which contained large amounts of *Cannabis* herb and resin and a water pipe, but no drugs. From the autopsy there was no evidence of natural or violent cause of death. Classical toxicological analysis of the specimens (blood, urine, kidney, liver, stomach) was negative for barbiturates and weak acids, neutral poisons, alkaline poisons, weak amines, benzodiazepine compounds, phenothiazines; for morphine, mephenon, palfrium, and other related narcotics, for alcohol and carbon monoxide. The only toxic substance identified (by thin-layer chromatography) was cannabinol in the urine of the deceased. The same cannabinol was identified chromatigraphically from the *Cannabis* herb and resin and combustion residues from the pipe, which were found in the room of the dead man (to the exclusion of any other toxic substances). Although the evidence presented is still presumptive, it does indicate that delta-9-THC might be a lethal compound in man as well as animals when present in high enough concentrations in the blood stream, and that such concentrations can be reached by inhalation of strong *Cannabis* preparations because of the rapid absorption of delta-9-THC by the lung. The report by Heyndrickx was corroborated by the observation of Gourves et al. (1971), who reported the case of a coma of 4-days' duration due to *Cannabis* intoxication in a 20-year-old French soldier. After recovery, the patient acknowledged having smoked nine to ten pipes of a mixture of tobacco and hashish with the intent of committing suicide, claiming that this method had been used by others. He admitted that each pipe contained 15 to 20 g of smoking mixture. Assuming (1) that the subject had smoked 180 g, (2) 5% delta-9-THC content for a potent hashish preparation, (3) a half-and-half mixture of tobacco and *Cannabis,* (4) 50% absorption of the drug by the lungs, the lethal intravenous dose of delta-9-THC in a 70-kg man would be of the order of 2000 mg or 30 mg/kg. LD_{50} (iv) in rats is 28.6 mg/kg.

These reports indicate that potent *Cannabis* preparations may be used in the drug subculture of Western Europe for suicidal purpose. Furthermore, several cases of accidental deaths occurring in children who had smoked hashish from a water pipe have also been reported in Egypt. The lack of more reports of severe cases of *Cannabis* intoxication from countries where this drug is abused might be misleading. Severe *Cannabis* intoxication with potent material occurs mainly in the developing countries where health facilities are seriously lacking. The causes of the many cases of coma or sudden death often go unrecorded. Hospitals are inadequate, understaffed, and rarely have emergency rooms. Even in Western countries, the statistics in an emergency ward or poison center show a number of cases which are reported as of "undetermined etiology."

However, the acute somatic toxicity of *Cannabis* extracts is quite low when compared with that of other simple chemical substances which are rapidly absorbed in their pure form in the gastrointestinal tract. These substances, which are readily available, would be used preferentially by those driven to commit suicide.

It should also be remembered that the lack of severe untoward physical effects of a psychotropic drug is poorly correlated with its psychotoxicity and its ability to disintegrate mental function, a condition which secondarily may cause bodily harm to self and others.

Subacute Toxicity

Studies have been performed on rats and monkeys which were administered by mouth for 90 to 104 days 50 to 500 mg/kg/day of either delta-9-THC or delta-8-THC. Other animals were given 150 to 1500 mg/kg/day of crude marihuana extract. A biphasic pattern of toxicity was observed in rats treated with all three substances. An initial period of 5 to 10 days of generalized depression was first observed, similar to that occurring after a single dose. Tolerance to these depressant effects developed gradually and coincided with the appearance of hyperactivity. The animals progressively displayed increased grooming, tremors, orientation movements, locomotor activity, and aggressiveness. When kept in cages together they inflicted severe mutilating wounds on each other. After 3 to 4 weeks of treatment, clonic and tonic convulsions were observed. Such behavioral aberrations have not been observed in animals given as much ethanol.

After 3 months of such treatment with the higher doses the animals succumbed. Pathological changes were present in bone marrow, spleen, adrenal cortex, and seminiferous tubules. In monkeys, initial depression, to which tolerance developed, was also observed. Hyperactivity in the primates was only observed with the higher dosage used (250 mg/kg/day). The daily dosage used in these experiments is far out of proportion to the heaviest chronic human consumption of *Cannabis* extracts. These studies, however, are of interest because they point out the primary and cumulative neurotoxicity of the psychoactive fractions of *Cannabis* extracts. This cumulative toxicity may be related to the storage of the cannabinoids in the fat depots of the body, from which they are slowly eliminated. It would appear that very large amounts of delta-9-THC are required to saturate the storage capacity of the tissues. It cannot be excluded that this storage capacity might also be reached in man over prolonged periods of chronic *Cannabis* consumption.

Chronic Toxicity

Systematic studies of the chronic toxicity of these components are not yet available in animal or man. Chronic toxicity studies are difficult to perform on animals with a drug which might have to be used by man for several decades before any sign of toxicity will become apparent. Man's life span outlasts that of all laboratory animals. Furthermore, his reaction to drugs, especially psychotropic ones, is quite different.

Among the vital organs affected by *Cannabis* one must consider the brain, which is the primary target; the liver and the lungs, where the active ingredients are metabolized; and the heart, which rapidly accelerates its rate in response to the drug.

Damage to the Brain?

The effect of chronic use of *Cannabis* on the most important organ of the human economy, the brain, has not yet been assessed. One of the main reasons is that present methods cannot establish histological damage produced in the central nervous system by psychotropic drugs.

These substances exert their action through molecular biochemical mechanisms which do not distort gross cell architecture. For instance, it has not been possible to establish any significant brain damage after chronic administration of opium or morphine-like drugs despite more than 50 years of study of opiates in animals and man.

Moreau (1845) recognized this fundamental fact when he said (about mental illness and hashish intoxication), "Yes, unquestionably there are modifications (I do not dare use the word 'lesion') in the organ which is in charge of mental functions. But these modifications are not those one would generally expect. They will always escape the investigations of the researchers seeking alleged or imagined structural changes. One must not look for particular, abnormal changes in either the gross anatomical or the fine histological structure of the brain; but one must look for an alteration of its sensibility, that is to say, for an irregular, enhanced, diminished or distorted activity of the specific mechanisms upon which depends the performance of mental functions."

Moreau's opinion was ignored by his contemporaries; it is widely accepted today by neurophysiologists and neurochemists who believe that a functional change in the brain is accompanied by one of the biochemical changes such as the turnover rate of neurohormones which regulate all of our thought processes. One cannot exclude the possibility that the repetitive impairment of these processes by frequent *Cannabis* intoxication during adolescence might after a few years induce permanent changes in patterns of thinking or of behavior. Such permanent changes would have to be related to permanent organic alterations.

One should therefore evaluate carefully the study of Campbell et al. (1971) which reports evidence of cerebral atrophy in 10 young men who smoked marihuana daily for 3 to 11 years. They had also taken amphetamines and LSD, but the regular smoking of *Cannabis* had been the main feature of their intoxication. These subjects presented enlargement of the cerebral ventricles measured after pneumoencephalography. Similar enlargements, which are indicative of brain atrophy, are observed in people aged 65 or older, those with Parkinson's disease, or subjects such as boxers who have presented multiple head trauma. The complaints of the *Cannabis* users who were studied included "headaches, memory loss for recent events, changes in personality and temperament, decreased clarity of thought and decreased desires to work." However, it would be premature to relate all of these symptoms, which have been reported by chronic *Cannabis* users from all over the world for many decades, to a single major organic lesion such as brain atrophy. In order to establish such a relationship, Campbell's observation would have to be confirmed on a much larger sample of marihuana users (at the exclusion of other drugs). Indeed, as pointed out earlier, the habitual usage of psychotropic drugs has never been related to gross anatomical changes of the brain.

Brain atrophy is a major nonspecific organic alteration. It certainly must be preceded by other more subtle cellular and molecular changes. The mechanisms by which these may be brought about by chronic *Cannabis* intoxication must be clarified.

Damage to the Lung

The possible damage to the lung should be next considered in the habitual smoker of *Cannabis* preparations. Reports from areas where potent preparations are used, such as India, Egypt, and Morocco, indicate that excessive smoking of the drug produces bronchial irritation, chronic catarrhal laryngitis, and asthma (Soueif, 1967; Benabud, 1957).

These symptoms have also been observed in 22 of 31 young American soldiers, 19 to 23 years old, who had smoked hashish for periods ranging from 6 to 15 months (Tennant et al., 1971). The material used was not assayed for delta-9-THC. The patients smoked 100 g or more a month. This corresponds to three to four 1-g cigarettes a day. Nine patients presented primarily bronchitis with respiratory wheezes and rales; one exhibited audible expiratory wheezing identical to asthma. Chest X-rays showed increased bronchiovascular markings. Sputum cultures yielded normal flora, and pulmonary function studies indicated mild obstructive pulmonary defects. Antibiotics did not improve the symptoms, but isoproteronol did. The patients were dyspneic and frequently disabled to the point that they could not function in "a normal working capacity"; four required hospitalization. Only a decrease of hashish consumption relieved the problems and improved pulmonary function. Twelve patients had recurrent rhinopharyngitis, and five others complained of related symptoms. They presented uvular edema which, according to the authors of the report, is a common symptom observed after the smoking of large amounts of hashish, and a more reliable clinical symptom than congestion of conjunctival vessels.

These ailments of the upper respiratory and bronchial tracts could not be causally related to any specific component of hashish, which contains many other substances in addition to delta-9-THC. Those substances which might act as allergens remain to be identified.

But steroids and triterpens, which are readily converted into carcinogenic agents, have been isolated from *Cannabis sativa* (Doorenbos et al., 1971). And it has already been reported that tar yield from marihuana smoke condensate is as carcinogenic to the mouse skin as smoke from the tobacco of commercial tobacco cigarettes (Magus and Harris, 1971).

Alveolar macrophages sampled from four nonsmokers and eight marihuana smokers in the United States presented significant structural and functional differences (Mann et al., 1971). The 12 subjects were 21 to 28 years of age; half were male and half female. The marihuana smokers had smoked a total of 1000 to 9300 marihuana cigarettes over a period of 2 to 8 years; three had also used hashish. There was a smaller percentage of macrophages in the fluid recovered from the lungs of *Cannabis* smokers than was recovered from nonsmokers.   In marihuana smokers, macrophages, which act as a primary pulmonary defense against inhaled organisms and particles, were replaced by other cell types.   This reduction contrasts with the greater volume and number of macrophages recovered by similar methods from tobacco smokers than nonsmokers.   There were also structural differences in macrophages from marihuana smokers which were confined to cytoplasmic inclusions.   Their phagocytic ability was not impaired.   A higher percentage of macrophages from smokers adhered to glass, indicating a difference in net negative surface change.   The significance of these changes is not clear, but it is at least indicative of subtle alterations which *Cannabis* extracts may produce at the cellular level.   It would therefore appear that chronic daily smoking of *Cannabis* preparations may be associated with damage to the lung and subtle cellular alterations which are not unlike those related to the heavy smoking of tobacco.

Damage to the Cardiovascular System

Significant tachycardia related to the dose administered is consistently observed during acute *Cannabis* intoxication.   The mechanism of this action is not clear, and its persistence among chronic heavy users remains to be systematically studied.   In the meantime, in view of the high incidence of acute cardiac accidents in the United States, the use of *Cannabis* derivatives by middle-aged men might present some hazard.

Chopra and Chopra (1957) report that in India, conjunctivitis was present in 72% of the chronic *Cannabis* users they examined.   The conjunctivitis consists of an active congestion in the transverse ciliary vessels accompanied by a yellow discoloration of the conjunctiva due to deposits of yellow pigment around the vessels.   Similar symptoms have not been reported from areas of chronic *Cannabis* intoxication of the Middle East.   The most serious vascular complications allegedly associated with the smoking of *Cannabis* extracts has been described by Sterne and Ducastaing (1960), who observed 29 cases of progressive obliterative arteritis of the lower extremities developing in young Moroccan males who were heavy smokers of *Cannabis* extracts (they smoked 10 to 15 pipes a day).   Evolution of the disease, which closely paralleled *Cannabis* intoxication, was lethal in 1 to 3 years in spite of repeated limb amputations.   According to Sterns and Ducastaing, *Cannabis*-induced juvenile arteritis is a common disease among North African Moslems, and contrasts with their otherwise low incidence of arteriosclerosis (15 times less than the local European population).   It is possible that the large amount of carbon monoxide absorbed under such conditions might also be a contributing factor of this condition which has not been reported elsewhere.

Damage to the Liver and Gastrointestinal Tract

The liver, in spite of its well-known resilience, might be affected by *Cannabis* extracts, especially after ingestion. A case of cirrhosis in a heavy user was observed by Kew and associates (1969). This observation led them to study 12 subjects who smoked *Cannabis* extracts but who had not taken intravenous drugs or used alcohol to excess. Eight showed "mild liver dysfunction," and biopsy in three showed "striking parenchymatosis degeneration." However, no laboratory evidence of liver disease was found in 31 heavy smokers of hashish by Tennant et al. (1971).

No liver dysfunction was present in 50 chronic marihuana smokers studied in California by Hockman and Brill (1971). Liver dysfunction was observed only in the subjects who associated *Cannabis* smoking and the drinking of alcohol.

The occurrence of diarrhea, abdominal cramps, and gastroenteritis has been reported in India, Egypt, and Morrocco among chronic users of strong *Cannabis* preparations, whether ingested or smoked. A pharmacological basis for the occurrence of these intestinal disorders might be the enterohepatic recycling of the metabolites of delta-9-THC. Chronic diarrhea and abdominal cramps associated with heavy smoking of hashish were reported in three young American soldiers. Weight loss was also a predominant finding in these patients (Tennant et al., 1971).

It would appear that many of the chronic toxic effects associated with the habitual (daily) usage of *Cannabis* preparations and described in the Middle Eastern countries are now starting to be observed in Western man. One could expect that as more potent *Cannabis* preparations become available in the United States, some of the toxic manifestations which have been described might become more frequent.

Teratogenicity

Experimental evidence concerning the teratogenic effect of *Cannabis* derivatives is not conclusive. Intraperitoneal injections to pregnant rats of 4 mg/kg of *Cannabis* resin from day 1 to day 6 of gestation produced a significant incidence of congenital malformations in the offspring (Persaud and Ellington, 1967). Similar observations were made on fetal hamsters and rabbits after maternal administration of large and multiple doses of resin (100 to 400 mg/kg) (Persuad and Ellington, 1968; Geber and Schramm, 1969*a,* 1969*b*). In contrast with these results, others have reported that administration of large amounts of delta-9-THC (10 to 200 mg/kg) in pregnant rats, hamsters, rabbits, and dogs did not result in abnormal offspring (Pace et al. 1971).

But a high incidence of neonatal deaths and some fetal abnormalities were reported by the same authors after administration of large doses of "marihuana extract distillate," MED, a concentrated extract of *Cannabis*. These results indicate that the teratogenic effect of *Cannabis* derivatives is not related to delta-9-THC but to another constituent of the plant. The lack of gross teratogenic effect of delta-9-THC is not due to a lack of passage of this agent through the placental barrier, as demonstrated in studies with labeled compounds. Delta-9-THC and its metabolites could therefore also exert their pharmacological effects on the fetus. But chromosome breakage, reported in man after LSD usage, has not been observed in preliminary studies of *Cannabis* users.

In countries where chronic *Cannabis* intoxication has prevailed for centuries, it is only the male population which has indulged in the use or abuse of *Cannabis* derivatives, usually of high potency. As a result, man was not exposed to the effects of *Cannabis* derivatives during his early intrauterine development. Such a situation would not prevail in Western countries where men and women share the same rights and participate in the same activities.

METABOLISM AND DISTRIBUTION

The availability of tagged delta-8- or delta-9-THC has only recently permitted the study of the distribution of these compounds and of their metabolites in different tissues and organs, as well as their elimination from the body.

These studies were performed on rats, mice, rabbits, and monkeys with ^{14}C- or trititium-labeled delta-8- or delta-9-THC administered intravenously. In spite of the high lipid solubility, delta-9-THC and its metabolites did not accumulate preferentially in neural tissue. The pattern of distribution and elimination of delta-9-THC and of its metabolites (Fig. 11) indicates that these compounds are stored preferentially in organs of absorption and metabolism (liver, lung, spleen) and in those most affected by the drug (brain, heart), as well as in the organs and products of elimination (liver—bile, kidney—urine).

Distribution

The radioactivity of whole-body homogenates of rats given 4 mg/kg (i.v.) of ^{14}C-THC declined experimentally, with a half-life of 16 hours (Klausner and Dingell, 1971). Fifteen minutes after the injection there was an accumulation of radioactivity (delta-9-THC and metabolites) in tissues with tissue-to-

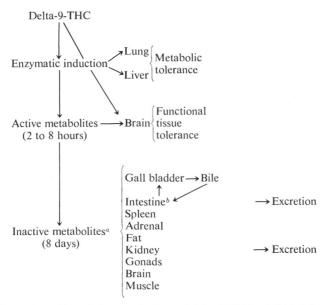

Fig. 11. Schematic outline of the metabolism of delta-9-THC. [a] Listed in order of decreasing concentration in various tissues. [b] Note entero-hepatic circulation.

plasma ratios of brain, 2.7; lung, 55.2; liver, 12.1; fat, 5.5; muscle, 3.0; kidney, 6.5; heart, 6.7; and intestine, 3.5. The relative distribution of radioactivity in the rabbit 3 days after intravenous administration of tritiated delta-9-THC reported by Agurell et al. (1970) is shown in Fig. 12. High concentrations are found in the organs of excretion, bile, gall bladder, kidney, and liver. High activity is also present in the spleen, adrenal glands, and fat. After 3 days comparatively little activity remains in the lung and brain. Fractionization of protein of rat and human plasma by ultracentrifugation after addition of delta-9-THC indicated that 90% of this compound was bound to protein, mostly to the lipoprotein. The rapid distribution of delta-9-THC from plasma into tissues can be explained by its intracellular binding. (Dingell et al., 1971). In the isolated perfused liver, delta-9-THC was localized in the nuclei and the microsomes.

Biotransformation of Delta-9-THC and Its Active Metabolites

The biotransformation of delta-9-THC is very complex, and many metabolites are formed. While nonpsychoactive polar metabolites remain in tissues and are slowly excreted in urine and feces, there is some evidence that psycho-

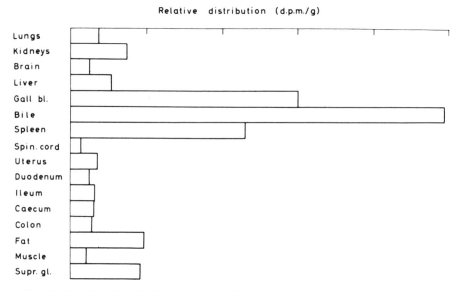

Fig. 12. Relative distribution of radioactivity in rabbit tissue 3 days after intra-venous injection of tritiated delta-9-THC (mean of four animals). Note high activity in gall bladder, bile, kidney, spleen, adrenal, and fat. (After Agurell, 1970.)

active metabolites of delta-9-THC might also be formed (Agurell et al., 1970; Truitt, 1970; Truitt and Anderson, 1971). They are 11-hydroxy-delta-8- or delta-9-THC, which can be produced by incubation of the delta-8- or delta-9-THC parent compound in liver homogenates. The pharmacological activity of these compounds resembles or even exceeds that of their precursors in mice (Truitt and Anderson, 1971) and in monkeys (Ben-Zvi et al., 1970).

It has also been shown that delta-9-THC is metabolized in the lungs of rats, where it produces two metabolites distinct from the 11-hydroxy compound produced in the liver (Nakazawa and Costa, 1971). The enzymes which metabolize delta-9-THC in the lung can be induced by methylcholantrene. This carcinogenic agent will therefore enhance the pharmacological effects of delta-9-THC in the rat. However, methylcholantrene will not change the metabolism of delta-9-THC in the liver.

Confirming Agurell's and Klausner's experiments, in which the highest level of radioactivity was found in the lungs of rats following intravenous injection of ^{14}C-labeled delta-9-THC, Ho et al. (1971) observed that ^{3}H-labeled delta-9-THC administered by smoking was retained preferentially in the lung. The radioactivity persisted in this tissue in greater amount than in any other analyzed after 24 hours.

Excretion

Very little delta-9-THC is excreted intact in the urine, which contains mostly polar metabolites. The relative fraction of polar metabolites of delta-9-THC excreted in urine or feces varies according to species. In the rat, 80% of his excretion occurs in the feces (Agurell et al., 1969; Klausner and Dingell, 1971). In the rabbit, most of the metabolites are excreted in the urine (Agurell, 1970). In both animals the total period of elimination is similar, exceeding 1 week. This prolonged retention is attributed to the fat solubility and protein binding of these compounds and to their recycling through the enterohepatic system, which delays considerably their fecal excretion. A large portion of the metabolites are excreted into the bile and then into the small intestine, from where they are reabsorbed. The metabolic products of *Cannabis* derivatives, which tend to accumulate in the body, do not contribute to their initial psychotoxic effect. But the effects due to their prolonged storage in lung, liver, kidney, intestine, and brain require careful evaluation.

Studies in man which will be subsequently discussed have corroborated the metabolic pattern observed in animals (Lemberger et al., 1971).

Distribution of Delta-9-THC in the Brain of the Nonhuman Primate

Distribution of delta-9-THC and its metabolites was studied in the brain of squirrel monkeys after intravenous administration of 2 to 30 mg/kg of tritiated delta-9-THC (McIsaac et al., 1971). The dose-response relationship noted with these increasing dosages was similar to that observed in man. Low doses had a euphoric, quieting effect, with disruption of perception; medium doses produced stimulation, excitation, lack of coordination, and hallucination. Higher dosages were accompanied by severe psychomotor incapacitation. A correlation was established between the distribution of delta-9-THC at different times in certain areas of the brain (Fig. 13) and concomitant behavior alterations. Fifteen minutes after administration of the drug, 79% of the radioactivity present in the brain was due to delta-9-THC, and the behavioral aberrations in the animals were maximal. This value declined to 50% at 4 hours; at the same time, the abnormal behavioral patterns subsided. Many of the behavioral effects were related not only to the distribution of delta-9-THC in the brain but also to changes in its distribution pattern at different times: Within 15 min after administration, the frontal cortex, which is the site of the higher functions of mentation, contained elevated concentrations of delta-9-THC. A similar distribution is observed with ^{14}C-labeled ethanol. Another similarity between delta-9-THC and ethanol is their

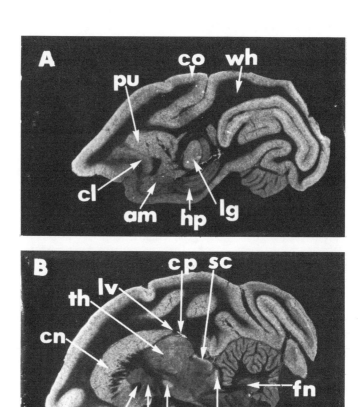

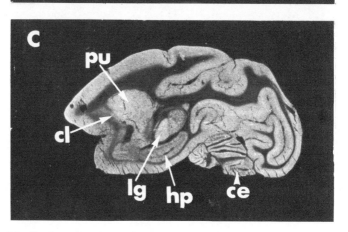

Fig. 13. Distribution of radioactivity (light areas) in monkey brain 15 min (A, B), 1 hour (C, D,), 4 hours (E), and 24 hours (F) after intravenous injection of ³H-delta-9-THC. ac, Anterior commissure; am, amygdala; ce, cerebellum; cl, claustrum; cn, caudate nucleus; co, cortex; cp, choroid plexus; dn, dentate nucleus; fn,

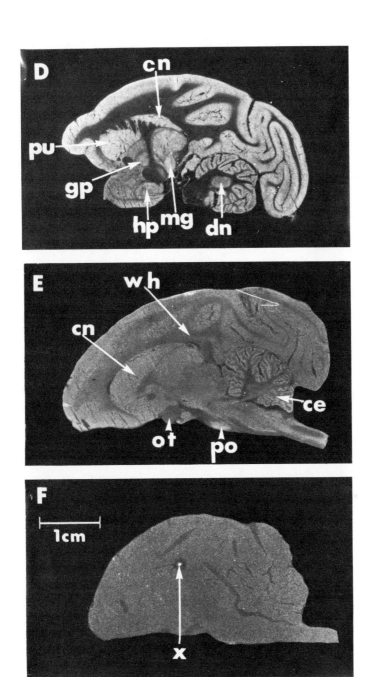

fastigial nucleus; gp, globus pallidus; hp, hippocampus; ic, inferior colliculus; lg, lateral geniculate nucleus; lv, lateral ventricle; mg, medial geniculate nucleus; ot, optic tract; po, pons; pu, putamen; sc, superior colliculus; st, subthalamic nucleus; th, thalamus; wh, white matter; x, artefact. (From McIsaac et al., 1971.)

marked accumulation in cerebellum and dental nuclei, which may be related to the lack of motor coordination produced by both substances. Fifteen minutes after delta-9-THC administration, lateral and medial geniculate nuclei had high concentrations of the drug. These structures, which have connections with the visual pathways, contained elevated delta-9-THC concentrations when visual perception appeared most distorted, and when the behavior of the animals suggested that they were hallucinating. High concentrations of the drug were also seen in the amygdala, hippocampus, superior and inferior colliculi. The amygdalal accumulation of delta-9-THC (and/or its metabolites) may be related to its reported anxiolytic and euphoric effect in man. It has been shown that antidepressant drugs used in man do accumulate in the amygdala. McIsaac concluded that "the extremely high concentration of delta-9-THC in the frontal cortex together with the hippocampal accumulation, makes it tempting to suggest that the interactions between these two areas play an important part in associating stimuli into a temporal context. It is well known that one of the chief effects of marihuana is distortion of time perception. Thus the typical disruption effect of delta-9-THC could well be attributed to its unique distribution in the central nervous system."

PHARMACOLOGY

The psychoactive component of *Cannabis* has many pharmacological properties, centrally acting, autonomic, and cardiovascular, which are common to stimulants, sedatives, tranquilizers, narcotics, analgesics, and hallucinogens. However, the chemistry and pharmacology, as well as the mechanism of action, of delta-9-THC are quite different from those of barbiturates, amphetamines, opiates, ethyl alcohol, or other hallucinogens.

Pharmacologists use in their experimental preparations much larger dosages of drugs than those used clinically for therapeutic purposes. This experimental attitude stems from the necessity of obtaining a maximal physiological or biochemical response which can be readily measured with methods which are still quite crude. Delta-9-THC, like any other drug studied pharmacologically, has been, therefore, used on experimental animals in dosages much higher than those which will produce in man a psychotoxic effect. These experimental studies are generally aimed at understanding the possible mechanism of action of these drugs. Delta-9-THC, like *Cannabis* extracts, acts primarily on the central nervous system and the behavior of experimental animals. Its second target organ is the richly innervated conductive system of the heart.

Effects on the Central Nervous System

The neurophysiological and neurohormonal mechanisms of brain function are poorly understood. In the brain, billions of nerve cells are constantly emitting coded signals which are transmitted through what resembles an intricate network of conductors, relays, and amplifiers. Transmission of the signals from one neuron to the other is mediated by neurohormones, norepinephrine, 5-hydroxytryptamine, and acetylcholine, which are stored in the synaptic vesiculae. The storage and retrieval of past signals, which characterize memory, involve the DNA and RNA of the neuron. The overall electrical activity of the brain can be recorded with the electroencephalogram (EEG), which results in patterns typical of gross brain activity such as wakefulness, sleep, or arousal. But there are no easy methods to measure the turnover rate of the neurohormonal transmitters which modulate the electrical activity of the brain.

In animals, *Cannabis* derivatives and delta-9-THC alter the overall electrical activity of the brain as measured by the EEG and polysynaptic reflex activity. These compounds will also change the delicate balance of neurohormones which characterizes the normally functioning brain; finally, the ratio of RNA to DNA, which appears to be related to a proper functioning of immediate memory, is also impaired by delta-9-THC.

Effects of Delta-9-THC on Polysynaptic Reflexes and EEG

Delta-9-THC and some of its synthetic derivatives inhibit in cats and dogs polysynaptic reflexes such as the flexion linguo-mandibular one and those involving the trigeminal system (Sampaio et al., 1967; Boyd and Merritt, 1965a). Since the tibialis nerve is unaffected, this effect is attributed to a specific central depressant action of THC localized in the forebrain area: Facilitation of reflexes induced by stimulation of this area is blocked by THC (Boyd et al., 1971). Like barbiturates, THC inhibits behavioral and EEG response to stimulation of the reticular activating system. However, THC also acts differently than barbiturates, since it also enhances a late phase of the evoked pattern in the polysensory cortex, displaying an ambivalent pattern of action, depressing total activity, and enhancing sensory input signals. This effect of THC in animals might correlate with the increased sensory awareness produced in man by this intoxicant. Accumulation of delta-9-THC in the structures of the brain connected with the visual and auditory pathways do correlate with increased visual and auditory sensitivity reported by man. The ambivalent action of THC is also apparent by its ability to enhance in mice the stimulation induced by amphetamine and caffeine (Phillips et al., 1971a).

Administration of delta-9- or delta-8- THC or of *Cannabis* extracts alter consistently electroencephalographic and electrocorticographic (ECoG) patterns in rats, cats, and rabbits. In the rat, marihuana extract distillate, 20 mg/kg given per os, or 2.5 to 10 mg/kg (i.p.) of delta-8- or delta-9- THC significantly decreases the integrated EEG voltage and produces, superimposed on this low voltage, high-voltage "spindle-like activity," suggesting increased excitability of neurons (Lipparini et al., 1969; Hockman et al., 1971). Tolerance develops to the depressant activity, and after 10 days of treatment the integrated voltage is no longer significantly lowered. But tolerance does not develop to the high-voltage spindle-like activity. The association of a reduction in the voltage EEG output with polyspike discharges is unique to this drug (Colasanti and Khazan, 1971). Such a pattern correlates with a central nervous system arousal during which the rats appear sedated. Similar spike and wave patterns were also observed in cats treated by intraperitoneal administration, or after inhalation of marihuana extract (with known delta-9-THC content) (Barratt et al., 1970). Slow waves with spikes were recorded after 10 days and were associated with progressive behavioral depression and withdrawal. Changes in EEG persisted for 22 days after the 3-week treatment with the highest doses (16 mg/kg/day, i.p.). Synchronization of the EEG changes by *Cannabis* derivatives could be in part related to the inhibition of the reticular arousal system produced by these substances. Other hallucinogens produce a desynchronization of the EEG.

Effects of Delta-9-THC on Metabolism of Brain Neurotransmitters

Attempts have been made to correlate these functional changes in brain activity and in behavior of rodents to alterations in the metabolism of brain neurotransmitters.

With large pharmacological doses administered to rats and mice (5 to 10 mg/kg, i.p. or 3 mg/kg, i.v.), some authors have reported an increase in brain 5-hydroxytryptamine (5-HT), while norepinephrine concentration and turnover rate had a tendency to be reduced (Holtzman et al., 1969; Sofia et al., 1971; Welch et al., 1971). These results are of interest since it has been shown that a rise in brain 5-HT with a slight decrease of norepinephrine is associated with the behavioral effect of hallucinogenic drugs. Since delta-9-THC does not inhibit monoamine oxidase, its inhibitory effect on the turnover rate of 5-HT has been attributed to a direct effect on the permeability of the vesicular membrane of the neuron.

Other authors have reported that smaller dosages of delta-9-THC (5 mg, i.p.) or 1 mg/kg, i.v.), which produced marked behavioral effects, did not alter the dynamics of the cerebral serotonergic system (Gallager et al., 1971). However, after repeated daily exposure of rats to the smoke of a cigarette containing delta-9-THC (10 mg), Ho et al. (1971) have reported significant changes in neurohormone metabolism in rats. While there were no changes in hydroxytryptamine and norepinephrine brain concentrations, there was a marked decrease in their metabolites, 5-hydroxyindoleacetic acid and normetanephrine. The decreases in the metabolites under the effects of delta-9-THC were interpreted as being due to a facilitation of their transport from the brain. Other studies with tritiated tyrosine showed that delta-9-THC significantly enhanced the turnover of brain norepinephrine, a pattern which could account for the stimulating effect of the drug. This increase of norepinephrine turnover in the brain would be related, according to Bein (1970), to an activation of tyrosine hydroxylase by delta-9-THC.

It has been reported that the concentration of another very important brain neurotransmitter, acetylcholine, is also increased by chronic administration of large doses of delta-8-THC or delta-9-THC to rats and monkeys.

Rises in brain 5-HT and acetylcholine have been previously correlated with sleep and sedation (decreased activity), and a decrease or increase in catecholamine levels has been shown to account for decreased or increased locomotor activity. But it is probably the combined effect of the changes in all three neurotransmitters which determines the ultimate neurophysiological and behavioral effects. At present the interrelationship between the turnover and metabolism of the basic neurotransmitters we have mentioned is not known during normal brain activity of sleep, wakefulness, or arousal. A biochemical interpretation of the alterations in brain activity produced by the cannabinoids lies, therefore, in the distant future. It might be very complex because of the multiple and contradictory effects of delta-9-THC on brain function and behavior.

Changes in the ratio of DNA to RNA concentration in the brains of rats and monkeys administered chronically large amounts of delta-9-THC have also been reported. These nucleic acids are involved in the storage of immediate memory, which is known to be impaired during *Cannabis* intoxication (Carlini and Carlini, 1965; Thompson et al., 1971).

Anticonvulsive and Analgesic Effects

It has also been reported that delta-9-THC has anticonvulsant and analgesic effects in rats and mice. The anticonvulsant action of delta-9-THC in mice required relatively high dosages to prevent electroconvulsive shock (effective dose$_{50}$ was 54 mg/kg, i.p.). This compound, like diphenylhydantoin, did not prevent seizures induced by strychnine or pentylenetetrazol (Sofia et al., 1971*b*).

Harris (1971) reports that the analgesic activity of delta-9-THC in rodents depends upon testing method, species used, solvent system, route of administration, and time of testing. In every instance, using the mouse tail-flick test or the hot plate test, very large doses (from 10 to 80 mg/kg, i.p.) were required. Harris concludes, "While delta-9-THC and delta-8-THC have some antinoceptive properties, they are inconsistent and have a profile different from that of known clinical analgesics."

In cats the analgesic dose was 1 mg/kg, which enhanced the excitory effect of morphine while reducing motor activity. (Kaymakcalan and Deneau, 1971). The dosage of delta-9-THC required to obtain anticonvulsant or analgesic action also produces other central nervous effects, which should limit its clinical usefulness. Therefore, synthetic derivatives of delta-9-THC free of untoward side effects will have to be developed for possible therapeutic applications.

Behavioral Effects

The effects of *Cannabis* derivatives on the central nervous system are accompanied by marked behavioral changes in animals. The changes are related to the species studied, the dosage used, the mode of administration, and the experimental setting. The overall picture is a mixture of depressant and stimulatory effects which are in keeping with the pharmacological action of *Cannabis* derivatives on the central nervous system. Rats given delta-9-THC intraperitoneally display increased or decreased spontaneous locomotor activity (Barry and Kubena, 1969). A dose of 2 mg/kg produces initial excitation followed by depression. A single dose of 10 to 20 mg/kg produces depression of activity, the rats appearing ataxic and flaccid, with some of them, however, reacting aggressively to external stimuli (Grunfeld and Edery, 1969). This dose disrupts learned behavior such as conditioned avoidance responses, but not reactions to unconditioned stimuli. Continuous administration of such elevated dosages produces tolerance and marked increase in locomotor activity and aggressive behavior (Thompson et al., 1971). It also appears that intragastric administration is more effective in producing reproducible effects than intraperitoneal administration and requires lesser dosage: The minimal dose of delta-8-THC to produce behavioral effects in mice and rats is 0.1 mg/kg, with the maximal effect occurring 2 hours after administration (Irwin, 1969). Repeated administration of delta-9-THC in the peritoneum produces chronic diffuse chemical peritonitis.

Effects of *Cannabis* derivatives on the social behavior of animals varies according to dosage and frequency of administration. A single administration tends to decrease aggressive behavior in rats and mice, which show less group aggregation and disruption of social hierarchies. Repetitive administration of large doses of delta-9-THC enhances aggressive and fighting behavior in rats. This increased aggressiveness had already been reported in starved rats given *Cannabis* extracts intraperitoneally.

Administration of delta-9-THC to rats (4 mg, i.p. or 2 to 32 mg, i.g.) for 30 days significantly decreased their food intake and weight gain. During that same period the animals developed tolerance to other behavioral effects of delta-9-THC. The weight loss suffered during delta-9-THC administration persisted during 30 days following the end of this treatment, while food intake was restored to control levels. It would seem that while tolerance to many of the behavioral effects of delta-9-THC develops rapidly in rats, the anorectic action of this agent is maintained (Manning et al., 1971).

Dogs (Harris, 1971) display a typical ataxia when treated acutely with marihuana extracts or delta-9-THC (0.5 to 1 mg/kg). These motor deficiencies, however, are accompanied by dysbarism, retching, and vomiting, and limit the usefulness of dogs in behavioral studies of this drug.

Behavioral tests such as operant schedules of the aversion or reward type have been used to assess the psychopharmacological action of the constituents of *Cannabis*.

Schedule-controlled behavior was studied in pigeons using key-pecking rates with a multiple fixed-ratio response, fixed-interval (5-min) schedule of food presentation. Effects of delta-9-THC and of two of its synthetic derivatives were measured 2 hours after intramuscular injections, which were performed once weekly for 7 weeks. A marked decrease in rate of responding developed under both schedules, along with tolerance and cross tolerance among the different cannabinoids used. The birds did not peck keys for 4 hours after the injection. As tolerance developed, normal rate of pecking gradually returned after 5 to 8 daily injections (McMillan et al., 1970).

The effects of synthetic tetrahydrocannabinols on patterns of operant behavior induced in rats by different schedules were difficult to interpret. Drug effects varied greatly with the type of schedule used and appeared, according to the test situation, to depress or stimulate learned behavior (Boyd et al., 1963; Carlini and Kramer, 1966).

Behavioral effects of delta-9- and delta-8-THC administered intraperitoneally were studied in rhesus and squirrel monkeys with operant conditioning techniques. Continuous avoidance behavior was induced by both compounds, and complex behavior involving memory and visual discrimination was markedly disrupted by these agents. Monkeys receiving 32 to 64 mg/kg of racemic delta-9-THC exhibited initial excitation, such as hand tremors, unusual limb positions, panic-like states, and apparent hallucinations. These symptoms, which lasted for 3 hours, were followed by depression. Nine of 14 animals died after receiving the higher dosage. The ambivalent effect of delta-9-THC was apparent in this study. A dose of 4 to 8 mg/kg reduced the response rate by 50% in a continuance avoidance schedule, while 16 to 24 mg/kg increased response rate by 200%. The social dominance hierarchy was not changed by the drug, but expressions of demeanor were changed, and the monkeys were less aggressive. In general, these substances caused stimulation, depression, apparent hallucinations, and the loss of motivation or ability to perform complex tasks (Scheckel et al., 1968).

Studies in chimpanzees given oral doses of 0.2 to 4.0 mg/kg of delta-9-THC showed that this compound can have both stimulating and depressing effects on reinforcement schedule-controlled operant behavior. A significant facilitation of differential reinforcement of low rate responding was obtained with an oral dose of 0.4 mg/kg of delta-9-THC, which is an effective oral dose in man (Ferraro et al., 1971).

Conrad et al. (1972) performed dose-related studies on timing behavior of chimpanzees which were given oral doses of 0.125 to 4.0 mg/kg of delta-9-THC. The animals presented stable efficient timing performances maintained by multilinked chained schedules of food reinforcement. Reinforcements decreased with increasing dose, because of decreased accuracy of the timing performances, which did occur. Higher doses exerted an effect for up to 3 days, a period of time which corresponds to the prolonged retention of delta-9-THC metabolites in the body. Drug effects were obtained with a dose level of 0.25 mg/kg, which is well within the dose range used by man.

All of these studies indicate that delta-9-THC, the major psychoactive compound of *Cannabis*, acutely or subacutely administered, produces in all animal species studied, marked and complex aberrations of spontaneous and of conditioned behavior. The possible additional toxic effects of the other cannabinoids and alkaloids present in *Cannabis* remained to be appraised as they became available for experimental studies.

Autonomic and Cardiovascular Effects

In dogs, delta-9-THC (1 to 10 mg/kg, i.v.) produces a decrease in systolic, diastolic, and mean arterial blood pressure, heart rate, cardiac output, and total peripheral resistance (Harris, 1971). The fall in blood pressure is prolonged (2 to 3 hours); it is not blocked by vagotomy or atropine, or by beta adrenergic blockade. In the normal Sherman rat, 10 to 20 mg/kg of delta-9-THC administered intragastrically does not change blood pressure but significantly decreases heart rate in normal animals; similar doses of the drug only lower blood pressure of spontaneous hypertensive rats in a transient way, because of rapid development of tolerance (Schwartz et al., 1972; Fig. 14A).

Bose (1963) reported that *Cannabis* extracts have a relaxing effect *in vitro* in smooth muscle of rabbit intestine and uterus, and antagonize the spasmogenic effect of carbachol and histamine. Gill and Paton (1970) also

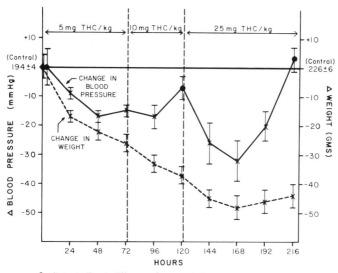

Fig. 14A. Effects of intragastric administration of delta-9-THC on the blood pressure of spontaneously hypertensive rats (SHR). Note the rapid development of tolerance to the drug (Nahas and Schwartz, 1972).

reported that delta-9-THC inhibited the contracture of ileum and aortic strip. Schwartz and Nahas (1972) observed that delta-9-THC 10^{-5} to 10^{-4} M *in vitro* inhibits the acetylcholine-induced contraction of uterine muscle strip in the rat (Fig. 14*b*). The same concentration also inhibits the contractile response of the aortic strip to serotonin. However, when THC was given intragastrically (20 mg/kg) and tissues removed, after the effects of the drug had become manifest, the results observed were opposite to those *in vitro:* the contractile effect of serotonin in the aorta, and of acetylcholine on the uterus, were significantly enhanced. A possible interpretation of these data might be that

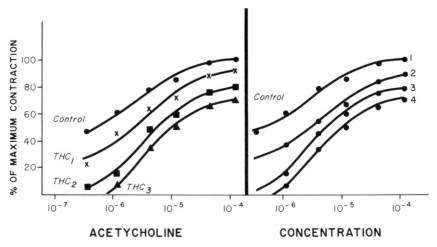

Fig. 14*b*. Inhibition by delta-9-THC of acetylcholine-induced contraction of uterine muscle strip (rat). Note that this inhibition is in part irreversible. (From Schwartz and Nahas, 1972.)

some active intermediary metabolites of delta-9-THC are formed *in vivo,* and have a different effect from those of the parent compound.

The cardiovascular effects produced by delta-9-THC in animals are difficult to correlate with those produced in man, where tachycardia is observed while blood pressure tends to increase, except in cases of massive intoxication where hypotension occurs.

Endocrine Effects

Cannabis extracts appear to alter carbohydrate metabolism in rabbits by increasing glycogenolysis and blood sugar levels (El-Sourogy et al., 1966). These effects have not been reported in man, except for an increase in glucose tolerance test as measured by standard clinical tests (Podolsky et al., 1971).

Delta-9-THC (4 to 16 mg/kg) produces in the rat a two- to threefold increase in plasma corticosterone mediated through the pituitary (Barry et al., 1970). The same dose produces an inhibition of antidiuretic hormone with a twofold increase of urine output. Large doses of delta-9-THC (10 mg/kg) or *Cannabis* extract reduce thyroidal uptake of radioiodine in the rat (Miras, 1965).

Cannabis extract or delta-9-THC produces hypothermia in mice, rats, cats, dogs, and monkeys (4 to 10 mg/kg, i.p.). A similar hypothermia has been reported in man only following massive intoxication (Gourves et al., 1971).

Interaction of Delta-9-THC with Other Drugs

Delta-9-THC administered to the dog in doses (0.1 to 0.3 mg/kg) which have little effect on cardiovascular or respiratory function potentiate the cardiovascular and respiratory effects of epinephrine and norepinephrine (Dewey et al., 1969 Dewey; et al., 1970d). Similar findings had been reported previously by Dagirmanjian and Boyd (1962) for the synthetic tetrahydrocannabinol DMHP.

In rodents, delta-9-THC significantly potentiates in a dose-related manner, sleeping time and immobility time produced by hexobarbital and by ethanol (Forney, 1971). Delta-9-THC also increases amphetamine- and caffeine-induced locomotor activity in mice (Garriot et al., 1967; Phillips et al., 1971a).

As we have seen, many of the drugs used commonly in daily therapy, such as barbiturates, antidepressants, analgesics, and anticoagulants, induce the same oxydative enzymes as delta-9-THC.

Delta-9-THC interacts with these drugs and alters their therapeutic action through metabolic competition. It was shown that THC (10^{-4} M) inhibits in the liver microsomal oxidation of aminopyrine by 50%, of hexobarbital by 58%, conjugation of estradiol by 25%, and of paranitrophenol by 18%— conversely, it enhances the reduction of paranitrobenzoic acid by 33% (Dingell et al., 1971).

Pretreatment of mice with phenobarbital, which enhances microsomal-induced drug metabolism, decreases by 50% the acute lethal toxicity of delta-9-THC in mice.

Tolerance to Delta-9-THC

It is now well established that a profound tolerance to the behavioral and pharmacological effects of delta-9-THC develops rapidly in all animal species tested with this drug: Birds, rats, dogs, and monkeys require a 10- to 20-fold increase in dosage within 5 to 15 days to continue to exhibit alteration of basic physiological or acquired learned responses. In addition to tolerance, delta-9-THC may induce in primates some symptoms of physical dependence and withdrawal reactions. These are rather mild in comparison with those developing after chronic ethanol or barbiturate intoxication, but tolerance to delta-9-THC is very marked, develops rapidly, and may make the animal quite refractory to the drug until toxicity ensues.

McMillan et al. (1970) have reported that pigeons displayed a marked tolerance to the behavioral effects of delta-9-THC. The effective dose (0.3–1 mg/kg), which completely eliminated a learned food-presentation schedule, could be subsequently and gradually increased over a 1-month period to 180 mg/kg. This dose, which is lethal to the nontolerant bird, could be increased further to 1600 mg/kg, a 6000-fold increase (Ford and McMillan, 1972). At this point, cessation of medication had no effect on the overt or operant behavior of the tolerant bird, which did not show any withdrawal symptoms. There was a long persistence of this tolerance, which was still present 30 days after cessation of the medication. A similar degree of tolerance was observed with delta-8-THC, and a cross tolerance between this compound and delta-9-THC was demonstrated.

Black et al. (1970) report the development in 7 weeks of similar tolerance to delta-9-THC in pigeons on schedule-controlled behavior and given a weekly intramuscular injection of delta-9-THC (10 mg/kg) or synthetic THC derivatives (DMHP and synhexyl). They demonstrated that tolerance and cross tolerance occurred among delta-9-THC and the synthetic derivatives, and that tolerance could be obtained even when medications were spaced a week apart.

Tolerance was also observed in the rat by Carlini (1968) and by Ford and McMillan (1971). Tolerance to the depressant effect of daily injections of delta-9-THC (125 mg/kg) on locomotor activity of the rat develops by the eleventh day. In the experiments of Ford and McMillan, a 10-fold tolerance to the behavioral effects of delta-9-THC was rapidly induced. An initial dose of 10 mg/kg i.p. markedly depressed the fixed-ratio response schedule of water reinforcement in trained rats. The dose was repeated and, as tolerance developed, increasd to 100 mg/kg within 20 to 30 days. No signs of withdrawal developed when medication was discontinued. In addition to this tolerance to the behavioral effects of delta-9-THC, rats also developed tolerance to its cardiovascular action. Initial treatment produced bradycardia, which was no longer present after a week. When the dose reached 16 mg/kg, tachycardia was noted. There was no change in blood pressure.

In the dog, marked tolerance to the behavioral and physiological effects of delta-9-THC developed rapidly (Harris, 1971). A dose of 2 mg/kg i.v. produced profound behavioral effects in dogs (ataxia, stupor, salivation). After the fourth daily administration, marked tolerance had developed, and the dose was gradually increased to 32 mg/kg. After an interruption of 10 days, during which no apparent signs of withdrawal were noted administration of delta-9-THC was resumed and increased to 160 mg/kg. This dose is four times the acute lethal intravenous dose in the dog.

Tolerance and physical dependence to delta-9-THC was demonstrated by Deneau and Kaymakcalan (1971) in six rhesus monkeys trained for intravenous self-administration of delta-9-THC. No monkey initiated self-administration over a 3-week period. Automatic injections were delivered at doses increasing from 0.4 to 1.6 mg/kg. Drug effects were ptosis, blank staring, scratching, and docility. Tolerance developed within a few days of each increase of dosage. When injections were stopped all monkeys showed abstinence symptoms, and two of the six animals initiated and maintained self-administration of THC. The abstinence symptoms appeared at 12 hours and lasted 5 days; they were yawning, anorexia, pilo erection, irritability, scratching, biting and licking fingers, pulling hair, tremors, twitches, shaking, photophobia, and apparent hallucinations.

If the psychoactive substance derived from delta-9-THC is an intermediary metabolite resulting from enzymatic induction, as suggested by some, tolerance to *Cannabis* would have a biochemical basis. The maximum turnover of this enzyme would be, in this case, a biochemical limiting factor controlling the development of tolerance with chronic usage of *Cannabis*. However, the nature of the tolerance which animals develop to delta-9-THC is not clear. It may be due in part to a change in drug metabolism, and to its more rapid disposition or elimination of the toxic. This hypothesis would be substantiated by the observation that mice pretreated with phenobarbitol, which increases microsomal drug metabolism, double their tolerance to a lethal dose of delta-9-THC; by contrast, SK 525-A, a compound which inhibits microsomal metabolism, potentiates considerably in the same animal THC-induced mortality. The very high tolerance developing in animals treated with delta-9-THC would indicate that, in addition to metabolic tolerance, this drug might also induce tissue or functional tolerance in the target organ. Cross tolerance has been found between delta-8- and delta-9-THC, between delta-9-THC and synhexyl, and between the dimethylheptyl analog and delta-9-THC. But there is no cross tolerance between delta-9-THC and LSD or mescaline. Since cross tolerance has been established for the two latter drugs, it would appear that tolerance to *Cannabis* must involve a different mechanism than that to mescaline or LSD. Cross tolerance between delta-9-THC and ethanol, and between delta-9-THC and barbiturates has been suggested by some.

The often-repeated claim that *Cannabis* does not induce tolerance has no pharmacological basis. Few compounds produce such a high degree of tolerance in so many species. Tolerance is one of the most striking features of the psychoactive substances of *Cannabis sativa* (McMillan, Dewey, and Harris, 1971).

Future Animal Research

The aim of future experimental studies on animals should be primarily to localize the molecular site where the cannabinoids act to perturb brain function after acute or chronic administration. It would appear that except for very high doses (10 to 100 mg/day of delta-9-THC) chronically administered, gross tissue pathological change is not observed, while profound behavioral aberrations are present. These behavioral abnormalities are multiple, do not follow any fixed pattern, and occur at low as well as high dosage with chronic or acute administration. They seem to be related to an interference of the cannabinoids with the free flow of the signals through the integrated structures of the brain which allows for the duplication of patterns of coherent behavior.

The broad ubiquitous effects of delta-9-THC on brain function indicate that it might impair the turnover of the neurotransmitters to be found in the multiple synapses of the central nervous system.

Another interesting area for research with *Cannabis* derivatives is to investigate the mechanism of the extraordinary tolerance which develops following chronic administration. The possible participation of the immune system should not be excluded.

THERAPEUTIC CLAIMS RECONSIDERED

The many therapeutic applications claimed for *Cannabis* preparations, from the treatment of tetanus to that of cholera, belong to the history of medicine (Mikuriya, 1969; Synder, 1971) and have been briefly reviewed in Chapter 1. Only one therapeutic property has really been proven: the antibiotic activity against gram-positive bacteria which is due to the nonpsychoactive, cannabidiol fraction of the plant. All other therapeutic claims have not been substantiated. This is especially true for delta-8- and delta-9-THC. The experimental results obtained with these two most important psychoactive ingredients of *Cannabis,* as well as with crude marihuana extract containing known amounts of the ingredients, have been inconclusive. These compounds will not rekindle the therapeutic potential of *Cannabis* for the treatment of common diseases and ailments affecting the central nervous system.

There are many unfavorable features inherent in the use of these psychoactive compounds as routine therapeutic agents in modern medicine. Their lack of water solubility precludes administration for rapid effect; their slow and uneven absorption in the gastrointestinal tract results in a delayed effect of 2 to 3 hours. Their absorption by smoking is more rapid but short-lived and this unusual method of drug administration might not be acceptable to all patients. Their uneven mode of action is accompanied by periods of waning and waxing. They have a prolonged half-life, and their metabolites accumulate in tissues for up to 1 week before being eliminated; there is rapid development of tolerance to their action, making a prolonged, uninterrupted course of therapy hazardous and ineffective.

All of these features would make it difficult to prescribe delta-8- or delta-9-THC in a quantitative way even if they had a unique specific therapeutic property. But this is not the case. All of the alleged therapeutic indications of delta-9- or delta-8-THC are met today by drugs which are more specific, more potent, easier to prescribe, administer, and control, have a mechanism of action better understood, and are free of psychotomimetic effects.

Good substitutes for the hypnotic, sedative, analgesic, tranquilizing, anti-convulsant, and relaxant drugs now available should have a rapid onset and a predictable duration of action; they should not give rise to rapid tolerance and should not be habit-forming or psychotomimetic.

The alleged hypotensive effect of delta-9-THC has never been clearly demonstrated in all animal species. Doses of 10 to 25 mg/kg i.g. lowers only transiently blood pressure of spontaneous hypertensive rats (Schwartz et al., 1972, Fig. 14A). A psychotomimetic dose of delta-9-THC does not always produce in man clear hypotensive effects, while it does induce a marked acceleration of heart rate, which is not desirable in the treatment of hypertension.

It was also suggested that *Cannabis* derivatives might be useful in the treatment of withdrawal symptoms to alcohol, barbiturates, or opiates. It has been established that the effects of *Cannabis* on psychomotor performance are potentiated by alcohol, but the mechanism of action of these two substances is quite different. A great degree of tolerance develops to both drugs, with the development of tolerance to delta-9-THC much more rapid. One report, by Thompson and Proctor (1953), claimed that pyrahexyl treatment with a synthetic *Cannabis* derivative (15 mg, 3 to 4 times daily) alleviated in 80% of the cases treated (59 of 70) withdrawal symptoms from ethanol intoxication. However, subsequent treatment with pyrahexyl was not continued beyond 5 days. Treatment by the same authors of withdrawal symptoms from morphine was less successful. It is evident that delta-9-THC cannot compete with methadone in the treatment of withdrawal symptoms from opiate intoxication.

Moreau (1845) was the first to assume that the "feeling of gaiety and joy" produced by *Cannabis* intoxication would be most valuable to treat "the fixed ideas of the depressives." He treated several such cases of deep depression with increasing dosages of hashish, but with little result. Moreau also tried hashish in the treatment of schizophrenia with disappointing results. He continued his trials on less sick "manic" patients, and reports that seven of them were cured.

One hundred years after, a similar lack of effectiveness of *Cannabis* derivatives on the depressive state was observed by Thompson and Proctor (1953), who treated 20 cases of depression with pyrahexyl. By contrast, Stockings

(1947) claimed a successful use of synhexyl (15 to 90 mg orally), another synthetic *Cannabis* derivative, in the treatment of "50 depressive patients" which included a large heterogenous group of subjects, affected with what the author calls "thalamic dysfunction." He states that 30 of 50 improved, but this study, with no control subjects and no objective measurements, is impossible to interpret. In any event, although an effective sedative drug might help common types of depression with anxiety, it cannot replace the tricydic antidepressants which are the agents of choice in the treatment of severe depressions.

Cannabis was prescribed in Hindu medicine not only to stimulate the appetite, as reported by Snyder (1971), but also to deaden the need for food or beverage by concentrating the mind on the eternal (Chopra, 1969). According to Chopra, the chronic user of ganja is thin and emaciated. By contrast, the contemporary grapevine also mentions the powerful stimulus of appetite that marihuana produces in the user. *Cannabis* is also supposed to improve the taste of food. All of these claims might be true in the context of the social setting where they developed. After a lively party ending late at night, where only tobacco has been smoked, everyone seems to have a ravenous appetite. But it would be difficult to substantiate the claim that *Cannabis* increases the appetite and might be a good drug to use in anorexia nervosa on the basis of well-controlled pharmacological studies on rodents: Rats given delta-9-THC decreased their food intake significantly; furthermore, the weight loss suffered persisted 30 days following the end of this treatment. The possibility that delta-9-THC could be used in the treatment of obesity was not suggested by the authors of this study (Manning et al., 1971).

Others have claimed that *Cannabis* derivatives could be useful in the treatment of migraine or facial neuralgia and as a sexual stimulant. There is little pharmacological basis for the first two indications. Delta-9-THC has weak analgesic activity, while the basic difficulty of formulating dosage and foreseeing the extent and reactions to its use remain important obstacles. The aphrodisiac properties of *Cannabis* derivatives have been reported throughout its long history. Many in the Orient still take *Cannabis* to increase their amorous prowess. Some youth claim today that their sexual performance and enjoyment is enhanced by the use of marihuana. The subjective impression of the slowing of time might indeed confer upon the performer a very unusual gratification if his orgasmic experience is extended from 30 sec to 30 min. However, the experimenter should be informed that this alleged effect of *Cannabis* is not dose dependent and occurs only with low dosage. Théophile Gautier (1846), a wild young French Romantic, stated that after taking a good dose of hashish "the hashish user would not lift a finger for the most beautiful maiden in Venice." Young French Romantics of the nineteenth century, like their ancestors, did not seem to need any special drug to enhance their many sensuous experiences. This tradition has prevailed in France. Moderate doses of *Cannabis* might act like ethanol. "It provokes and unprovokes: it provokes the desire, but it takes away the performance" (Shakespeare in *Macbeth,* Act 2, Sc. 3). The chronic use of *Cannabis,* according to Chopra (1969) and Benabud (1957), leads to a sad condition where a lack of desire is coupled with an inability to perform.

The only truly demonstrated therapeutic property of *Cannabis* is the antibacterial effect of cannabidiol. This effect has been demonstrated *in vitro,* and pharmaceutical preparations such as ointments for tropical application against staphylococcal infections have been proposed. Cannabidiol does not appear to have any particular advantage over the large number of powerful antibiotics presently available, but it might be a substance worthy of future study in bacteriology and microbiology.

The most biologically active molecules isolated from *Cannabis sativa* have not held their therapeutic promise. The curative properties attributed to this magic plant, first by Indian and Arabic folklore, then by the nineteenth century prescientific era of Western medicine, have proven to be quite illusory. Delta-9-THC is quite unlike digitoxin or reserpine, two biologically active molecules extracted from the foxglove leaf or from *Rawolfia serpentina.* Delta-9-THC does not meet any of the present-day pharmacological standards for safety, specificity, bio-availability, and effectiveness required for a new drug to replace those currently in use. The analog and homolog of delta-9-THC which have now been synthesized in large numbers might display the therapeutic properties which have been sought in vain for the psychoactive substances isolated from *Cannabis sativa.*

However, all of the synthetic THC derivatives which have been studied appear to have the same basic physicochemical and pharmacological properties as the parent compound; synhexyl, which was thought at first to be the natural active ingredient of *Cannabis* and was used as such in the La Guardia study, is weaker than delta-9-THC. Dimethylheptylpyran (DMHP), which was extensively studied in Seevers's laboratory, is a more stable, more potent (5-to-10-fold) cannabinoid than the naturally occurring one (Hardman et al., 1971). It is insoluble in water, induces marked tolerance, possesses the same pharmacological spectrum as delta-9-THC (hypotensive, hypothermic, anticonvulsant), and induces marked behavioral changes.

A single large dose of DMHP (10 mg/kg, i.v.) can render a dog unconscious for 5 to 6 days, after which recovery is uneventful. The broad disabling properties induced by this drug explains why it was studied extensively for possible application in chemical warfare. Smaller doses in cats and monkeys were lethal (Monroe, 1971).

Table 10

Drug Interactions with DMPH in the Dog[a]

Group no.	Drug no. 1, mg/kg, i.v. plus Drug no. 2,[b] mg/kg, i.v.	Behavioral responses	Mortality[c]/No. tested
1	DMHP, 1.0	Marked CNS depression for 24 hours; complete recovery in 3 days	0/3
2	Cocaine, 4.0	Immediate excitation, hyperpnea, then mild excitation for several hours	0/4
3	DMHP, 1.0, + cocaine, 2.0	DMHP sedation antagonized by cocaine; disorientation persists	1/4
4	DMHP, 1.0, + cocaine, 4.0	Cocaine induced convulsions in all dogs, sedation prominent 1 hour later	2/4
5	d-Amphetamine, 1.0	Hyperactivity, piloerection, mydriasis; complete recovery in <24 hours	0/3
6	DMHP, 1.0, + d-Amphetamine, 1.0	Amphetamine induced arousal which persisted for several hours	0/2
7	DMPH, 1.0, + d-Amphetamine, 2.0	Marked amphetamine arousal persisted for 3 hours	3/3
8	Caffeine, 10.0	Hyperactivity and muscle tremors which disappeared in 3–4 hours	0/2
9	DMHP, 1.0, + caffeine, 10.0	Caffeine induced arousal and tonic extensor convulsions	2/3
10	DMHP, 1.0, + nalorphine, 6.0	Nalorphine induced arousal, convulsions, and reversal of analgesia	1/4
11	Morphine SO$_4$, 2.0[d]	Emesis followed by CNS depression with recovery in 6 hours	0/2
12	DMHP, 0.1 + morphine SO$_4$, 2.0[d]	After morphine sulfate, emesis, ataxia, hyperreflexia, and respiratory stimulation; CNS depression and analgesia appeared to be enhanced after morphine sulfate	0/4

[a] From Hardman et al., 1971.

[b] Drug no. 2 was administered 3 hours after drug no. 1 when the full effects of DMHP were evident.

[c] Mortality was counted for 3 days after drug administration.

[d] Subcutaneously.

DMHP also interacts with many other common psychoactive drugs such as amphetamines and caffeine (Table 10). All of these features make these most potent derivatives of delta-9-THC unlikely to have any therapeutic applications.

CONCLUSION AND SUMMARY

Delta-9-THC, which appears to be the major psychoactive substance of *Cannabis,* presents the following pharmacological properties:

1. It is insoluble in water and body fluids.

2. It has a very high fat solubility and binds to plasma and cellular proteins.

3. It is slowly absorbed from the gastrointestinal tract and peritoneum.

4. It induces enzymes in lung and liver (nonspecific oxydases).

5. It has a prolonged half-life (greater than 24 hours).

6. Its metabolites accumulate in the brain and other tissues and are eliminated over a week in urine and feces.

7. *It rapidly induces marked tolerance in all animal species.*

8. It primarily affects the central nervous system, where it alters the turnover rate of the major neurotransmitters—norepinephrine, 5-hydroxytryptamine, and acetylcholine.

9. Its acute or chronic administration produces multiple behavioral aberrations in learned and evoked response.

10. It produces ambivalent action in the central nervous system, with stimulatory sensory effects combined or followed by depressant ones.

11. It interacts with other centrally acting drugs such as amphetamines, ethanol, and barbiturates.

12. It does not present any specific pharmacological property which could justify its use as a therapeutic agent more effective than any presently in use.

REFERENCES

Abel, E. (1969). Effects of the marihuana homologue, pyrahexyl, on a conditioned emotional response. *Psychonomic Sci.,* 16:1–44.

Abel, E., and Schiff, B. (1969). Effects of the marihuana homologue, pyrahexyl, on food and water intake and curiosity in the rat. *Psychonomic Sci.,* 16:38.

Agurell, S. (1970). Chemical and pharmacological studies of cannabis. In *The Botany and Chemistry of Cannabis,* C. R. B. Joyce and S. H. Curry (eds.). J. & A. Churchill, London, pp. 175–191.

Agurell, S., Nilsson, I. M., Ohlsson, A., and Sandberg, F. (1969). Elimination of tritium-labelled cannabinols in the rat with special reference to the development of tests for the identification of cannabis users. *Biochem. Pharmacol.,* 18:1195–1201.

Agurell, S., Nilsson, I. M., Ohlsson, A., and Sandberg, F. (1970). On the metabolism of tritium-labelled delta-1-tetrahydrocannabinol in the rabbit. *Biochem. Pharmacol.,* 19:1333–1339.

Barratt, E., Goolishian, H., Samuelson, G., and White, R. (1970). Panel report on action of marihuana. *Symposium in Mood Behavior and Drugs,* AAAS Meeting, Chicago, Dec.

Barry, H., III, and Kubena, R. (1969). Acclimation to laboratory alters response of rate to delta-1-tetrahydrocannabinol. *Proc. 77th Ann. Conv. Amer. Psychol. Ass.,* 4:865–866.

Barry, H., III, Perhach, J. L., Jr., and Kubena, R. K. (1970). Delta-1-tetra-hydrocannabinol activation of pituitary-adrenal function. *Pharmacologist,* 12:258.

Bein, H. J. (1970). In *The Botany and Chemistry of Cannabis,* C. R. B. Joyce and S. H. Curry (eds.). J. & A. Churchill, London, pp. 204–205.

Benabud, A. (1957). Psycho-pathological aspects of the cannabis situation in Morocco: Statistical data for 1956. *Bull. Narcotics,* 9:1–16.

Ben-Zvi, Z., Mechoulam, R., and Burstein, S. H. (1970). Identification through synthesis of an active delta-1,6-tetrahydrocannabinol metabolite. *J. Amer. Chem. Soc.,* 92:3468.

Ben-Zvi, Z., Mechoulam, R., Edery, H., and Porath, G. (1971). 6β-hydroxy-delta-1-tetrahydrocannabinol synthesis and biological activity. *Science,* 174:951–952.

Bicher, H. I., and Mechoulam, R. (1968). Pharmacological effects of two active constituents of marihuana. *Arch. Int. Pharmacodyn.,* 172:24–31.

Birch, E. C. (1889). The use of Indian hemp in the treatment of chronic chloral and chronic opium poisoning. *Lancet,* 1:625.

Black, M. B., Woods, J. H., and Domino, E. F. (1963). Some effects of ($-$) delta 9 *trans*-tetrahydrocannabinol and other drugs on operant behavior in rats. *Arch. Int. Pharmacodyn.,* 144:533–554.

Black, M. B., Woods, J. H., and Domino, E. F. (1970). Some effects of ($-$)-Δ^9-*trans*-tetrahydrocannabinol and other cannabis derivatives on schedule-controlled behavior. *Pharmacologist,* 12:258.

Borgen, L. A., and Davis, W. M. (1970). Effects of synthetic Δ^9-tetrahydro-cannabinol on pregnancy in the rat. *Pharmacologist,* 12:259.

Bose, B. C., Vijayvargiya, R., Saifi, A. Q., and Bhagwat, A. W. (1963). Chemical and pharmacological investigations of *Cannabis indica.* *Arch. Int. Pharmacodyn.,* 146:99–105.

Bose, B. C., Saifa, A. Q., and Bhagwat, A. S. (1964a). Observations on the pharmacological actions of *Cannabis indica,* Part II. *Arch. Int. Pharmacodyn.,* 147:285–290.

Bose, B. C., Saifa, A. Q., and Bhagwat, A. W. (1964b). Studies on pharmacological actions of *Cannabis indica* (Linn), Part III. *Arch. Int. Pharmacodyn. Ther.,* 147:291–297.

Boyd, E. S., Boyd, E. H., Muchmore, J. S., and Brown, L. E. (1971). Effects of two tetrahydrocannabinols and of pentobarbital on cortico-cortical evoked responses in the squirrel monkey. *J. Pharmacol. Exp. Ther.,* 176:480–488.

Boyd, E. S., Hutchinson, E. D., Gardner, L. C., and Meritt, D. A. (1963).

Effects of tetrahydrocannabinols and other drugs on operant behavior in rats. *Arch. Int. Pharmacodyn.,* 144:533–554.

Boyd, E. S., and Meritt, D. A. (1965a). Effects of a tetrahydrocannabinol derivative on some motor systems in the cat. *Arch. Int. Pharmacodyn.,* 153:1–12.

Boyd, E. S., and Meritt, D. A. (1965b). Effects of thiopental and a tetra-hydrocannabinol derivative on arousal and recruiting in the cat. *J. Pharmacol. Exp. Ther.,* 149:138–145.

Brooks, W. L. (1896). A case of recurrent migraine successfully treated with cannabis indica. *Indian Med. Rec.,* 11:338.

Brown, J. (1883). Cannabis: A valuable remedy in hemorrhagia. *Brit. Med. J.,* 1:1002.

Burstein, S. H., Menezes, F., Williamson, E., and Mechoulam, R. (1970). Metabolism of delta-I(6)-tetrahydrocannabinol, an active marihuana constituent. *Nature,* 225:87–88.

Buxbaum, D. (1969). Analgesic activity of tetrahydrocannabinol (THC) in rat and mouse. *Fed. Proc.,* 28:735.

Campbell, A. M. G., Evans, M., Thompson, J. L. G., and Williams, M. J. (1971). Cerebral atrophy in young cannabis smokers. *Lancet,* 7736: 1219–1224.

Carakushansky, G., New, R. F., and Gardner, L. I. (1969). Lysergide and *Cannabis* as possible teratogens in man. *Lancet,* 1:150–151.

Carlini, E. A. (1968). Tolerance to chronic administration of *Cannabis sativa* (marihuana) in rats. *Pharmacology,* 1:135–142.

Carlini, E. A., and Kramer, C. (1966). Effects of *Cannabis sativa* (marihuana) on maze performance of the rat. *Psychopharmacologia,* 7:175–181.

Carlini, E. A., and Masur, J. (1969). Development of aggressive behavior in rats by chronic administration of *Cannabis sativa* (marihuana). *Life Sci.* 8:607–620.

Carlini, G. R., and Carlini, E. A. (1965). Effects of strychnine and *Cannabis sativa* (marihuana) on the nucleic acid content in the brain of the rat. *Med. Pharmacol. Exp.,* 12:21–26.

Chopra, G. S. (1969). Man and Marihuana. *Int. J. Addictions,* 4:215–247.

Chopra, I. C., and Chopra, R. N. (1957). The use of cannabis drug in India. *Bull. Narcotics,* 9:4–29.

Christensen, H. D., Freudenthal, R. I., Gidley, J. T., Rosenfeld, R., Boegli, G., Testino, L., Brine, D. R., Pitt, C. G., and Wall, M. E. (1971). Activity of Δ^8- and Δ^9-tetrahydrocannabinol and related compounds in the mouse. *Science,* 172:165–167.

Colasanti, B., and Khazan, N. (1971). Changes in EEG voltage output of the sleep–awake cycle in response to tetrahydrocannabinols in the rat. *Pharmacologist,* 13:246.

Conrad, D. G., Elsmore, T. F., and Sodetz, F. J. (1972). Δ⁹-Tetrahydrocannabinol: Dose-related effects on timing behavior in chimpanzee. *Science,* 175:547–550.

Dagirmanjian, R., and Boyd, E. S. (1960). Peripheral effects of a tetrahydrocannabinol. *Fed. Proc.,* 19:267.

Dagirmanjian, R., and Boyd, E. S. (1962). Some pharmacological effects of two tetrahydrocannabinols. *J. Pharmacol. Exp.,* 135:25–33.

Dagirmanjian, R., and Hodge, H. C. (1970). Are biogenic amines involved in the mechanism of action of tetrahydrocannabinols? *Agents and Actions,* 1:46–48.

Davis, J. A., and Ramsey, H. H. (1949). Anti-epileptic action of marihuana-active substances. *Fed. Proc.,* 8:284–285.

Deneau, G. A., and Kaymakcalan, S. (1971). Physiological and psychological dependence to synthetic delta-9-tetrahydrocannabinol (THC) in rhesus monkeys. *Pharmacologist,* 13:246.

Dewey, W. L., Harris, L. S., Howes, J. F., Granchelli, F. E., Pars, H. G., and Razdan, R. K. (1970a). Pharmacology of some marijuana constituents and two heterocyclic analogues. *Nature,* 226:1265–1267.

Dewey, W. L., Harris, L. S., Howes, J. F., and Kennedy, J. S. (1969). Pharmacological effects of some active constituents of marihuana. *Pharmacologist,* 11:278.

Dewey, W. L., Kennedy, J. S., and Howes, J. F. (1970b). Some gastrointestinal and metabolic effects of two constituents of marihuana. *Fed. Proc.,* 29:650.

Dewey, W. L., Peng, T. C., and Harris, L. W. (1970c). The effects of (*l*)-*trans*-Δ⁹-tetrahydrocannabinol on the hypothalamo-hypophyseal-axis of rats. *Eur. J. Pharmacol.,* 12:382–384.

Dewey, W., Yonle, L., Harris, L., Reavis, W. M., Griffin, E. D., Jr., and Newby, E. V. (1970d). Some cardiovascular effects of *trans*-Δ-9-THC. *Pharmacologist,* 12:259.

Dingell, J. V., Wilcox, H. G., and Klausner, H. A. (1971). Biochemical interactions of delta-9-tetrahydrocannabinol. *Pharmacologist,* 13:296.

Domino, F., Hardman, F., and Seevers, H. (1971). Central nervous system actions of some synthetic tetrahydrocannabinol derivatives. *Pharmacol. Rev.,* 23:317–336.

Doorenbos, N. J., Fetterman, P. S., Quimby, M. W., and Turner, C. E. (1971). Cultivation, extraction and analysis of *Cannabis sativa* L. *Ann. N.Y. Acad. Sci.,* 191:3–12.

El-Sourogy, M., Malek, A. Y., and Ibrahim, H. H. (1966). The effects of cannabis indica on carbohydrate metabolism in rabbits. *J. Egypt. Med. Ass.,* 49:626–628.

Farlow, J. W. (1889). On the use of belladonna and cannabis indica by the rectum in gynecological practice. *Boston Med. Surg. J.,* 120:507–509.

Fere, C. (1901). Note sur l'influence du hachisch sur le travail. *Comptes rendus hebdomadaires des séances de la Société de Biologie* (2ème série), 3:696–700.

Ferenczy, L., Gracza, L., and Jakobey, I. (1958). An antibacterial preparatum from hemp (*Cannabis sativa* L.). *Naturwissenschaften,* 45:188–189.

Ferraro, D. P., Grilly, D. M., and Lynch, W. C. (1971). Effects of marihuana extract on the operant behavior of chimpanzees. Psychopharmacologia, 22:333–351.

Foltz, R. L., Fentiman, A. F., Jr., Leighty, E. G., Walter, J. L., Drewes, H. R., Schwartz, W. E., Page, T. F., Jr., and Truitt, E. B., Jr. (1970). Metabolite of (−)-trans-Δ⁸-tetrahydrocannabinol: Identification and synthesis. *Science,* 168:844–845.

Foltz, R. L., Kinzer, G. W., Mitchell, R. I., and Truitt, E. B., Jr. (1971). The fate of cannabinoid components of marihuana during smoking. *J. Anal. Chem.,* in press.

Ford, R. D., and McMillan, D. E. (1971). Behavioral tolerance and cross tolerance to 1-Δ⁹-tetrahydrocannabinol and 1-Δ⁸-tetrahydrocannabinol in pigeons and rats. *Fed. Proc.,* 30:279.

Ford, R. D., and McMillan, D. E. (1972): Further studies on the behavioral pharmacology of 1-delta-8 and 1-delta-9THC. *Fed. Proc.,* 31:506.

Forney, R. B. (1971). Toxicology of marihuana. *Pharmacol. Rev.,* 23:279–284.

Fox, R. H. (1897). Headaches, a study of some common forms with especial reference to arterial tension and to treatment. *Lancet,* 3:307–309.

Frankenheim, J., McMillan, D., and Harris, L. (1971). Effects of 1-Δ⁹- and 1-Δ⁸-*trans*-tetrahydrocannabinol on schedule-controlled behavior of pigeons and rats. *J. Pharmacol. Exp. Ther.,* 178:241–252.

Fraser, J. (1862). Treatment of tetanus with cannabis indica. *Med. Times Gaz.,* 1.

Gallager, D. W., Sanders-Bush, E., and Sulser, F. (1971). Dissociation between behavioral effects and changes in metabolism of cerebral serotonin (5HT) following delta-9-tetrahydrocannabinol (THC). *Pharmacologist,* 13:296.

Garattini, S. (1965). Effects of a cannabis extract on gross behavior. In *Hashish: Its Chemistry and Pharmacology,* G. E. W. Wolstenholme and J. Knight (eds.). Little, Brown and Company, Boston, pp. 70–82.

Garriott, J. C., Forney, R. B., Hughes, F. W., and Richard, A. B. (1968). Pharmacologic properties of some cannabis related compounds. *Arch. Int. Pharmacodyn.,* 171:425–435.

Garriott, J. C., King, L. J., Forney, R. B., and Hughes, F. W. (1967). Effects of some tetrahydrocannabinols on hexobarbital sleeping time and amphetamine induced hyperactivity in mice. *Life Sci.,* 6:2119–2128.

Gary, N. E., and Keylon, V. (1970). Intravenous administration of marihuana. *J. Amer. Med. Ass.,* 211:501.

Gautier, T. (1846). Le club des hachichins. In *La Revue des Deux Mondes,* Paris.

Gayer, H. (1928). Pharmakiologische wertbestimmung von oriental-ischem haschisch und herba cannabis indica. *Arch. Exp. Path. Pharmak.,* 129:312.

Geber, W. F., and Schramm, L. (1969a). Effect of marihuana extract on fetal hamsters and rabbits. *Toxicol. Appl. Pharmacol.,* 14:276–282.

Geber, W. F., and Schramm, L. (1969b). Teratogenicity of marihuana extract as influenced by plant origin and seasonal variation. *Arch. Int. Pharm.,* 177:224–230.

Gershon, S. (1970). On the pharmacology of marihuana. *Behavioral Neuropsychiat.,* 1:9–18.

Giarman, N. J., and Freedman, D. X. (1965). Biochemical aspects of the action of psychomimetic drugs. *Pharmacol. Rev.,* 17:1–26.

Gill, E. W., and Paton, W. D. M. (1970). Pharmacological experiments *in vitro* on the active principles of cannabis. In *The Botany and Chemistry of Cannabis,* C. R. B. Joyce and S. H. Curry (eds.). J. & A. Churchill, London, pp. 165–173.

Gill, E. W., Paton, W. D. M., and Pertwee, R. G. (1970). Preliminary experiments on the chemistry and pharmacology of cannabis. *Nature,* 228:134–136.

Goldstein, F. J. (1971). Marijuana. A pharmacological profile. *Amer. J. Pharm.,* 143:59–65.

Gourves, J., Viallard, C., LeLuan, D., Girard, J. P., and Aury, R. (1971). Case of coma due to *Cannabis sativa. Presse Med.,* 79:1389–1390.

Grunfeld, Y., and Edery, H. (1969).* Psychopharmacological activity of the active constituents of hashish and some related cannabinoids. *Psychoparmacologia,* 14:200–210.

Hardman, H. F., Domino, E. F., and Seevers, M. H. (1971). General pharmacological actions of some synthetic tetrahydrocannabinol derivatives. *Pharmacol. Rev.,* 23:295–315.

Harris, L. S. (1971). General and behavioral pharmacology of Δ^9-THC. *Pharmacol. Rev.,* 23:285–294.

Hecht, F., Beals, R. K., Lees, M. H., Jolly, H., and Roberts, R. (1968). Lysergic-acid diethylamide and cannabis as possible teratogens in man. *Lancet,* 2:1087–1090.

Hemenway, S. (1867). Poisoning by strychnine, successfully treated by cannabis. Pacific *Med. Surg.,* 10:113–114.

Henderson, A. H., and Pugsley, D. J. (1968). Collapse after intravenous injection of hashish. *Brit. Med. J.,* 3:229–230.

Heyndrickx, A., Scheiris, C., and Schepens, P. (1970). Toxicological study of a fatal intoxication in man due to cannabis smoking. *J. Pharm. Belg.,* 24:371–376.

Himmelsbach, C. K. (1944). Treatment of the morphine abstinence syndrome with a synthetic cannabis-like compound. *South. Med. J.,* 37:26–29.

Ho, B. T., Fritchie, G. E., Kralik, P. M., Englert, L. F., McIsaac, W. M., and Idanpaan-Heikkila, J. (1970). Distribution of tritiated Δ^9-tetrahydrocannabinol in rat tissues after inhalation. *J. Pharm. Pharmacal.,* 22:538–539.

Ho, B. T., Taylor, D., Englert, L. F., and McIsaac, W. M. (1971). Neurochemical effects of 1-delta-9-tetrahydrocannabinol in rats following repeated inhalation. *Brain Res.,* 31:233–236.

Hockman, C. H., Perrin, R. G., and Kalant, H. (1971). Electroencephalographic and behavioral alterations produced by Δ^1-tetrahydrocannabinol. *Science,* 172:968–970.

Hockman, J. S., and Brill, N. Q. (1971). Chronic marihuana usage and liver function. *Lancet,* 2:818–819.

Holtzman, D., Lovell, R. A., Jaffe, J. H., and Freedman, D. X. (1969). (l)-Δ^9-tetrahydrocannabinol: Neurochemical and behavioral effects in the mouse. *Science,* 163:1464–1467.

Hosko, M. J., and Hardman, H. F. (1971). Effect of delta-9-THC on cardiovascular responses to stimulation of vasopressor loci in the neuraxis of anesthetized cats. *Pharmacologist,* 13:296.

Howes, J. F. (1970). A study of two water soluble derivatives of delta-9-tetrahydrocannabinol. *Pharmacologist,* 12:258.

Idanpaan-Heikkila, J., Fritchie, G. E., Englert, L. F., Ho, B. T., and McIsaac, W. M. (1969). Placental transfer of tritiated (l)-Δ^9-tetrahydrocannabinol. *New Eng. J. Med.,* 281–330.

Irwin, S. (1964). Prediction of drug effects from animals to man. In *CIBA Foundation Symp.-Animal Behaviour and Drug Action,* A. V. S. deReuck and J. Knight (eds.). Little, Brown and Company, Boston, pp. 269–285.

Jaffe, P. G., and Baum, M. (1971). Increased resistance to extinction of an avoidance response to rats following the administration of hashish resin. *Psychopharmacologia,* 20:97–102.

Joachimoglu, G. (1965). Natural and smoked hashish. In *Hashish: Its Chemistry and Pharmacology,* G. E. W. Wolstenholme and J. Knight (eds.). Little, Brown and Company, Boston.

Kabelik, J., Krejci, Z., and Santavi, F. (1960). Cannabis as a medicament. *Bull. Narcotics,* 12:5–23.

Kaymakcalan, S., and Deneau, G. A. (1971). Some pharmacological effects of synthetic delta-9-tetrahydrocannabinol (THC). *Pharmacologist,* 13:247.

Kelley, W. M. (1883). Cannabis indica. *Brit. Med. J.,* 1:1281.

Kew, M. C., Bersohn, L., and Siew, S. (1969). Possible hepatotoxicity of cannabis. *Lancet,* 1:578–579.

King, A. B., and Cowen, D. L. (1969). Effect of intravenous injection of marihuana. *J. Amer. Med. Ass.,* 210:724–725.

King, L. J., and Forney, R. B. (1967). The absorption and excretion of the marihuana constituents, cannabinol and tetrahydrocannabinol. *Fed. Proc.,* 26:540

Klausner, H. A., and Dingell, J. V. (1971). The metabolism and excretion of Δ^9-tetrahydrocannabinol in the rat. *Life Sci.,* Pt. 1, 10:49–59.

Kubena, R. K., and Barry, H., III (1970). Interactions of delta-9-tetrahydrocannabinol with barbiturates and methamphetamine. *J. Pharm. Exp. Ther.,* 173:94–100.

Kubena, R. K., Cavero, I., Jandhyala, B. S., and Buckley, J. P. (1971). Certain respiratory and cardiovascular effects of delta-9-THC in dogs. *Pharmacologist,* 13:247.

Kubena, R. K., Perhach, J. L., and Barry, H., III (1971). Corticosterone elevation mediated centrally by Δ^1-tetrahydrocannabinol in rats. *Eur. J. Pharmacol.,* 14:89–92.

Lapa, A. J., Sampaio, C. A., Timo-Iaria, C., and Valle, J. R. (1968). Blocking action of tetrahydrocannabinol upon transmission in the trigeminal system of the cat. *J. Pharm. Pharmacol.,* 20:373–376.

Layman, J. M., and Milton, A. S. (1971). Some actions of delta-1-tetrahydrocannabinol and cannabidiol at cholinergic junctions. *Brit. J. Pharmacol.,* 41:379–380.

Lemberger, L., Weiss, J. L., Watanabe, A. M., Galanter, I. M., Wyatt, R. J., and Cardon, P. V. (1972). Delta-9-tetrahydrocannabinol: Temporal correlation of the psychologic effects and blood levels after various routes of administration. *New Eng. J. Med.,* 286:685–688.

Lipparini, F., DeCarolis, A., and Longo, V. A. (1969). A neuropharmacological investigation of some *trans*-tetrahydrocannabinol derivatives. *Physiol. Behav.,* 4:527–532.

Loewe, S. (1946). Studies on the pharmacology and acute toxicity of compounds with marihuana activity. *J. Pharmacol. Exp. Ther.,* 88:154–161.

Lomax, P. (1971). Acute tolerance to the hypothermic effect of marihuana in the rat. *Res. Comm. Chem. Pathol. Pharmacol.* 2:159–167.

McIsaac, W. M., Fritchie, G. W., Idanpaan-Heikkila, J. E., Ho, B. T., and Englert, L. F. (1971). Distribution of marihuana in monkey brain and concomitant behavioral effects. *Nature,* 230:593–594.

MacKenzie, S. (1887). Indian hemp in persistent headache. *J. Amer. Med. Ass.,* 9:731–732.

McMillan, D. E., Harris, L. S., Frankenheim, J. M., and Kennedy, J. S. (1970). (*l*)-Δ^9-*trans*-tetrahydrocannabinol in pigeons: Tolerance to the behavioral effects. *Science,* 169:501–503.

McMillan, D. E., Dewey, W. L., and Harris, L. S. (1971): Characteristics of tetrahydrocannabinol tolerance. *Ann. N.Y. Acad. Sci.* 191:83–99.

Magus, R. D., and Harris, L. S. (1971). Carcinogenic potential of marihuana smoke condensate. *Fed. Proc.,* 30:279.

Mann, P. E. G., Cohen, A. B., Finley, T. N., and Ladman, A. J. (1971). Alveolar macrophages. Structural and functional differences between non-smokers and smokers of marijuana and tobacco. *Lab. Invest.,* 25:111–120.

Manning, F. J., McDonough, J. A., Jr., Elsmore, T. F., Saller, C., and Sodetz, F. J. (1971). Inhibition of normal growth by chronic administration of delta-9-THC *Science,* 74:424–426.

Manno, B. R., Manno, J. E., Kilsheimer, G. S., and Forney, R. B. (1970). Response of the isolated, perfused rat heart to delta-9-THC. *Toxicol. Appl. Pharmacol.,* 16:97.

Mantilla-Plata, B., and Harbison, R. D. (1971). Phenobarbital and SKF 525-A effect on delta-9-tetrahydrocannabinol (THC) toxicity and distribution in mice. *Pharmacologist,* 13:297.

Martin, P. A. (1969). Cannabis and chromosomes. *Lancet,* 1:370.

Mattison, J. (1891). Cannabis indica as an anodyne and hypnotic. *St. Louis Med. Surg. J.,* 61:265–271.

Martinez, J. L., Jr., Stadnicki, S. W., and Schaeppi, U. H. (1971). Delta-9-tetrahydrocannabinol: Effects of I.V. infusion upon EEG and behavior of unrestrained rhesus monkeys. *Pharmacologist,* 13:246.

Mayor's Committee on Marihuana (1944). *The Marihuana Problem in the City of New York—Sociological, Medical, Psychological and Pharmacological Studies.* Cattell Press, Lancaster, Pa.

Mikuriya, T. H. (1969). Historical aspects of *Cannabis sativa* in Western medicine. *New Physician,* 18:902–908.

Mikuriya, T. H. (1970). Cannabis substitution, an adjunctive therapeutic tool in the treatment of alcoholism. *Med. Times,* 98:187–191.

Miller, J. (1900). Case of traumatic tetanus, following injury of the finger, treated by amputation of the injured part, the application of cold to the spine and the internal use of cannabis indica. *Monthly J. Med. Sci.,* 5:22–30.

Milzoff, J. R., Forney, R. B., Stone, C. J., and Allen, D. O. (1971). The cardiovascular effects of delta-9-THC in vagotomized rats. *Pharmacologist,* 13:247.

Miras, C. J. (1965). Some aspects of cannabis action. In *Hashish: Its Chemistry and Pharmacology,* G. E. W. Wolstenholme and J. Knight (eds.). Little, Brown and Company, Boston, pp. 37–52.

Monroe, R. (1971). Discussion of paper by E. F. Domino. *Ann. N.Y. Acad. Sci.,* 191:92.

Moreau, J J. (1845). *Du Hachisch et de l'Alienation Mentale: Etudes Psychologiques 34.* Librairie de Fortin, Masson, Paris.

Morrell, F. A., and Varsel, C. (1966). A total combustion product cigarette smoking machine—An analysis of radioactive cigarette paper, tobacco. *Science,* 10:45–50.

Nakazawa, K., and Costa, E. (1971). Induction by methylcholanthrene of Δ^9-tetrahydrocannabinol (Δ^9-THC) metabolism in rat lung. *Pharmacologist,* 13:297.

Neu, R. L., Powers, H., King, S., and Gardner, L. I. (1969). Cannabis and chromosomes. *Lancet,* 1:675.

Oliver, J. (1883). On the action of cannabis indica. *Brit. Med. J.,* 1:905–906.

O'Shaughnessy, W. B. (1842). Case of tetanus, cured by a preparation of hemp. *Trans. Med. Psychiat. Soc. Calif.,* 8:462–469.

Pace, H. B., Davis, W. M., and Borgen, L. A. (1971). Teratogenesis and marihuana. *Ann. N.Y. Acad. Sci.,* 191:123–131.

Parsons, L. S. (1862). Treatment of tetanus with cannabis indica. *Med. Times Gaz.,* 18.

Persaud, T. V., and Ellington, A. (1967). Cannabis in early pregnancy. *Lancet,* 2:1306.

Persaud, T. V., and Ellington, A. (1968). Teratogenic activity of cannabis resin. *Lancet,* 2:406–407.

Phillips, R. N., Neel, M. A., Brown, D. J., and Forney, R. B. (1971a). Enhancement of caffeine or methamphetamine stimulation in mice with aqueous-suspended delta-9-tetrahydrocannabinol. *Pharmacologist,* 13:297.

Phillips, R. N., Turk, R. F., and Forney, R. B. (1971b). Acute toxicity of Δ^9-tetrahydrocannabinol in rats and mice. *Proc. Soc. Exp. Biol. Med.,* 136:260–263.

Pirch, J. H., Barnes, P. R., and Barratt, E. (1971). Tolerance to EEG effects of marijuana in rats. *Pharmacologist,* 13:246.

Podolsky, S., Pattavina, C. G., and Amaral, M. A. (1971). Effect of marihuana on glucose tolerance test. *Ann. N.Y. Acad. Sci.,* 191:54–60.

Radosevic, A., Kupinic, M., and Grlic, L. (1962). Antibiotic activity of various types of cannabis resin. *Nature,* 195:1007–1009.

Razdan, R. K., and Pars, H. G. (1970). Studies on cannabis constituents and synthetic analogues. In *The Botany and Chemistry of Cannabis,* C. R. B. Joyce and S. H. Curry (eds.). J. & A. Churchill, London, pp. 137–149.

Reynolds, J. R. (1890). Therapeutic uses and toxic effects of cannabis indica. *Lancet,* 1:637–638.

Rolls, E. J., and Clark, D. S. (1954). Depersonalization treated by cannabis indica and psychotherapy. *Guy Hosp. Rep.,* 103:330–336.

Rosenkrantz, H., Thompson, G. R., and Braude, M. C. (1972). Development of formulations for the chronic oral and parenteral administration of marihuana constituents to laboratory animals. *J. Pharmaceut. Sci.,* in press.

Salustiano, J. et al. (1966). Effects of *Cannabis sativa* and chlorpromazine on mice as measured by two methods used for evaluation of tranquilizing agents. *Med. Pharmacol. Exp.,* 15:153–162.

Sampaio, C. A., Lapa, A. J., and Valle, J. R. (1967). Influence of cannabis, tetrahydrocannabinol, and pyrahexyl on the linguomandibular reflex of the dog. *J. Pharm. Pharmacol.,* 19:552–554.

Santos, M., Sampaio, C. A. M., Fernandes, N. W., and Carlini, E. A. (1966). Effects of *Cannabis sativa* on the fighting behavior of mice. *Psychopharmacologia,* 8:437–444.

Scheckel, C. L., Boff, E., Dahlen, P., and Smart, T. (1968). Behavioral effects in monkeys of racemates of two biologically active marihuana constituents. *Science,* 160:1467–1469.

Schildkraut, J. J., and Efron, D. H. (1971). Effects of Δ^9-tetrahydrocannabinol on the metabolism of norepinephrine in rat brain. *Psychopharmacologia,* 20:191–196.

Schwartz, I. W., Adamec, J., Manger, W. M., and Nahas, G. G. (1972). Effect of delta-9-tetrahydrocannabinol on the blood pressure of spontaneous hypertensive rats. *Circulation* (in press).

Smith, D. E., and Mehl, C. (1970). The analysis of marijuana toxicity. In *The New Social Drug,* D. E. Smith (ed.). Prentice-Hall, Inc., Englewood Cliffs, N.J., pp. 63–77.

Snyder S. H., (1971). *Uses of Marijuana.* Oxford University Press, New York.

Sofia, R. D., Dixit, B. N., and Barry, H., III (1771a). The effects of Δ¹-tetra-hydrocannabinol on serotonin metabolism in the rat brain. *Life Sci.,* 10:425–436.

Sofia, R. D., Solomon, T. A., and Barry, H., III (1971b). The anticonvulsant activity of delta-1-tetrahydrocannabinol in mice. *Pharmacologist,* 13:246.

Soueif, M. I., (1967). Hashish consumption in Egypt with special reference to psychological aspects. *Bull. Narcotics,* 19:1–12.

Sterne, J., and Ducastaing, C. (1960). Les arterites du cannabis indica. *Arch. Mal. Coeur,* 53:143–147.

Stockings, G. T., (1947). A new euphoriant for depressive mental states. *Brit. Med. J.,* 1:918–922.

Tart, C. T. (1970). Marihuana intoxication, common experiences. *Nature,* 226:701–704.

Tennant, F. S., Jr., Preble, M., Prendergast, T. J., and Ventry, P., (1971). Medical manifestations associated with hashish. *J. Amer. Med. Ass.,* 216:1965–1969.

Thompson, G. R., Rosenkrantz, H., and Braude, M. (1971). Neurotoxicity of cannabinoids in chronically treated rats and monkeys. *Pharmacologist,* 13:296.

Thompson, L. J., and Proctor, R. C., (1953). Pyrahexyl in treatment of alcoholic and drug withdrawal conditions. *N. Carolina Med. J.,* 14:520–523.

Tonge, S. R., and Leonard, B. E. (1971). Hallucinogens and nonhallucinogens: A comparison of the effects of 5-hydroxytryptamine and noradrenaline. *Life Sci.,* 10:161–168.

Truitt, E. B., Jr. (1970). Pharmacological activity in a metabolite of (1)-*trans*-delta-8-hydrocannabinol. *Fed. Proc.,* 29:619.

Truitt, E. B., Jr., and Anderson, S. M. (1971). Biogenic amine alterations produced in the brain by tetrahydrocannabinols and their metabolites. *Ann. N.Y. Acad. Sci.,* 191:68–72.

Wall, M. E., Brine, D. R., Brine, G. A., Pitt, C. G., Freudenthal, R. I., and Christensen, H. B. (1970). Isolation, structure, and biological activity of several metabolites of delta-9-tetrahydrocannabinol. *J. Amer. Chem. Soc.,* 92:3466–3468.

Webster, C. D., Willinsky, M. D., Herring, B. S., and Walters, G. C. (1971). Effects of 1-delta-1-tetrahydrocannabinol on temporally spaced responding and discriminated Sidman avoidance behavior in rats. *Nature,* 232:498–501.

Welch, B. L., Welch, A. S., Messiha, F. S., and Berger, H. J., (1971). Rapid depletion of adrenal epinephrine and elevation of telencephalic serotonin by (−)-trans-Δ⁹-tetrahydrocannabinol in mice. *Res. Comm. Chem. Pathol.*, 2:382–391.

Widman, M., Nilsson, I. M., Nilsson, J. L. G., Augurell, S., and Leander, K. (1971). Metabolism of cannabis IX. Cannabinol: Structure of a major metabolite formed in the liver. *Life Sci.*, 10:157–162.

Wikler, A., and Lloyd, B. J. (1945). Effect of smoking marihuana cigarettes on cortical electrical activity. *Fed. Proc.*, 4:141–142.

5

Clinical Pharmacology

As we have reviewed earlier, the symptoms of *Cannabis* intoxication have been known for centuries. The discovery of delta-9-THC as the major psychoactive agent in *Cannabis,* as well as the availability of techniques to measure its concentration, has given to the clinical pharmacologist the opportunity to study dose-response relationships of this drug.

Another important area which the clinical pharmacologist has investigated, using radioactively tagged material, is the metabolism and distribution of delta-9-THC. Analysis of these studies gives a better understanding of the mode of action of the drug through the formation of active and inactive metabolites.

The first clinical study with synthetic material was made by Isbell et al. (1967), who showed that the physical and psychological effects of *Cannabis* were related to the dose administered and confirmed the older observations of Moreau (1845) about the hallucinogenic properties of *Cannabis*. Isbell indeed concluded his study in a straightforward way: "The data in our experiments definitely indicate that the psychotomimetic effects of delta-9-THC are dependent on dosage and that sufficiently high dosage (15–20 mg smoked, 20–60 mg ingested) can cause psychotic reactions in any individual." Isbell therefore classified *Cannabis* among the hallucinogens.

Two subsequent studies, by Weil (1969) and by Crancer et al. (1969), however, made with unextracted, aged material containing a putative dose of delta-9-THC (5 to 66 mg) produced only mild symptoms of intoxication which were not related to the amount of drug administered. The results of these studies indicated that *Cannabis* was a "mild intoxicant" which produced effects not related to dosage, did not impair, and even improved performance of "chronic users." Following this work, a new pharmacological concept was introduced, that of "reverse tolerance."

From then on the great marihuana debate raged in the United States: Is *Cannabis* a hallucinogen? Or is it a mild intoxicant when used in a dosage likely to be taken by habitual users in the population at large?   The evidence to support these contradictory claims will be carefully scrutinized.

The difficulties of interpreting clinical studies with delta-9-THC are due to the many factors which influence the development of *Cannabis* intoxication in man (Table 11).   These factors are the dosage of active material (mostly delta-9-THC) in the preparation used, the route of intake (inhalation or ingestion), the previous experience of the subject with the drug, the frequency of intake, and the development of tolerance to the drug.   Individual genetic characteristics pertaining to enzyme induction by delta-9-THC and the formation of active metabolites are also very important.   Intake of other drugs which stimulate or inhibit enzyme induction modify delta-9-THC metabolism and its pharmacological activity.   The mood and expectation of the subject,

Table 11

Factors Influencing *Cannabis* Intoxication

---

1. Dose (amount of delta-9-THC)
2. Route of intake: inhalation; ingestion
3. Frequency of intake (development of tolerance)
4. Individual metabolism of delta-9-THC and formation of active metabolites
5. Associated intake of drugs interacting with delta-9-THC: alcohol, psychotropic drugs (barbiturates, amphetamines)
6. Mood of the subject (expectation)
7. Setting: group (interpersonal stimulation); solitary

---

as well as the setting in which the drug is taken, influence the psychological response.   It is apparent that all of these variables cannot be controlled even in the best clinical experiments.

When trying to determine the dosage administered to a subject, the clinical pharmacologist is faced with a difficult task: He has presently no way to measure the amount of active ingredients actually absorbed in the blood, because none of the available methods are sensitive enough.   Since all preparations are either ingested or smoked, the amounts absorbed by both routes vary considerably from one subject to the next.   And no clinical pharmacologist has yet felt free to administer delta-9-THC intravenously to man, except in tracer amounts, because of its insolubility in water.   But available techniques should allow investigators to measure accurately the amount of active ingredients present in the preparation they use.   With this measurement, imperfect as it is, dose-response relationships may be established, and the range of dosage required to produce euphoria, dysphoria, and hallucinations established.   This range has now been bracketed in a number of studies which will be reviewed; it is close to that determined by Isbell.

In addition to actual dosage delivered, the second factor to be considered in experimental studies of *Cannabis* in man is the personality of the subject and his previous knowledge or experience with the drug.

Previous *Cannabis* usage by a person modifies the subjective effects produced by the drug either in laboratory or social setting. But many investigators do not or cannot define what they mean by "use," "habitual use," "chronic use," or "experienced use" of the drug. It is impossible to ascertain the meaning of these words to describe accurately previous *Cannabis* use by the subjects enrolled in experimental studies. Other investigators define the dosage of *Cannabis* used in an experiment as one which will produce a "typical," socially acceptable "high," or a commonly experienced high, or a socially relevant dose. Such definitions are not quantitative enough to be scientifically acceptable. Many authors also speak of high, very high, moderate, and low dosages without specifying the actual amount administered.

In Isbell's studies, former narcotic addicts or prisoners were used as experimental subjects. They had a thorough previous knowledge of the subjective and intoxicating effects of drugs. Interpretation of the results observed in these subjects was criticized, and it was pointed out that such data might not apply to a more representative sample of the population at large. Similar criticisms should also be applied to other studies performed on young paid volunteers recruited from the student community, many of them enthusiastic marihuana smokers who are convinced that *Cannabis* is innocuous and are expecting pleasant effects from its use.

Jones (1971*a*, 1971*b*) performed unique studies on such a selected group of marihuana users who smoked relatively mild preparations (0.9% THC). He was able to distinguish the effects of the psychosocial factors associated with marihuana smoking from the pharmacological effects of the drug, or the "effects of the mind on marihuana."

The problem of tolerance to a drug which might be used habitually is of major importance. Can *Cannabis,* which rapidly creates tolerance in animals, be used frequently by man without having to increase dosage to produce the desired effect? Is chronic use of *Cannabis* associated with "reverse tolerance," and if so, by what mechanism? What about physical and psychological dependence? Investigators in clinical pharmacology must attempt to answer all of these questions, which sometime require critical comparison of present measurements with past observations.

METABOLISM AND DISPOSITION

Most significant studies were performed with tagged delta-9-THC administered intravenously (Lemberger et al., 1970, 1971). Results obtained confirmed those in animals: Delta-9-THC gives rise to polar metabolites which are slowly eliminated from the body (Fig. 15).

After intravenous administration of tracer amounts of ^{14}C-labeled delta-9-THC to subjects who had never previously used *Cannabis* extracts, the amount of this compound in plasma declines rapidly during the first hour, with a half-life of about 30 min. After 1 hour, the amount of delta-9-THC

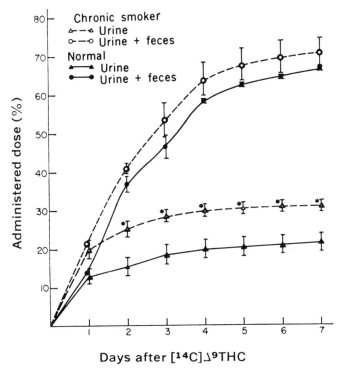

Fig. 15. Comparison of the cumulative excretion of radioactivity in three chronic marihuana users and three nonusers after intravenous injection of ^{14}C-labeled delta-9-THC. (From Lemberger, 1971a).

falls much more slowly (with a half-life of 56 hours). The decline of total radioactivity and of the more polar ether extractable metabolites in plasma is similar to that of delta-9-THC. A rapid initial decline precedes a much slower phase of disappearance from the plasma. Polar metabolites are formed rapidly and are present in plasma at higher concentrations than delta-9-THC. The initially rapid decrease of ^{14}C-labeled delta-9-THC in plasma represents redistribution of delta-9-THC from the intravascular compartment into tissues (including brain) and metabolism. These findings are

consistent with the reported clinical effects of a small dose of inhaled marihuana (containing approximately 5 mg or less of delta-9-THC), which are
maximum within 15 min, diminished between 30 min and 1 hour, and largely
dissipated by 3 hours. The slower decline of delta-9-THC in plasma ($t_{1/2} =$
56 hours) and of total radioactivity ($t_{1/2} = 67$ hours) presumably represents
retention and slow release of the drug from the tissues. Since delta-9-THC
is a nonpolar compound, it may accumulate in fat or other tissues such as
lung which have an affinity for the drug, and it has already been reported that,
in animals, after intravenous administration of delta-9-THC, much higher
levels of radioactivity were present in lung than in other tissues (Ho et al.,
1971).

Over a period of more than a week, Lemberger et al. (1971) showed that
about 30% of the administered radioactivity is excreted in the urine and 50%
in the feces. The finding that delta-9-THC and its metabolites persist in man
for long periods indicates that the drug and its metabolites may accumulate in
tissues when administered repeatedly. In chronic users, the half-life of the
slower phase of delta-9-THC in blood plasma is 28 hours (as opposed to 57
hours for nonusers). Apparent volume of distribution is similar in both
groups. Chronic users eliminate significantly more polar metabolites in the
urine and less in the feces than nonusers. The total amount of metabolites
eliminated in both groups is the same and requires more than 1 week. The
more rapid urinary elimination of delta-9-THC metabolites in chronic users
give a biochemical basis to the development of tolerance occurring with
Cannabis use.

TISSUE STORAGE OF CANNABIS DERIVATIVES

One of the deceptive aspects of Cannabis derivatives is that their polar metabolites are stored in body tissues for as long as a week, long after their psychoactive effect has been dissipated. Repeated administration of Cannabis
preparations at less than 1-week intervals results in the accumulation of metabolites in tissues, including brain. Long-term effects of a chronic accumulation of polar metabolites will have to be appraised with special attention
to memory, affectivity, and performance of complex tasks. Possible relationship between this accumulation and the development of the "amotivational
syndrome" should be investigated.

The possible adverse effects resulting from tissue storage of the metabolites
of Cannabis derivatives are now recognized by the cautious investigator. As a
result, the Food and Drug Administration (1971) has formulated the following regulations regarding the use of Cannabis for clinical investigation in man:

1. Oral doses of the extract, delta-8- or delta-9-THC may be given daily for a period not to exceed one week. Parenteral doses or prolonged oral doses may not be administered to human subjects.

2. Inhalation studies involving the smoking of the standard extract of marihuana, delta-8- or delta-9-THC may be performed for short periods, i.e., 3 days, and repeated after a washout period of 3 days.

3. Studies utilizing the smoking of whole plant material may be performed for a period up to one month."

If such regulations do permit assessment of the acute effect of known amounts of the active ingredient of *Cannabis,* they preclude studies of chronic experimental use in the foreseeable future.

Man is today making great attempts to limit the pollution of his environment, poisoned by the industrial wastes of an unbridled technology. When one considers the accumulation of the metabolites of *Cannabis* derivatives in body fluids, the possibility of a pollution of the internal milieu by these metabolites after prolonged use of *Cannabis* derivatives cannot be excluded.

ACTIVE METABOLITES

While nonpsychoactive polar metabolites remain in tissues, and are slowly excreted in urine and feces, there is evidence (reviewed in Chapter 4) that psychoactive metabolites of delta-9- and delta-8-THC might also be formed (Truitt, 1971; Nakazawa and Costa, 1971). These are the 11-hydroxy THC compounds.

The possible participation of active metabolites of delta-9-THC to the development of the psychic effects of *Cannabis* intoxication is supported by observations of Lemberger et al. (1971*a*). They administered orally, to a chronic user, tracer doses of ^{14}C-tagged delta-9-THC along with a pharmacological carrier dose (0.3 mg/kg). Very little delta-9-THC was present in the plasma throughout the 10-hour observation period, while large amounts of polar metabolites, including 11-hydroxy THC compounds were present (Fig. 15). Their plasma concentration correlated well with the time course of psychic effects of orally administered delta-9-THC as reported by Hollister, Richards, and Gillespie (1968) (Fig. 16).

The exact contribution of all of these metabolites to the multiple psychological and behavioral effects and aftereffects of *Cannabis* intoxication will be very difficult to assess. Nonspecific enzymes (oxidases) in the microsomal

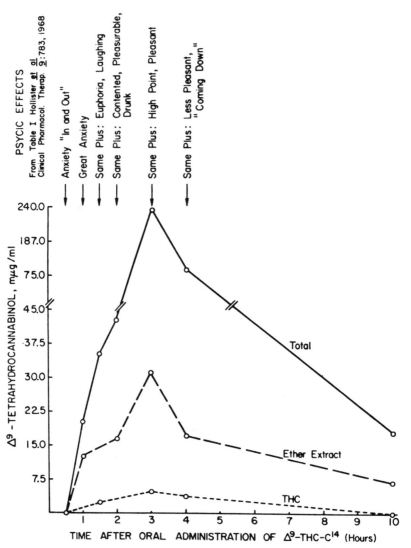

Fig. 16. Plasma levels of ^{14}C-labeled delta-9-THC, total radioactivity, and ether-extractable radioactivity after the oral administration of 0.3 mg/kg of delta-9-THC with 0.5 mg of ^{14}C-labeled delta-9-THC to a chronic *Cannabis* user. Blood samples were drawn at various times and plasma assayed for delta-9-THC, total radio-activity, and ether-extractable radioactivity. (From Lemberger, 1971.)

On the upper portion, the time course for the psychic effects of delta-9-THC after its oral administration (0.3 mg/kg) is described. (From Hollister, Richards and Gillespie, 1968.)

fraction of the cell are induced rapidly, *in vivo* and *in vitro,* to form these metabolites (Truitt, 1971). It is known that these same liver enzymes can be induced to higher rates of activity (initial methylation or hydroxylation steps) by repeated use of many other drugs, including barbiturates, antidepressants, tranquilizers, analgesics, and anticoagulants. Chronic administration of these drugs produces a metabolic tolerance due to an induction of an increased ac-

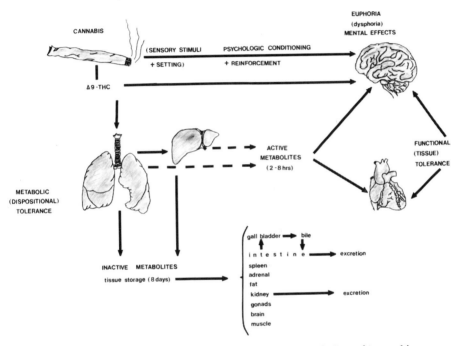

Fig. 17. Schematic representation of the multiple effects of *Cannabis* smoking on basic enzymatic and physiological mechanisms. These effects are mediated by delta-9-THC and possibly by active metabolites, and lead to the development of functional and metabolic tolerance.

tivity of these enzymes. All of these drugs interact with delta-9-THC and might alter its biotransformation and activity (Fig. 17).

The production of psychoactive metabolites of delta-9-THC by enzyme induction in liver and lung could account for the delayed appearance in many subjects of their first recorded manifestations of *Cannabis* intoxication. Few effects are reported when the drug is taken or smoked for the first time. They only appear after subsequent exposures, when the same dosage as taken the first time appears to be accompanied by greater effects. This phenomenon has been called "reverse tolerance." Pharmacologically, however, this so-called "reverse tolerance" is of brief duration and is followed by true tolerance. Indeed, as metabolic and functional tolerances rapidly develop to the drug, increments in delta-9-THC are required to obtain the same effects.

One may therefore expect the effects of delta-9-THC to vary considerably according to basal or induced activity of these enzymes in naive subjects, subjects taking *Cannabis* frequently, and subjects taking other drugs in addition.

PHYSICAL EFFECTS OF *CANNABIS* INTOXICATION

The Observations of Moreau

Moreau (1845) was the first to describe "the physical changes which ordinarily precede or accompany the mental problems caused by hashish." A careful observer, he noted a dose-response relationship between physical symptoms and dosage absorbed.

"With a weak dose, but still capable of profoundly changing the mind, physical effects are null, or at least so imperceptible that they would certainly go unrecognized if one who wants to experience them is not on the alert, and expecting their arrival. One might have an idea of this effect by recalling the feeling of well being, of pleasant expansiveness produced by a cup of coffee or tea taken at breakfast.

"By increasing the dose, this feeling becomes livelier and livelier, pervades all of your body and moves you more and more as though it were becoming profuse and were going to overflow. A light pressure is felt in the temples and the upper part of the skull. Respiration slows down, and the pulse rate accelerates, but feebly. A soft, gentle warmth comparable to that felt when taking a bath in winter, spreads throughout the body with the exception of the feet which usually become cold. The wrists and forearms grow numb, become heavier; it even happens that one shakes them instinctively as if to rid them of the weight that presses upon them. Then twitchings begin, principally in the lower extremities—they are vague, indefinable sensations that are characterized so well by their name. It is a sort of muscular quivering which the will has no power to control.

"Finally, if the dose has been considerable, it is not rare to see nervous phenomena appear which, in many ways, rather resemble choreic movements. Warm flushes suddenly invade your head in rapid spurts like steam escaping from the chimney of a locomotive. As I have heard it said several times, the brain boils over and seems to push against the top of the skull in order to escape. This sensation, which always causes a little fear no matter how accustomed one may be, is analogous to the noise that one hears when one's head is plunged into the water. Dizzy spells are rare; I have never had one. Buzzing in the ears, on the contrary is frequent. One feels anxiety at times, a sort of anguish, and a feeling of constriction in the epigastric area. Second only to the brain, it is in this region that hashish seems to produce the greatest effects.

"A young physician once said that he believed that he was seeing nervous currents circulating through the branches of his solar plexus. Heartbeats seem to have an unusual amplitude and resonance, but if one places his hand in the precordial region, one is easily reassured that the heart is not beating more strongly or faster than usual. Spasms in the limbs sometimes become very strong without actually turning into real convulsions. Action of the flexor muscles predominates. If one lies down, which one almost always feels in the need of doing, the calves bend involuntarily under the thighs, the forearms over the arms, which touch the sides of the chest, the head bends and sinks between the shoulders; the energetic contractions of the pectoral muscles interfere with the expansion of the thorax and stop the breathing. These symptoms are brief. They cease abruptly, only to suddenly reappear after intervals of perfect calm of a few seconds at first—then of several minutes —of a half-hour—of an hour—as one moves further away from the moment of their first appearance. The muscles of the face, particularly those of the jaw, may be also seized with spasmodic movements. On one occasion, I felt a real trismus. The hands seem to contract by themselves in order to grasp and tightly squeeze things.

"Such are all, or nearly all, the physical disorders caused by hashish, from the mildest to the most intense. They all relate to the nervous system. They develop much later than the mental disturbances: these faculties can be profoundly changed without giving rise to organic symptoms. Those who are in the habit of using hashish know very well how to avoid them. It is easily done by graduating the dose, and one can always become initiated into the marvels of hashish intoxication without purchasing this pleasure at the cost of any unpleasant nervous manifestation. It seems that the causal agent (the drug) acts directly on the faculties of the mind without the mediation of the organs, as in the case of mental illness."

These observations of Moreau were confirmed 100 years later when investigators were able to measure the physical changes produced by *Cannabis* intoxication.

Clinical Recording of the Physical Effects of Cannabis Intoxication

Subjects given *Cannabis* derivatives to smoke or ingest present very few physical changes which can be recorded objectively. Such changes were studied systematically for the first time by the investigators appointed by Mayor Fiorello La Guardia to study marihuana intoxication in the city of New York. Increased heart rate and dilation of conjunctival blood vessels are the most consistently observed changes following *Cannabis* intoxication. These measurable manifestations are not accompanied by any specific biochemical alterations in body fluids identifiable by present techniques.

Cardiovascular Effects. Cannabis derivatives acutely administered to Western smokers cause a significant increase in heart rate. The degree of tachycardia, which is related to the dose of delta-9-THC absorbed, reaches a maximum 30 min after smoking and persists for more than 40 min. In one study 65% of the increase in heart rate observed could be associated with the concentration of delta-9-THC in the cigarette (Johnson and Domino, 1971). Linear dose-response curves were obtained on heart rate of subjects smoking marihuana cigarettes containing 1 to 6.5 mg of delta-9-THC. Standardized smoke administration was delivered by a means of a spirometer (Fig. 18). A reproducible dose effect was observed in individual subjects, while variance between subjects in their heart rate response to marihuana inhalation was great. No difference was found between experienced and inexperienced smokers. Marihuana smoking suppressed the normal sinus arythmus as well as the bradycardia associated with the Valsalva maneuver. With the highest delta-9-THC concentration (6.5 mg), maximum heart rates were in the range of 140 to 160/min (Renault et al., 1971).

The increase in pulse parallels the intensity of the subjective effects. If the drug induces anxiety, a marked increase in heart rate occurs—while if it induces somnolence or sedation, a moderate rise is observed.

It should be noted that this increase in heart rate, which is the most consistently observed physical manifestation of *Cannabis* intoxication, was first reported only in 1940 by the authors of the La Guardia Report. None of the previous studies of *Cannabis* intoxication, such as the Indian Hemp Drug Commission Report of 1894 or subsequent ones from India or the Middle East, mentioned this basic physiological change. Since it is unlikely that ac-

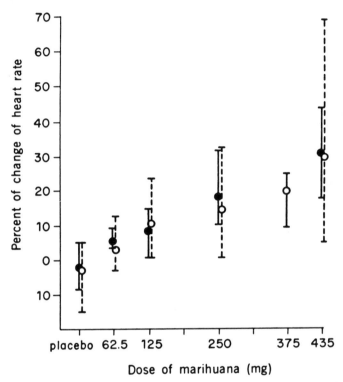

Fig. 18. Dose-response increase in heart rate following increasing doses of smoked marihuana. (From Renault et al., 1971.)

celeration of heart rate is specific to American users of *Cannabis,* one can surmise that physical examination of *Cannabis* users in other countries was not systematically performed.

In the study by Johnson and Domino (1971), changes in electrocardiogram were minimal, but premature ventricular contractions were observed in 2 of 15 subjects who smoked cigarettes containing 10 mg or more of delta-9-THC. Allentuck (1941) also reported in a few instances "a temporary sinus tachycardia or sinus bradycardia." By contrast, Isbell and Hollister did not report any arythmias occurring in the subjects they studied. In view of the high incidence of acute cardiac pathology in the United States, however, a systematic evaluation of the effects of *Cannabis* intoxication on the heart seems to be urgently warranted.

Changes in blood pressure have also been reported following *Cannabis* intoxication. Reports are conflicting. Isbell et al. (1967), who studied prisoners, experienced marihuana users, given 10 to 30 mg of delta-9-THC orally, reported no change or a decrease in blood pressure. So did Hollister (1971*a*), who studied student volunteers given larger doses (30 to 70 mg of delta-9-THC). With the higher dose, two of the subjects developed orthostatic hypotension. By contrast, Johnson and Domino report a significant rise in systolic and diastolic blood pressures when doses greater than 10 mg of delta-9-THC were inhaled. Allentuck, in the La Guardia Report, also states that "the increase in pulse rate was usually accompanied by a rise in blood pressure," and Williams et al. (1946), in his study of 17 subjects smoking marihuana *ad lib.* observed a slightly increased blood pressure. The significance of these conflicting reports is not clear. They indicate, in any event, that delta-9-THC might have variable and complex actions on blood-pressure regulating mechanisms, which preclude its use as an effective hypotensive agent in the treatment of elevated blood pressure. This is more so the case because effects on blood pressure due to *Cannabis* can only be observed with a dosage of delta-9-THC which produces marked mental and behavioral alterations.

Conjunctival blood vessel congestion is one of the most constant recognizable signs following marihuana smoking. This congestion is related to the dose of the drug; it lasts longer than the increase in heart rate produced by *Cannabis* intoxication, and is still apparent 90 min after smoking has terminated, but subsides in the following 24 hours. The mechanism of action is not known; it is not related to an irritation from smoke of the cigarette, but rather to direct action of the delta-9-THC on the conjunctival vessels. The active congestion of the transverse ciliary vessels has been reported in India among chronic users of *Cannabis* (ganja). It is accompanied by a yellow discoloration of the conjunctiva due to deposition of a yellow pigment around the vessels, and is reported to be still present years after the drug was withheld (Chopra, 1969).

Neuromuscular Changes. Cannabis intoxication does not alter deep tendon patellar or Achilles reflexes, unlike LSD, which produces a hyperreflectivity. In contradiction to earlier reports, pupil diameter is not changed following *Cannabis* intoxication. There is a muscle weakness which can be measured objectively by the ergograph test (Hollister et al., 1968). Ptosis of the eyelids is also observed (Domino, 1971), as well as an impairment of body and hand steadiness. The ataxia is in general in all directions rather than predominant in any particular axis; it can be ascribed to both the central and peripheral nervous system effects of *Cannabis,* which acts on the cerebellum and on the neuromuscular junction.

Electroencephalographic Changes. These changes, observed in occasional users smoking cigarettes containing a putative dose of 7.5 to 22.5 mg of delta-9-THC, are not very pronounced; they consist of an increase in percent time of alpha band and an associated reduction in theta and beta bands. However, another experiment performed by these same authors on chronic users showed that marihuana smoked for 10 to 22 days by four previous heroin addicts produced dysphoria and EEG synchronization (Volavka et al., 1971).

Effects on Sleep. Tart and Crawford (1970) report the effects of marihuana intoxication in sleep patterns in 150 experienced smokers. They report that moderate levels of marihuana intoxication have a sedative effect, but that high levels may overstimulate, ward off drowsiness, and make sleep poorer.

Other Neural Changes. Nausea with vasomotor imbalance and vomiting is often reported by inexperienced subjects using *Cannabis* extracts. Dryness of the mouth and nasopharyngeal mucosa is usually reported by the *Cannabis* smoker. This symptom might not be entirely due to the irritation of the smoking process and has been related to an atropine-like substance present in the smoke, which could cause a decrease in salivary flow (Gill et al., 1970).

Hepler and Frank (1971) reported that 9 of 11 subjects, after smoking 2g of marihuana containing .9% delta-9-THC in a water pipe, presented a significant decrease in intraocular pressure.

Alteration of Glucose Metabolism. Endocrine Studies. Many subjects have reported an increased appetite after *Cannabis* use, especially for sweets. This subjective symptom is not related to changes in blood sugar levels, which remain constant at times when the cardiovascular and psychological effects of the drug are maximal. However, an abnormal glucose tolerance test has been reported in "chronic" marihuana smokers.

Podolsky et al. (1971) studied the prolonged oral glucose tolerance test (G.T.T.) on four chronic marihuana smokers (21 to 24 years of age). Fasting blood sugar was measured, (1) after a week of abstaining from marihuana smoking (control), (2) following a week of daily smoking (1 cigarette with 1% delta-9-THC). G.T.T. deteriorated after the period of smoking (from 106 to 142 mg% at 30 min and from 107 to 130 mg% at 1 hour). Fasting blood glucose levels were not significantly different. There was no impairment of insulin release or elevation of growth hormone.

In studies where a single dose of 15 to 70 mg of delta-9-THC was ingested, there were no changes in plasma cortisol levels, platelet serotonin, blood chemistry and hematology, or urinary catecholamines excretion. Creatinine and phosphorous clearance were temporarily decreased, a phenomenon which has been observed with LSD (Hollister, 1968).

CLINICAL STUDIES WITH SMOKED *CANNABIS* EXTRACTS OR SYNTHETIC DELTA-9-THC

The Technique of Smoking the Marihuana Cigarette

Smoking is a common method of inducing *Cannabis* intoxication; it is the method of choice of marihuana users in the United States because a swift effect can be obtained with a small amount of the substance. Administration of the drug by vaporization approximates intravenous administration in rapidity of effect, though not in dosage. Sophisticated, experienced smokers who have not developed tolerance to the drug claim that they are able to titrate the amount which they need in order to obtain the desired effect. *Cannabis* cigarettes or "joints" are quite different from tobacco cigarettes, and the amount of substance available for smoking varies greatly. Most of these cigarettes are handmade; the dried material is unevenly packed in rectangular pieces of paper which are sealed over the chopped weed with saliva. The quality and porosity of the paper will determine the rate of consumption of the cigarette and the amount of air which enters the smoke stream. The method of smoking is quite particular, a deep inhalation which is held in the lungs as long as possible. The aim is to absorb as much of the intoxicating substance as possible, regardless of the discomfort, and attempts are made to limit "side-stream smoke," the smoke which escapes inhalation. All of the smoke is trapped in the tracheobronchial tree and nasopharynx, where it produces irritation and causes the novice smoker to cough and gag. The experienced smoker learns to overcome this natural reflex; furthermore, he will inhale with the smoke some cooler ambient air, a process which seems to increase the absorption of active material by the mucous membrane lining the respiratory tree. The *Cannabis* vapors are kept in the lung voluntarily as long as the subject can hold his breath. Some experienced smokers use the Valsalva maneuver, a forced expiration against a closed mouth and nose, so that the positive pressure in the airways increases absorption of inhaled smoke into the pulmonary circulation. After such a maneuver, very little visible smoke is exhaled. The act of smoking *Cannabis* is a rather contrived experience in breath holding, aimed at obtaining optimal absorption of the intoxicating material. This method, when well performed, is quite efficient, as shown by the rapid appearance of the physiological and psychological effects of *Cannabis* intoxication.

The Absorption of the Active Ingredient from the Smoke

The amount of active material absorbed in the blood stream is, in part, a function of the method of smoking. Therefore the experience of the smoker and his motivation to perform a given task influence the amount of inhaled smoke stored in the lungs. The amount of inhaled smoke may vary considerably, from 15 to 100 ml per inhalation. To control this variable it is important to measure tidal volume as well as amount of smoke inhaled and breath-holding time. Even so, different subjects will not have the same efficiency in delivering the active ingredients contained in their cigarette to their pulmonary vessel, through an optimal distribution of smoke in their lungs. This efficiency has been estimated to be between 20 and 50%, according to the experience of the smoker and the anatomical and physiological characteristics of his heart and lungs, and also the amount of the active *Cannabis* con-

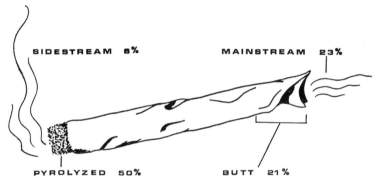

Fig. 19. Distribution of delta-9-THC in smoke of a marihuana cigarette consumed under standard conditions in the Batelle Laboratory, on a smoking machine. (From Truitt, 1971.)

stituents which can be transferred into the smoke. It is therefore difficult to gauge quantitatively the physiological and psychological effects of the same amount of *Cannabis* smoked by different subjects. And it is difficult to obtain typical dose-response curves, since the ultimate dose absorbed from the smoke tends to vary with each individual.

The relationship between the active constituents of the *Cannabis* cigarette and the chemical by-products which may be produced in the burning process of smoking (pyrolysis) was discussed in Chapter 3. The experiments performed by Manno et al. (1970) and by Truitt (1971) indicate that after ensuring complete smoking of the cigarette end, approximately 50% of the delta-9-THC originally present in the cigarette is delivered unchanged in the smoke (Fig. 19). Assuming that mainstream smoke (which is inhaled) accounts for 90% of the smoke produced by the burning cigarette, the maximum efficiency of delivery of delta-9-THC by an experienced smoker would be 45%, providing the entire cigarette is burned.

If the cigarette is not entirely consumed, as much as 50% of the delta-9-

THC may accumulate in the unburned end or "roach." In this case, the efficiency of transfer of delta-9-THC will be further decreased to 22%. Since half of the delta-9-THC may remain in the butt of a *Cannabis* cigarette, it is important in clinical experiments that all smokers consume their cigarettes to the same length. If they do not, the remaining butts should be weighed, and the delta-9-THC measured and subtracted from the original amount present in the cigarette.

The exact amount of delta-9-THC absorbed from a cigarette into the blood stream has not yet been accurately determined. The only precise manner is to use an isotope (^{14}C or ^{3}H) labeled compound in the cigarette. With such a method the exact amounts of delta-9-THC present in side-stream and mainstream smoke and in body fluids can be measured. An accurate estimate of the half-life, lung absorption, distribution, and excretion of delta-9-THC and its metabolites can be established and compared with the same factors when the drug is given orally or intravenously.

Some investigators have compared, in double-blind experiments, the effects of smoking *Cannabis* extracts of different potency in experienced and novice subjects with the effects produced by a placebo. Chronic *Cannabis* smokers claim that they are able to identify the cigarette containing psychoactive ingredients. It has been proven that this is not the case, especially when the cigarettes contain small doses of toxic material (1% delta-9-THC or less) (Jones, 1971a). The characteristic smell of burning *Cannabis* is not related to its active cannabinoids and cannot be an index of potency. It has been reported that a satisfactory placebo can be made with *Cannabis* from which the psychoactive ingredients have been extracted with petroleum ether. Known amounts of delta-9-THC can also be added to this same material. Placebo and drug-containing cigarettes prepared with this method had similar appearance, taste, smell, and burning characteristics. Other plant substances, such as oregano, catnip, tobacco, pansy, and other herbs have been tried as placebos, but have not been found satisfactory.

It is generally agreed that delta-9-THC is three to four times more potent when smoked than when taken orally. Smoking produces, within a few minutes, effects which last from 1 to 4 hours, according to dosage and many other individual and social factors. Oral dosage of greater potency is felt only after 1 hour but lasts for 6 to 8 hours. Some experienced smokers claim that they are able to titrate the amount of smoke absorbed in order to obtain the desired effect. Such claims are difficult to prove and to generalize to all smokers who are not strong-willed. Indeed, it is known that tolerance to *Cannabis* consumption does develop.

The reasons for the greater potency of smoked *Cannabis* in comparison with the preparation administered orally are not clear. It has been shown that the efficacy of the transfer of delta-9-THC from cigarette to the lung may vary from 10 to 50%. The fact that delta-9-THC may possibly induce in the lung active metabolites might be a reason for the greater activity of smoked marihuana. The by-products of ingested *Cannabis* first go through the liver, where some may be inactivated. The exact mechanisms of action of ingested and smoked *Cannabis* will be clarified only after completion of tracer studies.

The amount of active ingredients transferred through smoking *Cannabis* depends on many factors, including the method of smoking, the expertise of the smoker, the amount of mainstream smoke which can be trapped in the lung, the amount of side-stream smoke, and the amount of psychoactive substance trapped in the unburned cigarette end. It is very difficult to keep all of these factors uniform from one subject to the next, especially when dealing with inexperienced smokers. All of the studies performed must be analyzed very carefully to determine if the actual potency of the cigarette used was accurately assessed, and if all the variables that have been mentioned were properly controlled, since variations in the technique of smoking will produce significant variations in dose delivery. Unfortunately, a significant number of clinical studies did not control these important variables. As a result, the reported results are misleading; see, for example, Table 12, where the results of the first two studies are at variance with the subsequent ones, where the actual dosage of delta-9-THC was ascertained. (Note the dose-response relationship in the later studies.)

The Weil Study on the Clinical and Psychological Effects of Marihuana Smoking

The first laboratory study made by Weil et al. (1968) on smokers using marihuana cigarettes containing putative doses of 4.5 to 18 mg of delta-9-THC illustrates the uncertainties inherent in clinical investigations performed with *Cannabis* of uncertain potency. In this study nonusers experienced few subjective effects, demonstrated impaired performance on simple intellectual and psychomotor tests, moderate acceleration of heart rate (not dose related) and injection of the conjunctivae. "Experienced users" presented increases in heart rate higher than those observed in nonusers and not dose related, reported a subjective "high" and a "slight improvement" of their performance (pursuit rotor test and digit-symbol substitution test). On the basis of these observations, Weil et al. concluded that "marihuana is a relatively mild intoxicant," a view which can be shared only by all those who read their report. And readers were many, since Weil's paper was published in *Science,* was extensively quoted in Grinspoon's article on marihuana in *Scientific American* (1969), and was the subject of a feature article on the front page of *The New*

Table 12

Comparative Changes in Heart Rate Observed after Smoking Marihuana Cigarettes Containing Different Dosages of Delta-9-THC

Authors	Subjects	Dose Delta-9-THC (mg) in cigarettes	Heart rate				Psychomotor performance	
			Average increase (beats/min)	Time (Min)	Duration (Min)	Dose dependence	Change[a]	Dose dependence
Weil et al. (1968)	"Naive"	4.5 (alleged)	16	15	>90	No	Impaired (1)	Yes
		18.0 (alleged)	16	15	<90		Impaired (1)	
	"Chronic"	4.5 (alleged)	32	15	>90	No	Not changed (1)	No
		18.0 (alleged)	—	—	—		Not changed (1)	
Crancer et al., (1969)	"Naive"	22.0 (alleged)	?	?	?	?	Not changed (2)	No
	"Chronic"	22.0 (alleged)	?	?	?	No	Not changed (2)	
		66.0 (alleged)	?	?	?		Not changed (2)	
Isbell and Jasinski (1969)	"Experienced"	5.0	40	60	>240	Yes	Impaired (3)	Yes
		15.0	65	60	>240		Impaired (3)	
Manno et al. (1970)	"Experienced and naive"	5.0	16	20	>60	Yes	Impaired (4)	Yes
		10.0	36	20	>60		Impaired (4)	
Johnson and Domino (1971)	"Experienced"	1.5–5.0	10–20	5	>90	Yes	Not changed (5)	
		10.0–30.0	40–60	20	>120		Not performed	—
Dornbush et al. (1971)	"Experienced"	7.5	3–5	Immediate	20	Yes	Not changed (6)	Yes
		22.5	18–26	Immediate	60		Impaired (6)	
Renault et al. (1971)	"Inexperienced and experienced"	1.87	7[b]	10–20	>60	Yes	Not performed	—
		3.75	15[b]	10–20	>60			
		6.50	22[b]	10–20	>60			
Jones (1971a)	"Frequent"	9.0	17.3	30	—	—	Not impaired (7)	—
	"Infrequent"	9.0	32.0	30	—	—	Impaired (7)	

The results of the first two studies are at variance with the subsequent ones where the actual dosage of delta-9-THC was ascertained. Note the dose-response relationship in the later studies.

[a] (1) Pursuit rotor performance; (2) driving simulation; (3) questionnaire; (4) pursuit meter; (5) auditory and visual threshold; (6) reaction time, short-term memory; (7) digit symbol substitution, complex reaction time.

[b] assuming resting heart rate of 70/min.

York Times. This paper certainly contributed to the widely held belief in the United States that marihuana is a mild intoxicant with few untoward effects.

However, it is now apparent that the dose of psychoactive material absorbed in this study must have been quite low. All of the subsequent studies in which delta-9-THC was actually measured indicate that dosages similar to those used by Weil produced much more significant impairment in psychomotor performance and much more important dose-related increases in heart rate. On the basis of the experience of another investigator who used similar aged, unextracted natural material, the reported dose of delta-9-THC utilized by Weil might have been seven times lower than that actually assumed. However, in the discussions of his results, Weil does not mention at any time that the dosage he used might have been lower than assumed, in spite of the fact that he did not observe a dose-response increase in heart rate. It is clear from Weil's study that a scientist should not interpret as a reliable index of *Cannabis* intoxication the subjective feeling of a person who claims that he is experiencing a "normal social marihuana high."

The Crancer Study on the Effects of Marihuana on Driving Performance

A similar criticism can be made of the simulated driving study of Crancer et al. (1969), also published in *Science* and quoted in part in *Scientific American*. Driving skills of subjects were tested with a driving simulator after they had consumed enough alcohol to approximate concentrations of 100 mg/100 ml plasma or had smoked 2 marihuana cigarettes containing putative doses of 22 mg of delta-9-THC. Such a dose, in the careful studies of Isbell et al. (1967) reported two years earlier produced, when "smoked," hallucinations, depersonalization, and derealization. Furthermore, all of the subjects in Crancer's study were favorably disposed towards marihuana, and some might have been tolerant to its effects while having a bias against alcohol. Under conditions of "marihuana intoxication," speedometer errors were increased (the subjects did not watch the speedometer carefully), but driving was not otherwise impaired. By contrast, profound impairment was observed with the large doses of alcohol administered (equivalent to 0.7 to 0.9 ml of 95% ethanol per pound). Crancer and associates also tested four inexperienced users, who showed either no change or negligible improvement in their scores. They also gave to four "habitual users" three times the dose used in their first experiment (66 mg of delta-9-THC), and these subjects did not show any significant driving impairment. Crancer concluded "that impairment in simulated driving performance is not a function of increased marihuana dosage or inexperience with the drug." He does not discuss the discrepancy between his study and that of Isbell. However, he is careful not to state that the use of marihuana will not impair actual driving on the road, or that it is safer to use than alcohol. But some of the readers of his paper were less cautious.

Grinspoon (1969), discussing the Crancer study, stated, "It was found that marihuana causes significantly less impairment of driving ability than alcohol does." Grinspoon also relies heavily on the studies of Weil and Crancer in his book *Marihuana Reconsidered* (1971), where he asserts that "if an habitual or relatively frequent user has a specific self- or other-assigned task to carry out he will be able to do so as effectively while experiencing a "social marihuana high" as he would if he were entirely drug-free and in some cases he may perform more efficiently or accurately." This book was hailed in *The New York Times Book Review* (1971) as presenting "the best dope on pot so far."

John Kaplan devotes five pages of his book, *Marihuana—The New Prohibition* (1971), to the Crancer study, prefacing this section with the following statement: "There is at least some evidence that the marihuana-using driver is a much less serious problem than his alcohol-using counterpart. Probably the most dramatic evidence of this is the study by Crancer. . . ." This statement immediately follows another equally misleading one: "Experimental research does reveal that marihuana does not impair the reflexes." Such observations contrast with those of Isbell, who reported that smoking cigarettes containing 16 mg delta-9-THC was accompanied by hallucinations and, in one instance, by psychotic episodes. No such symptoms were reported by Weil, who used a putative dose of 18 mg, or by Crancer, who used alleged doses of 22 to 66 mg of delta-9-THC. It would appear that somebody must be wrong.

The Crancer study is also quoted in another widely circulated monograph on *Cannabis* by Schofield (1971), a British psychologist. "This experimental study has shown that *Cannabis* has very little effect on driving ability."

The 1971 N.I.M.H. Report to Congress on Marihuana and Health also reports uncritically the Crancer study and concludes that "the legal level of alcohol intoxication (used in the study) is probably higher than typical levels of social use of alcohol. By contrast, the use of marihuana used in this research may have more closely approximated a typical level of social marihuana use." If the authors of the N.I.M.H. report are correct, marihuana used socially in the United States is more closely related to lawn grass than to the drug-type of *Cannabis sativa* which has been used through the centuries for its intoxicating properties.

The Dose-Related Studies of Isbell and Forney

Isbell used delta-9-THC which had been prepared and assayed by Korte from the Institute of Organic Chemistry of Bonn University in Germany.

Forty healthy former opiate addicts serving prison sentences and abstinent from all drugs were studied. In addition to physical changes (such as rectal temperature, pulse rate, blood pressure, pupillary diameter), subjective effects were evaluated by means of a questionnaire containing 63 questions. This questionnaire permits assessment of personality and mood alterations typically considered to be important determinants of drug effects. Thirty questions were selected from the "general drug," "marihuana," and LSD scales of the Addiction Research Inventory, while the remaining 33 questions dealt with alterations in mood, distortion, and sensory perceptions, alterations in body-image illusions, delusions, and hallucinations, and were designated as the psychotomimetic scale. A dose of 0.05 mg/kg of delta-9-THC smoked or 0.12 mg/kg ingested produced euphoria as well as time-sense and perceptual changes. A dose of 0.2 to 0.25 mg/kg smoked or 0.3 to 0.48 mg/kg ingested was accompanied by marked distortion in visual and auditory perception, derealization, depersonalization, and hallucinations. Isbell also established that for each subject physical changes (increases in pulse rate) and psychological changes were dose dependent. In a subsequent study he compared delta-9-THC (15 to 225 μg/kg smoked) and LSD (0.5 to 1.5 μg, i.m.) in the same eight subjects. While the objective effects of both drugs were markedly different, the subjective effects could not be readily distinguished by using the special drug scales developed at the Addiction Research Center. Two patients of 10 withdrew after experiencing psychotic reactions following THC. Both drugs were shown to be psychotomimetics—LSD was 160 times as potent as THC on the psychotomimetic scale and 150 times as potent as THC on the general drug scale. But patients tolerant to LSD were not cross tolerant to THC, indicating that the mental effects of the two drugs are mediated by different mechanisms.

The pioneering observations of Isbell on the adverse effects of delta-9-THC on mental performance were substantiated by subsequent well-controlled studies performed by Forney's group (1971). They compared the effect of placebo cigarettes with those containing marihuana extracts containing 10 mg of delta-9-THC, THC being assayed by the investigators themselves with the use of gas chromatography. These authors had demonstrated in previous studies that a cigarette containing 10 mg of delta-9-THC, smoked with maximum efficiency, will deliver to the subject 5 mg of THC.

Cannabis impaired performance significantly on a pursuit meter as well as on five of nine performance tests done under conditions of delayed auditory feedback. Many more subjective symptoms were reported by those who smoked *Cannabis* than by those who smoked the placebo cigarettes, and all were able to identify the active cigarettes without error. However, half of the group also reported that the placebo cigarettes were active, which confirms the studies of Jones regarding the unreliability of subjective identification of

Cannabis intoxication induced by smoking, because of the associated sensory perceptions which favor psychological conditioning. With available techniques, it was not possible to detect any cannabinols in the blood or urine of the subjects who smoked the *Cannabis*.

A subsequent study made by the same group cast still more uncertainty on the validity of the results reported by Weil and Crancer. Twelve volunteers smoked placebo or marihuana cigarettes calibrated to deliver 2.5 or 5 mg of delta-9-THC, which amounts to the same or half the putative doses used by Weil et al. (1968), and one-quarter to one-sixth of the putative doses used by Crancer et al. (1969). In the course of the experiments the subjects were also given fruit juice or ethanol so as to produce a concentration of 50 mg/100 ml of plasma. All subjects who smoked *Cannabis* presented a significant decrease in motor and mental performance which was equal to or greater than the dose produced by the alcohol. Alcohol produced an additive effect on performance impairment.

Hollister, a seasoned clinical pharmacologist specializing in the study of marihuana, commenting on the Crancer study, has this to say: "We simply asked our subjects when they were high (on marihuana), 'Do you think you could drive a car?' Without exception the answer from those who had really gotten high has been 'no' or 'you must be kidding.' "

In another study, 10 experienced marihuana smokers who smoked 2 to 3 cigarettes each containing an alleged dosage of 3.9 mg of delta-9-THC had only minimal effects (jocularity, loosening of associations). When the material smoked was reanalyzed, a 10-fold decrease of its original potency was recorded. It is also probable that the lack of untoward effects of *Cannabis* in psychomotor performance reported in the studies of Weil and Crancer might have been caused by the subthreshold amounts of delta-9-THC present in the material they used. This psychoactive substance is inactivated by exposure to air, moisture, and light. It is therefore important for each investigator to assay the material he uses by independently calibrated techniques, as was done by Isbell et al. and by Forney et al.

A careful analysis of the studies performed on marihuana smokers illustrates the uncertainties inherent in smoking the unextracted *Cannabis* weed available in the United States. A great deal of this weed contains little or no delta-9-THC or rapidly loses its potency if not properly stored. The deceptive aspect of many of the studies (see Table 2) conducted with smoked marihuana is now quite apparent, because the following factors were not ascertained: (1) the amount of active ingredients in the cigarette; (2) the fraction of the psychoactive material absorbed by the subject; (3) the extent of the placebo effect or psychological conditioning produced in "habitual smokers" by the smoking process. Only double-blind studies performed with carefully titrated extracted material indistinguishable from a placebo gave an opportunity to distinguish drug effect from psychological and emotional learned response. Such studies were performed by Jones (1971*a*, 1971*b*).

The Experiments of Jones on Casual and Habitual Marihuana Smokers

Jones has attempted to distinguish the effects of the psychological and emotional conditioning associated with marihuana smoking from the pharmacological effects of the drug. His studies were performed over a period several years on a large sample of young marihuana smokers from the San Francisco area.

One hundred paid student volunteers from the University of California who had smoked marihuana intermittently or daily for 3 years were given a 1-g marihuana cigarette containing either 0.9% delta-9-THC or a placebo. The amount absorbed by each individual smoker could not be assessed, and was probably quite different from one to another, but it could not have been greater than 4 to 5 mg (50% of the amount present in the cigarette). The subjects were asked to rate the subjective estimation of their intoxication on a scale from 0 to 100. The mean rating of the group was 61 for marihuana and 34 for the placebo—but there was considerable overlap in individual ratings. Placebo was rated from 0 to 90, *Cannabis* from 0 to 95. Many subjects estimated that placebo and marihuana cigarettes were equal in potency. This was especially true for the frequent users of *Cannabis* (more than 1 cigarette a day) who had developed a tolerance to the drug and rated placebo 52 and marihuana 48. For these "experienced, sophisticated users of *Cannabis*," the olfactory, oral, and upper airway sensory perceptions associated with smoking were sufficient to recapture the euphoric sensations they had felt in previous intoxications.

By contrast, infrequent smokers (less than 2 cigarettes a month), rated the marihuana significantly higher (67) than the placebo (22). This well-documented observation is at variance with the new *Cannabis* folklore entertained by "marihuana smokers" (Goode, 1970), who claim that the experienced smoker is able to judge the intoxicating quality of the grass. "The greater the amount of experience with the drug," says Goode, "the less likely it is that the subject has experienced either no reaction or nothing but a placebo reaction. In fact, the likelihood that a given person who has smoked marihuana more than a dozen times thinks that he has been high without actually experiencing what a truly experienced user would call a high, is practically nil." This possibility is far from nil, as shown by the studies of Jones. The frequent users, on the average, rated the effects of placebo and marihuana cigarettes similarly. As Jones says, "There may be a credibility gap in the marihuana culture." "The marihuana smoker makes the same misjudgment of psychotropic drug effects frequently made by consumers and professionals alike" (Lennard et al., 1971).

The importance of psychological conditioning in frequent marihuana smokers was further illustrated by the fact that they gave a low rating (32) to delta-9-THC (25 mg) administered orally. When these frequent users of *Cannabis* did not experience the familiar oral and nasal sensory perceptions associated with smoking, they were unable to recapture a euphoric state of mind, and their physical or pharmacological tolerance to *Cannabis* became apparent. Many of these students had developed physical tolerance to *Cannabis* without even knowing it. Instead of increased sensitivity to *Cannabis,* the data of Jones suggests that tolerance to the physiological and psychological effects of marihuana develops in frequent users. Pulse-rate increase was significantly smaller and decrease in salivary flow was less marked in the frequent users than in infrequent users. Psychomotor performance, as measured by complex reaction time and digit-symbol substitution, was significantly impaired only in occasional smokers. Jones also demonstrated that marihuana smokers experienced greater euphoria and less dysphoria when they smoked in groups than when they smoked alone. Jones concludes, "These data suggest that marihuana, when smoked at 'socially relevant doses,' produces a level of intoxication that allows the attitude of the subject, his set and expectations, the setting and his past experience to interact in a complex way to determine how the subjective state will be labeled and reported. Many people have uncritically accepted the belief that the drug has specific effects on behavior and experience, and that these can be readily identified. Although at high doses such a model may be valid, at the doses most youthful drug users are discussing, there is ample evidence that the effects of psychoactive drugs on behavior and experience are often independent of the drugs' pharmacologic effects."

The pattern of response of the smokers studied by Jones is consistent with the model in which the smoker may obtain intermittent response from delta-9-THC, but where much of the behavior and subsequent response is maintained by conditioned reinforcement, "such as the ritual of lighting up in group, and the associated stimuli of smell, taste and visual perception."

Jones criticizes the investigators who depend upon a subjective response to gauge *Cannabis* intoxication. "They do so at the risk of studying behavior in a non-specific psychological state rather than the pharmacological action of marihuana." Many physicians will agree on this point.

But Jones claims that the researcher must also attempt to "quantify the effect of interpersonal stimulation and the effects of subject expectation on the pharmacological action of *Cannabis.*" By doing so, the researcher will be able to relate in "a meaningful way" the pharmacological effects of *Cannabis* to a given subjective state. Such complex investigations are of great interest from a scientific viewpoint, and will require formidable academic talent and financial outlay. But one fails to see how such studies will answer the basic question asked of the physician: Does *Cannabis* represent a hazard to the health of man and especially of growing man?

The criterion used by Jones to define marihuana dosage is somewhat fragile, since he speaks of a "social relevant dose." How can such a dose be defined in terms of the present unstable student milieu? Jones criticizes the investigators who interpret experimental data on the basis of subjective response of the *Cannabis* smoker, but he accepts the criterion of the "social relevant dose," which is a still more uncertain yardstick.

The Smoking of Marihuana, "a Mild Intoxicant," or an "Hallucinogen"

Weil et al. (1968) state that "the researcher who set out with prior conviction that hemp is psychotomimetic or a mild hallucinogen is likely to confirm his conviction experimentally, but he would probably confirm the opposite hypothesis if his bias were in the opposite direction." This statement is quite pertinent, but it is equally true that the psychotomimetic effect of a drug can certainly not be established if one uses a compound from which the basic psychotropic ingredient is missing. It is unfortunate that Weil's studies, which were so widely heralded by the lay and scientific press as indicating that *Cannabis* is a mild intoxicant, were done with plant material which seemed to contain subthreshold dosages of intoxicating substance. Not only were the investigators who performed these studies somewhat deceived by this deceptive weed, but they in turn deceived thousands of educators and students and millions of young people and laymen. The doses of delta-9-THC in the *Cannabis* used in the studies reporting minimal psychological effects were either assayed in the laboratory by ultraviolent absorption spectrophotometry or by the National Institute of Mental Health (N.I.M.H.). It is now established that it is not possible to separate quantitatively various cannabinoids present in *Cannabis* by ultraviolet absorption spectrophotometry. Furthermore, discrepancies have been reported between assays performed first at the N.I.M.H. with gas chromatography and subsequently at private laboratories (samples of marihuana allegedly containing 1.3% delta-9-THC were found to have only 0.2% delta-9-THC). These discrepancies might be due to spontaneous inactivation in the crude material of delta-9-THC during transport or storage.

One wonders why the studies by Crancer and Weil were so widely publicized by the scientific and lay press, while those by Manno and Isbell went practically unnoticed except by the few thousand readers of the *Journal of Clinical Pharmacology and Therapeutics* or the still fewer who read *Psychopharmacologia.* And why do many investigators still fail to recognize the methodological shortcomings of the early studies of Weil and Crancer? Snyder, for instance, in his 100-page book, *The Uses of Marihuana,* devotes four pages to Weil's study, and two pages to Crancer's. He accepts uncritically their results and not once raises the possibility that these authors might have used marihuana containing subthreshold dosage of delta-9-THC in studies where dose-response relationships were not observed. Snyder notes the discrepancies between the results of Weil and Crancer and those observed by Clark et al. (1968, 1970) and by Forney (1971), who reported significant psychomotor impairment caused by smaller doses of delta-9-THC. Such discrepancies lead Snyder to state: "The reader is free to choose from among the findings of Weil, Clark, and Kiplinger groups those which agree with his own viewpoint." Such a statement ignores the basic scientific method, which has always narrowed down differences on the basis of careful factual interpretation of objectively measured data. To suggest that the reader may be free to choose according to his own viewpoint or preconceived ideas is to invite polarization in a debate already too emotionally charged.

CLINICAL STUDIES WITH ORAL DOSES OF CANNABIS OR OF DELTA-9-THC

All of the recent studies performed on volunteers given oral doses of *Cannabis* material assayed for delta-9-THC content, or known amounts of synthetic delta-9-THC, yield more uniform results than the studies performed with smoked material. For one thing, the psychological conditioning which affects marihuana smokers is not operative.

The findings of the first study performed by Isbell on former narcotic addicts serving prison sentences have already been mentioned. They have been in the main largely confirmed by other groups who used, in addition to synthetic THC, crude marihuana extracts carefully assayed for THC content. Hollister et al. (1968) used a group of student volunteers who ingested doses of 30 to 70 mg of THC, which corresponds to about twice the dosage used by Isbell. Perceptual and psychic changes reported by the subjects indicated more pronounced euphoria than that experienced by the prisoners studied by Isbell in a correctional institution. Sleepiness was observed more consistently, with deep sleep following the higher dose. Time sense was altered, hearing was less discriminate, and visual distortion was common. Depersonalization and difficulty in concentrating and thinking were predominant.

Many of the symptoms produced were like those elicited by the psycho-tomimetics LSD, mescaline, and psilocybin, but Hollister observed fewer of such effects than Isbell did. Hollister also studied the effect of synhexyl, a synthetic delta-8-THC homolog, which was extensively studied for possible clinical application. Similar effects were reported with this compound, but three times greater dosage was required.

Mechoulam (1970) reports that one of his subjects after ingesting 20 mg of delta-9-THC "fell into a panicky nearly psychotic state and needed help by the attendant psychiatrist." The other volunteers reported general feeling of euphoria, increased sensitivity to sound, mental confusion and depersonaliza-tion.

Zeidenberg (1971) reports that one of four volunteers (residents in psychia-try) after ingesting 15 mg of delta-9-THC experienced most of the perceptual distortions reported by Hollister, but with dysphoria and later had moderate depression. He became paranoid, had feelings which were borderline de-lusional and "that he felt psychotic and had a thought disorder." The three other subjects enjoyed their experiences which included many of the symptoms discussed by Moreau (euphoria, temporal and sensory distortions, deperson-alization).

In a study performed by a group from the N.I.M.H., 20 mg of delta-9-THC (putative dosage) was administered to 32 prisoners, paid volunteers who were ignorant of the nature of the drug under study, and who were studied in a neutral setting (Waskow et al., 1970). These subjects presented very mild physiological changes, with increases in heart rate much smaller than those reported by Isbell with similar or even lower dosages, raising the ques-tion of the real potency of the drug administered. They felt, nevertheless, "considerable somatic discomfort, dizziness, weirdness, dream-like state, visual changes, alteration in time sense, and cognitive impairment." The feeling of euphoria, though present in some subjects, was not predominant.

In the studies of Hollister, repetitive psychometric tests of arithmetic ability or free-hand drawing were impaired in different ways, indicating slowing of performance against time and loss of finer judgment. Subjects studied by the N.I.M.H. groups showed that only accuracy of serial addition was im-paired but that other simple cognitive measurements (ability to say the alpha-bet or count backward) were not altered.

Studies were also performed on volunteers given placebos or oral doses of crude marihuana extracts assayed for delta-9-THC content, which ranged from 5 to 60 mg. In general, the effects produced by these extracts were comparable to those produced by similar amounts of synthetic delta-9-THC. Ingestion of extracts containing the equivalent amounts of 20, 40, and 60 mg of delta-9-THC produced impairment of short-term memory; these impairments did not follow a smooth time function but were episodic, brief in duration, and not always under volitional control; they were accompanied by intermittent lapses of memory. Furthermore, oral doses of marihuana extract containing 40 to 60 mg of delta-9-THC significantly impaired the social coordination of cognitive operations during a task that required sequential adjustments in reaching a goal. This disintegration of sequential thought is related to impaired immediate memory and is associated with disorganized speech and thinking. Disturbance of this type has been called "temporal disintegration." *Cannabis* does, therefore, interfere with the cerebral mechanism which controls the selection of information deriving from immediate memory storage. The influence of chronic *Cannabis* intoxication on that mechanism, which is so important in the learning process during the formative school years, is not known, but one cannot exclude the possibility that it could be significantly impaired. The temporal incoordination of recent memory with a task to achieve may account in part for the speech pattern of the marihuana user, who is not able to coordinate recent memory with immediate temporal goals. The intoxicated subject forgets what he is about to say, and he has a strong tendency to discuss matters that have nothing to do with the preceding sentence because the logical sequence of his thought escapes him. He acknowledges that he needs to exert a considerable effort in order to recall from one moment to the other the logical thread of what he is in the process of expressing.

Clark and Nakashima (1968) also used oral marihuana extracts on volunteer subjects never exposed before to *Cannabis* and studied their discriminatory and retentive faculties. They observed the disruptive effects of *Cannabis* in sequential thought which suggest impairment of rapid decision making and of short-term memory. They noted important variations in the same subject and from one subject to another as far as the dose required to impair individual performance. These authors conclude: "These results are consistent with those reached when studying the influence of drugs such as LSD on such a complex state as behavior which is influenced by a multitude of nonpharmacological factors. It is impossible to predict the effect of marihuana on different individuals or on the same individual at different times and in different circumstances. This impossibility to predict the effects of *Cannabis* still increases the dangers of using that drug."

In a subsequent experiment with a dose of *Cannabis* equivalent to 0.66 mg/kg of delta-9-THC, they observed significant impairment in complex reaction time, digit-code memory, time estimation, hand steadiness, and reading comprehension. The sporadic nature of the effect was noted, with lapses in psychomotor response as attention waned.

These studies with ingested *Cannabis* extract confirm the psychotomimetic properties of *Cannabis* first described by Moreau. They indicate the greater danger of using this route of administration, which requires larger dosage and is accompanied by much less psychological conditioning and therefore a more rapid development of tolerance.

RELEVANCE OF LABORATORY EXPERIMENTS WITH *CANNABIS* AND ITS ACTUAL USE

Some investigators question the relevance of experiments performed on volunteers in a laboratory setting with "large doses of strong, synthetic material" to the social use of marihuana smoked in an amount sufficient to produce a "normal, socially acceptable high."

Jones (1971*a*) claims, for instance: "To do socially relevant experiments with marihuana in the laboratory one must have some idea of what dose people are smoking in a 'typical, social situation.' "

How "typical" of *Cannabis* use is the social situation on a California campus in 1970? Patterns of behavior on an American university campus do change rapidly as they reflect alterations in political, religious, and economic factors. What is typical today may be atypical tomorrow. Should one therefore plan on yearly studies of marihuana use in a student community to keep up with the different interactions that changing social factors have on the pharmacological effects of *Cannabis?* Is it not on the quicksand characteristic of adolescent behavior on a university campus that one can establish typical patterns of *Cannabis* use. How can one generalize from the "typical" use of marihuana in a California university in 1970, to the "typical" use of marihuana elsewhere in America or in the rest of the world? The social relevance of the experimental study of a drug is based on its prospective value for the individual and society over a period of time which spans a lifetime. Such a study must attempt to answer, not elude, the following question: "To what extent does the chronic use of *Cannabis* harm man and society?"

Jones's study contains exceedingly socially relevant data which should outlast the "typical social situation" of the California student milieu of 1970 and will endure in any social situation throughout the world: (1) That tolerance develops to daily marihuana users in spite of self-denial; (2) That daily users "tend to have poorer work histories, school performance, and social adjustments."

Other investigators were given the task of evaluating the "biomedical effects of marihuana on man in the military environment" (Federation of American Societies for Experimental Biology, 1971). After reviewing all of the experimental evidence, which indicates that marihuana disintegrates mental function, they were still not convinced that *Cannabis* intoxication might impair psychomotor performance in a military situation. Indeed, they concluded, "the results of laboratory testing procedures of a man's performance may not reflect his performance using sophisticated military equipment in field operations. Therefore, model field exercises must be conducted with military equipment and include command responsibilities, judgment, and execution of commands to determine the effects of marihuana on man in the military environment. The unique facilities and experience at the Army Edgewood Arsenal with incapacitating agents provide an unparalleled opportunity for studies of the effects of marihuana on human performance." However, one might surmise that the effects of marihuana use on the performance of American soldiers in Vietnam, which have been the subject of several military reports (Colbach, 1971; Joel Kaplan, 1971), might have helped to assess the effect of this drug on the performance of complex tasks in a combat situation. These reports are not discussed in this survey except the report of Talbott and Teague (1969) on marihuana-induced psychoses in 12 soldiers in Vietnam, which is briefly dismissed with the comment, "Additives may have produced the psychotic-like effects in military personnel who had smoked marihuana in Vietnam."

In civilian life, however, as shown by Hollister (1968) and Tart (1970), it is possible through the use of questionnaires to gather a basic group of symptoms which can be specifically tabulated for the different psychotropic drugs. It can now be reported that the clinical symptoms observed and described in laboratory studies of *Cannabis* intoxication are quite similar to those described by those who use the drug socially. One such questionnaire shows that the most common symptoms reported are floating sensations, depersonalization, weakness, relaxation, perceptual changes in vision, hearing, and touch, subjective slowing of time, loss of attention and immediate memory, difficulty of concentration, euphoria, and sleepiness. Other answers indicate increased insight and enhanced sexual performance and enjoyment, claims which cannot be verified in the ordinary laboratory. Another questionnaire study of 42 randomly selected students who had used marihuana indicate the following results: 90% had experienced minor changes in perception (seeing colors or objects as more intense); about half had experienced major perceptual changes (hallucinating colors or designs); and 40% had experienced hallucinogenic reactions. These were as frequent among those who had not used mescaline or LSD as among those who had, and it was not necessary to have used marihuana a great many times to present these reactions. It was concluded from these questionnaires that *Cannabis* is a hallucinogen, a statement which concurs with that made by Moreau after he experienced the drug himself in 1840. All of these inquiries indicate that the respondents to the questionnaire corroborated experimental observations and had experience with the same range of dosage used in the laboratory. Some of the dosages used were larger than required to produce a "normal, socially acceptable high," since hallucinogenic responses were frequently reported (Hollister, 1971a).

INTERACTION OF CANNABIS WITH OTHER DRUGS

It has been demonstrated in the experimental animal that delta-9-THC interacts with many commonly used psychotropic drugs: It acts synergistically with amphetamines and caffeine. It potentiates the depressant action of barbiturates and ethanol (see Chapter 4). In man, a similar potentiating effect between *Cannabis* preparations and ethanol has been observed (Manno et al., 1971), and there is good reason to believe that interactions between *Cannabis* preparations and barbiturates, caffeine, and amphetamine are also present. In addition to all of these drugs so commonly used in our society, one should mention the antihistamines, tranquilizers, phenothiazine, benzodiazepine, imipramines, and butyrophenones. The resulting interactions of delta-9-THC and other cannabinoids with these drugs, which may stimulate or inhibit the same enzyme systems, must be carefully appraised. Indeed, it has already been established that regular users of *Cannabis* do not abstain from smoking cigarettes or drinking alcoholic beverages. They are also prone to experiment and use other psychotropic drugs (see Chapter 7). The frequent daily smokers studied by Jones used more hallucinogens, alcohol, and tobacco than occasional smokers. The marihuana smoker also tends to be a heavy smoker of tobacco cigarettes. The mere act of smoking may enable him to recapture, through psychological conditioning associated with similar sensory perceptions, some of the pleasant effects of *Cannabis* intoxication. It will be of interest to study the interaction of tobacco and *Cannabis* on lung and heart function.

The use of multiple drugs by daily chronic smokers of marihuana in the United States is so prevalent that it led Mirin et al. (1971) to the following conclusions: "It is difficult to assess the effects of marihuana per se in many heavy users, since what is observed is a multiple drug abuse syndrome."

TOLERANCE

That tolerance to *Cannabis* may develop in man as it does in animals was first indicated by the 1894 report of the Indian Hemp Drug Commission:

"Powerful and noxious drugs are occasionally introduced into the pipe; but this practice is confined to those excessive consumers *on whom hemp alone has ceased to produce the desired effect* of exhilaration or stupefaction." Evidence derived from observations made in India suggest that tolerance develops with chronic use of potent preparations. It would indeed appear doubtful that Indian smokers of ganja or charas could consume daily an estimated average of 700 mg of delta-9-THC, as reported by Chopra and Chopra (1939), without having developed some tolerance (Table 13). A similar dose in a novice would produce acute psychotomimetic toxic effects. This tolerance would explain why chronic users of *Cannabis* may use large amounts of potent preparations without suffering any apparent severe somatic toxicity. These older reports have been corroborated by more recent ones. Morrow, who performed psychomotor tests on nonusers and habitual users of *Cannabis,* states in the La Guardia Report that "Non-users generally seem to be more affected by the drug when it is ingested than are users." Williams and co-workers (1946) reported that the repeated administration to volunteers of synhexyl (a synthetic derivative of *Cannabis* which could be given in known amounts) or the *ad lib.* smoking of marihuana cigarettes resulted in decreasing effects within 4 to 6 days. The subjects requested an increase in dose; during the experimental period, which lasted 39 days (Table 14), the number of cigarettes smoked daily by the subjects increased, and the users experienced "euphoria for several days," then "general lassitude and indifference." These observations indicate that chronic marihuana smokers may well develop tolerance to the psychological as well as the physiological effects of *Cannabis* intoxication.

Wilson and Linken (1968) reported from England that a few adolescent *Cannabis* users tend to use increasing doses. These chronic smokers, who find great difficulty in breaking the habit and do not particularly enjoy their dependent needs, appear to suffer from some degree of psychic dependence coupled with a requirement for fairly high doses of the drug.

Miras (1969) reported that "hashish smokers he has known in Greece for 20 years are able to smoke at least 10 times as much as other people. If a beginner smoked the same quantity he would collapse."

The rapid development of tolerance to *Cannabis* preparations is noted in a report describing the respiratory complications of 31 young American soldiers stationed in Germany. They smoked monthly, for 6 to 15 months, 100 g or more of hashish, probably smuggled from North Africa or the Middle East. "Every patient described the development of this hashish tolerance as one which simply occurred by consuming increasing amounts over a few weeks' period" (Tennant et al., 1971). This amount corresponds to 3 to 4 cigarettes a day containing 1 g of hashish, which would represent 20 to 70

Table 13

Estimates of Amount and Delta-9-THC Content of *Cannabis* consumed per day[a]

Country	Preparation	Median daily dose		Maximum daily dose		Reference[c]
		Weight (g)	Delta-9-THC (mg)[b]	Weight (g)	Delta-9-THC (mg)[b]	
Egypt	Hashish[d]	1.1	55	4	200	Soueif, 1967
Egypt	Hashish	—	—	4	200	Abdulla, 1953
India	Bhang	1.3	13	—	—	Chopra, 1940; Chopra and Chopra, 1939
	Bhang	6.0	60	24	240	Indian Hemp Drug Commission, 1894
	Ganja	1.2	36	—	—	Chopra, 1940
	Ganja	1.9	57	—	—	Chopra, 1969
India (Bengal)	Ganja	1.0	30	12	360	Indian Hemp Drug Commission, 1894
India (Punjab)	Ganja	2.2	66	—	—	Indian Hemp Drug Commission, 1894
India	Ganja or charas	0.5	15[e]	—	—	Chopra, 1935
India	Ganja or charas	5.0	150[e]	24	720[e]	Chopra and Chopra, 1939
Morocco	Kif	6.0	60	18	180	Sigg, 1963
South Africa (*ad lib.* experiments)	Dagga	1.3	13	2	20	Pretoria Mental Hospital Report, 1938
United States (*ad lib.* experiments)	Marihuana	2.5	25	10	100	Siler et al., 1933
	Marihuana	8.5	85	13	130	Williams et al., 1946
	Marihuana	4.2	42	8	80	Mayor's Committee on Marihuana, 1944
United States	Marihuana	2.5	25	5	50	Charen and Perelman, 1946
	Marihuana	4.0	40	5	50	Mayor's Committee on Marihuana, 1944
	Marihuana	1.5	15	—	—	Williams et al., 1946

[a] From W.H.O. Technical Report Series No. 478, 1971.
[b] The estimates of delta-9-THC content are based on the rough guide of 1%, 3%, and 5% for marihuana, ganja, and hashish, respectively.
[c] References to this table are found in Chapters 1, 6, and 7.
[d] Not necessarily used daily.
[e] Delta-9-THC estimate based on ganja.

TABLE 14

Physiologic and Mental Effects of Marihuana Smoking on Six Patients Who Smoked Daily an Average of 17 Marihuana Cigarettes (of Unknown Potency) for 39 days[a]

Measure	Interval	Marihuana	Synhexyl
Rectal temperature	Daily	Increased slightly	Decreased slightly
Pulse rate	Daily	Increased for 3 weeks, then returned to normal	Increased initially, then decreased below normal
Respiratory rate	Daily	No change	Decreased
Systolic blood pressure	Daily	Slightly increased	No change
Body weight	Daily	Increased	Increased
Caloric intake	Daily	Initial increase, then progressive decline	
Sleep	Daily	Increase	Increase
Mood	Daily	Euphoria for several days, then general lassitude and indifference	Euphoria for 3 days, then increased lethargy and general loss of interest
Coordination	Daily	No change	No change
Confusion	Daily	Mild	Mild
General intelligence tests	Baseline before medication; 14 days on medication; 3 days after discontinuation	Slightly impaired	Slightly impaired
Rote memory	Baseline before medication, 14 days on medication, 3 days after discontinuation	No change	No change
EEG	14 days on medication	Not consistent, tendency toward slowed alpha frequencies	
		Increased and decreased alpha percentages	Decreased alpha frequencies and occasional delta in 2 of 6
	5 days after discontinuance	Normal	Normal

[a] These changes were quite comparable to those observed in six other subjects who ingested a daily dose of 60 to 2400 mg of synhexyl, a synthetic derivative (from Williams et al., 1946).

mg of delta-9-THC. Such a figure corresponds to the one given by Chopra (1969) for the dose used by chronic users of ganja in India.

A candid report from Israel by Freedman and Peer (1968) is indicative of the development of tolerance to *Cannabis* (Table 15). Seven of 21 pimps or prostitutes with little or no high school education (aged 18 to 42, median age 28) studied in Israel admitted to having to increase the dose of hashish they were taking. "When your body gets used to it you want it stronger, the body needs more and more." "You start off with a small cigarette, then a big one, then a narguila" (water pipe). The remainder in this group (14) claimed that they used the same amount of hashish. However, if one takes into account the age of the hashish user and the length of his habit, it can be observed that all of the members of the group (five) who had used hashish more than 12 years also admitted using opium.

All of this data is in agreement with the marked development of tolerance to *Cannabis* derivatives in animals. It does not support the concept of "reverse tolerance" suggested by Weil et al. (1968) and entertained uncritically by many other authors. This condition has been described by habitual smokers of marihuana who claim that following initial exposure to the drug, they will need a lesser amount to become intoxicated. As a result they report that they do not feel constrained to increase the dose of *Cannabis* in order to obtain the desired effect. This so-called "reverse tolerance" might be explained by a combination of enzymatic induction necessary for the production of "active metabolites" and also by a conditioned reinforcement produced by the smoking process. However, it is short lived: as drug intake continues, half-life of delta-9-THC metabolites significantly shortens in plasma and their kidney excretion is markedly increased ("metabolic tolerance"). In addition, it is likely that tissue tolerance develops in the brain to the psychoactive metabolites of delta-9-THC ("functional tolerance") (Fig. 17). The combined development of metabolic and functional tolerance in chronic users of *Cannabis* will eventually predominate over psychological conditioning and increments in drug intake will be required to obtain the desired effects.

Such a conclusion, which could be inferred from the older observations in the literature, is also borne out by the double-blind studies of Jones (1971) on American chronic marihuana smokers (average length of drug use, 5.2 years): "Performance and physiological measurements demonstrate differences between frequent and infrequent users and are consistent with the development of tolerance to some of the effects of marihuana in frequent users. There is a diminished drug effect in the frequent (daily) users both on physiological and behavioral measurements."

Jones adds the following comment: "If tolerance to behavioral and physiologic effects developed without tolerance to the desirable subjective effects,

TABLE 15

Profile of 21 Hashish Users in Israel[a]

	Age	Years of education	Country of origin	Year of immigration	Family status	Status of parent family	Drugs used	Number of years of hashish use	Number of years of "criminal" behavior
Male	19	7	Iraq	1950	Bachelor	Father and mother living	Hashish	2	4
	28	6	Syria	1953	Married	Mother dead	Hashish and alcohol	11	13
	24	7	Yemen	1953	Bachelor	Father and mother divorced	Hashish	5	8
	30	4	Morocco	1952	Bachelor	Father dead	Hashish and alcohol	10	11
	27	5	Israel (Turkey)	—	Divorced	Mother dead	Hashish	7	11
	20	7	Israel (Iraq)	—	Bachelor	Father and mother living	Hashish	4	4
	33	3	Turkey	1949	Married	Father and mother dead	Hashish, opium, and alcohol	13	13
	42	0	Morocco	1948	Married	Father dead	Hashish, opium, and alcohol	20	22
	37	3	Morocco	1957	Married	Father and mother dead	Hashish, opium, and alcohol	15	16
	32	3	Morocco	1958	Married	Father dead	Hashish and alcohol	13	13
	30	3	Turkey	1952	Bachelor	Father and mother divorced	Hashish, opium, and alcohol	12	15
	21	7	Turkey	1955	Bachelor	Father dead	Hashish	3	5
	34	0	Morocco	1949	Deserted	Father dead	Hashish, opium, and alcohol	9	11
Female	34	0	Morocco	1951	Married	Mother dead	Hashish and opium	10	16
	28	12	Israel (Germany)	—	Deserted	Father and mother living	Hashish	4	6
	18	7	Tripoli	1955	Bachelor	Father dead	Hashish	1	2
	33	0	Morocco	1952	Married	Mother dead	Hashish	11	12
	28	10	Rumania	1948	Divorced	Father dead	Hashish	12	12
	36	7	Rumania	1950	Divorced	Father and mother dead	Hashish and opium	18	18
	21	8	Germany	1948	Bachelor	Father dead	Hashish	3	4
	20	8	Israel (Rumania)	—	Bachelor	Father dead	Hashish	2	2

[a] From Freedman and Peer (1968).

Cannabis would perhaps be a useful drug. This would be a situation similar to that seen in tobacco smoking. Unfortunately, it appears that tolerance to the sought-after subjective effects also occurs with marihuana."

It is well known that a few strong-willed, motivated persons, endowed with powerful detoxifying enzyme systems, can control for many years the amount of drugs (including opiates and cocaine) they can take in order to obtain the desired effect. Such persons, such as the French artist and author Jean Cocteau, or the mysterious Mr. X interviewed by Grinspoon, fall out of the normal range of any random population sample; rapid tolerance to psycho-active drugs is most likely to develop in the average human being, especially if he is an adolescent with a labile personality and an uncertain future, or if he belongs to the underprivileged groups which today are striving for a better life. It is very doubtful that the use of *Cannabis* will help them achieve this goal. It is now well established that pharmacological tolerance develops to delta-9-THC and *Cannabis*. The tolerance to smoked *Cannabis* can be controlled by casual users for some time through psychological conditioning.

However, all pharmacological and clinical evidence presently available indicates that frequent (daily) users of *Cannabis* develop tolerance to the physiological as well as the psychological effects of the drug. This tolerance to *Cannabis* gives a physiological basis to the necessity for the frequent smoker to increase dosage, or to use more potent psychotropic drugs such as other hallucinogens or the opiates.

The popular belief that "there is little or no tendency to increase dosage of *Cannabis* since there is little or no development of tolerance" (W.H.O. Expert Committee, 1964) must be revised. Such a belief is currently reinforced by all of the statements contained in the books on *Cannabis* available in 1971 to the English reader (John Kaplan, 1971; Snyder, 1971; Grinspoon, 1971; Schofield, 1971).

PHYSICAL AND PSYCHOLOGICAL DEPENDENCE: THE MARIHUANA HABIT

A misconception seems to have penetrated into the minds of many psy-chologists and physicians that "addiction," meaning physical dependence accompanied by withdrawal symptoms, is the main criterion by which the potential harm of a drug to the individual or to society should be gauged. One must be very careful about drawing too sharp a line between physical and psychological dependence. There is no complete dichotomy between mind and body. Psychological function also has physiological and bio-chemical bases. The desire for instant gratification is a profound psychological reinforcer. Physical dependence does not develop with central nervous system stimulants such as cocaine, which is known to create in an individual one of the most enslaving types of drug dependence. Addiction to a drug is not a function of the ability of the drug to produce withdrawal symptoms. Drug dependence results basically from the reproducible interaction between an individual and a pleasure-inducing biologically active molecule. The common denominator of all drug dependence is the psychological reinforcement resulting from reward associated with past individual drug interaction and the subsequent increasing desire for repeated reinforcement (Seevers, 1970). On this basis it is deceptive to categorize marihuana as a "soft," acceptable drug.

The example of Freud, who recommended cocaine to his friend Von Fleishl to help him withdraw from morphine addiction, should be kept in mind. With this new drug Von Fleishl was able to withdraw from morphine; but he used cocaine instead, and ever-increasing doses until he was in a state of constant intoxication. As a result of this sad experience, Freud, even when he suffered from cancer, did not take pain-killing medications except aspirin (Lennard, 1971). As Jones, his biographer, says, "Freud, like all good doctors, was averse to taking drugs" (Jones, 1953). The example of cocaine clearly demonstrates that a strong psychological reinforcement is the only necessary requirement to perpetuate a most compelling form of drug addiction.

While *Cannabis* users develop tolerance to the drug, they do not present any significant physical dependence identifiable by specific withdrawal symptoms similar to those occurring with heroin or ethanol. The symptoms observed following discontinuation of heavy use are relatively mild. Loss of appetite, insomnia, and irritability are well tolerated, but it is well documented that *Cannabis* may create a state of psychological dependence which is an important obstacle to discontinued usage.

In India, "chronic hemp habituation," says Chopra (1969), "is a self-inflicted disease. It is progressive and seldom abates by itself. The urge to smoke may become so great that the individual inhales until he loses consciousness. Repeated use of the drug leads to a craving and psychological dependence."

Soueif (1967) reports that in Egypt 65% of the consumers of hashish declared they were unable to stop although they expressed a wish to discontinue their habituation. According to Soueif, "Among hashish users there is a definite pattern of oscillation of temperamental traits, swinging between two opposite poles, that of social ease, a desire to mix acquiescence and elation (euphoria) when under immediate drug effects and that of ascendancy, seclusiveness, negativism, depression of the mood and pugnacity (which may be considered as main components of a psychic withdrawal syndrome) when the subjects are deprived of the drug. This pattern of oscillation of the subject's personality, between the drugged state and the state of deprivation from the drug, may be considered as the behavioral core of a state of psychic dependence. One of the most salient characteristics of this state is a need to continue taking the drug not only to attain the feeling of well being but also to avoid feeling low."

The Israeli users of hashish studied by Freedman and Peer (1968) resemble closely, in this respect, their Egyptian neighbors. Half of those questioned acknowledged candidly that they could not give up hashish. Some of the answers of these Israeli *Cannabis* smokers are revealing: "Maybe somebody with a strong character can quit. Because all you do is to smell it and you're back smoking." Eleven of 21 said: "You can kick the habit, and you don't need the hospital—it's only hard the first month." However, when the members of the group were asked, "Do you know of cases where people who quit went back to smoking again?" 20 of 21 answered that they knew such people, because "you always go back to it—you can't stop." This statement contrasts with the preceding one because "it is easier to be frank when talking about others than when talking about one's self." Two-thirds of the group believed that it would be worthwhile stopping, "because it finishes you off and makes you lazy too. You have to either give up the drug or your future. It can affect your health sometimes, because it's a drug. A person is always like a drunk—high—doesn't know what is happening with him and it interferes with his future. It louses up your family life, kids, doesn't let you get ahead and make a living." Such statements are not the rule among young habitual *Cannabis* smokers in Western culture. Many of them strongly deny any ill effect on performance or interpersonal relationships. The observations of Yardley (1968), who was a proctor in 1965 at Oxford University, are indicative of the self-deception experienced by students who fall into the habit of using *Cannabis* regularly. "Every one of those who were regular takers seemed to be convinced that *Cannabis* was not habit forming; that they had not developed any real habit of taking it; and that they could give up the drug at any time at will; that it was a cleaner practice than the taking of alcohol; and that it should be legalized. But most of those who had become accustomed to taking this drug regularly had to call on professional help to give it up. Furthermore, it was plain that those who did take it regularly tended gradually to increase their consumption and a certain number of them, small but perhaps significant, graduated to hard drugs."

Man is a creature of habit, and Americans are not immune from the marihuana habit. This habit has been reported among American smokers between 20 and 30 years of age who usually have a history of 4 to 5 years of marihuana use (Scher, 1970). They describe a decreasing interest in the use of marihuana, but seem completely unwilling or unable to discontinue use of the drug. They develop diminished pleasure from the drug, requiring more (a stronger amount or a different variety) to produce the "high"—all signs of the same increased tolerance which now becomes so apparent in frequent users. The American soldiers stationed in Germany studied by Tennant et al. (1971) did not wish to give up hashish smoking in spite of the impairment to their health which resulted from using the drug. They presented ailments ranging from acute bronchitis, sinusitis, rhinopharyngitis, abdominal cramps, and diarrhea, conditions which led them to consult a physician or to be hospitalized. However, despite the morbidity that these patients attributed to hashish smoking, none expressed a willingness to stop. It had become "a habit" just like "smoking tobacco." Furthermore, in order to sustain their habit, they had to become traffickers of the drug.

Cannabis derivatives are not addictive in the same sense as opiate derivatives are, but they certainly are habit forming.

CONCLUSION

All of the clinical investigation performed with *Cannabis* derivatives in the past 4 years has added little which was not been known since Moreau's reports.

The major advance has been the studies of the drug's metabolism with radioactivity tagged delta-9-THC. Numerous active and inactive metabolites are formed in lung and liver through enzymatic induction. Inactive metabolites are stored in tissues for days.

Another advance has been a better quantitation of the amount of drug required to obtain a measurable psychological and physiological response. On the basis of these criteria it would appear that the dose-response relationships for delta-9-THC first established by Isbell could now serve as general guidelines in clinical investigation. The controversial results obtained by some of the clinical investigators who used nonextracted *Cannabis* herb, in which the active ingredients appeared to have lost their potency, should not be forgotten. All of the *Cannabis* derivatives used in clinical investigations, either crude plant, plant extract, or delta-9-THC, should be tested before experimental use for actual potency. Acute laboratory experiments such as those described, which are rarely accompanied by any serious untoward effects, cannot answer the question of the extent of untoward effects resulting from chronic use of *Cannabis*.

Clinical studies have confirmed the development of tolerance to the physiological and psychological effects of *Cannabis* preparations in man. These observations are indicative of the profound biochemical changes occurring in the target organs. Development of tolerance to *Cannabis* gives a physiological basis to the necessity of increasing the dosage of the compound to obtain the desired effect and to the subsequent use of more potent drugs when they are available.

The French psychiatrist Delay (1965) has attempted to categorize all

Table 16

Classification of Psychotropic Drugs According to the Main Effect
of a Single Effective Dose[a]

Psycholeptics (depress mental function)	Psychoanaleptics (stimulate mental function)	Psychodysleptics (disintegrate mental function)
General anesthetics	Stimulate alertness: amphetamines	Hallucinogenics LSD
Hypnotics: Barbiturates	Stimulate mood (antidepressants): MAO inhibitors	Psilocybine Mescaline
Neuroleptics: Phenothiazine Butyrophenones Reserpine	Tricyclic compounds (impramine, lithium)	*Cannabis* derivatives: Hashish Marihuana
Tranquilizers Anticonvulsants Antiparkinsonians Anticholinergics Antihistamines	Convulsant drugs (metrazol) Local anesthetics (cocaine) Psychostimulants (caffeine)	Opiate derivatives Morphine Heroin Depersonalizing drugs: Phencyclidine
Analgesics Antipyretics Ethyl alcohol Bromides		

[a] This effect depends upon individual traits (age, sex, endocrine function, metabolism) and the environment. Many of these drugs, depending on the dose, may have multiple actions (after Delay, 1965).

psychotropic drugs into three main groups according to their predominant effect when given in a single effective dose: psycholeptics, which depress; psychoanaleptics, which stimulate; and psychodysleptics, which disintegrate mental function (Table 16). *Cannabis* preparations containing psychoactive delta-9-THC are hallucinogenic. It seems, therefore, appropriate to have classified *Cannabis* derivatives in Delay's functional nomenclature among the "psychodysleptic" drugs which "disintegrate mental function and produce a distortion of judgment and memory with impairment in evaluating the reality situation."

SUMMARY

Clinical studies with measured amounts of delta-9-THC, performed mostly on student volunteers in the United States, indicate the following:

1. The first widely publicized studies claimed that smoked marihuana containing 5 to 66 mg of delta-9-THC was a "mild intoxicant." It appears that these studies were performed with unextracted material containing, in reality, much lower amounts of delta-9-THC.

2. The half-life of delta-9-THC in blood plasma is 28 hours for chronic marihuana smokers, as compared to 57 hours for nonusers. Apparent volume of distribution is similar in both groups. Chronic users eliminate significantly more polar metabolites in the urine, and less in the feces, than nonusers. The total amount of metabolites eliminated in both groups is the same and requires more than 1 week. Repeated administration of cannabinoids at less than 1-week intervals will therefore result in accumulation of metabolites in tissues and body fluids.

3. Delta-9-THC is three to four times more active when smoked than when ingested.

4. Tachycardia, which is dose related and lasts throughout the period of intoxication, is the most significant clinical feature observed after administration of delta-9-THC or *Cannabis* extracts. A dose-related conjunctival injection is also observed.

5. Delta-9-THC, administered acutely in doses of 5 to 10 mg smoked or 15 to 30 mg ingested, significantly decreases psychomotor performance and produces a significant impairment of immediate memory storage.

6. Doses of 10 to 20 mg smoked or 20 to 60 mg ingested may produce in normal subjects a brief psychotic-like state with panic reaction, delusions and hallucinations. But euphoria usually predominates over dysphoria and the pleasant feelings experienced by the users tend to create a positive reinforcement.

7. Frequent (daily) users of *Cannabis* develop physiological and psychological tolerance to the drug, leading to increased dosages and to the use of more potent psychotropic drugs such as LSD or opium derivatives.

8. Although *Cannabis* users do not develop any physical dependence identifiable by a specific withdrawal symptom, they do present a psychological dependence to the drug.

These studies in clinical pharmacology underline the potential health and social liabilities associated with *Cannabis* intoxication. All of the major effects of *Cannabis* derivatives justify their classification in Delay's functional nomenclature of psychotropic drugs among the "psychodysleptic" compounds which "disintegrate mental function."

REFERENCES

Abel, E. (1970). Marijuana and memory. *Nature,* 227:1151–1152.

Abramson, H. A., Jarvik, M. E., Kaufman, M. R., Kornetsky, C., Levine, A., and Wagner, M. (1955). Lysergic acid diethylamide (LSD-25). Physiological and perceptual responses. *J. Psychol.,* 39:3–60.

Allentuck, S. (1941). Medical aspects of the marijuana problem in the city of New York. In *The Marihuana Papers,* D. A. Soloman (ed.). The Bobbs-Merrill Co., Inc., Indianapolis, Ind., pp. 269–284.

Allentuck, S., and Bowman, K. M. (1942). The psychiatric aspects of marihuana intoxication. *Amer. J. Psychiat.,* 99:248–251.

Baker, A. A., and Lucas, E. G. (1969). Some hospital admissions associated with cannabis. *Lancet* 1:148–152.

Baker-Bates, E. T. (1935). A case of *Cannabis indica* intoxication. *Lancet,* 1:811.

Beringer, K. (1932). Zur klinik des hashischrausches. *Der Nervenaryt,* 5:337–350.

Brill, N. O., Crumpton, E., Frank, I. M., Hochman, J. S., Lomas, P., McGlothlin, W. H., and West, L. J. (1970). The marijuana problem. *Ann. Intern. Med.,* 73:449–465.

Bromberg, W. (1934). Marihuana intoxication: A clinical study of *Cannabis sativa* intoxication. *Amer. J. Psychiat.,* 91:303–330.

Burns, J. J. (1967). Symposium on drug interactions. *The Pharmacologist,* 9:77–81.

Caldwell, D. F., Myers, S. A., and Domino, E. F. (1970). Effect of marihuana smoking on sensory thresholds in man. In *Psychotomimetic Drugs,* E. H. Efron (ed.). Raven Press, New York, pp. 299–321.

Caldwell, D. F., Myers, S. A., Domino, E. F., and Merriam, D. E. (1969). Auditory and visual threshold effects of marihuana on man. *Percept. Motor Skills,* 29:755–759.

Chopra, G. S. (1969). Man and marijuana. *Int. J. Addict.,* 4:215–247.

Chopra, R. N., and Chopra, G. S. (1939). The present positions of hemp drug addiction in India. *Indian J. Med. Res. Mem.,* 31:1–119.

Christiansen, J., and Rafaelsen, O. J. (1969). Cannabis metabolites in urine after oral administration. *Psychopharmacologia,* 15:60–63.

Clark, L. D., Hughes, R., and Nakashima, E. N. (1970). Behavioral effects of marihuana: Experimental studies. *Arch. Gen. Psychiat. (Chicago),* 23:193–198.

Clark, L. D., and Nakashima, E. N. (1968). Experimental studies of marihuana. *Amer. J. Psychiat.,* 125:135–140.

Colbach, E. (1971). Marijuana use by GIs in Viet Nam. *Amer. J. Psychiat.,* 128:96–99.

Council on Mental Health and Committee on Alcoholism and Drug Dependence (1967). Dependence on *Cannabis* (marihuana). *J. Amer. Med. Ass.,* 201:368–371.

Crancer, A., Jr., Dille, J. M., Delay, J. C., Wallace, J. E., and Haykin, M. D. (1969). Comparison of the effects of marihuana and alcohol on simulated driving performance. *Science,* 164:851–854.

Delay, J. (1965). Psychotropic drugs and experimental psychiatry. *Int. J. Neuropsychiat.,* 1:104–117.

Dinnerstein, A. J. (1968). Marihuana and perceptual style. A theoretical note. *Percept. Motor Skills,* 26:1016–1018.

Domino, E. F. (1971). Neuropsychopharmacologic studies of marijuana. Some synthetic and natural THC derivatives in animals and man. *Ann. N.Y. Acad. Sci.,* 191:166–191.

Dornbush, R. L., Fink, M., and Freedman, A. M. (1971). Marijuana, memory and perception. *Amer. J. Psychiat.,* 128:194–197.

Eddy, N. B., Halbach, H., Isbell, H., and Seevers, M. (1965). Drug dependence: Its significance and characteristics. *Bull. W.H.O.,* 32:721–733.

Edwards, G. (1968). The problem of *Cannabis* dependence. *Practitioner,* 200:226–233.

F.D.A. Announcement (1971). Clinical studies with marihuana and tetrahydrocannabinol currently being allowed by the Food and Drug Administration. *Clin. Pharmacol., Therap.,* 12:1019.

Federation of American Societies for Experimental Biology (1971). *A Review of the Biomedical Effects of Marihuana on Man in the Military Environment.* Bethesda, Md.

Fisher, S. (1970). Nonspecific factors as determinants of behavior response to drugs. In *Clinical Handbook of Psychopharmacology,* A. DiMascio and R. I. Shader (eds.). Science House, New York, pp. 17–39.

Ford, R. D., and McMillan, D. E. (1972) Further studies on the behavioral pharmacology of 1-delta-8 and 1-delta-9-THC. *Fed. Proc.* 31:506.

Forney, R. B. (1971). Toxicology of marihuana. *Pharmacol. Rev.,* 23:279–284.

Fraser, J. D. (1949). Withdrawal symptoms in *Cannabis* indica addicts. *Lancet,* 2:747.

Freedman, H., and Rockmore, N. (1946). Marihuana: A factor in personality evaluation and Army maladjustment. *J. Clin. Psychopathol.,* 7:765–782.

Freedman, I., and Peer, I. (1968). Drug addiction among pimps and prostitutes in Israel. *Int. J. Addictions,* 3:271–300.

Gaskill, H. S. (1945). Marihuana, an intoxicant. *Amer. J. Psychiat.,* 102:202–204.

Gill, E. W., Paton, W. D. M., and Pertwee, R. G. (1970). Preliminary experiments on the chemistry and pharmacology of cannabis. *Nature,* 228:134–136.

Goddard, J. L. (1971). Review of *Marihuana Reconsidered,* by Lester Grinspoon. *N.Y. Times Book Review,* June 27, p. 1.

Goode, E. (1970) *The Marihuana Smokers.* Basic Books, New York.

Grinspoon, L. (1969). Marihuana. *Sci. Amer.,* 221:17–25.

Grinspoon, L. (1971). *Marihuana Reconsidered.* Harvard University Press, Cambridge, Mass.

Haertzen, C. A. (1966). Development of scales based on patterns of drug effect, using the Addiction Research Center Inventory (ARCI). *Psychol. Rep.,* 18:163–194.

H.E.W. Report to Congress (1971). *Marihuana and Health.* U.S. Government Printing Office, Washington, D.C.

Hepler, R. S., and Frank, I. (1971). Marihuana smoking and intraocular pressure. *J. Amer. Med. Ass.,* 217:1392.

Hepler, R. S., Frank, I., and Ungerleider, J. T. (1971). The effects of marihuana smoking on pupillary size. *Amer. J. Ophthal.,*

Hockman, C. H., Perrin, R. G., and Kalant, H. (1971). Electroencephalographic and behavioral alterations produced by delta-1-tetrahydrocannabinol. *Science,* 172:968–970.

Hollister, L. E. (1968). *Chemical Psychoses: L.S.D. and Related Drugs.* Charles C. Thomas, Springfield, Ill.

Hollister, L. E. (1969a). Steroids and moods: Correlations in schizophrenics and subjects treated with lysergic acid diethylamide (LSD), mescaline, tetrahydrocannabinol, and synhexyl. *J. Clin. Pharmacol.,* 9:24–29.

Hollister, L. E. (1969b). Criminal laws and the control of drugs of abuse: An historical view of the law (or, it's the lawyer's fault). *J. Clin. Pharmacol.,* 9:345–348.

Hollister, L. E. (1970). Tetrahydrocannabinol isomers and homologues: Contrasted effects of smoking. *Nature,* 227:968–969.

Hollister, L. E. (1971a). Marihuana in man: Three years later. *Science* 172:21–24.

Hollister, L. E. (1971b). Hunger and appetite after single doses of marihuana, alcohol and dextroamphetamine. *Clin. Pharmacol. Ther.,* 12:44–49.

Hollister, L. E. (1971c). Actions of various marihuana derivatives. *Pharmacol. Rev.,* 23:349–358.

Hollister, L. E., and Gillespie, H. K. (1969). Similarities and differences between the effects of lysergic acid diethylamide and tetrahydracannabinol in man. In *Drugs and Youth,* J. R. Wittenborn, H. Brill, J. P. Smith, and

S. A. Wittenborn (eds.). Charles C. Thomas, Springfield, Ill., pp. 208–211.

Hollister, L. E., and Gillespie, H. K. (1970). Marihuana, ethanol and dextroamphetamine. Mood and mental function alterations. *Arch. Gen. Psychiat. (Chicago)*, 23:199–203.

Hollister, L. E., and Moore, F. (1967). Urinary catecholamine excretion following lysergic acid diethylamide in man. *Psychopharmacologia (Berlin)*, 11:270–275.

Hollister, L. E., Moore, F., Kanter, S. L., and Noble, E. (1970). Delta-1-tetrahydrocannabinol, synhexyl and marihuana extract administered orally in man: Catecholamine excretion, plasma cortisol level and platelet serotonin content. *Psychopharmacologia*, 17:354–360.

Hollister, L. E., Richards, R. K., and Gillespie, H. K. (1968). Comparison of tetrahydrocannabinol and synhexyl in man. *Clin. Pharmacol. Ther.*, 9:783–791.

Hollister, L. E., Sherwood, S. L., and Cavasino, A. (1970). Marihuana and the human electroencephalogram. *Pharmacol. Res. Commun.*, 2:305–308.

Hollister, L. E., and Sjoberg, B. J. (1964). Clinical syndromes and biochemical alterations following mescaline, LSD, psilocybin and a combination of the three psychotomimetic drugs. *Compr. Psychiat.*, 5:170–178.

Hughes, J. E., Steahly, L. P., and Bier, M. M. (1970). Marihuana and the diabetic coma. *J. Amer. Med. Ass.*, 214:1113–1114.

Indian Hemp Drug Commission (1969). *Report on Marihuana of the Indian Hemp Commission, 1893–1894.* Thomas Jefferson Publishing Company, Silver Springs, Md.

Isbell, H. (1971). Clinical pharmacology. *Pharmacol. Rev.*, 23:337–338.

Isbell, H., Gorodetsky, G. W., Jasinski, D., Claussen, U., Spulak, F., and Korte, F. (1967). Effects of (−) delta-9-*trans*tetrahydrocannabinol in man. *Psychopharmacologia*, 11:184–188.

Isbell, H., and Jasinski, D. (1969). A comparison of LSD-25 with (−) delta-9-*trans*tetrahydrocannabinol (THC) and attempted cross tolerance between LSD and THC. *Psychopharmacologia*, 14:115–123.

Johnson, S., and Domino, E. F. (1971). Some cardiovascular effects of marihuana smoking in normal volunteers. *Clin. Pharmacol. Ther.*, 12:762–786.

Jones, Ernest (1953). *The Life and Work of Sigmund Freud.* Basic Books, New York.

Jones, R. T. (1971a). Marihuana-induced "high": Influence of expectation, setting and previous drug experience. *Pharmacol. Rev.*, 23:359–370.

Jones, R. T. (1971b). ᵛTetrahydrocannabinol and the marihuana-induced social "high" or the effects of the mind on marihuana. *Ann. N.Y. Acad. Sci.,* 191:155–165.

Jones, R. T., and Stone, G. C. (1970). Psychological studies of marihuana and alcohol in man. *Psychopharmacologia,* 18:108–117.

Joyce, C. R. B., and Curry, S. H. (eds.) (1970). *The Botany and Chemistry of Cannabis.* J. & A. Churchill, London.

Kalant, H. (1969). Marihuana and simulated driving. *Science,* 166:640.

Kaplan, H. S. (1971). Psychosis associated with marijuana. *N.Y. State J. Med.,* 71:433–435.

Kaplan, John (1971). *Marihuana—The New Prohibition.* World Publishing Company, New York.

Kaplan, Joel H. (1971). Marijuana and drug abuse in Vietnam. *Ann. N.Y. Acad. Sci.,* 191:261–269.

Kiplinger, G. F., and Manno, J. E. (1971). Dose-response relationships to *Cannabis* in human subjects. *Pharmacol. Rev.,* 23:339–348.

Korte, F., and Sieper, H. (1965). Recent results in hashish analysis. In *Hashish: Its Chemistry and Pharmacology,* G. E. W. Wolstenholme and J. Knight (eds.). Little, Brown and Company, Boston, pp. 15–20.

Lemberger, L., Axelrod, J., and Kopin, I. J. (1971*a*). Metabolism and disposition of delta-9-tetrahydrocannabinol in man. *Pharmacol. Rev.,* 23:371–380.

Lemberger, L., Silberstein, S. D., Axelrod, J., and Kopin, I. J. (1970). Marihuana: Studies on the disposition and metabolism of delta-9-tetrahydrocannabinol in man. *Science,* 170:1320–1322.

Lemberger, L., Tamarkin, N. R., Axelrod, J., and Kopin, I. J. (1971*b*). Delta-9-THC metabolism and disposition in long-term marihuana smokers. *Science,* 173:72–74.

Lemberger, L., Weiss, J. L., Watanabe, A. M., Galanter, I. M., Wyatt, R. J., and Cardon, P. V. (1972): Delta-9-tetrahydrocannabinol: Temporal correlation of the psychologic effects and blood levels after various routes of administration. *New Eng. J. Med.,* 286:685–688.

Lennard, H. L., Epstein, L. J., Bernstein, A., and Ransom, D. C. (1971). *Mystification and Drug Misuse.* Jossey-Bass, San Francisco.

Lerner, M., and Zeffer, J. T. (1968). Determination of tetrahydrocannabinol isomers in marihuana and hashish. *Bull. Narcotics,* 20:53–54.

McGlothlin, W. H., Arnold, D. O., and Rowan, P. K. (1970). Marihuana use among adults. *Psychiatry,* 33:433–443.

Mann, P. E. G., Cohen, A. B., Finley, T. N., and Ladman, A. J. (1971). Alveolar macrophages. Structural and functional differences between non-smokers and smokers of marijuana and tobacco. *Lab. Invest.,* 25:111–120

Manno, J. E., Kiplinger, G. F., Haine, S. E., Bennett, I. F., and Forney, R. B. (1970). Comparative effects of smoking marihuana or placebo on human motor and mental performance. *Clin. Pharmacol. Ther.,* 11:808–815.

Manno, J. E., Kiplinger, G. F., Scholtz, N., and Forney, R. B. (1971). The influence of alcohol and marihuana on motor and mental performance. *Clin. Pharmacol. Ther.,* 12:202–211.

Mayor's Committee on Marihuana (1944). *The Marihuana Problem in the City of New York—Sociological, Medical, Psychological and Pharmacological Studies.* Cattell Press, Lancaster, Pa.

Mechoulam, R., Shani, A., Yagnitinsky, R., Ben-Zvi, Z., Braun, P., and Gaoni, Y. (1970). Some aspects of cannabinoid chemistry. In: *The Botany and Chemistry of Cannabis,* edited by C. R. B. Joyce and S. H. Curry, pp. 93–117, J. & A. Churchill, London.

Melges, F. T., Tinkelberg, J. R., Hollister, L. E., and Gillespie, H. K. (1970a). Marihuana and temporal disintegration. *Science,* 168:1118–1120.

Melges, F. T., Tinkelberg, J. R., Hollister, L. E., and Gillespie, H. K. (1970b). Temporal disintegration and depersonalization during marihuana intoxication. *Arch. Gen. Psychiat. (Chicago),* 23:204–210.

Meyer, R. E., Pillard, R. C., Shapiro, L. S., and Mirin, S. M. (1971). Administration of marihuana to heavy and casual marijuana users. *Amer. J. Psychiat.,* 128:198–203.

Miras, C. J. (1969). Experience with chronic hashish smokers. In *Drugs and Youth,* J. R. Wittenborn, H. Brill, J. P. Smith, and S. A. Wittenborn (eds.). Charles C. Thomas, Springfield, Ill., pp. 191–198.

Miras, C. Simon, S., and Kiburis, J. (1964). Comparative assay of the constituents from the sublimate of smoked cannabis with that from ordinary cannabis. *Bull. Narcotics,* 16:13–15.

Mirin, S. M., Shapiro, L. M., Meyer, R. E., Pillard, R. C., and Fisher, S. (1971). Casual vs. heavy use of marihuana, a redefinition of the marihuana problem. *Amer. J. Psychiat.,* 127:1134–1140.

Mohan, H., and Sood, G. C. (1964). Conjugate deviation of the eyes after *Cannabis* indica intoxication. *Brit. J. Ophthal.,* 48:160–161.

Moreau, J. J. (1845). *Du Hachisch et de l'Alienation Mentale: Études Psychologiques.* Libraire de Fortin, Masson, Paris (English edition: Raven Press, New York, 1972).

Myers, S. A., and Caldwell, D. F. (1969). The effects of marihuana on auditory and visual sensation: A preliminary report. *The New Physician,* 18:212–215.

Nakazawa, K., and Costa, E: (1971). The pharmacological implications of delta-9-tetrahydrocannabinol metabolism by lung: Effects of 3-methylcholanthrene. *Ann. N.Y. Acad. Sci.,* 191:216–221.

Newman, R. H., Jones, W. L., and Jenkins, R. W. (1969). Automatic device for the evaluation of total mainstream cigarette smoke. *Anal. Chem.,* 41:543–545.

Palmer, E. L. (1949). *Fieldbook of Natural History.* McGraw-Hill Book Company, Inc., New York.

Parker, C. S., and Wrigley, F. J. (1950). Synthetic *Cannabis* preparations in psychiatry: Synhexyl. *J. Ment. Sci.,* 96:276–279.

Pillsbury, H. C., Bright, C. C., O'Connor, K. J., and Irish, F. W. (1969). Tar and nicotine in cigarette smoke. *J. Ass. Offic. Anal. Chem.,* 52:458–462.

Pivik, T., Zarcone, V., Hollister, L. E., and Dement, W. (1969). The effects of hallucinogenic agents on sleep. *Psychophysiology,* 6:261.

Podolsky, S., Pattavina, C. G., and Amaral, M. A. (1971). Effects of marihuana on glucose tolerance test. *Ann. N.Y. Acad. Sci.,* 191:54–60.

President's Commission on Law Enforcement and Administration of Justice, N. deB. Katzenbach, Chairman (1967). *Task Force Report: Narcotics and Drug Abuse.* U.S. Government Printing Office, Washington, D.C.

Renault, P. F., Schuster, C. R., Heinrich, R., and Freeman, D. X. (1971). Marihuana: Standardized smoke administration and dose effect curves on heart rate in humans. *Science,* 174:589–591.

Rodin, E. A. and Domino, E. F. (1970). Effects of acute marihuana smoking on the electroencephalograms. *Electroenceph. Clin. Neurophysiol.,* 29:321.

Rodin, E. A., Domino, E. F., and Porzak, J. P. (1970). The marihuana-induced "social high": Neurological and electroencephalograph concomitants. *J. Amer. Med. Ass.,* 213:1300–1302.

Roland, J. L., and Teste, M. (1958). Le cannabisme au Maroc. *Maroc-Med.,* 387:694–703. [This same article appears under the name of Benabud, A. (1957). Psycho-pathological aspects of the cannabis situation in Morocco: Statistical data for 1956. *U.N. Bull. Narcotics,* 9:1–16.]

Scher, J. M. (1970). The marihuana habit. *J. Amer. Med. Ass.,* 214:1120.

Schick, J. F., Smith, D. E., and Meyers, F. H. (1968). The use of marijuana in the Haight-Ashbury subculture. *J. Psychedelic Drugs,* 2:49–66.

Schofield, M. (1971). *The Strange Case of Pot.* Penguin Books, Middlesex, England.

Schwartz, I., Manger, W. M., and Nahas, G. G. (1972): Some cardiovascular effects of delta-9-THC on normal and hypertensive rats. *Circulation* (in press).

Schwartz, I., and Nahas, G. G. (1972): Effects of delta-9-THC on contractility of smooth muscle in vivo and in vitro. *Proc. Soc. Expr. Biog. Med.,* (in press).

Seevers, M. H. (1970). Drug dependence and drug abuse, a world problem. *Pharmacologist,* 12:172–181.

Smith, D. E. (1968). Acute and chronic toxicity of marijuana. *J. Psychedelic Drugs,* 2:37–41.

Snyder, S. H. (1970). What have we forgotten about pot? *The New York Times Magazine,* December 13, p. 26.

Snyder, S. H. (1971). *The Uses of Marijuana.* Oxford University Press, New York.

Soueif, M. I. (1967). Hashish consumption in Egypt with special reference to psychological aspects. *Bull. Narcotics,* 19:1–12.

Soueif, M. I. (1971). The use of cannabis in Egypt: A behavioural study. *Bull. Narcatics,* 33:17–28.

Talbott, J. A., and Teague, J. W. (1969). Marihuana psychosis: Acute toxic psychosis associated with the use of cannabis derivatives. *J. Amer. Med. Ass.,* 210:299–302.

Tart, C. T. (1969). *Altered States of Consciousness.* John Wiley & Sons, New York.

Tart, C. T. (1970). Marihuana intoxication: Common experiences. *Nature,* 226:701–704.

Tart, C. T., and Crawford, H. J. (1970). Marijuana intoxication: Reported effects on sleep. *Psychophysiol.,* 7:348.

Tennant, F. S., Jr., Preble, M., Prendergast, T. J., and Ventry, P. (1971). Medical manifestations associated with hashish. *J. Amer. Med. Ass.,* 216:1965–1969.

Tinklenberg, J. R., Melges, F. T., Hollister, L. E., and Gillespie, H. K. (1970). Marihuana and immediate memory. *Nature,* 226:1171–1172.

Truitt, E. B., Jr. (1971). Biological disposition of tetrahyrocannabinols. *Pharmacol. Rev.,* 23:273–278.

Volavka, J., Dornbush, R., Feldstein, S., Clare, G., Zaks, A., Fink, M., and Freedman, A. M. (1971). Marijuana, EEG and Behavior. *Ann. N.Y. Acad. Sci.,* 191:206–215.

Waller, C. W. (1970). *Supplies for the Marihuana Program—Report to the Committee on Problems of Drug Dependence.* Nat. Acad. Sci., NRC, 6394–6396.

Waskow, I. E., Olsson, J. E., Salzman, C., and Katz, M. M. (1970). Psychological effects of delta-9-THC. *Arch. Gen. Psychiat.,* 22:97–107.

Weil, A. T. (1969). Cannabis. *Science J. (London),* 5A:36–42.

Weil, A. T. (1970). Adverse reactions to marihuana: Classification and suggested treatment. *New Eng. J. Med.,* 282:997–1000.

Weil, A. T., and Zinberg, N. E. (1969). Acute effects of marihuana on speech. *Nature,* 222:434–437.

Weil, A. T., Zinberg, N. E., and Nelson, J. M. (1968). Clinical and psychological effects of marihuana in man. *Science,* 162:1234–1242.

White, R. B., Goolishian, H., and Barratt, E. S. (1970). Dilemmas encountered by the marihuana researcher (1970): Paper presented at the 46th Annual Conference of the Central Neuropsychiatric Association, Galveston, Texas, October 16.

W.H.O. Expert Committee on Addiction-Producing Drugs (1964). *Thirteenth Report.* World Health Organization Technical Report Series No. 273, Geneva.

Wikler, A. (1970). Clinical and social aspects of marihuana intoxication. *Arch. Gen. Psychiat. (Chicago),* 22:320–325.

Williams, E. G., Himmelsbach, C. K., Wikler, A., Ruble, D. C., and Lloyd, B. J., Jr. (1946). Studies on marihuana and pyrahexl compound. *Public Health Rep.,* 61:1059–1083.

Wilson, C., and Linken, A. (1968). *The Use of Cannabis in Adolescent Drug Dependents.* Pergamon Press, Oxford.

Yardley, D. C. M. (1968). Legal aspects of drug dependence in relation to student drug abuse. In *The Pharmacological and Epidemiological Aspects of Adolescent Drug Dependents,* C. W. M. Wilson (ed.). Pergamon Press, Oxford.

Zeidenberg, P., Clark, C. W., Jaffe, J., and Malitz, S. (1972). Effect of oral administration of delta-9-THC on four normal human volunteers. (In preparation).

6

Cannabis Intoxication and Mental Illness

The discrepancy between the marked psychological and emotional alterations and the slight physical symptoms associated with *Cannabis* intoxication
represent another aspect of its deceptive nature. Many people today believe
that since no apparent gross physical damage results from the absorption of
Cannabis derivatives, there is little or no danger associated with their use.
They are mistaken: *Cannabis* and all other hallucinogens have a common
characteristic, their psychotoxicity and their ability to disintegrate mental
function, which is not accompanied by any major alterations of the vital
physiological functions. Mental illness, especially in the young, is also
characterized by a similar discrepancy between the functions of the mind,
which are markedly impaired, and those of the body, which are well preserved.

The analogy between the symptoms present during acute *Cannabis* intoxication and those of mental illness was first noted by Jacques-Joseph Moreau
(1845). Not only did this pioneering physician and psychiatrist take *Cannabis* extracts himself and record their effect in detail, but he advocated their
use by his students so that they could gain more insight into mental illness.
His observations and conclusions are so pertinent that they will be recalled
at some length. All of the acute psychotomimetic effects which have been
subsequently described by numerous experimenters and patients in India,
Egypt, Morocco, England, and the United States are in keeping with the
symptoms Moreau observed in himself.

HASHISH AND MENTAL ILLNESS: THE EXPERIENCES AND OBSERVATIONS OF MOREAU

Jacques-Joseph Moreau (1804–1884)

Moreau was born in 1804 in Montresor, a small town in the Loire valley.
His father, an officer in the armies of Napoleon, fought in many battles,

and retired after Waterloo to devote himself to the study of mathematics. Moreau first studied medicine in Tours, near his home town, hence the surname he added to his own when he later went to Paris. His first teacher was a very famous clinician of his time, Bretonneau. The period was still the prescientific era of medicine, which was based primarily on the study of gross anatomy and pathology. Physiology as a science did not exist. One man could still learn everything which was known about medicine, and Moreau attempted to do just that. Psychiatry had hardly emerged as a specialty.

When he was 20 years old he went to Paris to complete his studies and earned his degree of doctor of medicine. At 22 he applied for the position of assistant physician in the largest mental hospital in France, which was just outside Paris, L'Asile d'Aliénés de Charenton. The director of the hospital was Jean Etienne Esquirol, one of the first physicians to consider mental patients as sick people who are not possessed by demons, should not be shackled, and should be treated with care, concern, and kindness. Moreau learned a great deal from his famous master and from his associates, including Pinel and Aubert.

At that time a prolonged voyage to a distant and exotic land in the company of a psychiatrist was a customary treatment for mental illness among the wealthy people of France and Europe. Moreau accompanied patients to Egypt and the Orient. During his trips he observed that the Arabs used hashish as an intoxicant as commonly as the Turks or Chinese used opium and the Europeans used alcoholic beverages. Moreau was impressed by the unusual effects of this substance on the mind and on the behavior of Oriental people. Back in Paris in 1840, the year of Esquirol's death, Moreau was appointed physician of the new Bicêtre mental hospital. He decided then to experiment systematically with hashish and began the first recorded clinical experiments on the psychopharmacology of *Cannabis* extracts.

Moreau seems to have prepared his own hashish. He used a crude preparation, the fat-extracted material which the Arabs call "dawamesc." "The flowering tops of the plant are boiled in water to which fresh butter has been added. When this concoction has been reduced by evaporation to a syrupy liquid, it is strained through a cloth. One thus obtains a butter of greenish color which contains the active ingredient. This extract is never absorbed in its pure form because of its obnoxious and nauseous odor. It is sweetened with sugar and flavored with scented fruit or flower extracts. When freshly prepared the finished product is not too unpleasant to the taste, but it becomes rancid." "However," according to Moreau, "this extract keeps its intoxicating properties for as long as ten years."

Moreau might have prepared his own extracts in order to avoid the many additives (ginger, cinnamon, cloves, and powder of cantharides) added by the Arabs. However, he had to start with imported plants of *Cannabis*. His attempts, with his friend Aubert, to grow the plant near Bicêtre yielded a variant which contained minimal active ingredient, insufficient to produce intoxication.

Moreau claims that one has to ingest an amount of his hashish preparation equal to a walnut (30 g) to obtain any results. Because such a large dose was necessary, Moreau's extract could not contain more than .5% delta-9-THC: in 30 g this would amount to 150 mg of the drug, a very large dose. With one-half or one-quarter of this dose, says Moreau, ". . . one will feel happy and gay, and one might have a few fits of uncontrollable laughter." But it is only with much higher dosage (which Moreau and his pupils ingested) that one obtains the profound effects designated in the Orient by the word "fantasia."

Moreau and his pupils went about their experimentation in a very systematic way. They took many different doses of hashish. The pharmacist of the hospital, after a specially high dosage (3 doses or about 90 g) presented for 3 days a psychotic episode, with hallucinations, incoherence, and great agitation. All the experimenters took notes during their intoxications, giving detailed accounts of all their symptoms. They observed each other carefully, exchanged and discussed their impressions, feelings, and thoughts during and after hashish intoxication.

As a result of this experimentation in the clinical pharmacology of hashish, Moreau published in 1845 a book, *Hashish and Mental Alienation*. Alienation was the common medical term to describe mental illness or madness. No better account of the acute effects of *Cannabis* intoxication on mental function has been given since Moreau's own descriptions, which will be summarized here.

"Hashish Intoxication and Mental Illness"

Moreau candidly describes the purpose of his experimentation with hashish.

> "Most psychiatrists have carefully described the infinite variety of symptoms of the many patients with whom they have lived, but I do not know one who, in speaking of madness, has given us the benefit of his personal experience, or described it from the point of view of his own perceptions and sensations. Only curiosity originally led me to experiment upon myself with hashish. Later, it was difficult to forget the exciting memory of some of the effects I owed to this drug. But, from the very outset, I was motivated by another reason: I had seen in hashish, or more specifically in its effect upon the mental faculties,

a powerful and unique method of exploring the genesis of mental illness.

"Madness most frequently explodes without the afflicted being warned by any appreciable impairment of the organism, and his physician is unable to relate it to any physical malfunction. This is a first point of similarity between the effects of hashish and mental illness. The cause is obvious, but the origin remains unknown. This is what most often happens when that cause acts directly on the organ of the mind. We shall see that the manifestations of hashish intoxication are completely analogous to those reported by mental patients. Mental patients and eaters of hashish express themselves similarly when they want to convey their experiences; it seems that both groups have been under the same morbid influence.

"I have compared the principal characteristics observed in mental illness to the symptoms caused in me by hashish intoxication. The insights provided by my own study gave me a better understanding of mental illness."

Moreau next lists the eight cardinal symptoms which are either observed during hashish intoxication or reported by mental patients. They are, in order of increasing mental disorganization:

Unexplainable feeling of bliss, happiness
Excitement; dissociation of ideas
Errors of time and space appreciation
Development of the sense of hearing; the influence of music
Fixed ideas (delusions)
Damage to the emotions
Irresistible impulses
Illusions; hallucinations

Feeling of Happiness

"It is a feeling of physical and mental comfort, of inner satisfaction, of intimate joy; that you seek mainly to understand or analyze that for which you cannot find the cause. You feel happy; you proclaim it with exuberance; you seek to express it with all the means at your disposal; you repeat it to the point of satiety. But to say how and why you are happy, words are not enough. Finding myself in this situation one day and despairing of being understood by words alone, I uttered cries or rather howls. Imperceptibly, following this

febrile and nervous feeling of happiness which shakes convulsively all of your sensitivity, there descends a soft feeling of
physical and mental fatigue, a kind of apathy, of unconcern, an
absolutely complete calm to which your mind abandons itself
with great delight.   It seems that nothing can impair this still-
ness of the soul and that you are inaccessible to sadness."

"I doubt that the most unfortunate news could draw you out
of that imaginary beatitude which one is unable to appreciate
unless he has experienced it.

"External circumstances will confer to these feelings of happiness a still greater intensity by directing them towards a goal.
One imagines what pleasant sensations can add to this state of
bliss and how much more the joys of hashish can be increased
by external impressions, by direct excitations of the senses or
by arousing feelings by natural means.   At that time, the rapture of hashish intoxication, taking shape and form will assume
the dimensions of madness.

"It is really happiness that hashish gives, and by that I mean
totally mental joys, not at all sensual as one might be tempted
to believe.   It is a very curious fact from which one can draw
strange conclusions: All joy, all contentment, even though
their cause is strictly mental, and our most spiritual, idealistic
enjoyments could well be in reality only purely physical sensations, developed in the core of our brain exactly like those produced by hashish.   At least, if one relies on subjective feelings,
no distinction can be made between these two orders of sensation and in spite of the diversity of causes to which they are
related the eater of hashish is happy not like the ravenous man
who is famished and satisfies his appetite, or like the hedonist
who satisfies his desires, but like the man who hears news that
overwhelms him with joy, like the miser counting his treasures,
like the gambler favored by luck, like the ambitious man intoxicated by his success.

"The symptoms we have just described also occur frequently
at the beginning of mental illness: They are the feelings of
happiness, of intimate joy in which the sick find so much hope,
so much confidence in the future and which, alas, are only
precursory symptoms of more violent insanity."

Moreau gives several examples of mental patients who in the course of their
illness experienced great joy with no apparent reason.   It was a young

woman of fine, observing mind, convalescing from "a mania" secondary to childbirth who told Moreau: "In the night, I woke up with a feeling of comfort I cannot describe. I felt happy as I never had. My happiness, my joy, were overflowing and I felt a need to share them with my surroundings. I waited impatiently for daylight to announce the good news. I was wild with delight; I wanted to embrace everybody, even my servants."

Moreau agrees with his teacher, Esquirol, who made similar observations and who believed that such episodes of unexplainable elation often precede the onset of mental illness. He concludes: "One of the effects of hashish, which is generally the most unbelievable experience, is precisely the state of bliss, of fantastic happiness. However, we also see this effect occurring under the influence of the numerous and varied factors that create mental illness. In this respect, mental patients and hashish users present a perfect resemblance."

Excitement; Dissociation of ideas

"The slightest event can interfere with the functioning of our mental faculties and as Pascal said, 'the wing of a fly is enough to disturb the most profound schemes of a genius at work.' In the waking state, when we wish to think of something, to ponder a subject, it almost always happens that we are distracted by some extraneous idea. But that idea only crosses our mind without leaving any trace, or it is easy for us to reject it and the train of our thoughts is not interrupted.

"One of the first noticeable effects of hashish is the gradual weakening of the power that we have to orient our thoughts as we wish. Imperceptibly, we feel ourselves overwhelmed by strange ideas unrelated to those on which we want to concentrate. These ideas, which we do not want to recall, crop up in our mind, one knows not why or how, become more and more numerous, livelier and sharper. Soon one pays attention to them; one follows them in their most extravagant associations, in their most impossible and fantastic creations. If by an effort of will you recover the broken thread of your thoughts, the ones you have rejected will return to your mind but from an already remote past, with the fleeting, nebulous form of dreams from an agitated night.

"In hashish intoxication, the ideas that occur in the mind in the dream state merge fantasy and reality in a curious fashion and relate much more to the past than to the present. You forget those things that at the present most excite your interest and even stir your feelings the most violently, that absorb all your attention when you are in your waking state to think only of those which are already prescribed in your mind. Memory is the source upon which these new ideas originate and the liveliness, the brilliance, the multiplicity of images and of pictures greatly excite the imagination which associates them to one another and gives birth to new productions.

"We live in the present by an act of will that directs our attention toward objects that have a current interest for us. Through memory we live in the past; through memory, we can start over our existence from the time when we became aware of ourselves.

"Through imagination, we live in the future and create for ourselves a new external world. Through imagination, the ego seems to transform himself, as imagination changes at will things, people, time, and places.

"The action of hashish weakens the will—the mental power that rules ideas and connects them together. Memory and imagination then predominate; present things become clear to us, and we are concerned entirely with things of the past and of the future.

"So long as the disorder has not gone beyond certain bounds, one readily recognizes the mistake in which one is temporarily involved; there occurs an uninterrupted succession of false ideas and true ideas, of dreams and of realities, which constitute a sort of composite state of madness and reason and make a person seem to be mad and rational at the same time."

In more severe intoxication, "consciousness is carried away by the whirlwind and is led by one's dream. Lucid moments are briefer and briefer; we abandon ourselves entirely to our inner feelings; our eyes and our ears have not stopped functioning, but they admit only those impressions furnished by memory or imagination. In other words, we fall asleep while dreaming."

Moreau compares the dream state of hashish intoxication with the twilight of consciousness of the person who while still asleep is aware that he is dreaming and wishes to prolong his dream. Superimposed on the dream state and the free flowing of the stream of consciousness there is a state of emotional lability and an exacerbation of sensory perceptions.

"The train of our ideas can be broken by the slightest thing; we undergo the most contradictory influences. We turn in all directions. By a word, a gesture, our thoughts can be directed in succession to a multitude of diverse subjects with a speed and yet with a clearness that is marvelous. A deep feeling of pride takes hold of you with the growing exaltation of your faculties which you feel are growing in energy and power. Depending on the circumstances, on the objects that you see, and the words that you hear, you will experience the most vivid feelings of happiness or sorrow, the most contradictory passions with unusual violence. From irritation, one can pass rapidly to fury, from discontent to hate and desire for revenge, from the calmest love to the wildest passion. Fear becomes terror, courage a dedication that none can stop and that ignores danger. Groundless suspicions may become convictions. The mind tends to exaggerate in all areas; the slightest excitation rarely fails to carry it away. Those who use hashish in the Orient, when they want to abandon themselves to the rapture of hashish intoxication, exert an extreme care to eliminate anything that might turn their madness into depression, or might arouse anything other than pleasant and tender feelings. They take advantage of all the practices that the corrupt customs of the Orient place at their disposal. In the depths of their harem, surrounded by their women, under the spell of the music and the suggestive dancing performed by the dancing girls they relish the intoxicating hashish; and aided by their expectations, they are transported into the midst of the countless wonders that the Prophet has gathered in his paradise."

Moreau concludes that this aspect of *Cannabis* intoxication, with its composite mental excitement where "fragments" of the imagination constantly interact with enhanced sensory perception, recalls the symptoms of "manic" madness in all its details.

"I have not just observed this picture in myself; I have seen several persons who after taking hashish also displayed it in the intoxicated state, and I swear that it was impossible to see the slightest difference between these persons and the patients for whom we care in our asylums."

Errors of Time and Space

"Under the influence of hashish, the mind can fall into the strangest errors concerning time and space. Time seems at first to drag with a slowness that exasperates. Minutes become hours, hours, days. Soon, with more and more exaggeration, all precise ideas of the duration of time escape us, the past and the present are merged. The speed with which our thoughts follow one another and the resulting dream state explains this phenomenon. Time seems longer than when it is measured by terrestrial clocks because the actions or the facts contained in an interval of time, by virtue of their intensity, extend the limits of this interval.

"I was still unacquainted with the effects of hashish when while walking across the Street of the Opera one night, I was struck with the length of time that it was taking me to reach the other side. I had only taken a few steps and it seemed to me that I had been there for two or three hours. I stared at the people, who were numerous as usual. I noticed that some people were passing me, while I was passing ahead of others. I tried in vain to undeceive myself. I hastened my step in vain—time did not pass more rapidly.

"It seemed to me that the crossing was endless, and that the side toward which I walked was retreating at the same rate as I was advancing. Several times, I felt this kind of illusion in strolling the boulevards. Seen at a certain distance, people and things appeared to me as though I was observing them through the large end of binoculars.

"We will remember that T. Gautier, seeking to estimate the duration of a hashish crisis, calculated that 'it was about three hundred years. Sensations followed one another so rapidly that true appreciation of time was impossible. Once the crisis was over, I saw that it had lasted one quarter hour.'

"The phenomenon we have just described may be compared with certain extravagant ideas that are sometimes encountered in psychotics. Some of them believe they are a hundred, a thousand years old—some even say they are eternal. The young woman I mentioned earlier believed in the first days of her manic illness that she had no age. She imagined that she had lived in all the historical periods which she could remember. 'I accused those who surrounded me of stealing from me the measure of time; for me, it no longer exists, I told them. My days and nights passed in an instant too rapidly for me to be able to carry out all the vast plans that filled my mind. I refused to recognize my mother for the reason that I could not have a mother younger than I was.'

"The action of hashish could not cause impressions as distorted as those I have just indicated. With the awareness of himself one easily recognizes the illusion by which psychotics are naturally deceived and one avoids drawing, as they do, extravagant conclusions. However, let us not forget that the source of this illusion is in both cases the same excitement."

Development of the Sense of Hearing; The Influence of Music

Moreau first recalls, despite their poetic exaggeration, the words that Gautier used to describe this phenomenon:

"My hearing was fantastically sharpened. I heard the sound of colors—green, red, blue and yellow sounds in perfectly distinct waves. . . . An overturned glass echoed through me like thunder . . ."

"I have observed these effects in several people," adds Moreau. "I have witnessed their cries of joy, their songs, their tears and their lament, their deep depression or their foolish mirth, depending on the harmonic mode in which sound reached their ears.

"Pleasant or unpleasant, happy or sad, the emotions that music creates are only comparable to those one feels in a dream. It is not enough to say that they are more vivid than those of the waking state. Their character is transformed, and it is only upon reaching a hallucinatory state that they assume their full strength and can induce real paroxysms of pleasure or pain. At that moment, the immediate, direct action of the harmonics and the actual auditory sensations are combined with the most varied and fiery emotions which result from the associations of ideas created by the combination of sounds.

"One day, I had taken a strong dose of hashish. I was surrounded by close friends whose kindness I knew well. I had asked them to observe me scrupulously, to keep an accurate account of my words and gestures. When I had reached a sufficiently high state of intoxication, in order to subdue the mettle of my ideas and feelings by imparting to them a single direction, I begged a young lady artist of great distinction, to sit at the piano to play a sad and melancholic tune. She chose a waltz by Weber. From the first notes of this tune, so deeply imprinted with sorrow, I felt a chill go through my entire body. My excitement changed abruptly in character. Totally concentrated like a fire in me, the waltz evoked in me only sad thoughts and distressing memories. The faces of several people surrounding me reflected the sinister mood of my imagination. These people were just serious; others who were laughing and staring at me seemed to be making faces and threatening me. They terrified me, and I conjectured that they were hostile toward me. I closed my eyes in order not to see anyone and stretched on a couch. I collected myself as best I could, to concentrate entirely on my inner thoughts, but then a sadness, a somber melancholy, a painful anxiety overtook me to such a degree that I felt my chest so compressed that I nearly stopped breathing. My tears flowed profusely and had I been alone, I would have cried aloud. I could not stand it any longer and felt the need to get rid of this awful nightmare. The prayer from the opera *Moses* gradually restored calm in my soul. It seemed that my chest was freed from the weight that was oppressing it. I had that physical and mental feeling of comfort that one experiences upon waking from a bad dream or that one enjoys at the end of a bout of fever.

"I had not been deceived for a moment by my illusions, although these illusions had affected me like reality itself. I listened with delight to religious tones that stirred memories that I had thought to be extinct for years—pleasant feelings that are known only in early childhood and are smothered so fast by doubt and skepticism as soon as we take our first steps into real life. Then I had the idea of kneeling in front of the piano, and there in profound meditation, my eyes closed and my hands clasped, I waited until the music had ceased. An instant later I arose as if waking with a start. My ears had suddenly been struck by rhythms of the waltz. Looking around me, I was astonished to see everyone sitting quietly. 'You do not dance! You can listen to this music and sit quietly like statues!'

"It seemed to me that electric currents were running through all my limbs and forcing them to move rhythmically as if I had been bitten by a giant spider. I asked the mistress of the house to waltz with me. I waltzed for more than a quarter of an hour, half asleep. At each moment, I felt that the floor was disappearing from under my feet for a period of time which I could not estimate. It seemed that my will had nothing to do in the rapid whirl that transported me and that my body irresistibly obeyed the sound waves coming from the piano, just like the spinning top of a child spins, while under the blows of his whip. I did not miss a beat and exchanged a few words with the lady who was waltzing with me.

"This rather violent exercise did not cause me the slightest fatigue. Nevertheless, it made me sweat a great deal, and my crisis, which had lasted about four hours, ended here."

Moreau explains the causes of the rapture produced by music during hashish intoxication. There is first a physical, "organic," basis to this condition, and *Cannabis* must stimulate the organs associated with hearing.

"The overstimulation that hashish causes in the whole nervous system is felt most particularly in the portion of this system concerned with the perception of sounds. Hearing acquires an unbelievable sensitivity. The sounds spread even to the epigastric center; they expand or compress the chest, accelerate or slow the heartbeat, and convulsively set in motion the whole muscular system or benumb it."

In the second place, Moreau stresses the power of music to stimulate the imagination and to recall old memories, which confers to harmony its social significance. "To feel music it must be understood, which is to say that sounds must be associated with familiar ideas." On his travels through the Middle East, Moreau had noticed that European military music was poorly appreciated by the native Arabs, who by contrast showed great pleasure upon hearing the discordant sound of a "poor little flute." "Music plays a minimal part in the emotions you feel, memory and imagination do most of the recollection." Stimulation of memory and imagination by hashish also explains the influence of music on the hashish experience. "Memories of mourning and death ally themselves immediately with sad songs, happy thoughts with gay songs, religious memories with religious songs, and these thoughts and memories exert an almost unlimited influence upon one's judgment."

"When conscious thinking is obliterated by hashish, the mind abandons itself entirely and unreservedly to impressions which are no more considered in perspective and assume a greatly exaggerated importance."

The stimulation of memory and imagination, combined with an increased sense of hearing, are not the only factors contributing to the extraordinary perception of music during hashish intoxication. The special "dream state" produced by hashish also explains the strange effect of music on the mental faculties which have been previously changed by this drug.

> "The overstimulation of memory and imagination, great enough to leave but little room for external stimuli, combined with the confusion of judgment and the turmoil of ideas, results in what I have called 'the dream state.' In this state the sensations produced by music are changed in such a way that, despite having originated in the real world, they resemble those imaginary creations which occur in the dream state. They have all the characteristics of hallucinations.
> "In this manner we can explain the strength of the sensations, the rapture, the kind of ecstasy that music causes in those who have taken hashish. All of these are due to the overstimulation of the sense of hearing, of memory and of imagination associated with the dream state. It is a fact of subjective observation that the sensations and emotions particular to the dream state reach sometimes such intensity and power that nothing in waking life can be compared to them."

Fixed Ideas (Delusions)

"This intellectual lesion, so frequent in mental illness, is also caused by hashish, but only when intoxication has progressed to an advanced stage, a stage which one would seldomly reach deliberately."

Moreau experienced delusions only once, when he was first experimenting with the drug and might have absorbed too large a dose. The idea occurred to him that he had been poisoned by his colleagues, and this idea progressively took hold of his mind, dominating all other thoughts in the most absolute manner. He even accused his colleague, Dr. Aubert-Roche, of being an assassin. The denials he received only strengthened his conviction, and he could not recognize the absurdity of his thought. Another delusion, much more extravagant, followed: He was dead, his soul had left his body, and he was on the verge of being buried.

> "When the 'excitement' of hashish intoxication is less intense, delusions are still numerous, but they are fleeting. It is only with difficulty and in the case of a serious disturbance that they penetrate deeply into one's thinking and remain there for some time. At first they are strongly opposed

by the inner feeling, by the awareness that is so solidly implanted amidst all the disturbance caused by hashish.

"In the case of mental illness, delusions are essentially characterized by their total and exclusive domination over the mind, as if they had absorbed the individual's personality. Delusions caused by hashish are similar. They can only exist with their distinctive characteristics when the consciousness and the ego are impaired and involved in the overall disintegration of the mind.

"We all have fantastic ideas crossing our mind, of power, love, wealth, immortality; in the waking state—in our state of reflective power and complete independence, of self-power— we consider all of these fantasies playing in our mind as if they were in some way alien to us. The slightest impulse of our will makes them change endlessly. Like images from a kaleidoscope moved by the hand, we clear them away without any effort.

If, as a result of the action of hashish, this intellectual capacity weakens and completely disappears, temporarily or permanently, immediately the fantasy that had only crossed our mind before is transformed into a conviction, a fixed idea, because our judgment, directed by inner consciousness, cannot combat it, accuse it of error and discard it. With hashish, unless intoxication is excessive, the delusions are very short-lived. You catch yourself at times imagining the most incredible things, the strangest monstrosities, to which you surrender body and soul. Then suddenly, on the stroke of lightning, conscious thinking returns: you take hold of yourself, you recognize the error in which you had indulged. You were crazy and you have become reasonable. But you remain convinced that in pushing things a little farther the delusion had a good chance of completely dominating you, for a period of time which cannot be foreseen."

Moreau attributes the appearance and fixation of delusions in the mind to a primary "excitement" of brain function which he "wishes eagerly to explain clearly." His usual insight leads him to define the basic cause of delusions in terms which modern psychopharmacologists would not reject. This phenomenon of mental excitement "which precedes delusion I would willingly call a dissolution, *a molecular disintegration of intelligence,* if I dared explain it as I feel it. A delusion is the result of this intellectual disintegration, a result which persists even when this disintegration has stopped and intelligence has in a way integrated itself again: it is the motivating idea of a dream which survives the dream that had given birth to this idea."

When Moreau examines the circumstances under which delusions develop among mental patients presenting depression ("melancholy"), he finds, preceding the acute depressive episode, an original "shock to the brain," such as fainting, loss of consciousness accompanied by complete impairment of the thought processes, and dissociation of ideas.

He believes, as did his teacher Esquirol, that the delusions experienced by many psychotics are preceded by "a confusion of all the elements of intelligence and a general disorder of the mind."

"I call attention to the observations of physicians who have considerable experience with psychotics. When their patients were in a condition to understand them, the physicians often asked them: 'How did your illness begin? How could you put in your head such absurd, extravagant ideas?' Answer: 'I became so sad, I was so sick that I was completely confused; I was no longer normal; I had lost my bearings; my ideas were all upside down; I did not know what I was saying or doing, and I imagined that. . . .' This is the start of the delusion which will later dominate all thought processes and will survive the general confusion, the upheaval of the faculties of the mind. Delusions do not always rapidly overwhelm the intelligence of mental patients. Sometimes delusions will have to struggle with the inner consciousness: this is the moment of uncertainty, of indecision, of anxiety, of extreme flight of ideas. These delusions follow patterns of waning and waxing, disappearing and reappearing with still greater intensity.

"A further proof that an overall confusion of the mind constitutes the basic source of all delusions is that psychotics will frequently forget their prevailing delusions to adopt new ones more related to current preoccupations: A lady believes that her husband wants to shoot her; she escapes from her castle and throws herself in a well; she is told that if one wanted to kill her, poison would be easier; immediately she is afraid of being poisoned and refuses all food. A man, in a depression, believes that he is dishonored; after having tried in vain to reassure him, he is given the comfort of religion; immediately he is convinced that he is damned.

"Once the regular chain of orderly association of ideas is

broken, the strangest and most extravagant thoughts, the strangest combinations of ideas, are formed and establish themselves in the mind. The most insignificant reason may give birth to them. When the psycho-cerebral disturbances which underlie the formation of delusions subside progressively, it is the conviction and the immovable tenacity upon which they rested which will disappear, rather than the ideas themselves. These ideas will just become more and more similar to the simple erroneous ideas and misconceptions from which no one escapes even in the most perfect state of mental health.

"Subjective observation by the inner consciousness of the mental processes in hashish intoxication has also enabled me to establish that dissociation of ideas and the resulting dream state were the primary source of delusions. Delusions can only be the result of a profound and radical change in the intelligence, of a general upheaval of our mental faculties. A delusion is not an error in thinking. A psychotic does not make a mistake. He functions in an intellectual sphere essentially different from our own. He has a conviction against which neither the reason of someone else, nor his own, can prevail; no more than any reasoning, any thought of the waking state can rectify the reasoning and thinking of the dream state. The same difference exists between the psychotic and the same man as between the man who dreams and the man who is awake.

"Delusions are only separated parts, temporary manifestations of a dream state that extends into the waking state."

By a systematic analysis into the origin of delusions as they appear under the influence of hashish or in the course of mental illness, Moreau became convinced of the primary organic nature of mental disturbances.

Disturbance of the Emotions

Moreau first describes, by using his own "subjective awareness," the labile emotional state associated with *Cannabis* intoxication.

"With hashish, the emotions display the same degree of overexcitement as the intellectual faculties. They have the mobility and also the despotism of the ideas. The more one feels incapable of directing his thoughts, the more one loses the power to resist the emotions they create. The violence of these emotions is boundless when the disorder of the intellect has reached the point of incoherence.

"In order to study these emotions better, we shall examine them separately: (1) those related to things past, but which we remember, and (2) those related to the present or that affect us at that very instant and for the first time.

"In this second catgory we include the irritability that leads us to eagerly seize any reason to excite our anger, our hate, and all our worst instincts, that strained sensitivity that causes us to exaggerate our feelings of friendship, of gratitude, our joy, our sadness, our hopes, our fears, our terrors. Under such a disposition a cause which in the waking state would at the most dissatify us enrages us. We will easily control the rage that we feel growing in our heart but because of our awareness of the situation we will think of the most extreme ways to satisfy it. If something frightens us, we are soon assailed by fears, unexplainable anxieties which cast a dark shroud on all our surroundings. One day in the midst of a strong hashish intoxication my ears were suddenly struck by the sounds of bells. This was hardly an hallucination but, being in a bad mood, I associated to this sound the idea that it was sounding for a funeral.

"Like the ideas to which they relate, emotions overpower the intellect because their action is exerted alone, without the discriminating influence that reflective thought, in the waking state, always exerts against them. These emotions are blind instinctive drives in which consciousness has no part."

Moreau believes that this unbalanced emotional state cannot be related to any "main injury to the emotions," as many of his contemporaries thought. He attributes the emotional lability of hashish intoxication to the primary "pathological state" of the intellect created by the drug.

"So long as the association of ideas is regular, so long as the uncontrollable speed of perception does not disturb the mind, emotions—gay or sad, hateful or kind—are in no ferment. They remain under the control of the will. The dream state which is the necessary consequence of hashish intoxication unleashes all of the power of emotions."

Similar disorders of the emotions were observed by Moreau in his mental patients.

"Nothing compares with the mettle and violence of emotions in manics except the extreme incoherence of their ideas. Every time their emotions are openly and forcefully expressed it must be attributed to their state of mental excitement. At this moment we have under observation a lady who, for several months, has been under the spell of delusions and imaginary terrors. She was calm enough for about the first month in the institution. She had to be questioned a great deal to obtain a few words concerning her dominant thoughts. Then, under the influence of very cold weather, an active state of excitement developed. Her thoughts were disjointed and rapid, her movement jerky. All her limbs shook with tremors. The fears, the imaginary terrors of this patient were paramount; it was the state of a person who all of a sudden is seized by the greatest terror, who, in illness, does not know what he is saying or doing."

Moreau attributed the emotional instability of his patient to a primary disturbance of the intellect. In taking this stand he disagreed with the prevailing view held by all his famous contemporaries such as Pinel and Esquirol. These authors believed in the existence of "a primary damage of the emotional faculties" without any lesion of the intellect, inasmuch as the patient with such a disease entity is often ready to justfy his feelings. Moreau rejects this stand: "Only the intellect is basically damaged in mental illness; the disorder of the feelings is secondary to the disorder of the thoughts. The impairment of judgment, the dissociation of ideas, is the primary source of all damage to the emotions."

He describes the power of *Cannabis* to stimulate emotions from past memories and to confer on them a new life.

"The exciting action of hashish is also exerted on feelings which had been experienced long ago and had only left slight memories in the mind. A feeling which one thought was completely gone suddenly revives another which had been left dormant in the depths of the mind and it surges with such intensity that one believes himself to be under a spell. This is particularly true of feelings of love, probably because of desire for happiness caused by hashish. The vitality of memories, which gives a sort of actuality to things past, and the imagination, which likes to embellish the object of our affections, confer new dimensions to the feelings of love."

But in the state of hashish intoxication experienced by Moreau, "the effects of the drug on feelings of love are exclusively intellectual. The imagination bears all the cost; the senses are in no way involved. Plato himself could not have dreamed of passions purer, more ethereal, than those kindled by hashish."

Irresistible Impulses

"Impulses, those instinctive urges which build up in us almost without our knowledge, acquire under the influence of hashish an extraordinary driving power, one that is irresistible if the toxic action is very strong. Impulses are like passions; they draw their strength from the excitement, the mental disturbance that prevents regular, free association of ideas. They have their periods of waning and waxing and are only irresistible at the height of the excitement."

As Moreau recalls, "Seeing an open window in my room I got the idea that if I wanted I could throw myself from that window. Though I did not think I would commit such an act, I asked that the window be closed: I was afraid I might get the idea of jumping out the window. Deep down in my fear, I felt a growing impulse, and I had an intimate feeling that I might have followed it with a stronger 'excitement.' The action of hashish is not continuous. During the brief period of remission, the same thought was in my mind, but not the fear of giving in to the absurd idea of throwing myself out the window. It was difficult to explain to myself how such a fear had occurred to me, but this same fear reappeared with the return of the 'excitement.' "

Moreau observed very similar manifestations in mental patients: "The actions of psychotics are not always irresistible, although in no case can they be held responsible. Often these actions are only the logical consequence of false convictions. At other times, a particular disposition of his intelligence will thrust the patient, without any possible resistance, to all his impulses. He will then act without knowing or realizing what he is doing. These patients then act mechanically, as if they obeyed a dream, according to their favorite expression."

"These patients," says Esquirol, "are unhappy about the directions in which they are so irresistibly drawn, but all acknowledged that they felt something inside that they could not explain, that their brain was encumbered, that they felt an unexpressible turmoil in exercising their reason."

Moreau disagreed with his contemporaries, who believed that some mental patients presented a primary disturbance of the instincts without any impairment of their judgement. "Neither the will nor the instinctive drives become irresistible as a result of an injury specific to them. There is a basic lesion of judgement, a lesion that is profound but so transitory that the patients themselves can hardly describe it. It is from his lesion, his excitement, that all the manifestations of psychosis are derived. 'Excitement' of the brain can be brought about by a multiplicity of causes, such as alcohol intoxication, which makes one submit with an extreme facility and an irresistible urge to impulses that until then were controlled and resisted. In the Orient, *Cannabis* extract, opium, thorn apple, and other substances are used to produce this 'excitement' of the intellect. We can induce this excitement with external agents; experience has proved for a long time that pathological causes, developed in the very core and depths of the body, can also produce the same excitement with an even greater intensity and with changes of which only nature knows the secret."

Illusions, Hallucinations

These two serious manifestations of mental illness derive from the same basic mental change of cerebral excitement "which carries the seed of all mental pathology as the trunk of a tree, its branches, its leaves, and its flowers are contained in the grain."

Illusions of Hashish Intoxication

"Progressively, as 'excitement' grows, our mind shuts itself off from external impressions to concentrate more and more on subjective ones; as this kind of metamorphosis takes place, we are drawn away from real life to be thrown into a world where the only reality is the one created by our memories and our imagination; progressively, one becomes the toy, first of simple illusions and then of true hallucinations which are like the remote sounds, the first lights, which are coming to us from an imaginary and fantastic world.

"When any sort of thing, alive or lifeless, strikes our sight, or when a sound, such as the song of a bird strikes our ears while the 'excitement' is still weak, we feel that two distinct phenomena are occurring in our mind:

1. We have seen, we have heard, clearly and distinctly as we do in the waking state.

2. Then suddenly, as the result of certain similarities of which we may or may not be aware, the image of another object and the sensation of another sound are awakened within us. As a result of these intracerebral impressions, due to the

action of memory and imagination, the mind pauses, shortly fusing the two sensations into a single one, covering over the real sensation with the imaginary one and projecting the latter upon the external object.

"Therefore, an illusion is made of two component parts:

1. a sensory impression

2. a cerebral sensation (immediately deriving from the former) and which is totally due to the action of the imagination There lies its essential psychic nature.

"The external features of an illusion, with the numerous varied forms that it is likely to assume, will be necessarily borrowed from the particular nature of the mood and habitual thoughts of a person. It is understandable that images or ideas that have made the strongest impression on the mind are the first to be awakened or that the cerebral fibers that vibrate most often are more readily disturbed than others."

Visual Illusions

"We often see the face of a person totally unknown to us but which resembles the face of a familiar person. This resemblance, however slight, is enough to recall from our mind the memory of that person; this memory has all the vividness of the sensory impression, for the mind perceives it in the same manner as it perceives in the dream state.

"From that moment, what we have seen with the eyes of the mind is put in the place of what we have seen with the eyes of the body. The creations of our imagination have taken the place of reality. And if all reflective thinking is denied to us by the violence of the cerebral disturbance due to hashish intoxication, the two sensations are fused into a single one, and the error is inevitable.

"It has happened to me many times that being in a rather lively state of intoxication and looking attentively at a portrait I saw all of a sudden the portrait come to life. The head moved slightly and seemed to want to detach itself from the canvas. The entire face took an expression that only life may confer; the eyes especially were alive; I saw them turning in their orbits to follow all my movements. The first time I had such an experience without expecting it I could not retain a cry of fear. I retreated several steps, crying, 'It is prodigious! That portrait is alive! It is magic!' I repeated this experience two or three times in order to explain this phenomenon to myself and analyze it in cold blood. Then I realized that I gradually ceased to see the image that was in front of my eyes. Imperceptibly I was seeing it only as if it were floating in the clouds of a faint dream. Finally I saw in a dream the very same person represented on the painting and who, like all the figments of the imagination, impressed me more vividly than the real vision of the portrait."

In another visual illusion, Moreau, before experiencing the effects of hashish, observed attentively a very fine engraving depicting a cavalry battle:

"We sat down at the table. From my place I was turning my back to the engraving. After repressing several times the intoxication that was gradually seizing me, I suddenly stood up and, placing my hand behind my head, I cried, 'I do not like horses that kick, even on a painting.' I pointed with my finger to one of the horses on the picture: 'I feel that one of them hit me with his hoof.' These words were greeted with great laughter. I laughed with everybody; then, collecting myself, I found within me the image of a spirited jumping horse, but a pale and fleeting one like the impressions from a dream when one wakes up. My illusion was nothing else than a dream, but that dream had been as rapid as a thought, and an external cause, a sensory impression, had provoked it. This last feature, which did not distinguish my illusion from an ordinary dream, was in fact a true manifestation of mental illness.

"When the visage of an old woman evoked in me the youngest and most attractive face, I felt perfectly that the subjective image which my overactive imagination had made me see in a dream was taking the place of the real image. I told myself there were two explanations to this illusion: (1) in taking hashish, I thought that all sensations had to be pleasant, that I must see everything as if it was beautiful; (2) the image of a pretty woman, by the admiration it creates and the emotion it causes, engraves itself spontaneously and deeply in our mind and consequently may be reproduced with great ease.

"All these examples of visual illusions have the same character. Excitement is the basic, generative fact of the illusion, whose nature will then be modified by the person's particular character and the bend of his usual or predominant ideas. Whatever the condition of our mind, whatever emotions stir us, if there is no excitement, no intoxication, we shall not be able to have illusions. But as 'excitement' develops the resulting illusions will invariably reflect the nature or the ideas and feelings which are most prevalent in us at that time.

"The user of hashish will be influenced by everything that strikes his eyes and his ears. A word, a gesture, a look, a sound, or the slightest noise, in directing his attention in a given direction, will confer to all his illusions a special character.

"A few words were enough to make me change from the greatest happiness to the deepest depression. And this depression reflected upon all the objects that surrounded me and distorted them. It was a plaid beret that offered me the features of a bloody face; it was a stove full of glowing coal that I saw in a glass of lemonade. Finally there was a light that multiplied into ten or twelve others which were then placed around a bier in which I imagined myself lying."

Auditory Illusions. According to Moreau, illusions of hearing are infrequently caused by hashish intoxication. Rarely are sounds distorted. However, sounds may be amplified, or give rise to emotions or thoughts which are colored by the prevailing mood. Moreau recalls going to a reception while he was under the influence of hashish.

"First of all I was overwhelmed by many visual illusions, which did not bother me, but I found that everyone was talking—or, rather, yelling—at the top of their lungs, which was terribly irritating. After about a half-hour, which seemed like a century, I found a pretext and walked out.

"Sometimes sounds are not only exaggerated; they multiply as if repeated by an echo that amplifies them. One evening in a garden I did hear very distinctly the songs of a vast flock of birds. The garden was small; there was only one bird in it. It was a nightingale which sang intermittently. But I heard a continual twittering. I covered my ears; I continued to hear it, but less clearly. That same evening I heard some shooting, followed by buzzing sounds made by large crowds. For a moment, overcome by this illusion, I cried out: 'Listen! I hear gunshots! There is a riot!' Swiftly realizing my mistake, I looked for the cause of the noise. I learned that a servant had dropped an object while tidying up a room which had an open window overlooking the garden where we were.

"Another time, hearing the bells ringing in a nearby church, I asked what it could be. Somebody answered, 'Someone has probably died.' Immediately, the last word echoed five or six times in my ears, as if each person in the room had, in turn, repeated it in a more and more dismal tone. At that time I was not completely sure of the innocuity of hashish. I feared I had taken too high a dose, which explains the sad nature of this illusion. This illusion was very painful to me; I advise all those who want to experiment with hashish to take all necessary measures to avoid experiencing such illusions."

Moreau displays great insight as he analyzes the different component parts of auditory illusions, which, like visual ones, include:

"1. A sensory impression, which is the true physical sensation.

2. A second sensation that follows the first immediately, a sensation totally in the mind and purely subjective.

3. A temporal error of the mind that confounds the two sensations—or, rather, forgets the first one and only retains the second, from which results the distorted perception."

This is the first definition known to this author of what psychologists today call "temporal disintegration." The mental condition created by *Cannabis* intoxication is characterized by an impairment of immediate memory and a disintegration of sequential thought which is essential for the proper interpretation of sensory perception.

"As rapidly as these three phases of an illusion succeed each other, the mind perceives them distinctly, not at the very moment the manifestation occurs but immediately after; it is the impression of a dream that remains in the mind and which harkens back to it. If we were to give a faithful account of this impression we would say, 'I dreamed that I heard . . . ,' a true statement that a psychotic changes to '*I heard*,' because he is deprived of his awareness and necessarily confuses the dream state with the waking state."

Illusions of General Sensibility (Awareness of Body Image). These illusions cannot be accounted for by the analytic study to which Moreau subjected auditory and visual ones.

"When I felt my body grow in size, inflate like a balloon, this sensation, however unusual, could not be distinguished from ordinary sensations. It was impossible to distinguish, as in the case of visual or auditory illusions, the actual sensation from the creation of the imagination. Illusions of general sensibility are the result of special sensory alterations as real as those that take place in normal sensations. Only the origin of these changes differs. Contrary to what happens in ordinary sensations, it is not in the peripheral parts of the organs or at the nerve endings that one first instinctively locates the source of the abnormal sensation which forms illusion. This sensation is concentrated entirely in the brain. It is in the central nervous system that it first develops, and then irradiates to the organs.

"Thus, when I felt my body inflate, I passed my hands over my body and I was not able to confirm this sensation. My hands informed me that my body had kept its usual size at the very moment that I felt it increase excessively. This contradiction between my touch and my subjective perception created the strangest ambiguous experience in me.

"I felt so light that my feet hardly touched the ground when I walked, and I heard distinctly and with some pain resounding in my head, the sound of my steps on the ground. I felt also mildly a sensation well known to hashish users: sudden flushes of pleasant warmth rose to my head. My brain seemed to enlarge and I thought I was taking off from the ground."

The sensory illusions reported by psychotics are similar, according to Moreau, to those produced by hashish, provided the dose absorbed is large enough to create a cerebral disturbance which obliterates awareness.

"Supposing a degree of intellectual disturbance sufficiently intense to obliterate in me all consciousness, as happens among psychotics, we may well imagine that my illusions might have become the point of departure of delusions similar to those seen in psychotics. I could have believed myself transformed into a bird or a balloon, afraid of being carried away by a gust of wind or punctured by the slightest shock or burned by a spark. If the intoxication was intense enough I might believe I had the power of rising into the air, of flying through space like a bird.

"It is exactly what happened to the young man who thought he had been changed into a steam engine piston.

"Several persons, after taking hashish, claimed that their brains started boiling and the tops of their head rhythmically rose and dropped as if lifted by sprays of steam. I myself felt a similar sensation. It is one of the sensations which most frightens those not yet accustomed to hashish."

Moreau distinguishes illusions from delusions or fixed ideas, which need not be triggered by sensory stimuli. He also distinguishes illusions from hallucinations. In illusions, the mind is still on the border of a dream state, and the imagination has not yet shaken off its dependence on external stimuli. The illusion is confined within certain limits like the activity of the senses to which it is related: Imagination acts within the limits of the sensory activity; visual and auditory impressions trigger the appearance of the dream and of the resulting illusion.

Hallucinations. By contrast, hallucinations include all the faculties of the mind; their only limits are those that nature has placed upon the activity of mental functions. As a result, all mental manifestations may be "hallucinated," not only those related to the perception of sounds or images. Hallucinations are the most striking manifestations of the cerebral disturbance or "excitement" which is produced by hashish intoxication or by mental illness in which the dream state takes precedence over the conscious state.

"The 'hallucinator' hears his own thoughts as he sees and hears the creations of his imagination, as he is moved by the impressions he uncovers in his memory.

"As the action of hashish is more keenly felt, one passes imperceptibly from the real world into a fictitious world without losing consciousness of oneself. In a way there exists a sort of fusion between the dream state and the waking state. One dreams while awake.

"One evening I was in a salon, in a reunion with close friends. We played some music which helped greatly to stimulate all of my faculties. There came a moment when all my thoughts and memories carried me back to the Orient. I spoke enthusiastically of the countries where I had traveled; I glibly told of several episodes that had most impressed me during my trip. As I was telling of my departure from Cairo to Upper Egypt, I suddenly stopped and shouted, 'Here! Here! I am now hearing the song of the sailors rowing on the

Nile: Al bedaoui! Al bedaoui!' I repeated this refrain as I
had done in the past.

"It was an hallucination because I heard clearly and distinctly the songs that in the past had so often struck my ears.

"This was the first time I experienced this manifestation in
such a distinct and clear-cut manner and despite the disturbance of my thoughts, which were whirling in my mind, I applied myself to study this hallucination as precisely as I could.

"I first tried to provoke other hallucinations by turning my
attention to other thoughts and evoking other memories. It
was impossible. In spite of myself, I was constantly brought
back to the same subject; but the hallucination had stopped,
although the chain of memories connected to it had been re-
linked.

"This hallucination had only left in my mind the fleeting
memory of a dream. I perceived only a difference in the degree of intensity between the memory and the impression itself.

"I dreamed I heard: I believed that I was hearing with
that full and complete conviction that one has when dreaming.
Such was the invariable response that I made to myself when
I sought to account for what I had felt. So I was dreaming;
that conclusion resulted from the clearest, most precise testimony from my inner consciousness. I responded with complete presence of mind to the questions that were asked concerning the songs I said I was hearing. Several times I had
the occasion to assure myself that other hallucinators experienced impressions of this type. They invariably described
these same impressions: 'I dreamed that I saw; I dreamed
that I heard; and yet I knew perfectly well where I was, who
was around me. It is unbelievable.'

"My concept of the pathogenesis of hallucinations did not
at first come to me as clearly as I have just expressed it.
Many experiences were necessary to dispel the errors similar
to those made by psychotics who have lost all awareness of
their conditions.

"Several times, when the excitement was not very pronounced, the sounds that I heard seemed to resound in my
head; but it was only a vague impression. At other times I
was inclined to believe that I was the one who was talking.
But I corrected this mistake as soon as I really started to talk.
Exactly the same thing happens in the dream state; it is our

own thoughts that we express and to which we respond when we converse with other people in dreams. These are various impressions that we have formerly received which repeat themselves and which we associate and combine in all sorts of ways. All these manifestations derive essentially from the dream state, and one should not mistake them for the hearing of voices when the intellectual faculties have not undergone a change.

"At times in the waking state it happens that we are suddenly awakened by voices that we had been hearing in a dream. And we are as keenly impressed by these voices as if they were real, to the extent that we have to think for a few moments in order to convince ourselves that we were dreaming.

"Let us suppose now that these manifestations recur intermittently and that in the intervals we are perfectly lucid. We will then have an idea of what happens in hashish intoxication and in other mental disturbances where hallucinations occur.

"We have only mentioned auditory hallucinations. Our observations apply equally to visual ones. They are two manifestations in nature, namely simple accidents of a dream state.

"Every time we have observed hallucinations we have inevitably found the 'dynamic nervous lesion' that the action of Indian hemp has taught us to recognize and which is the primordial disturbance of all the other pathological phenomena of the mental faculties."

The Primary Organic Nature of Mental Illness

By a systematic analysis of the symptoms described by mental patients considered in the light of his own observations during hashish intoxication, Moreau became convinced of the primarily organic nature of mental illness. This conviction brings him to point out "the little differences between the folly of the 'demented' (schizophrenic) and that of the manics. The difference in the two conditions being more a matter of degree of the same basic lesion on the combined mental faculties." He tries to define this abnormal cerebral condition "as a general state of excitement of mental faculties, a rapid and confused agitation of ideas, a dynamic nervous lesion, a kind of oscillatory movement of nervous activity" (Fig. 20). This functional lesion cannot exist, according to Moreau, independently of the brain. It is linked

Fig. 20. A schematic representation of Moreau's concept of mental illness, showing its analogy with hashish intoxication.

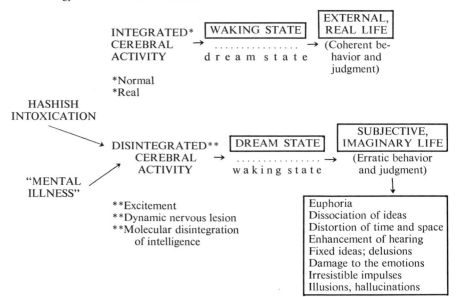

to a completely material and molecular change, however imperceptible its nature, "imperceptible as the changes that take place in the intimate texture of a rope upon which one applies vibrating motions of variable intensity."

"The existence of this organic change is revealed to us with complete certainty by subjective observation; but how are we to discover its traces when life is gone from the organs, even supposing that this change can leave traces? Take apart, piece by piece, the keyboard that gives so discordant sounds when touched by inexperienced hands, and you will look in vain for the cause of the disharmony that offended your ears. Similarly in your search for the cause of a psychosis you would look in vain at the inner texture (histology) of the brain which will have presented a functional disturbance for some time."

And what are the causes of this primordial change in brain activity? Moreau mentions the small number of known reasons such as physical, mental, and pathological changes which abruptly shock mental faculties and exaggerate their action. In his opinion, "the psychological reasons that appear so frequently in the development of madness are only secondary and have an occasional value. They do not contain in themselves the power necessary to cause the disease. There is almost always a latent, more or less pronounced, organic predisposition. That is why one sees the most insignificant psychological reason trigger the explosion of the most violent disturbances. Perhaps this explains why, when we see 'psychological reasons' triggering so easily mental disturbances, methods of the same nature are so ineffective in curing them."

And finally, Moreau recognizes our ignorance concerning the great number of other possible organic causes of mental illness. He hints at some which will be recognized more than a century later as probable enzymatic changes.

> "We completely ignore the greater number of causes, those
> which are hidden, and made (synthetized) in the secret depth
> of our tissues, which are discharged from one system into an-
> other and are transmitted by inheritance."

Moreau's generalizations created great controversies among his contemporaries, who defined insanity as a purely functional disturbance of intelligence and classified the manifestations of mental illness in a strictly symptomatic way according to the different categories of the mind: there were the lesions of the emotions, the lesions of the will, the lesions of the instincts.

To formulate his hypothesis of the primarily organic nature of mental illness, Moreau utilized to the fullest possible extent all of the tools available to him in 1840: *Cannabis,* the only psychotomimetic drug at his disposal; his own extraordinary insight; and his keen sense of clinical observation. Now, some 130 years later, in spite of all the many investigative tools in neurophysiology, neurochemistry, and psychopharmacology at their disposal, psychiatrists are still pondering the basic nature of mental illness and the validity of Moreau's theory.

And no one is ready to answer Moreau's following query: "What is the lesion of the brain, what is the disposition of cerebral molecules which may be correlated with the false convictions, the erroneous ideas which are common to all of us, from the most learned to the most ignorant?"

PSYCHOPATHOLOGICAL EFFECTS

It is clear from the observations of Moreau and of the French Romantics, and from the experiences of Taylor (1849) and Ludlow (1857), that ingestion of *Cannabis* extracts might precipitate episodes of acute mental confusion reminiscent of an acute brain syndrome. Their intensity was enough to discourage Taylor and Gautier (1846) from repeating a second time their hashish experiences. The hashish eaters, Ludlow and Baudelaire (1858), who continued to absorb *Cannabis* extracts for some time, eventually gave up the drug, convinced of its destructive effect on the creative faculties of the mind.   Moreau mentions only one acute psychotic episode among his associates who had taken hashish; all the others kept their self-awareness and their consciousness while being transported in the fantastic world created by the drug.   They did not choose to use *Cannabis* as a pleasure-inducing substance, but as a method to explore mental pathology.   None of them absorbed the drug over a prolonged time and on a regular basis, and its chronic effect on mental function could not be assessed.   However, Moreau mentions that "one of the determining causes of insanity among the Orientals is the excessive use of hashish" and that large amounts of the drug could readily induce a true psychotic episode "for a period of time which cannot be foreseen."

The widespread use of *Cannabis* extracts in the nineteenth century for therapeutic purposes, in Europe and the United States, was not accompanied by any report of adverse acute or chronic mental reactions.

Until recently, the only reports of the adverse effects of *Cannabis* on mental functions came from India or the Middle East.   They were not sufficiently substantiated to convince a number of American psychiatrists that the use of *Cannabis* might produce mental pathology.

Other physicians (Deniker and Ginestet, 1969), after studying the observations of the hashish eaters of the nineteenth century, believed that young persons with labile personalities and lacking a strong ego might not be able to cope with the profound disturbances of the mental process produced by *Cannabis* intoxication and might present acute adverse reactions.

Such acute adverse reactions have been described repetitively and with increasing frequency over the past 25 years, as *Cannabis* intoxication has appeared on the American scene.   They resemble those described earlier in India and Morocco.

More recently, the syndrome of mental and physical deterioration first reported by Moreau (1845) and attributed to chronic *Cannabis* intoxication, and confirmed by Chopra (1969), Miras (1969), and Benabud (1957), has appeared in England and the United States.

Acute Adverse Effects of *Cannabis* Intoxication

The acute adverse effects of *Cannabis* intoxication are now well documented.   They were first reported in the United States by Bromberg (1934) and by Walton (1938).   They vary in intensity, as described by Bromberg, from anxiety states (Keeler, 1967) to panic reactions and reactive emotional states (Weil, 1970), to acute toxic psychosis (Talbott and Teague, 1969; H. S. Kaplan, 1971).   Many factors influence onset and intensity of these reactions, such as dosage absorbed, prevailing mood of the subject, and social setting.

Panic Reactions. Panic reactions are those most frequently reported in the United States, where *Cannabis* preparations are often mild. They are characterized by a state of reactive fear and helplessness, with the feeling of impending death or of becoming insane. But the patients are not disoriented and relate their distress to consumption of the drug. They respond to gentle and firm reassurance. This conditions usually occurs in first-time users, but has also been seen after multiple use.

These panic reactions were described by Moreau (1845) who, when he started experimenting with hashish, thought that he had been poisoned by his friends. Ames (1958) reports that one of 10 volunteers given orally 0.24 to 0.46 g of *Cannabis* extract experienced an episode of intense anxiety.

The following case was reported by Weil (1970) as an example of such a panic reaction:

> "A 37-year-old housewife was persuaded by her 15-year-old daughter to 'turn on' by eating candy made with hashish. She had never tried *Cannabis* before and agreed to do so out of 'curiosity' although she was very apprehensive. The daughter ate three times as much candy as the patient and became 'pleasantly high' for about 6 hours. The patient, 1 hour after ingesting the candy, felt her heart racing and thought she was going to have a heart attack. She became panicky and lay down without telling her daughter what was wrong. Shortly afterward she felt 'flushed and dizzy' and became convinced that she was poisoned. Finally, she got the daughter to call a family physician, who persuaded the patient to take a taxicab to a nearby emergency ward. When the physician arrived at the hospital he found her in *a state of nervous collapse* with a regular *heart rate of 140*. He ordered an intramuscular injection of chlorpromazine and had her admitted to a psychiatric bed. *She remained agitated and depressed for 4 days* and was discharged on the fifth day with no aftereffects. The daughter, who had taken three times the dose of hashish, had a 'good time' that lasted about 6 hours."

A very similar case is reported from India by Chopra (1971):

> "S. S., age 37, a school teacher. Out of curiosity he took 15 grains (900 mg) of bhang in the company of his brother

who consumed 360 grains. He had never taken the drug before. While his brother felt happy, exhilarated, and high, he
felt dizzy and experienced a sinking sensation and felt that he
was going to die. There was an inner struggle between his
will and feelings. His face was flushed, he had an *excessively
high heartbeat,* and upon examination, he was found to be
suffering from *nervous collapse.* He was given chlorpromazine intramuscularly. *He remained agitated and depressed
for four days,* after which recovery followed. His brother enjoyed the euphoria of the drug for six hours and did not suffer
from any adverse effects."

The similarities of these two case reports, written by different physicians
and occurring in people of different sex, and with major differences in culture
and background, are really striking. They are indicative of the deceptive,
unpredictable nature of *Cannabis* preparations which at certain times, in
certain individuals, even closely related, will produce such paradoxically
different results, conferring to some happiness and joy and striking others
with promise of doom.

Acute Toxic Psychosis. It seems now to be well established that administration of *Cannabis* preparations may also be followed by acute toxic psychosis.
Toxic psychosis or acute brain syndromes are temporary malfunctions of the
brain. The reaction is nonspecific and can occur with many intoxicants and
medications, including *Cannabis.* The clinical manifestations resemble the
delirium of high fever: confusion, prostration, disorientation, derealization,
and at times auditory and visual hallucinations. The appearance of such
toxic psychosis were first reported in India, where there had always been a
popular belief that prolonged and "excessive" use of *Cannabis* preparations
led to mental disorders. The conclusions of the Indian Hemp Drug Commission had tempered this popular idea by stating that "moderate use of
hemp drugs produced no injurious effect except in persons with specially
marked neurotic diathesis. Excessive use indicated and intensifies mental
instability." Excessive and moderate use were not defined. However, at the
turn of the century, Ewens (1904) and Robertson-Milne (1906) described
"a toxic insanity" mainly related to "excessive use of hemp."

In the La Guardia study, six of the 77 subjects, after taking 4 to 8 g of
marihuana concentrate, developed "toxic episodes" which included euphoria
and anxiety states, disorientation, and mental confusion. In three cases the
effects were brief and in three they developed on a background of previous
mental pathology. The authors concluded that "given the potential personality make up, and the right time and environment, marihuana may bring

out true psychotic state." This statement was interpreted by many as indicating that *Cannabis* would act only as a precipitating factor and induce an acute psychotic episode only in subjects already predisposed. A similar conclusion had been reached by the Indian Hemp Drug Commission.

This view is also still shared by some American psychiatrists (L. Grinspoon) who have taken a permissive view toward marihuana use. Grinspoon admits that *Cannabis* may precipitate, in "susceptible" people, one of several types of mental dysfunctions, such as a toxic psychosis. He does not clearly spell out what he means by "susceptible" people as opposed to the "normal" personality. But it would appear that a large percentage of adolescents anywhere in the world, and in America especially, are "susceptible." In America, 20 to 30% of the young people come from divorced parents, a large number have suffered the humiliation associated with poverty or racial discrimination; they all feel threatened by pollution, social inequities, the consequences of senseless wars, atomic destruction, and unemployment. It would certainly be possible to say that all people are "susceptible" at one time or another in their lives, but especially in adolescence.

Nicholi (1971) reports that of 1454 undergraduates who withdrew from Harvard over a 5-year period, 43% left for psychiatric reasons. All of these students had very unusual intellectual endowments. But Grinspoon, who teaches at Harvard, does not mention what the effect of marihuana smoking might produce in these "susceptible" students, who represent a significant portion of the student body. Furthermore, these "susceptible" personalities are more likely to use marihuana in order to withdraw from the pressing problems of everyday living.

A careful assessment of the literature indicates that the consumption of *Cannabis* preparations is associated, in some subjects who appear normal, with all of the manifestations of severe acute toxic psychosis. DeFarias (1955) reports the appearance of mental confusion and hallucinations with fear of impending death in a Brazilian Indian who had smoked 2 g of *Cannabis*. Nine other subjects who had smoked equal amounts of the drug did not present any untoward effects.

Talbott and Teague (1969) reported cases of acute toxic psychosis which developed in 12 soldiers in Vietnam after smoking a single cigarette of marihuana which was known to be potent. One of them killed his comrade with a blast from his tommy gun and boasted afterwards that he had just murdered Ho Chi Minh. These psychotic states, which lasted from 3 to 11 days, might have been influenced by the wartime setting, but the authors stated that "*Cannabis* was directly and essentially involved in the development of the (psychotic) syndrome." These authors, though recognizing the possible precipitating factors of combat conditions in the production of such psychotic states, suggested that a similar syndrome was quite likely to occur in the United States.

This prediction was borne out by H. S. Kaplan (1971), who reports five cases of psychosis associated with marihuana use at dose levels that are generally socially acceptable in the New York area. She states that this reaction, marked by symptoms of paranoia, depersonalization, and hallucinations that rarely last more than 1 week, is indistinguishable from an acute schizophrenia reaction: Perceptual and cognitive as well as effective functions are disrupted; perceptions of all sensory modalities, including the sense of time, may be distorted. The patients are oriented; their consciousness is not impaired; they fear "they are going crazy," but do not attribute their difficulty to *Cannabis*.

The following is one of the cases reported by Kaplan:

> "A twenty-seven year old female, married social worker with three children smoked marijuana in the presence of her husband and her sister and the latter's husband. The patient is intensely competitive with her sister who is extremely prominent. This was the patient's first exposure to marijuana. She stated that after smoking three or four 'joints,' she began to experience intense fear, spatial distortion, and paranoid symptoms. These symptoms lasted for four days at which time she was flown to New York City for treatment. Treatment consisted of assurance and of 25 mg of chlorpromazine at bedtime for four days, which was sufficient to control the symptoms. The patient recovered with no residual pathologic condition within twenty-four hours after initiation of treatment. Follow-up after one and a half years revealed no recurrence. She has not used marijuana since this episode. Family history is negative for overt psychosis, but the father is reported to be 'very nervous.' The patient had no previous history of psychiatric illness. On examination shortly after the episode no signs of psychosis were noted. The patient is a very sensitive and emotionally labile person, whose psychologic functioning is generally excellent."

Most of the patients, says Kaplan, recover from this frightening experience without damage within a few days. However, occasionally the psychotic episode is prolonged, and some of the mental problems such as phobias or inhibitions developed during the acute episode persist.

Weil reports an acute toxic psychosis, not as serious, in a 24-year-old law student who smoked marihuana daily and "never had difficulty with it." One evening he absorbed a ½-in. cube of powdered hashish in coffee on an empty stomach, in order to duplicate Baudelaire's hallucinatory experiences. He did—within 1 hour he felt "higher than ever after smoking hashish and also very sick." He could not make sense of what people were saying or what was happening. He went to bed and lay in misery for 6 hours, seeing crawling patterns on the walls and having unpleasant voices calling him. He could not recognize or talk to the people who visited him. He fell asleep, had horrible nightmares, and felt exhausted on awakening. He ached all over and had a headache and a hangover for a day and a half.

The cases reported by Kaplan and by Weil are similar to some reported by Chopra (1971) in his study of 200 adverse psychotic reactions occurring among users of *Cannabis,* observed in Calcutta over a 5-year period. Sixty-eight of these patients (37%) were in good health, had no personality problems and no history of mental problems. An invariable element was the history of their use of *Cannabis.* The symptoms of these patients simulated toxic psychosis, and were so similar and uniform as "to give a reasonable supposition of a definite cause." There were no other concomitant factors beyond the use of the drug. This eliminated the possibility of toxic psychosis resulting from other causes.

The toxic episodes lasted from a few hours to a few days, and were followed by a "90% recovery rate" after the drug was withdrawn.

The following is a typical case reported by Chopra:

> "S. M., a teacher. He had been smoking ganja for nine months and had then given it up for a few months. During a visit to a friend, he suddenly began smoking ganja again. He experienced hallucinogenic effects, developed signs of psychotic decompensation, and was brought to the clinic suffering from acute paranoid schizophrenia. He was given phenothiazines in large doses, and psychotherapy, and showed remarkable improvement. He recovered completely in about three weeks and was discharged."

In all African countries where *Cannabis* is used extensively, toxic psychosis attributed to the use of the drug is reported. In South Africa, mental hospitals have reported that 2 to 3% of their admissions were due to dagga smoking. In Nigeria (Asuni, 1964; Lambo, 1965), 14% of the psychotic admissions were users, and one half of these admissions were related directly to *Cannabis* intoxication. One-third of the acute toxic psychoses reported by Asuni and Lambo occurred among students and schoolboys. Recovery was not always rapid, requiring in some cases up to 12 months. In Morocco, Benabud (1957) reports that 27% of the 2300 patients admitted at Berrechid Psychiatric Hospital in 1956 suffered from what may be considered acute toxic psychosis. He also states that there are three times more men than women in mental hospitals, because only men smoke hashish.   It must also be emphasized that all these acute brain syndromes occurred in the age group between 20 and 30 years.

These acute psychotic episodes, whether they occur in the United States or India, are not always necessarily related to excessive consumption.   Further-

Table 17

Age of Patients Admitted to Berrechid Psychiatric Hospital (Morocco) with Acute Toxic Psychosis
Associated with *Cannabis* Intoxication[a]

18–20 years	10
21–25 years	29
26–30 years	38
31–35 years	33
36–40 years	7
41–50 years	9
51–60 years	4

[a] From Christozov (1965).

more, contrary to the opinion of Weil (1970), they may also occur after marihuana has been smoked as well as ingested.

The data reported by Christozov (1965) indicates that hospitalization of patients admitted to Berrechid Hospital with acute toxic psychosis associated with *Cannabis* intoxication occurs mostly among the younger age groups, 20 to 30 years old (Table 17).   But the incidence of the acute toxic episode does not seem to be related to the duration of the period of *Cannabis* intoxication (Table 18).   Tennant and Groesbeck (1972) report 13 cases of acute toxic

Table 18

Duration of *Cannabis* Usage Preceding Admission
of Patients with Acute Toxic Psychosis to
Berrechid Psychiatric Hospital
(Morocco)[a]

Duration	Number of patients
6 months	7
1 year	5
2 years	7
3–5 years	13
6–8 years	11
9–11 years	9
12–14 years	11
15–25 years	10

[a] From Christozov (1965).

psychosis (with paranoia and hallucinations) in American soldiers who had smoked 5 to 30 g of hashish in a few hours. In addition, 85 cases of toxic psychosis were observed by the same authors after simultaneous consumption of hashish and alcohol or other drugs.

The occurrence of such acute episodes is relatively infrequent in the United

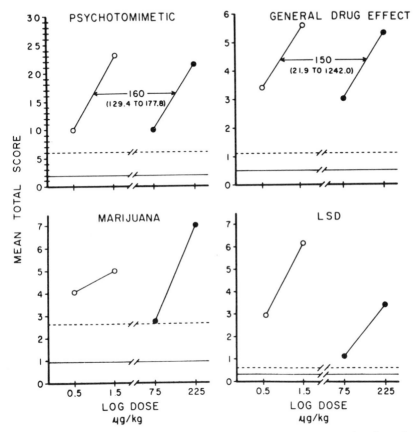

Fig. 21. Responses on the four scales of subjective effects: psychotomimetic scale, the general drug effect scale, marijuana scale, and the LSD scale by Isbell and Jasinski (1969) for the comparison of LSD administered i.m. with Δ9-THC by smoking. Solid lines represent the mean placebo response, with broken lines representing the 95% confidence limits of the mean placebo response. Numbers represent the relative potency expressed as μg/kg of Δ9-THC smoked equivalent to 1 μg/kg LSD i.m. in 8 subjects. Open circles represent the mean number of responses to LSD at the doses indicated. Solid circles represent the mean number of responses to THC. The figures in the arrows on the psychotomimetic and general drug scales represent the relative potency of LSD as compared with THC, with the confidence limits being shown in parentheses underneath.

States when one considers the extensive use of the drug. However, they may occur unpredictably in apparently healthy young people following administration of a dosage originally intended to "induce a socially acceptable high."

Acute Toxic Psychosis Following Administration of Cannabis *Extracts or Synthetic Delta-9 THC.* It has been observed by a number of investigators that delta-9-THC, like other tetrahydrocannabinol derivatives, is a hallucinogen (Fig. 21). Given in sufficient amounts (15 mg smoked, 40 mg ingested), delta-9-THC may produce acute psychotic reactions (Isbell and Jasinski, 1969; Jasinski et al., 1971) not unlike those reported by Allentuck (1944) and Ames (1948), who used crude extracts on their volunteers.

Delayed Effects

Flashbacks: Recurrence of Hallucination. The effects called flashbacks or abreaction syndrome may occur days, weeks, or even months after administration of a single dose of the drug and in the absence of any new intoxication. They are charactized by the sudden reappearance of the symptoms of the *Cannabis* intoxication, such as euphoria, anxiety, or hallucinations. In addition, marihuana smokers who try other hallucinogens, such as LSD or mescaline, recapture the effects of these drugs when they take *Cannabis*. The following is a case history given by Weil (1970):

> "M. N., a 49-year-old psychiatrist, had smoked marihuana about once a week for 3 years; he used it as a recreational intoxicant and enjoyed its 'relaxant effects.' Then he tried LSD out of curiosity and found the experience 'unpleasant.' Subsequently, he discovered that he could no longer enjoy marihuana because whenever he smoked it he re-experienced the LSD effects. He now does not smoke marihuana at all and has not tried any other psychoactive drugs."

Tennant and Groesbeck (1972) report that 15 soldiers under the influence of hashish recalled hallucinations experienced on a previous LSD "trip." But no flashback could be documented under the influence of *Cannabis* alone.

Precipitation of an Underlying Psychosis

There has been and still is some disagreement concerning the ability of acute *Cannabis* intoxication to trigger a psychotic episode in a stable, well-structured personality (Dally, 1967; Smith and Mehl, 1970). But everyone concurs in the opinion that marihuana may trigger a psychosis in unstable predisposed patients presenting a schizophrenic profile. Some believe that such an occurrence might have happened anyway, and that *Cannabis* cannot be incriminated as the major precipitating agent. Others hold the opinion that many people who have a predisposition for mental illness do not develop any of its overt manifestations, and that *Cannabis* will precipitate an ailment which would not have occurred or would have occurred at a later time.

Incidence of Acute Untoward Effects

Except for toxic psychosis, the occurrence of untoward effects associated with *Cannabis* intoxication is not infrequent. Keeler et al. (1971) reports that 40% of a group of students who used marihuana regularly had presented hallucinations. Halikas et al. (1971), in a survey of 100 regular marihuana users, report that 16% (one in six) report some adverse effects. During the period of intoxication some report anxiety and sadness, aggressive feelings, memory impairment, feelings of derealization, and visual and auditory hallucinations. When intoxication has subsided, depression, poor driving, anxieties, and hallucinations are mentioned. But all of the subjects also reported, as did the majority of smokers, pleasurable effects of peace, relaxation, and euphoria which were strong enough to override the negative effects associated with the drug. And none of the subjects interviewed manifested the desire to give up *Cannabis*. A similar attitude was reported by Keeler (1967) among students who had suffered adverse reactions following marihuana intoxication. The positive reinforcement of the euphoriant effect of the drug far outweighs its most common adverse effects. This is even true of the more serious mental effects of *Cannabis* intoxication, such as acute psychotic episodes. According to Chopra and Benabud, such disorders do not deter *Cannabis* users from resuming their habits.

Adverse effects from the use of other drugs, such as alcohol and tobacco, which induce a measure of euphoria rarely discourage their willing victims. It is at this juncture that the power of psychological dependence comes into play, a phenomenon which can lead to chronic use of the drug. And *Cannabis* extracts produce a much greater euphoric state than alcohol or tobacco; they induce an inner gratification which certainly acts as a major positive reinforcement.

Chronic Effects

Prolonged Psychotic Reaction. Following chronic use of *Cannabis,* episodes of psychosis lasting for several months have been described in patients who do not present any previous history of mental illness. Weil describes one such occurrence:

> "G. M., a 24-year-old writer with no psychiatric history, had smoked marihuana frequently for 1 year. Then she began experimenting with hallucinogens with her boyfriend. She took LSD 3 times and mescaline once. Three months after her last hallucinogenic experience (she continued to smoke marihuana), she broke off her relation with her boyfriend and returned to her parents' home in New York. Shortly after her arrival there, on a weekend night, she got very high on marihuana by herself and to her surprise began to re-experience hallucinogenic symptoms. Over the next 48 hours she suffered a severe psychotic decompensation and had to be hospitalized involuntarily. A diagnosis of acute paranoid schizophrenia was made, and high doses of phenothiazines were begun. After 4 weeks she was able to be discharged to outpatient therapy. One year later she suffered a second psychotic break requiring hospitalization for 7 months. She is now attending graduate school and is still receiving phenothiazines and psychotherapy. She has not used marihuana or other psychoactive intoxicants since the onset of her illness."

Spencer (1970) reported nine cases of "*Cannabis*-induced psychosis" observed within a 6-month period in Jamaica. They occurred in nine male patients aged 18 to 24 who were chronic marihuana smokers and had to be hospitalized for 4 to 8 weeks in a psychiatric ward. None of these subjects had any personal or family history of mental illness. The acute psychotic episode was sudden and marked by aggressive behavior, gross psychomotor activity, grandiose delusions, disturbance of sleep, and amnesia of the onset of the illness. Treatment consisted of phenothiazines, hypnotics, and in four cases electroshock therapy. Following the acute phase of the illness, there was persistence of amnesia, flattening of affect, poor motivation, and thought fragmentation.

Chopra (1971) also reported prolonged psychotic episodes in chronic *Cannabis* users with no previous episodes of psychotic illness and no history of family mental pathology. These patients presented amnesia, mental disorientation, strong morbid delusions, agitation, and insomnia, as well as acute maniacal and paranoid reactions. This condition may continue for weeks or months, require therapy with phenothiazines, and subside slowly with possible relapse. The following is one of his case reports:

> "M. D., age 25, a riksha puller. He had a history of fre-
> quent indulgence in large doses of bhang and charas. After
> an excessive use of charas he threw his sister's child from the
> roof of his house, injuring her seriously. Noisy, restless,
> filthy, incoherent, he had no idea of what he had done. He
> recovered after two months and remained normal for one year,
> when he again obtained some charas. Within a few hours
> after smoking the drug, he displayed the previous symptoms.
> He again recovered within four months. There was no previ-
> ous history of psychosis."

Tennant and Groesbeck (1972) report an acute schizophrenic reaction in 115
American soldiers in Germany, who had consumed 25 to 200 g hashish
monthly for three to six months. Treatment with chlorpromazine for one
to three weeks was not effective and all required medical evacuation to the
United States for long-term psychiatric hospitalization. Only 3 of the 115
consumed hashish exclusively; the others were multiple drug users. Since
the drug era started in the U.S. Army in West Germany (1968), persistent
schizophrenic reactions have more than quadrupled (from 18 in 1968, to
77 in 1971).

Mental and Physical Deterioration (Amotivational Syndrome). In his
report, "Research on the Insane in the Orient," Moreau describes the mental
and physical deterioration which results from "lengthy abuse of hashish"
and which has been recently observed in the United States, according to West
(1970), and given the less judgmental name of "amotivational syndrome."

> "A state of constant disappearance of spontaneity of ac-
> tions, willpower, ability to make decisions; psychic anomalies
> visible by an expressionless physiognomy, a depressed, lax
> and languid countenance, dull eyes rolling unsteadily in their
> orbits, or with a 'robot like' immobility, drooping lips, slow
> movements without energy, etc. These are some of the symp-
> toms characteristic of the excessive use of hashish. We have
> had occasions to observe several cases of this."

Moreau stressed that this condition is brought about only by excessive abuse
going on for a great number of years. He even takes, at that time, a benign
view of hashish, "this marvellous substance to which the Orientals owe in-
describable delights." While stating "that all Moslems eat hashish, and that
a very great number are addicted to it to an unbelievably high degree," he
seems to underestimate the incidence of undesirable mental and social effects
caused by the drug in the native Egyptian population.

Similar states of lethargy, social deterioration, and drug preoccupation have been described among chronic users in India (Chopra and Chopra, 1967), in Morocco (Christozov, 1965), and Egypt (Souief, 1967).

"The chronic hashish smoker," says Miras (1969)," is apathetic, depressed and tired, his need for increased doses grows stronger and his reveries occupy the greatest part of the day. He has little hope for recovery, since the change in his personality, character and physical activity is deep. He does not have the withdrawal symptoms of the opiate, but he has anxiety, nervousness, tiredness, and fears. He is thin and undernourished with an apathetic grayish-yellow complexion, careless about his personal hygiene and diet. He is useless to both himself and the community."

The 1972 "Marihuana and Health" report to Congress states: "Heavy patterns of *Cannabis* use comparable to those seen in the East have not yet developed in the West." This statement ignores the study performed by the United States Army, between September 1968 and September 1971, on an American Army population in West Germany (Tennant and Groesbeck, 1972): 110 soldiers who had smoked 2 to 50 g of hashish (5–10% delta-9-THC) daily for 3 to 12 months presented a chronic intoxicated state characterized by apathy, dullness, and lethargy, with mild to severe impairment of judgment, concentration, and memory. These patients had intermittent episodes of confusion, inability to calculate, slowed speech; they exhibited poor hygiene, lost interest in appearance, proper diet and personal affairs. After discontinuation of hashish, a number of subjects presented intermittent residual symptoms analogous to those of organic brain disease. Seventy soldiers who did not discontinue hashish consumption had to be discharged because they "did not function in a working capacity."

In spite of the relatively recent appearance of widespread *Cannabis* intoxication in the United States and the low potency of most of the marihuana available, a similar syndrome has been described among young Americans who have used the drug over 3 to 5 years. The following description is given by Smith and Mehl (1970) as "a loss of desire to work, to compete, to face challenges. Interests and major concerns of the individual become centered around marihuana and drug use becomes compulsive. The individual may drop out of school, leave work, ignore personal hygiene, experience loss of sex drive and avoid social interaction."

A similar individual stagnation is described by West (1970), who suggests that it might be due to a "biochemical scarring of the brain."

> "There are many young people, including some of the brightest, who have been using marihuana now more or less regularly for 3 to 4 years. Addiction or even habituation is

denied. The smoking is said to be simply for pleasure. Untoward effects are usually (not always) denied. But the experienced clinician observes in many of these individuals personality changes that may grow subtly over long periods of time: diminished drive, lessened ambition, decreased motivation, apathy, shortened attention span, distractibility, poor judgment, impaired communication skills, less effectiveness, magical thinking, derealization and depersonalization, diminished capacity to carry out complex plans or prepare realistically for the future, a peculiar fragmentation in the flow of thought, habit deterioration and progressive loss of insight. There is a clinical impression of organicity to this syndrome that I simply cannot explain away. There are too many instances of youngsters who should be getting their Ph.D.'s by now who are drifting along smoking marihuana and gradually developing these symptoms. Some of them at least are not schizophrenic, not psychopathic, not avitaminotic, not using other drugs, not simply "dropping out" by choice. And a few of the brightest ones will even tell you, 'I can't even read a book from cover to cover and grasp its meaning any more. I tell myself that I really don't care what's in it; that their topics are not important. But I really can't do it. Of course, I really don't care.' "

The description of West would fit the case report of Kolansky and Moore (1971) selected among six similar individuals who displayed general deterioration of school work, inability to concentrate or to pay attention in class, decreased memory, disturbance of abstract thinking and speech, gradual decrease in academic standing, apathy, indifference, passivity, withdrawal from social activities, and limitation of interest.

"A 19-year-old college freshman arrived on time for psychiatric consultation, dressed in old, torn, dirty clothes. He was unkempt, with long hair that was uncombed, and disheveled. He talked in a slow, hesitant manner, frequently losing his train of thought, and he could not pay attention or concentrate. He tried hard to both talk and listen, but had difficulty with both. He had been an excellent high school athlete and the highest student in his class in a large city. He was described as neat, orderly, and taking pride in his appearance, intellect, and physical fitness. During the last half of his senior year, he began casual (one or two marihuana cigarettes each weekend) smoking. By the time of the evaluation in the middle of his first college year, he was smoking several marihuana cigarettes daily. While in college, he stopped attending classes, didn't know what his goals were, and was flunking all subjects. He partook in no athletic or social events, and was planning to drop out of college to live in a young, drug-oriented group."

White et al. (1970) report on a group of 19 young hospitalized patients (14 to 20 years old) suffering behavior disorders. Eight had used only marihuana and the other 11 had consumed it along with LSD and amphetamines, a common form of association in the Western world. These patients had lost motivation to pursue school work and other constructive activities, presented primitive and magical modes of thought and low tolerance to frustration. Sixteen showed subtle abnormal EEG patterns particularly related to the temporal lobes.

These subtle changes in personality and behavior observed in all chronic *Cannabis* users are consistent with the accumulation of delta-9-THC metabolites in the tissues of the organism, including the brain.

EFFECTS OF *CANNABIS* INTOXICATION ON ADOLESCENT BRAIN FUNCTION

The brain has strong regulatory mechanisms which permit the individual to perceive himself in relation to the outside world and the outside world in relation to himself in a real, objective, verifiable scientific manner. Moreau clearly showed how hashish dissolves these mechanisms, altering both our own image and the image we have of the outside world. Such mechanisms are progressively and slowly developed through childhood, puberty, and adolescence.

It would seem evident that repetitive *Cannabis* intoxication should be accompanied by most serious adverse effects in adolescents who are attempting to structure their personalities in the world around them at a time when their vulnerable brains are in the process of integration. Recent reports substantiate this view.

Kornhaber (1971) studied a group of 50 patients 13 to 18 years old who had smoked a minimum of 2 cigarettes of marihuana daily 4 days a week for 1 year, believing the drug to be harmless. Some of them also used LSD. Kornhaber believes that "marihuana facilitates decrease in attendance, inattention to time, impulse or desire." Kornhaber concludes, "Marihuana is toxic to the human nervous system during growth and development; the biologically active substance it contains provokes an organic brain syndrome, the severity of which will depend upon individual vulnerability, dose of drug, psychological state, and frequency of use." He also adds that cessation of the drug is accompanied by functional improvement. This opinion is also shared by Kolansky and Moore (1971), who believe that *Cannabis* intoxication damages psychological growth, development, and maturation of the adolescent. Marihuana accentuates the inconsistencies of behavior, the lack of control of impulses, the vagueness of thinking, and the uncertainties of body identity.

Kolansky and Moore report on the adverse effects of chronic use of *Cannabis* on adolescent development. The following are two of the cases they discuss:

> "A bright 16-year-old boy smoked marihuana for 18 months. He had a B average prior to smoking. He was well liked by teachers and peers, seemed happy, and appeared to have no more difficulties than other adolescents prior to smoking marihuana. He said that he began to smoke because his friends did. He felt that it was safe, believing marihuana was harmless. As he began to notice some apathy, loss of goal direction, and increasing depression, he still felt that marihuana was not harmful.
>
> "Upon examination, he attempted to win over the psychiatrist with a pleasant, willing, cooperative manner. There was, however, mild disorientation, feelings of omnipotence, and a feeling of isolation.
>
> "In psychological testing, he had bright-normal scores on the Wechsler–Bellevue intelligence scale. He showed poor attention span and concentration and poor retention of acquired, as well as of accumulated knowledge. There was evidence of tenuous control of impulses. Reality testing was impaired. The psychologist reported 'early signs of personality decompensation in that he retreated into himself. He functioned at a level of early childhood, believing in his own omnipotence. This state might result in further impulse-motivated behavior so that he would probably commit further asocial and/or anti-social acts prior to becoming severely depressed.' "
>
> "Shortly after a 14-year-old boy began to smoke marihuana, he began to demonstrate indolence, apathy, and de-

pression. Over a period of eight months, his condition wors-
ened until he began to hallucinate and to develop paranoid
ideas. Simultaneously, he became actively homosexual.
There was no evidence of psychiatric illness prior to smoking
marihuana and hashish. At the height of his paranoid delusions, he attempted suicide by jumping from a moving car he
had stolen. He was arrested, and during his probation period,
he stopped smoking and his paranoid ideation disappeared.
In two six-month follow-up examinations, he was still showing some memory impairment and difficulty in concentration.
Of note was the fact that he still complained of an alteration
in time sense and distortion of depth perception at the time
of his most recent examination."

The authors of this study conclude that the moderate to heavy use of marihuana in adolescents without predisposition to mental illness impedes mental
integration, and development of the personality and may lead to mental illness and deterioration. The alteration of one's own image produced by *Cannabis* would be specially disruptive to the adolescent, who is attempting to
build his personality. The distortion of the outside world produced by *Cannabis* would be a further source of confusion. *Cannabis* use may then lead
to an interruption of the integrative mechanisms of brain function which
otherwise should lead the adolescent toward adulthood.

These reports are similar to those of Campbell et al. (1971), describing
young *Cannabis* smokers in England. For example:

"A 22-year-old unemployed man complained of difficulty in
recalling recent events, and also of periods of amnesia with occasional headaches. He described permanent alteration of
vision after some years of drug abuse, with alteration of bright
lights into colours: 'On a sunny day I have a lot of extra
colour without drugs—that's very nice.' There was no history
of birth injury, trauma to the head, or significant past illness.

"He had a 7-year history of drug abuse, starting with *Cannabis* and amphetamine at age 15. *Cannabis* remained the
chief drug, although he had also taken a large amount of LSD
and occasional barbiturates. He left school aged 15 and then
had 4 months at sea with the Merchant Navy. Since then he
had been unable to hold any job for long, and has not worked
for the past 4 years. Over the previous 18 months his mental
state had rapidly deteriorated, with intermittent confusional
states and paranoid psychosis. There seemed to be a striking
difference between the bright lively youngster of 14 who was

interested in fishing and shooting and was able to strip down and maintain a motorcycle, and the retarded, slothful, emotionally labile, and intolerant man of 22. He had no abnormal neurological signs."

CONCLUSION

The brain is the organ of the mind. Can one repetitively disturb the mental function without impairing the brain?

The brain, like all other organs of the human body, has very large functional reserves which allow it to resist and adapt to stressful abnormal demands. It seems that chronic use of psychotropic drugs, including *Cannabis* derivatives, slowly erodes these reserves.

SUMMARY

1. The mental effects of acute *Cannabis* intoxication were definitively described by Moreau's own observation in 1845. He emphasized the similarity between the symptoms present during *Cannabis* intoxication and those of mental illness (unexplained euphoria, dissociation of ideas, errors in time and space, hallucinations, delusions), indicating the psychotomimetic nature of this drug.

2. All of these effects have been described subsequently by many authors or subjects who have smoked or ingested sufficient amounts of psychoactive doses of delta-9-THC in a laboratory or a social setting (equivalent to 10 to 20 mg smoked, 20 to 60 mg ingested).

3. Panic reactions and acute toxic psychoses, especially in unfavorable settings, do occur, infrequently but also unpredictably. But euphoria usually predominates over dysphoria, and the pleasant feelings experienced by the users tend to create a positive reinforcement.

4. *Cannabis* use may precipitate an underlying psychosis.

5. Recent reports confirm older ones made over the centuries, and indicate that the daily use of *Cannabis* preparations (containing 1 to 5% delta-9-THC) is associated with mental and physical deterioration as well as social stagnation.

6. *Cannabis* intoxication will have most serious adverse effects in adolescents (13 to 18 years old) who are attempting to structure their personalities in the world around them when their vulnerable brains are in the process of integration.

REFERENCES

Allentuck, S. (1944). Medical aspects. In *The Marihuana Problem in the City of New York* (Mayor's Committee on Marihuana), Cattell Press, Lancaster, Pa.

Ames, F. (1958). *Cannabis sativa* and its role in the model psychoses. *J. Ment. Sci.,* 104:972–999.

Asuni, T. (1964). Socio-psychiatric problems of cannabis in Nigeria. *Bull. Narcotics,* 16:17–28.

Bartolucci, G., Fryer, L., Perris, C., and Shagass, C. (1969). Marihuana psychosis: A case report. *Canad. Psychiat. Ass. J.,* 14:77–79.

Baudelaire, C. (1858). De l'idéal artificiel. *La Revue Contemporaine,* Paris.

Benabud, A. (1957). Psychopathological aspects of the cannabis situation in Morocco: Statistical data for 1956. *Bull. Narcotics,* 9:1–16.

Boroffka, A. (1966). Mental illness and Indian hemp in Lagos. *E. Afr. Med. J.,* 43:377–384.

Bouquet, J. R. (1951). Cannabis. *Bull. Narcotics,* 3:22–45.

Bromberg, W. (1934). Marihuana, A psychiatric study. *J. Amer. Med. Ass.,* 113:4–12.

Campbell, A. M. G., Evans, M., Thompson, J. L. G., and Williams, M. J. (1971). Cerebral atrophy in young cannabis smokers. *Lancet,* 7736:1219–24.

Charen, S., and Perelman, L. (1946). Personality studies of marihuana addicts. *Amer. J. Psychiat.,* 102:674–782.

Chopra, G. S. (1969). Man and marihuana. *Int. J. Addictions,* 4:215–247.

Chopra, G. S. (1971). Marihuana and adverse psychotic reactions. *Bull. Narcotics,* 28:15–22.

Chopra, I. C., and Chopra, R. N. (1967). The use of cannabis drug in India. *Bull. Narcotics,* 9:4–29.

Chopra, R. N., Chopra, G. S., and Chopra, I. C. (1942). *Cannabis sativa* in relation to mental diseases and crime in India. *Indian J. Med. Res.,* 30:155–171.

Christozov, C. (1965). L'aspect marocain de l'intoxication cannabique d'après des études sur des malades mentaux chroniques: 1ere partie et 2eme partie. *Maroc. Med.,* 44:630–642; 866–899.

Collet, C. G. (1962). *Candidature de J. Moreau au Prix Montyon.* Presses Universitaires de France, Paris.

Conos, B. (1925). Trois cas de cannabisme avec psychose consecutive. *Bull. Soc. Path. Exot.,* 18:788–793.

Curtis, H. C., and Wolfe, J. R. (1939). Psychosis following the use of marihuana with report of cases. *J. Kansas Med. Soc.,* 40:515–517, 526–528.

Dally, P. (1967). Undesirable effects of marijuana. *Brit. Med. J.,* 3:367.

Deakin, S. (1880). Death from taking Indian hemp. *Indian Med. Gaz.,* 15:71.

DeFarias, C. (1955). Use of maconha (*Cannabis sativa* L.) in Brazil. *Bull. Narcotics,* 7:5–19.

Defer, B., and Diehl, M. L. (1968). Les psychoses cannabiques aigues: A propose de 560 observations. *Ann. Med. Psychol.,* 2:260–266.

Deniker, P., and Ginestet, B. (1969). Pharmacologie humaine de l'usage incontrôlé des drogues psychodysleptiques. *Laval Med.,* 40:25–36.

Dhunjibhoy, J. E. (1930). A brief resumé of the types of insanity commonly met with in India with a full description of "Indian hemp insanity" peculiar to the country. *J. Ment. Sci.,* 76:254–264.

Dinshaw, V. (1896). Complete aphonia after ganja-smoking recovery. *Indian Med. Rec.,* 11:14.

Dobell, H. (1863). On some effects of *Cannabis indica. Med. Times Gaz.,* 2:245–246.

Douglas, J. (1883). On the use of Indian hemp in chorea. *Edinburgh Med. J.,* 14:777–784.

Ewens, G. F. W. (1904). Insanity following the use of Indian hemp. *Indian Med. Gaz.,* 39:401–413.

Favazza, A., and Domino, E. F. (1969). Recurrent LSD experience (flashbacks) triggered by marihuana. *Univ. Mich. Med. Cent. J.,* 35:214–216.

Fischlowitz, G. G. (1896). Poisoning by *Cannabis indica. Med. Rec.,* 50:280–281.

Gary, N. E., and Keylon, V. (1970). Intravenous administration of marihuana. *J. Amer. Med. Ass.,* 211:501.

Gautier, T. (1846). Le club des hachischins. In *Le Revue des Deux Mondes,* Paris.

Gourves, J., Viallard, C., LeLuan, D., Girard, J. P., and Aury, R. (1971). Case of coma due to *Cannabis sativa. Presse Med.,* 79:1389.

Graff, H. (1969). Marihuana and scopolamine high. *Amer. J. Psychiat.,* 125:1258–1259.

Grinspoon, L. (1971). *Marihuana Reconsidered.* Harvard University Press, Cambridge, Mass.

Grossman, W. (1969). Adverse reactions associated with cannabis products in India. *Ann. Intern. Med.,* 70:529–533.

Halikas, J. A., Goodwin, D. W., and Guze, S. B. (1971). Marihuana effects, A survey of regular users. *J. Amer. Med. Ass.,* 217:692–694.

Hamaker, S. T. (1891). A case of overdose of *Cannabis indica. Ther. Gaz.,* 7:808.

Henderson, A. H., and Pugsley, D. G. (1968). Collapse after intravenous injection of hashish. *Brit. Med. J.,* 3:229–230.

Heyndrickx, A., Scheiris, C., and Schepens, P. (1970). Toxicological study of a fatal intoxication in man due to cannabis smoking. *J. Pharm. Belg.,* 24:371–376.

Indian Hemp Drug Commission (1969). *Report on Marihuana of the Indian Hemp Drug Commission 1893–1894.* Thomas Jefferson Publishing Co., Silver Springs, Md.

Ireland, T. (1893). Insanity from the abuse of Indian hemp. *Alienist and Neurologist,* 14:622–630.

Isbell, H., and Jasinski, D. R. (1969). A comparison of LSD-25 with $(-)$-Δ^9-trans-tetrahydrocannabinol (THC) and attempted cross tolerance between LSD and THC. *Psychopharmacologia,* 14:115–123.

Jasinski, D. R., Haertzen, C. A., and Isbell, H. (1971). Review of the effects in man of marihuana and tetrahydrocannabinols on subjective state and physiologic functioning. *Ann. N.Y. Acad. Sci.,* 191:196–205.

Kaplan, H. S. (1971). Psychosis associated with marijuana. *N.Y. State J. Med.,* 71:433–435.

Keeler, M. H. (1967). Adverse reactions to marihuana. *Amer. J. Psychiat.,* 124:674–677.

Keeler, M. H. (1968). Marihuana induced hallucinations. *Dis. Nerv. Syst.,* 29:314–315.

Keeler, M. H., Ewing, J. A., and Rouse, B. A. (1971). Hallucinogenic effects of marijuana as currently used. *Amer. J. Psychiat.,* 128:105–108.

Keeler, M. H., and Reifler, C. B. (1967). Grand mal convulsions subsequent to marihuana use. *Dis. Nerv. Syst.,* 28:474–475.

Keeler, M. H., Reifler, C. B., and Liptzin, M. B. (1968). Spontaneous recurrence of marihuana effect. *Amer. J. Psychiat.,* 125:140–142.

Keup, W. (1970). Psychotic symptoms due to cannabis abuse. *Dis. Nerv. Syst.,* 31:119–126.

Kew, M. C., Bersohn, L., and Siew, S. (1969). Possible hepatotoxicity of cannabis. *Lancet,* 1:578–579.

King, A. B., and Cowen, D. L. (1969). Effect of intravenous injection of marihuana. *J. Amer. Med. Ass.,* 210:724–725.

Kolansky, H., and Moore, W. T. (1971). Effects of marihuana on adolescents and young adults. *J. Amer. Med. Ass.,* 216:486–492.

Kornhaber, A. (1971). Marihuana in an adolescent psychiatric outpatient population. *J. Amer. Med. Ass.,* 215:1000.

Lambo, T. A. (1965). Medical and social problems of drug addiction in West Africa. *Bull. Narcotics,* 17:3–14.

Layman, J. M., and Milton, A. S. (1971). Some actions of D1-tetrahydrocannabinol and cannabinol at cholinergic junctions. *Brit. J. Pharmacol.,* 41:379–380.

Ludlow, F. (1857). *The Hasheesh Eater: Being Passages from the Life of a Pythagorean.* Harper and Row, New York.

Marcovitz, E., and Myers, H. J. (1944). The marihuana addict in the army. *War Med.,* 6:382–391.

Marten, G. W. (1969). Adverse reaction to the use of marihuana. *J. Tenn. Med. Ass.,* 62:627–630.

Mayor's Committee on Marihuana (1944). *The Marihuana Problem in the City of New York—Sociological, Medical, Psychological and Pharmacological Studies.* Cattell Press, Lancaster, Pa.

Minter, L. J. (1896). Indian hemp poisoning. *Brit. Med. J.,* 11:1773–1774.

Miras, C. J. (1969). Experience with chronic hashish smokers. In *Drugs and Youth,* J. R. Wittenborn, H. Brill, J. P. Smith, and S. A. Wittenborn (eds.). Charles C. Thomas, Springfield, Ill., pp. 191–198.

Moreau, J. J. (1845). *Du Hachisch et de l'Alienation Mentale.* Libraire de Fortin, Masson, Paris (English edition: Raven Press, New York, 1972).

Nicholi, A. M., II (1971). Harvard's dropouts attributed largely to mental illnesses. *World Medical News,* June 14.

Peebles, A. S. M., and Mann, H. W. (1914). Ganja as a cause of insanity and crime in Bengal. *Indian Med. Gaz.,* 49:395–396.

Perna, D. (1969). Psychotogenic effect of marihuana. *J. Amer. Med. Ass.,* 209:1085–1086.

Persyko, I. (1970). Marihuana psychosis. *J. Amer. Med. Ass.,* 212:1527.

Pillard, R. C. (1970). Marihuana. *New Eng. J. Med.,* 283:294–303.

Pond, D. A. (1948). Psychological effects in depressive patients of the marihuana homologue synhexyl. *J. Neurol. Neurosurg. Psychiat.,* 11:271–279.

Porot, A. (1942). Le cannabisme. *Ann. Medicopsychol.,* 1:1–24.

Pretoria Mental Hospital Medical Staff (1938). Report of an investigation: Mental symptoms associated with the smoking of dagga. *S. Afr. Med. J.,* 12:85–88.

Robertson-Milne, C. J. (1906). Hemp and insanity. *Ind. Med. Gaz.,* 41:129.

Roland, J. L., and Teste, M. (1958). Le cannabisme au Maroc. *Maroc. Med.,* 387:694–703.

Scher, J. M., (1970). The marihuana habit. *J. Amer. Med. Ass.,* 214:1120.

Smith, D. E., and Mehl, C. (1970). An analysis of marihuana toxicity. In *The New Social Drug*, D. E. Smith (ed.). Prentice-Hall, Inc., Englewood Cliffs, N.J.

Sonnenrich, C., and Goes, J. F. (1962). Marijuana and mental disturbances. *Neurobiologia*, 25:69–91.

Soueif, M. I. (1967). Hashish consumption in Egypt with special reference to psychological aspects. *Bull. Narcotics*, 19:1–12.

Spencer, D. J. (1970). Cannabis induced psychosis. *W. Indian Med. J.*, 19:228–230.

Sterne, J., and Ducastaing, C. (1960). Les arterites du *Cannabis* indica. *Arch. Mal. Coeur.*, 53:143–147.

Stockings, G. T. (1947). A new euphoriant for depressive mental states. *Brit. Med. J.*, 1:918–922.

Talbott, J. A., and Teague, J. W. (1969). Marihuana psychosis: Acute toxic psychosis associated with the use of cannabis derivatives. *J. Amer. Med. Ass.*, 210:299–302.

Taylor, M. (1849). *Flight from Reality*. Duell, Sloan and Pearce, New York.

Tennant, F. S., and Groesbeck, C. J. (1972). Psychiatric effects of hashish. *Arch. Gen. Psychiat.*, 27:133–136.

Thompson, L. J., and Proctor, R. C. (1953). Pyrahexyl in treatment of alcoholic and drug withdrawal conditions. *N. Carolina Med. J.*, 14:520–523.

Walton, R. P. (1938). *Marihuana, America's New Drug Problem*. J. B. Lippincott Co., Philadelphia.

Warnoch, J. (1903). Insanity from hasheesh. *J. Ment. Sci.*, 49:96–110.

Weil, A. T. (1970). Adverse reactions to marihuana: Classification and suggested treatment. *New Eng. J. Med.*, 282:997–1000.

West, L. J. (1970). On the marihuana problem. In *Psychotomimetic Drugs*, D. Efron (ed.). Raven Press, New York.

White, R. B., Goolishian, H., and Barratt, E. S. (1970). Dilemmas encountered by the marihuana researcher (1970): Paper presented at the 46th Annual Conference of the Central Neuropsychiatric Association, Galveston, Texas, October 16.

Wurmser, L., Levin, L., and Lewis, A. (1969). Chronic paranoid symptoms and thought disorders in users of marihuana and LSD as observed in psychotherapy. *Nat. Acad. Sci.* (*US*), *Bull. Problems on Drug Dependence*, 6154–6177.

7

Social Aspects

CANNABIS USE IN POOR AGRARIAN SOCIETIES

It has been reported that *Cannabis* preparations are used, often daily, by a significant fraction of the poor agrarian classes of India, Egypt, Morocco, and Jamaica. In these countries such extracts are smoked daily, not for pleasure but as an aid to perform most menial tasks. No tendency to increase dosage is reported when it has reached an equivalent concentration of 100 to 200 mg of delta-9-THC, and no other drugs are taken in conjunction with *Cannabis,* since it is the only one available. In these countries *Cannabis* is used for the same reasons that coca leaves are used in Peru or opium in the Far East.

We have seen that a marked and rapid tolerance develops to *Cannabis* extracts in experimental animals (Chapter 4), and the development of tolerance has also been clearly documented in man (Chapter 5). It would therefore appear that daily smoking by man of amounts equivalent to 100 to 200 mg of delta-9-THC should be accompanied by a marked degree of tolerance. Under such conditions the true pharmacological effects of daily use of *Cannabis* by the poor peasants or laborers of the underdeveloped countries might be quite subdued and similar to those of a "placebo." The effects produced by the consumption of such extracts might be primarily the result of psychological and social conditioning.

In this case, it seems that the interaction between *Cannabis* and man results in a kind of symbiosis which allows him to tolerate better the drugs as well as the dreariness of his daily existence. A similar interaction between man and opium seems to prevail among the destitute workers of the Far East, as reported in the 1950 edition of the *Encyclopedia Britannica.*

"So far as can be gathered from the conflicting statements published on the subject, opium smoking may be regarded much in the same light as the use of alcoholic stimulants. To the great majority of smokers who use it moderately it appears to act as a stimulant, and to enable them to undergo great fatigue and to go for a considerable time with little or no food. According to the reports on the subject, when the smoker has plenty of active work it appears to be no more injurious than smoking tobacco. In a large dock company in the Far East where 5,000 laborers were employed, the managers were unable to pick out any opium-smokers who, by any difference in physique, capacity for work or in behaviour, were different from the non-smokers. When carried to excess, opium-smoking becomes an inveterate habit; but this happens chiefly in individuals of weak will power who would just as easily become the victims of intoxicating drinks, and who are practically moral imbeciles, often addicted also to other forms of depravity. The effect in bad cases is to cause loss of appetite, a leaden pallor of the skin and a degree of leanness so excessive as to make its victims appear like living skeletons. All inclination for exertion gradually becomes lost, business is neglected, and certain ruin to the smoker follows."

If in this text the word *opium* was replaced by *Cannabis,* it could have been written by any of the proponents of marihuana use in the United States. However, two points deserve emphasis when one describes the pattern of daily *Cannabis* use in poor countries. First, the resulting existence of a man daily dependent on *Cannabis* is stabilized at a marginal subsistence level. Second, *Cannabis* is the drug of choice, to the exclusion of others. The association of other drugs such as alcohol results in rapid physical and mental deterioration (Roland and Teste, 1958; Bouquet, 1951). Such a pattern of *Cannabis* use seems to have little similarity to that which prevails among a section of the Western adolescent culture. The adoption by Western man of a similar habit can be interpreted as a symptom of regression. It is also indicative of his deep-seated dissatisfaction with the world in which he lives.

CANNABIS AND ADOLESCENT CULTURE IN THE WESTERN WORLD

The use of *Cannabis* and other drugs by adolescents in Western countries is the end result of a sequence of events set in motion by the social and cultural developments of modern society.

The use of drugs by young people to alter consciousness is not new. More than a century ago, medical students and other youths held ether parties or "jags," well before the introduction of this agent as an anesthetic. Dr. Long attended such ether frolics before administering ether to a friend prior to an operation for removal of a growth on the neck. This introduced a new era in anesthesiology (Goodman and Gilman, 1965).

Pescor (1943) was the first to document statistically the vulnerability of adolescents and young people to the abuse of psychotropic drugs. He reports:

> "While no age is exempt from drug addiction, there is, nevertheless, a heavy concentration of cases in the decade 20 to 29 years, more than half of the patients being victimized during this period. A substantial percentage of adolescents (19 years of age or less) also yielded to the temptation of using drugs. On the other hand, very few individuals became addicted after the age of 50. Therefore, drug addiction seems to be a greater potential danger to youthful individuals than to older men. Youth characteristically seeks adventure, excitement, new thrills, anything but settling down with one sexual partner to the hum-drum business of making a living and rearing a family. Drugs offer new thrills and an escape from uninteresting reality. Furthermore, drugs act as a balance for those unfortunate individuals who, after they are cut adrift from parental protection, are unable to decide upon a career or to carve a niche for themselves in the social structure. This state of indecision and dissatisfaction is bound to be reflected in emotional upsets which are relieved, at least temporarily, by alcohol or drugs."

These early observations of Pescor were borne out in succeeding decades as more and more drugs which could induce instant gratification and new thrills became available in a society which seemed to offer less and less rewarding tasks to its young members. The use of drugs has become more and more a part of adolescent culture. Miras (1969) states that in Greece, "More susceptible to hashish abuse are youngsters who are highstrung, emotionally unstable, unreasonably unhappy, and with a tendency to illusion and daydreaming. Many of them are trapped in hashish smoking through the feeling of self-confidence it gives, the illusion of increased ability and sexual drive, as well as the pleasant reveries—all produced by the drug at a certain stage." We will now attempt to analyze some of the factors which have contributed to the "drug explosion" among American and other Western adolescents, and to the increased acceptance of *Cannabis* into their lives.

Permissive Education

According to some educators over the age of 40, the permissively brought up young people of America have been given too much too soon, and have not been offered any guidelines. In many instances, a major goal of progressive education is the instant and effortless gratification of the school child. Disciplined scheduling is frowned upon as preventing self-realization of the child. The fear of fostering a "destructive guilt complex" in the young leads to the withholding of traditional verbal reproach or light spanking. Many of these oversensitive, spoiled youths are unable to develop their own resources and resilience, and their threshold to frustration and boredom is dangerously lowered. They are not taught the discipline of hard work; they are not told that the learning process is in most instances a hard one.

Probing of the Unconscious

The use of hallucinogens such as *Cannabis* and LSD or mescaline, which allegedly "expand consciousness," has been advocated as a research method by experimental psychologists and some psychiatrists. The "expansion of consciousness" produced by these drugs is not far removed from the psychoanalytic therapeutic goal of "making the unconscious conscious." In too many cases, especially in adolescents who are in the process of integrating their personality, confusion and irrationality may follow, particularly because of the nondirective, nonjudgmental approach of many present-day psychotherapeutic techniques. In both instances a destructuring of the hierarchical functions of the mind occurs.

Some psychiatrists justify the use of *Cannabis* by students. According to Greenwald (1968), "Marihuana restores to the student his ability to feel in an often hostile environment and the liberating action of that drug is going to allow him to experience more intimate social contacts." Many psychoanalysts in the past vigorously protested against the treatment of mental illness based on psychotropic drugs, such as phenothiazines and antidepressants, which help patients recover a better appreciation of reality and tend to obliterate past experiences. The "chemical lobotomy" which such agents may produce is criticized by the psychiatrist who wishes to see his patient gaining insight into his problems rather than repressing them with drugs. Yet some psychoanalysts, like Grinspoon, have adopted today a benign view of hashish intoxication and are willing to accept the use of a psychoactive agent which selectively acts on basic brain mechanisms, disrupts thought processes, and creates a chemical gratification as well as departure from reality.

Many young people are encouraged to use *Cannabis* by the permissive attitude of some psychiatrists, especially in the climate of revolt against family and social structures that exists today. An officer of the narcotics squad in Englewood, New Jersey, told the author that many of the young people he had apprehended for carrying marihuana showed him newspaper clippings quoting the statements of some "prominent doctors" claiming that marihuana was less dangerous than cigarettes and alcohol and that since it is said the drug should be legalized they were not committing a felony.

However, we have already seen that many psychiatrists (Deniker and Ginestet, 1969; Olivenstein, 1970; West, 1970; Robins et al., 1970) and psychoanalysts (Kolansky and Moore, 1971), in view of clinical observations of their young patients, believe that marihuana is particularly dangerous for the psychological and emotional development of adolescent man. These studies indicate that *Cannabis* only intensifies psychiatric problems by decreasing contact with reality and impeding social or professional integration. Such warnings seem to go mostly unheeded by a large number of young people, who often prefer to follow the pronouncements which are more to their own liking.

Drug Availability and Opportunity

Availability of the drug and opportunity to take it often determine whether the curious insecure adolescent will embark on using marihuana or pills or both, rather than trying to solve the often boring tasks and problems he encounters in his family or at school. Because of biological transformations, an adolescent is naturally unstable and insecure. The more often drug taking is physiologically rewarded by the achievement of the desired goal of feeling "high" or "stoned" or "getting away from it all," the more often the user will tend to take drugs. The discovery that he can achieve immediate gratification relatively effortlessly reinforces the adolescent's tendency to forego any striving for long-term goals (Fig. 22).

Fig. 22. Vulnerability of the adolescent to the use of cannabis

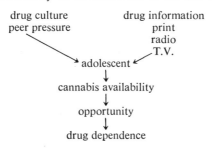

Soueif (1971) reports that in Egypt 42% of 850 users started taking *Cannabis* before the age of 20, and one-third of these before 16 years of age. This early onset of *Cannabis* usage was associated with exposure to the influence of a drug-consuming person within the family circle: the existence of a father or a male relative known to be using hashish himself was definitely related to the subject becoming a hashish taker. Other motives were: conformity to a group of friends, euphoria, curiosity, and trying to appear like "real men." Furthermore, the frequency of drug taking per month and of attempts at interrupting hashish use was found to be related to age of onset of the habit. The earlier the onset, the higher the frequency of drug taking and the fewer the attempts at interruption.

Grinspoon (1971) ignores availability and opportunity as factors leading to drug use among adolescents when he suggests that the temptation of a child to smoke marihuana will be diminished as soon as *Cannabis* is legalized and readily available. According to Grinspoon, the child, knowing he will be permitted to smoke pot when he reaches the magic age of informed decision (18 years old) won't care any more to smoke a joint with his little neighbor pal, in imitation of their big brothers and/or sisters. According to this new theory of child behavior, the temptation of a child to smoke a marihuana cigarette should be no different from the temptation to drive the family car, which is legal only at age 18! All available evidence indicates that for most children smoking a marihuana cigarette from an available pack on a desk is much more like reaching for the forbidden cookie jar on the shelf. In both cases the rapid gratification which results remains the motivating force.

Cannabis and Revolt Against Society

Young people emerging from a protected childhood are appalled to discover the many unresolved contradictions of modern American society in the areas of race relations, distribution of wealth, health care, urban congestion, environmental pollution, and foreign policy. Thus it is often claimed that drug use is only a symptom of maladjustment such as psychological disturbances or a sympton of social injustice. The removal of these symptoms should therefore be the best remedy for drug dependence. But the problem is not as simple as it appears. It is obvious that drug use or alcohol abuse may be symptomatic of underlying psychological disorders or social inadequacies. But habitual use of one drug (toxicomania) is in itself an identifiable clinical syndrome with its own dynamics. The reasons which induced the subject to start using a drug may not play much of a part in the continued use of it. Repetitive use of a drug induces a psychological and physiological conditioning which has no relationship to the initial cause which triggered the

habit.   Once this conditioning, which involves the imprinting of basic biological memories at a very elementary neuronal level, is established, the exertion
of "free" will may be significantly impeded.

For instance, many youths start smoking cigarettes at age 12 because they
want to look grown up.   Ten years later, when the young smokers have
reached adulthood, their original goal is achieved, and they should not need
to smoke and should be ready to stop.   But very few do so.   The physical
and psychological conditioning instilled in the intervening years has created
a new physiological milieu which makes it very difficult to stop smoking at
any time in their lives.   They are likely to say "I wish I could stop" or "I
will stop tomorrow" or "for New Year's."   The same pattern may occur with
marihuana smoking.

The following is a case report from Glatt (1969) which describes the progressive development of compulsive drug dependence in a young student.
Drug taking was first a way of expressing his revolt.

> "In my second year at the school I concluded that if I could
> not be an outstanding success I could at least make a strong
> play for the position of Public Enemy Number One . . .
> and I threw myself into . . . rowdyism, . . . rebelliousness,
> and irresponsible horseplay with all the vigour which I con-
> spicuously failed to display on the sports field.   That hap-
> pened at the age of 12 years, a few years before I started to
> smoke marijuana.
>
> "Having been introduced to marijuana I began to smoke
> socially . . . and we began to conduct small . . . smoking
> parties and get high. . . .   I was a social smoker who would
> never have considered solitary indulgence. . . .   Later, how-
> ever, when abroad and feeling isolated, a couple of cigarettes
> soon put matters right, enabling me to remove myself mentally
> from my surroundings. . . .   I found it remarkably effective,
> and travelling to Paris I bought a lot of the stronger hashish.
> . . . I also allowed myself to be talked into taking quantities
> of strange tablets. . . .   The point is that, before entering
> the drug sub-culture, I would never have agreed to exceed the
> stated dose of an unknown pill.   I suppose that it was at this
> time that I lost my independence from drugs.   Previously, I
> had been in control of the situation but I had now abandoned
> myself to the world of drugs.
>
> ". . . The digestion of a great deal of jazz literature had
> given me a somewhat romanticized vision of the possible ef-

fects of smoking marijuana, but this was countered by arguments opposing the use of drugs. I was aware that some medical opinion thought that cannabis was relatively harmless, and an article in the *Guardian* advocating the legalization of it seemed to me to justify experiments in this field. . . ."

The original psychological disturbance or social inequity which might have triggered the inception of *Cannabis* use has little to do with the subsequent biological conditioning which develops in a subject who may have become conditioned to take drugs for pleasure, even though this was not his original intention.

The true revolutionaries of Moscow and Peking whom I have met are quite aware of this possibility. While advocating the free use of drugs in the bourgeois society which they wish to destroy, they themselves strictly abstain from their use and forbid their use by their followers.

Cannabis Intoxication—A Substitute for a Religious Experience

All traditional religions are based on a set of beliefs which have a mystical appeal and underpin a code of ethics to which all believers are required to conform. Most of these beliefs seem irrelevant in the scientific age, where only what may be objectively observed holds any reality. Keeping in step with the times, many of the churches have become social clubs and their pastors editorial commentators of current events. In the process they have lost their mystical appeal. Rules governing behavior are all but ignored, with the acceptance of provisional or situational ethics where personal situations and individual judgment prevail over the clearly delineated commandments.

With no sense of purpose and no meaning in their lives, many adolescents wish to escape a harsh world in which they feel alienated and for which they have not been prepared. They turn toward drugs, which give their lives the dimension they cannot find through the free play of the mental faculties within their particular social context.

In 1936 de Felice pointed out in his book, *Sacred Poisons, Divine Raptures,* that the drug experience, inasmuch as it confers on the individual the feeling of greater, superhuman power, has a religious connotation. The lack of formal religious ties or religious interest among students using marihuana was later reported by Robbins et al. (1970) and by Crompton and Brill (1971). The extent to which *Cannabis* can replace a true religious experience, is, however, open to question. How can this drug lead to a fuller understanding of the universe in which we live, since it depresses some parts of the brain and at the same time causes other parts of the brain to interpret falsely information received from the sensory organs about the world around us?

Man has a very deep craving to go beyond the narrow bonds of a mortal existence. Modern man escapes this permanent and fundamental drive no more than his ancestors did. When the rising generation uses drugs to quench its thirst for evasion, it is reverting to an old mystical practice in which the most primitive tribes have always indulged. It is also obvious that such practices, which do not ennoble man, can only prevent him from reaching a truly lofty goal. But youth is still willing to take the risk of damaging his future for the sake of passing exaltation of his imagination.

There exists a great spiritual ardor and enthusiasm in the unsatisfied youth seeking drug-induced transcendence. This should not be forgotten. The rigid teetotaler who ignores the disquieting yearning of adolescence and is satisfied to condemn flatly without an attempt at understanding shows little heart or imagination.

Théophile Gautier (1846) expressed quite simply this deep-seated human desire for fulfillment when he commented on his experience with hashish: "The yearning for an ideal is so powerful in man that he strives as much as possible to loosen the ties which link the spirit to the body; and since a pure mystical experience is out of the reach of most of us, man will drink joy, he will smoke oblivion and will eat folly, under the form of wine, of tobacco and of hashish."

Drug use in the adolescent culture of Western society simply proves that man cannot live by bread alone. When adolescents are not offered a challenging ideal or a striking example, they are attracted to drugs and to all kinds of individual and group inebriations. But how can they gratify their instinctive desire to fulfill themselves by sinking below their true selves?

DRUG INFORMATION AND DRUG EDUCATION

Drug Information and the Drug Culture

Drug use, including *Cannabis* intoxication, would not spread to the same extent and with such rapidity if information were not made so easily available by the mass media. Demand for a desired drug increases as a consequence of the amount of information accessible to the public.

The sensationalism of most popular newspapers and magazines has contributed to the creation of a culture which has some knowledge of the actual and potential effects of drugs, but is interested in the psychedelic rather than the therapeutic aspects of drug action.

> "In 1966 the American periodical *Playboy* contained an article on hallucinogens. This mentioned that a certain kind of morning glory seed was a hallucinogen, and all that was needed was a 50-cent packet of seeds to enter a state of intoxication of the LSD-type. A youth in a Swedish town read the article, went to the seed shop, bought a few packets and tried them out. A little temporary epidemic of abuse developed around him, comprising a handful of teen-age boys. At this point a journalist on the local daily paper wrote about the epidemic, and the next day a big evening paper in Stockholm had half a page on the subject. The following day it was hardly possible to buy a packet of morning glory seeds anywhere in Sweden" (Bejerot, 1970).

The same author conjectures, with good reason, that there would have been an epidemic of *Cannabis* usage at the time of Gautier and Moreau (1844) if the mass media had been in existence at that time.

An adolescent has the opportunity, by looking through any popular magazine, to saturate himself with knowledge of the esoteric action of drugs; lay and professional advertising make the names of the drugs known and enable interested individuals to become familiar with them. In a society already prone to taking drugs and pills, the desire for practical knowledge about drug action is the next step. Knowledge about drugs associated with the desire to experiment with them in order to experience a supranormal state creates a demand for the desired drug which can be satisfied only through black market suppliers.

It is well established that the level of sophistication about drug abuse among young people who have become involved in the drug scene is generally higher than their nondrug-using classmates. Adolescents, having learned and experimented with drugs in peer groups which accept and promote use of drugs, thereby create a drug culture. Development of drug dependence is a logical result of the drug culture.

Misleading information about *Cannabis* has been widely circulated among the young by such publications as *The Marihuana Papers* (Solomon, 1966), *The Book of Grass* (Andrews and Vinkenoog, 1967), and *The Marihuana Smokers* (Goode, 1970). The causes of this ignorance are multiple but are due primarily to a superficial and careless analysis of the facts, and a reliance on old and new folklore. To these popular stereotypes, still more has been added by books written by authors from prestigious universities (Harvard, Johns Hopkins, Stanford, Oxford). As long as misinformation on problems such as tolerance, toxicity, and psychopharmacological effects of *Cannabis* persists, it will be difficult to have a calm, dispassionate debate on the fundamental issues of *Cannabis* intoxication.

Drug Education

There is a need for wider professional and lay education about the dangers of taking drugs without informed medical advice. However, this information must be given with care. Too often education is the mere dispensation of objective information. Many young people report that only after hearing or reading about drugs do they decide to experiment themselves and find out "really what it is all about."

The first prerequisite of drug education is that it be based on correct, proven facts. The assertion that marihuana is harmless is incorrect. Nothing is more dangerous than a substance which is alleged to be harmless, since one is, therefore, not on guard against it and will use it readily. One need only recall the old story of the Trojan Horse as well as the fact that many chemicals prove to be great hazards to health only after many years of use.

The mere knowledge that a drug such as *Cannabis* has pleasurable strange effects creates in the mind of most adolescents the secret desire to use it. The desire will become overwhelming if associated with the knowledge that this drug is "relatively" harmless as claimed by so many science writers and educators.

Although it seems reasonable to presume that information on the hazards of drug abuse would reduce the likelihood of experimentation or actual dependence, the truth of the matter is that scientific knowledge alone does not keep people from abusing psychotropic drugs. Few adolescents will attempt to make an informed decision, that is to say, a truly objective assessment of whether the long-term effects and complications caused by the drug may not be more troublesome than the original stress and passing euphoria.

Educators are aware that knowledge is no substitute for maturity. "Wisdom entereth not into a malicious soul, and science without conscience spells but destruction of the spirit" (Rabelais, 1542). This was the final advice of Gargantua to his son Pantagruel before he started on the road to learning all of the knowledge of the time, already a monumental task. "The best deterrent to drug abuse is education that strengthens an individual's code of values and increases his ability to assess the consequences" (Levy, 1971). This statement implies that an individual already possesses a code of values. Knowledge alone is not enough; it is not a substitute for maturity, motivation, and ability to overcome stress and frustration. The medical profession, the most knowledgeable about drugs, has one of the highest levels of drug addiction. Educators know very well that exposure to objective facts, with careful avoidance of judgmental tones, may not always be a very effective method in drug education and that it might be illusory to think that every school child will choose only what is best for himself.

The functions of the brain are to feel and to think in harmony. When these two functions are integrated at the highest level in any human activity, a measure of truth is achieved and great joy may result. There is no pharmacological substitute for such human achievement. As Haldane, the British biochemist who made so many contributions to our knowledge of genetics, states in an article written just before his death, entitled "A Scientist Looks Into His Own Grave," "I have tried morphine, heroin, opium, and ganja. The alterations of my consciousness due to these drugs were trivial compared with those produced through my work."

CANNABIS AND ACADEMIA

It would be difficult to prove that the effects of *Cannabis* intoxication on society are reflected primarily by the increased incidence of violent crime which we observe today. As pointed out by Murphy (1963), the incidence of overt criminal behavior related to *Cannabis* use occurs only with the development of panic reactions or acute psychoses, which are not frequent. The long-term untoward effects of *Cannabis* on society are more subtle and hidden. One might well ask to what extent the use of *Cannabis* for pleasure might not erode the position of leadership normally imparted to the more educated members of society.

The use of *Cannabis* by academia seems to be acceptable in America today as it is in some intellectual circles of England (Bewley, 1966). Lindesmith (1969) mentions the following story told by one of his acquaintances, a professor in a large American university who is nationally known and respected in his profession:

> "Last New Year's Eve, two of his friends, one the head of a department in his University, the other a lawyer, gave a cooperative New Year's Eve party. At the party they provided for their guests, the usual assortment of alcoholic beverages, plus marihuana. About half the guests 'turned on' with alcohol, the other half with marihuana.
>
> "The professor then told this episode to his dentist who in

turn suggested that he might try some really high quality marihuana of the Mexican variety. Acapulco gold. The dentist,
it turned out, was growing his own supply. The professor admitted that he had not smoked pot at the New Year's party,
but he had tried it before with some police officer friends,
members of a narcotic squad who furnished the marihuana
from confiscated supplies."

"This is by no means," says Lindesmith, "an isolated or unrepresentative
instance, and many others of a similar nature have been or could be reported.
One of the most remarkable was the fourteen minute televised version of a
'Pot Party at a University' film by Chicago's WBBM-TV station, in the vicinity
of Northwestern University on November 1–2, 1967."

It is possible for a group of intellectuals with important assets of talent and
ability to use with taste and discrimination, for their own comfort and pleasure, psychotropic drugs including *Cannabis*. Many of them, after a number of
years, may outgrow the marihuana habit, and find nonpharmacological ways
to gratify themselves. But what about those who by birth or opportunity do
not possess such resources? What about those who must be satisfied with a
routine and uninspiring occupation? Will they outgrow or control as readily
the chemical gratification so easily offered by *Cannabis,* especially if this drug
has become socially acceptable because of its use by those in the professions
and the universities? As a facetious Englishman remarked, "And what happens when grass hits the grass roots? Who will do the hard work?"

Medical Students and Cannabis Use

In the spring of 1970, a survey at four medical schools (Lipp et al., 1971)
in different geographical regions of the United States indicated that *Cannabis*
use ranged from 17% of the students at one school to 70% at another. Over
500 students in the four schools had used marihuana at least once, and 114
said they had used the drug more than 100 times. There was a difference in
use according to the social patterns of the geographical areas, rather than
according to age, sex, or marital status. Marihuana use was more prevalent
on the Eastern and Western seaboards than in the Midwest area. Medical
student opinion of marihuana varied according to geographical region. In
schools with a high percentage of marihuana use, information obtained from
personal experience with *Cannabis* rated higher than information gathered
from medical school teaching. In all schools students rated peers' opinions
(40 to 65%) and "mass media" (40 to 49%) as more dependable sources

of information than medical school teaching (10 to 41%), and "authority figures" had the lowest rating (18 to 32%) (Table 19).

Table 19

Percent Rating by Medical Students of Their Sources of Information Concerning *Cannabis*[a]

Source	School				% of sample
	A	B	C	D	
1. Peers	65	40	61	52	55
2. Professional readings	61	46	55	62	56
3. Media	40	45	42	49	44
4. Personal experience	46	10	41	30	32
5. Medical school teachings	13	41	10	36	25
6. Authority figures	32	25	21	18	24

[a] After Lipp et al. (1971).

For any other drug, medical students depend on their teachers as their primary source of information. Marihuana, of all the drugs, has a privileged position. While 23% of the medical students interviewed believed that *Cannabis* is relatively harmless, 46% thought it should be restricted according to strength. In a survey conducted by Solursh et al. (1971) on senior medical students in Ontario (Canada) and California, a clear majority of both groups expected no significant effect of moderate *Cannabis* use on either physical or mental health of the user. Moderate use was defined as "one to three cigarettes, shared, about once a week." Very few pharmacologists could dispute this last statement, provided the marihuana cigarette used contained 1% or less delta-9-THC. But many will question the assumption that moderate use could last for any prolonged period in the population at large because of the remarkable tolerance which develops to this drug.

The authors conclude, "There is a vast gulf between the position of the medical profession and the position of medical students. We the authors generally agree with the students we surveyed and disagree with the position of established medicine." (Lipp et al., 1971).

The opinion of these medical students in 1970 faithfully reflects the misinformation about *Cannabis* that the American scientific and lay press of 1968 to 1970 have disseminated with considerable assistance from the other mass media. We have seen that this information underplayed the health hazards of *Cannabis* intoxication and did not discuss the fundamental social issues underlying the widespread availability of psychotropic drugs.

This misinformation about *Cannabis* is due primarily to a casual and somewhat careless analysis of the facts. And Lipp et al., speaking for the medical students, says "If medical authorities cannot convince medical students to refrain from using marihuana, persuading the population at large seems unlikely. If medical students, with their excellent intelligence, cannot be convinced, it behooves medical educators to wonder why." Medical educators do wonder why their younger colleagues express such sanguine views in reference to a toxic substance which carries a serious potential hazard to mental health, if it is not very cautiously, sparsely, and infrequently used.

To state that "there have been no studies that can clearly relate any dangerous effects to most casual users of this drug in the quantities that are consumed in most social settings" is to take a very narrow view of the overall problem. The social settings referred to by Lipp et al. are the comfortable homes or apartments of affluent medical students. The "casual" user is a motivated, intelligent young person smoking marihuana for pleasure. There are many social settings which should be considered, and many other more justifiable reasons for persons to absorb psychotropic drugs.

Are medical students willing to see marihuana become freely available so that they might use it for pleasure every week or 2 weeks, even if such free availability would cause a very large number of less fortunate adolescents to use the drug daily and impair their health? Medical students must ask themselves what might happen to their society if *Cannabis* were made available, as alcohol and cigarettes are, without practical restriction or limitation. This question might seem unfair, but the medical profession cannot ignore it. Traditionally, the aim of medicine has been to protect the health of man, especially of growing man, and to achieve this goal preventive medicine should become more and more the aim of the physician.

The use of *Cannabis* by medical students carries an additional serious hazard which Benson ignores, namely, drug dependence among physicians. Medical students should think of themselves and their future careers when they indulge in the use of psychotropic drugs. Indeed, numerous studies have indicated that physicians are prone to drug use and dependence, because of easy access to drugs, and also because of the considerable pressures and responsibilities which accompany their daily tasks. The use, by medical students under stress, of mind-altering drugs—depressants and stimulants, which induce tolerance—tends to create an unhealthy pattern of response: The association of drug use with a pleasurable sensation is engraved in the mind of the user as an effective way of reversing a bad mood.

In future years, the physician confronted with conflicting situations is bound to remember the pleasant easy solution afforded by drug taking, and he will be tempted to use it again. Physicians, like all men, are weaker than they wish to think they are (Farnsworth, 1970). Most medical students seem to accept this proposition for all psychotropic drugs with the exception of *Cannabis*. Aren't they mistaken in using this deceptive drug because of its alleged harmlessness?

Many physicians have deluded themselves in using many other drugs which seemed harmless, as reported in the study of Vaillant et al. (1970). This prospective study, carried out over a 20-year period, compares a group of 45 physicians with a group of 89 matched control subjects. As college sophomores, both groups had been selected for the study because of better than average physical and psychological health. The physicians used significantly more tranquilizers, sedatives, and stimulants than their nonmedical counterparts (Table 20).

Table 20

Maximum Use of Mood-Altering Drugs by 45 Physicians
and 89 Controls During a 20-Year Period[a]

Category	Use of Amphetamines (%)		Use of tranquilizers[b] (%)		Use of sedatives (%)	
	Physicians	Controls	Physicians	Controls	Physicians	Controls
1 No mention of use	78	96	73	85	33	65.0
2 "Occasional" use (one mention)	18	2	9	8	27	25.0
3 "Occasional" use (two mentions)	—	—	—	—	22[c]	4.5
4 Regular use	4	2	18	7	13	4.5
5 Abuse	0	0	0	0	5	1.0

[a] After Valliant et al. (1970).

[b] Two doctors used imipramine, two doctors used chlorpromazine, and one control used chlorprothixene; all the rest used "minor" tranquilizers.

[c] The increased number of physicians falling in groups 3, 4, and 5 is significant at 0.001 level of confidence (chi-square test); one control was lost to follow-up observation.

Vaillant et al. conclude by asking medical schools to "assume greater responsibility for teaching their students that they represent a high-risk population for drug abuse, and that, unchecked, the virtues of the good physician can increase the risk. No physician, whatever his rationalization, should write a prescription for himself for a drug that will make his brain feel better, sleep better, or work better. This will not be easy for the student to hear; he will use his excellent intelligence to argue that his instructor is overcautious. But in our group of 45 physicians, preselected for psychologic soundness, self-medication with drugs or alcohol was the cause of one-third of the total time that this group spent in the hospital."

Cannabis and Alcohol

It is frequently stated that *Cannabis* is "less dangerous than alcohol." This comparison is erroneous and misleading. One cannot compare a plant like *Cannabis* with its dozens of complex chemical constituents to a single well-identified chemical substance such as ethanol. At best, *Cannabis* extracts could be compared with wine. But it is also very difficult to compare delta-9-THC and alcohol, two substances which are very different in chemical structure, physical properties, metabolism, distribution, and pharmacological and physiological effects.

The statement so often repeated of the greater "safety" of *Cannabis* as compared to alcohol refers to the occasional weekly or monthly use of a few milligrams of delta-9-THC as opposed to the frequent immoderate use of hundreds of grams of alcohol. Chronic *Cannabis* intoxication is achieved by absorbing daily variable amounts of *Cannabis* extracts containing 70 to 100 mg of delta-9-THC. Chronic alcoholism is achieved by daily absorption of 100 to 200 ml of ethanol (100,000 to 200,000 mg).

There are distinct, measurable differences in the effects of marihuana and alcohol on brain function. No impairment in short-term memory has been reported in alcoholics without a history of blackouts, despite blood alcohol levels of 200 mg/ml. This fact has been confirmed in monkeys given doses of alcohol of 1 to 3.5 gm/kg and which had to perform a delayed matching-to-sample task (Mello, 1972).

Tinklenberg (1972) compared the effects of alcohol and *Cannabis* on 12 college-educated men in their twenties who had been screened for good physical and mental health. They were given 0.35 mg/kg of delta-9-THC, 0.7 ml/kg of ethanol, or a placebo. It was observed that marihuana was more disruptive of tasks requiring appropriate temporal sequencing and that it induced greater variability in cognitive performance. Electrocortical measurements showed that marihuana consistently increased amplitude of the visual averaged potentials and of the contingent negative variation, while alcohol decreased these amplitudes.

Alcohol is rapidly and entirely eliminated or metabolized within 8 to 10 hours after its absorption, has a half-life of 4 hours. Delta-9-THC has a half-life of 2 to 3 days and its metabolites, which are slowly excreted over a week, accumulate in tissues and body fluids. Daily use of alcohol, amounting to 20 to 50 ml a day, does not accumulate in tissues. It would seem that *Cannabis* cannot become a substitute for alcohol on a daily basis.

Daily use of *Cannabis* would appear to be fraught with hazard because of the rapid development of tolerance, which leads to chronic self-administration of amounts which could produce in a few years significant mental deterioration. This same tolerance may lead the *Cannabis* user to experiment with other, stronger hallucinogens or other, more potent psychotropic drugs.

Another factor which makes it difficult to compare *Cannabis* and alcohol is that intake of alcohol may be readily quantitated just by the amount ingested, since all of it is absorbed into the blood stream. However, it is not possible to quantitate or titrate even roughly the amount of delta-9-THC which ultimately reaches the blood after being absorbed from a smoked cigarette or material ingested. One has to depend on a purely subjective feeling of "high," which is not necessarily related to the amount of psychoactive material absorbed (Jones, 1971). For such reasons, it is much more difficult to control the amount of delta-9-THC absorbed from *Cannabis* preparations than to control the amount of alcohol one will absorb.

Another misleading aspect of the comparison between alcohol and *Cannabis* is that both compounds are not taken entirely for the same reasons. Few people admit to taking alcoholic beverages, especially the weaker ones such as wine, in order to become inebriated. These beverages have been used in the Western world over the centuries by those who wish to enhance the taste of food and enjoy the innumerable forms of fermented beverages available, each one for a special occasion. Appreciation of fine wines and brandies is an art which takes many years to acquire.

Alcohol is a most useful pharmacological agent and solvent which enters into the composition of innumerable pharmaceutical and biological preparations. It is an essential chemical substance. Socially, alcohol has been used for several thousand years and, in spite of its abuse, for which man has paid and continues to pay an exorbitant price, it has not stymied the development of Eastern or Western European countries or of North America. *Cannabis,* on the other hand, has little or no pharmaceutical usefulness and no industrial application. And it has been used for centuries in countries which are now called underdeveloped after having displayed brilliant periods of development.

Cannabis is used only for its euphoric psychotropic effect and for the alterations of perception it induces. There is no such thing as a little bit of marihuana. Achievement of a high is what is sought by the user, which is similar to being quite intoxicated with alcohol. Isn't being "stoned" the equivalent of being drunk? The smoke is not especially enjoyable, nor is the method of smoking. When administered orally, the unpalatable taste must be masked by strong beverages or sweets. One takes *Cannabis* as a drug for its after-effects, not for the pleasurable sensations it induces in the process of taking it.

Young people today prefer *Cannabis* to alcohol. They may obtain greater, longer-lasting euphoric effects than those derived from much larger quantities of alcohol and without the unpleasant side effects that follow excessive libation. "The pleasure of smoking marihuana has convinced many students that this drug is better than alcohol" (Greenwald, 1968). Just because *Cannabis,* when available, is preferentially used by the young, it represents a much greater abuse potential and consequently a greater danger to health in that age group than does alcohol. Unlike wine, one cannot take a little marihuana day in and day out without running the risk of rapidly developing tolerance to this drug.

The major physical and psychological disabling effects of chronic alcohol intoxication are mostly observed when man reaches forty or fifty. The disabling effects of chronic *Cannabis* intoxication are observed much sooner, between 20 and 30 years of age.

Some advocates of *Cannabis* use have claimed that marihuana, if freely available, might become a substitute for alcohol. They refer to the study of Carstairs (1954), who reported on the exclusive use of marihuana taken in moderation for religious purposes by 85 Brahmans of a small village of 2400 inhabitants in northern India. Carstairs claims that the use of bhang by the Brahmans was less disruptive, less unseemly, more in harmony with the highest ideas of their race than the use of alcohol practiced by another elite group, the Rajputs of the same village. However, it is clear that the use of *Cannabis* described by Carstairs in the unique cultural context of the impermeable Hindu caste system is oriented entirely toward achievement of a traditional religious and cultural goal.

The use of *Cannabis* by the Brahmans may be compared to that of peyote in the Native American Indian Church (*Hospital Tribune Report, 1971a*). In both instances a psychotropic drug is taken in a very formal religious context, and emphasis is placed on communion rather than on withdrawal, on adherence to the standards of a closed society rather than of the freeing of impulses. In both instances strict abstinence from alcohol is advocated and practiced. The use of bhang by the Brahmans to enhance meditation, to be more ascetic in their religious observance, is a far cry from the use of marihuana just for pleasure or fun among American youth as described by Becker (1963) or Goode (1970). In the Western world, the use of marihuana for pleasure is associated with the use of alcohol. Almost all of the surveys where the use of both drugs has been cross-tabulated have indicated that there is clearly an association between drinking alcohol and smoking marihuana. Usually, use of tobacco is also associated (Blum, 1969; Mirin et al., 1971).

In Moslem North Africa, wine and alcohol were strictly forbidden by religion, and *Cannabis* was consumed at the exclusion of fermented beverages. However, as a result of earlier French influence, large vineyards were planted and wine became available. Today most *Cannabis* users also take wine or alcohol (Christozov, 1965) in spite of the religious interdiction. This is a clear example that when a pleasurable substance becomes readily available it is widely used.

The regulations of the Food and Drug Administration, issued in 1971, regarding the use of *Cannabis* for clinical investigation in man, certainly indicate that chronic absorption of *Cannabis* extract might be hazardous. They state: "Oral doses of the extract, delta-8- or delta-9-THC (not to exceed 30 mg) may be given daily for a period not to exceed one week. *Parenteral doses or prolonged oral doses may not be administered to human subjects."* This statement is indicative of the hazards of oral chronic absorption of *Cannabis.* The F.D.A. has not yet issued any similar warning concerning clinical investigation with ethanol, which may be orally administered indefinitely without any ill effect at a daily dosage of 10 to 30 ml.

However, in 1971, Grinspoon states: "No amount of research is likely to prove that *Cannabis* is as dangerous as alcohol and tobacco." American society has already enough problems with alcohol, tobacco, and pollution. It is now facing a serious problem of drug dependence in its population at large. Will these problems find an easier solution after marihuana has been made freely available? Can American society really afford, in spite of its extraordinary resiliency, to legitimize the use of *Cannabis,* and still keep its identity?

If we cannot tell our children not to smoke marihuana because we are drinking immoderately, it is high time that we scrutinize our patterns of drinking and that a concerned society review its laws controlling the sale and distribution of alcoholic beverages, as well as its ultimate goals and values.

The Use of Cannabis for Pleasure

Some sociologists and psychiatrists are taking an optimistic view of the passing away of a Puritan society based on an obsolete Protestant ethic oriented toward outward achievement. They envision the emergence of an age of economic abundance, where automation will provide a guaranteed annual income with sufficient goods and services for all as well as greatly increased leisure time. With the coming of this New Kingdom, the pursuit of happiness which is embedded in the American Constitution as a sacred fundamental right will become a goal in itself, and will include the use of pleasurable drugs. The old value system which demands that pleasure be earned through work would become obsolete (McGlothin and West, 1968).

Becker (1963) has analyzed the process which is followed and the conditions which must be fulfilled when an individual is introduced to the use of marihuana for pleasure. Becker employs the term "use for pleasure" to emphasize the noncompulsive and casual character of the behavior. The individual must undergo a sequence of changes in his attitude to, and his experience with, the drug in order that he may finally appreciate the full effects which are described as pleasurable by experienced smokers. If the individual undergoes all the processes described by Becker, and maintains the attitude developed during them as his experience with the drug increases, he becomes willing and able to use the drug for pleasure when the opportunity presents itself.

The process of initiation into the use of marihuana for pleasure is outlined below:

1. The drug must be smoked properly. Joachimoglu (1965), Miras (1969), and Isbell et al. (1967) have emphasized the importance of deep and rapid inhalation in their experimental investigations of *Cannabis*.

2. The individual must absorb sufficient *Cannabis* to produce psychopharmacological effects; he must also be able to recognize the symptoms and their connection with his use of the drug. It is not enough that the effects be present; the user must be able to point them out to himself and consciously connect them with his smoking of marihuana before he can appreciate the experience of being high. In order to continue use of the drug, it must be used in a manner so that it produces effects, the effects must continually be appreciated when they occur, and as new ones develop they must be appreciated. With increasing experience the user develops a greater appreciation of the drug's effects; he continues to learn to get high.

3. The user must learn to enjoy the effect he has learned to experience. *Cannabis*-produced effects are not automatically nor necessarily pleasurable. The taste for such experience is socially acquired. In the early stages these effects may be unpleasant and frightening. The experienced user can reassure the novice when the unpleasant effects appear and teach him to regulate the amount he smokes so as to avoid any severely uncomfortable symptoms while retaining the pleasant ones. Finally, the new user may be taught to redefine his attitude towards what he previously considered to be unpleasant effects, so that they become acceptable and desirable. If this redefinition does not occur, use of the drug will cease. For such a redefinition to occur the individual must participate in the drug with other more experienced users. Where participation is intensive, experience is encouraged, and pleasure is educated.

The consequence is that the individual consciously uses the drug for the pleasure to which he has been educated by the culture with which he is associated. Considerations of expediency, long-term effects, legal and general disapproval of *Cannabis* use, and morality, may interfere with or inhibit further use, but use of the drug continues to be a possibility in terms of the individual's conception of the drug and his culture's acceptance of and belief in it.

Becker's approach implies a perfectly "cool," well-controlled individual, liberated from the structures of a bourgeois society, and finding a new life style in the pursuit of his own pleasure, which he may share with others as long as the sharing is an added source of gratification. The more the subject is liberated from the taboos of the old society, from his own hang-ups, from the hypocritical values of his family and parents, the greater the chance of experiencing pleasure and fun from *Cannabis.*

It does not seem to occur to Becker or Goode that physical tolerance to the effects of *Cannabis* does occur and that its chronic use might lead to increasing dosage, and to the use of stronger drugs. The physiological and pharmacological aspects of drug use in general and of *Cannabis* in particular are also ignored by Becker and Goode. In addition to the physical tolerance to *Cannabis* which the habitual user will develop, and which we have previously described, there are also the physiologically untoward effects of acute and chronic intoxication with *Cannabis.* That these effects were ignored by Becker and Goode might be indicative of the low potency of the material used by their subjects. Indeed, none of these authors ever attempt to define the chemical nature of the "marihuana" smoked in their studies.

Becker describes the use of *Cannabis* for pleasure as if the mind were disconnected from the body. He gives little importance to the basic physiological mechanisms which are triggered when one uses *Cannabis* to obtain pleasurable feelings and sensations. The basic neural structures which control the final dispensing of pain and pleasure have been clearly demonstrated in the experimental animal (Olds and Milner, 1954) and give strong support to the pain-and-pleasure theory of behavior. These also exist in man. The repetitive triggering of these mechanisms by *Cannabis* results in biochemical changes associated with patterns of behavior which become imprinted in the nervous system. The demand for the pleasurable sensations caused by *Cannabis* will require in time larger and larger amounts of the drug. A biological urge will develop to substitute more potent drugs for *Cannabis,* in order to reach a similar feeling of detachment from the world.

Even a sociologist such as Schofield (1971), who takes a mild view of *Cannabis* intoxication, recognizes that this weed is far from an ideal recreational drug. "The pro-pot lobby has tended to oversell the advantages of pot with dreamy descriptions of getting high and self-admiring talk about lovely people who take it. It is a mistake to claim too much for *Cannabis,* for there are several drawbacks. Its effects are unpredictable and its action imprecise. For many it does not work at all, and for others its effects are variable. It depends too much upon the mood of the user at the time he takes it. Regular users say it does not help them when they are depressed. An antagonistic person in the *Cannabis* circle can spoil it for others. A few people have had a frightening experience while under the influence of *Cannabis*."

If modern man needs a pharmacological euphoriant to forget the frustrations of daily life, he should utilize a substance less deceptive than delta-9-THC and less hazardous to the integrity of brain function. The development of such a substance, predicted for 1984, (Orwell, 1949), which may be heralded by the scorces of psychotropic agents synthesized in the past 20 years and widely used by man today, would represent a major challenge to the ingenuity of the organic chemist. Such a substance should make one feel relaxed and happy and remove aggressive feelings so as to favor pleasant social gatherings. It should not induce tolerance or dependence of a physical or psychological nature and should not have any undesirable side effects.

Soma, synthesized by the imagination of Huxley (1946), is the first such hypothetical drug to give great pleasure harmlessly. "One cubic centimeter cures ten gloomy sentiments," says the assistant predestinator of the *Brave New World*.

The hazards of such preparations were pointed out in perspectives of the future by writers of science fiction. The cheery gum of Pohl and Kornbluth (1969) is so relaxing that people chew it continually and no longer bother to work. Pohl's "coffiest drink" is such a delicious beverage that once people start drinking it they continue to do so for the rest of their lives.

An additional hazard would be, of course, the dispensation of such pleasurable substances by regulatory government agencies (such as the F.D.A. or the F.B.I.) to condition man's behavior and abridge his freedom. Such a move would merely defeat the very goal of those who advocate, in the name of individual liberty, the free use of psychotropic drugs (Lindesmith, 1965).

Cannabis As a "Social Drug"

According to Bouquet (1951) and my own observations (1971), a few users of *Cannabis* extracts in North Africa, where the drug is still socially acceptable in some circles, do manage to regulate and restrict the consumption of their favorite preparations at festive special occasions, to the exclusion of any other psychotropic drugs. John Kaplan (1971) claims that this type of marihuana use, though not typical in Oriental countries, "would be the American pattern." This assimilation of patterns of *Cannabis* use in North Africa and America is for many reasons fraught with great uncertainty. The potency of the *Cannabis* used in both countries is quite different. Kaplan seems to assume that only marihuana of low potency will be used by the American people. On what basis?

The people of the United States have not given an example of restraint in the use of any other drugs made available to them for medical and nonmedical purposes. This is true for barbiturates and tranquilizers, alcohol and tobacco, amphetamines and opiate derivatives. In no country in the world have opiates been abused in a more destructive way. On what basis, therefore, is Kaplan justified in implying that marihuana will become the only drug widely used with restraint and moderation in the United States by the population at large as soon as it becomes a "legal" staple of known THC content?

Nevertheless, this assumption is widespread, as indicated by the following extract from an article in the *American Journal of Psychotherapy* (Lesse, 1971):

> "For all practical purposes, marihuana has joined alcohol as another universally available euphorizing agent, and shortly it will have the same acceptance as alcohol. It has been estimated that within a few years after receiving legal sanction between 30 and 40 million people will be users of marihuana and approximately 1% of those will become frequent or even habitual users or 'potheads.' "

The figure of 1% seems very low in view of the much larger percentage of heavy users of tobacco and alcohol among those who consume these freely available social drugs.

The evidence at hand would justify an opposite conjecture stated by Seevers (1970), and which some physicians call Seevers's law: "When *Cannabis* (or any other psychotropic drug) is easily available, it is abused on a large scale." Furthermore, almost everyone would agree that the use of this social drug would have to be curtailed to a much greater extent than tea, coffee, cigarettes, or even wine. Except for Leary (1966), none of the protagonists of *Cannabis* have yet suggested that this social drug might also be shared in the family circle, as wine is in Jewish and Christian celebrations. No one is suggesting that the traditional birthday champagne be replaced by an elixir of *Cannabis*. As a "social drug" *Cannabis* preparations would be limited to relatively few social occasions in which the whole family would not be invited to participate.

Cannabis and Multiple Drug Use

All available evidence indicates that in countries like the United States, where many psychotropic drugs are available, the smoking of marihuana is associated with multiple drug use. Indeed, all of the surveys performed among marihuana users in the past 5 years indicate that the habitual use of

Cannabis is associated in a statistically significant way with the use of other psychotropic drugs.

Soueif (1971), after comparing in Egypt 850 hashish users with 839 subjects who did not use the drug, concluded "Cannabis users tend to seek agents acting on the central nervous system more than non-users do." In his series, more hashish takers (22.7%) than controls (9.1%) were found to be alcohol drinkers, in a country where this beverage is not socially accepted. Hashish users also tended to take coffee and tea more than controls did. Tobacco smoking was much more prevalent among *Cannabis* users (91.6%) than among controls (32.4%). The majority of the *Cannabis* users reported taking coffee and tea and smoking tobacco before they started to take hashish. The frequent American smokers of marihuana studied by Jones (1971) present similar traits. "The frequent users used the drug longer (5.2 years), had greater experience with alcohol and hallucinogens, and smoked more tobacco."

In his extensive student survey, Blum (1969) reports that more students had used marihuana than any other illicit drug, and more than any other illicit drug it was correlated with other illicit drug use. And Blum states "that an initial interest in drugs can lead to expanding drug interests and commitments to a life style in which drugs play a predominant role." Other studies indicate that frequent regular users of marihuana are more likely to experiment with other more potent drugs than occasional users. Crompton and Brill (1970) report in their survey of college students that 100% of daily users of marihuana use other drugs, in contrast to 84% of weekly smokers and 22% of monthly marihuana users. Only 20% of students who merely tried marihuana had used other drugs, and no other drugs were used by those who did not smoke marihuana. The other drugs tried by marihuana users were, in order of frequency, hallucinogens (LSD, mescaline), barbiturates, amphetamines, hashish, and opiates. Another study of nine colleges by Mizner et al. (1970) reported a similar pattern. The development of tolerance to *Cannabis* which is now so well documented in animal and man gives a biological basis to this tendency of regular users to experiment with more potent psychotropic preparations to obtain the desired effect. If this was the case one would expect that, if available, other stronger hallucinogens such as LSD or mescaline rather than opiates would be the drugs of choice in alumni marihuana smokers. Recent surveys have indicated that these drugs were in fact those most frequently associated with habitual *Cannabis* use. These surveys also confirmed that if one is a regular smoker of marihuana, one is likely to go on and at least experiment with other more powerful psychotropic drugs.

Mirin et al. (1971), in a study of 12 heavy marihuana smokers (Table 21) conclude: "A certain percentage of the drug-using population readily falls

Table 21

Pattern of Drug Abuse in 12 Daily Users of Marihuana[a]

	Mean age at first use[b] (years)	Duration of use (years)
Alcohol	15.0	9.8
Marihuana	20.4	4.4
Amphetamines	20.6	4.2
Hallucinogens	21.5	3.3

[a] From Mirin et al. (1971).
[b] Current mean age of heavy users is 24.8 years (range: 22–29).

into a pattern of frequent marihuana use, followed shortly by use of other drugs. Consequently, it is difficult to draw conclusions about the effects of heavy marihuana use per se, since what we observe here is a multiple abuse syndrome."

Table 22

Multiple Drug Use in 106 Adult Marihuana Smokers[a]

Drug used	No.	%	Medical use No.	Medical use %	Nonmedical use No.	Nonmedical use %
"No psychedelic drugs"	28	26				
"Psychedelic experience"	78	74				
LSD	65	61				
Experimental use[b]	25	24				
Moderate use[c]	28	26				
Heavy use[d]	12	11				
Mescaline	67	64				
Experimental use[b]	38	36				
Moderate use[c]	24	23				
Heavy use[d]	5	5				
Amphetamines	64	60				
Opium	29	27				
Heroin and morphine	6	6				
Tranquilizers	50	47	40	38	10	9
Barbiturates	47	44	33	31	14	13
Pain medication	71	67	65	61	6	6

[a] From Carlin and Post (1971).
[b] Experimental use, 1–5 times.
[c] Moderate use, 6–50 times.
[d] Heavy use, 50 times or more.

The prevalence of this syndrome in the United States would make it difficult to study the effects of chronic marihuana use in the country. The study of Carlin and Post (1971) surveyed 106 marihuana users of an average age of 24.5 years, and comprising 60% students, 23% employed, and 17% unemployed or "drop outs." A majority (74%) admitted using other psychotropic drugs. The most frequently used were the hallucinogens mescaline or LSD (Table 22). Sixty percent experimented with amphetamines, 27% with opium, and 6% with heroin. Compared to the earlier survey of Blum (1969), the present results would include a greater average use among marihuana users of hallucinogens and opium. Moreover, the study of Josephson et al., reported in the *Hospital Tribune* (1971b) on drug use among 35,000 high school students aged 12 to 17 years in four regions of the United States confirm the pattern observed among adult marihuana smokers. Fifteen percent of all the school children interviewed admitted using marihuana, and

Table 23

Multiple Drug Use Among Americans 12 to 17 Years Old[a]

| | Nonusers[b] of marihuana | Marihuana users | |
| | | Experimenters[c] | Occasional[d] and Frequent[e] users |
Percentage who have . . .	(1424)	(158)	(103)
Smoked cigarettes	22%	91%	78%
Drunk liquor apart from family	45	91	93
Tried other drugs[f]			
Heroin	1	0	12
LSD	1	0	55
Glue	3	10	37
"Downs" or barbiturates	1	18	71
"Ups" or amphetamines	1	38	74
Tried one or two of the five drugs	2	35	29
Tried three or more of the five drugs	1	6	51

[a] From Josephson et al., as reported in *Hospital Tribune* (1971b).

[b] This is based on a weighted sample of 1701 (the actual number interviewed was 498). The totals of nonusers and marihuana users do not add up to 1701 because not all respondents provided information about their behavior with regard to the drug.

[c] Experimenters were those who had used marihuana one to nine times.

[d] Occasional users were those who had used marihuana from 10 to 59 times.

[e] Frequent users were those who had used marihuana 60 times or more.

[f] Eighteen percent of the occasional and frequent marihuana users did not answer the question about heroin use; 12% of the occasional and frequent users did not answer the question about use of glue. The percentage of nonusers of marihuana, experimenters, or occasional and frequent users who did not answer questions about other drugs in no case exceeded 6%.

the report emphasized the close relationship between the use of *Cannabis* and experimentation with other psychotropic drugs, including heroin (Table 23).

Furthermore, the influx of European *Cannabis* smokers to certain areas of North Africa, where the drug is easily available, has resulted in a close association between Europeans and Africans. In exchange for *Cannabis* preparations, the Europeans initiate their African companions to the pleasures of LSD, amphetamines, and opium (Teste, 1972).

Cannabis, the Use of Opiates, and Escalation

The use of opiates by chronic frequent *Cannabis* users was already mentioned in the Indian Hemp Drug Commission Report (1893) (see p. 263). It was later reported in the study of Freedman and Peer (1968) among chronic hashish users in Israel (Table 15). All hashish users who had smoked the drug for more than 12 years also reported using opium. A positive correlation between length of hashish consumption and opium usage was clearly established by Soueif (1971) in Egypt: 31.6% of 850 hashish users admitted taking opium (Fig. 23). More heavy (daily) users (34.3%)

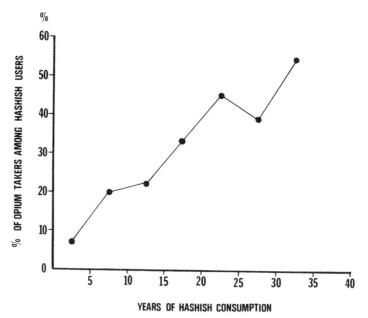

Fig. 23. The positive relationship between opium taking and duration of hashish consumption among 850 hashish users in Egypt (Soueif, 1971).

than moderate (less than daily) users (25.7%) also indulged in opium. Opium taking was also found to be more prevalent among urban habitués (34.5%) than among the rural group (28%). Opium is more available in the city than in the rural areas. Soueif's observations give strong support to the escalation theory formulated by some pharmacologists and especially by Paton (1969) (Fig. 24). Pillard (1970) has also emphasized that all of the surveys on the use of *Cannabis* among young people of England and the United States have established a statistical relationship between marihuana and the use of other drugs, legal and illegal, including opiates.

Chapple (1966) also noted that 88% of 80 heroin or cocaine users had previously taken *Cannabis*. Most of the subjects (80%) shifted from *Cannabis* to the more potent drugs between age 20 and 34. Ball et al. (1968), in their studies of opium addicts admitted to Fort Worth and Lexington penitentiaries, showed a positive association between marihuana and opiate use in 16 states with high addiction rates.

Of course, a statistical relation does not prove a causal one, and as we have already mentioned, stronger hallucinogens would be the drugs of choice for *Cannabis* users who have developed tolerance to this drug.

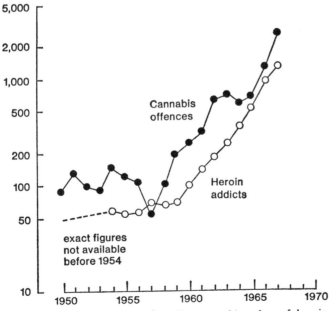

Fig. 24. Comparison between *Cannabis* offenses and number of heroin addicts in England (Paton, 1968).

The fact remains, however, that a significant number of marihuana smokers and users of other hallucinogens turn to opiates. Idanpaan-Heikkila and Schoolar (1971), in a study of 72 multiple-drug users, suggests that the young hallucinogen users who turn to heroin (21% in this survey) have a character disorder or sociopathy, in contrast with the pure hallucinogen users in whom schizophrenia prevails.

Some authors, such as Grinspoon and Snyder, are far from convinced that *Cannabis* smoking leads to multiple drug use and use of stronger drugs. For instance, the fact that a large number of heroin addicts have tried *Cannabis* first is dismissed by Grinspoon with the comment, "doubtless, they all drank milk, ate food, read comic books, wore clothes and rode bicycles before they used *Cannabis* or heroin, yet so far as I know no one has maintained that any of these activities lead to the use of heroin." This is a frequent but incorrect argument which ignores a basic pharmacological fact: The development of somatic functional tolerance to *Cannabis* drives a significant number of users to increase dosage in order to obtain the desired effect. This does not occur with milk drinkers, comic readers, and bicycle riders. Grinspoon also overlooks the other fact, so clearly documented in all studies we have reported, which indicates that the individual who takes one psychotropic drug for pleasure is prone to experiment with others.

Pillard (1971) demonstrates the superficial aspect of Grinspoon's argumentation which ignores some of the statistical techniques (such as contingency tables) that are available in order to distinguish significant correlates, such as marihuana and opiate taking, from insignificant correlates, such as marihuana and milk drinking. It has been shown that LSD usage in a sample of 243 American students can be clearly correlated with marihuana usage (chi square, with Yate's correction, 17.9, $P < 0.001$). However, all LSD users in this sample of students had also used alcohol, but here the relation is not significant (chi square less than 1). The proportion of alcohol users (or milk drinkers) in the American population is so high that just by chance most drug users will be included. All the data available from all over the world indicates that *Cannabis* usage is related to the usage of other central nervous system acting drugs when these are available.

The claim so often repeated that *Cannabis* is not "addictive" and that its use may be discontinued without any accompanying physical distress seems to be one more argument for the users to pursue their habits. They act as if they will be able to stop when the time comes without any difficulty; but they tend to postpone the time of decision to the indefinite future. In addition, the habitual use of *Cannabis* creates in the user a pattern of behavior which is biologically determined and therefore more difficult to discontinue in the absence of very strong motivation or of a substitute.

Becker discards with the following argument the possibility that users of *Cannabis* for pleasure will use opiates: If an individual is smoking *Cannabis* for pleasure, the ability to perceive the effects of the drug must be maintained; if the individual starts to use opiates he loses his ability to appreciate the pleasurable effects of *Cannabis* and becomes unable to distinguish its effects from those of the opiate. Becker's argument implies, as we have already seen, that the brain "receptors" related to pleasurable sensations will be selectively and specifically stimulated within a given social setting in a close to identical fashion by the same dosage of *Cannabis*. Such a concept is not compatible with our knowledge of the marked functional tolerance induced by *Cannabis* and other hallucinogens.

All available evidence indicates that regular *Cannabis* consumption conditions the user psychologically as well as pharmacologically to the use of other mind-altering drugs. And from a physiological point of view, multiple drug use with the resulting drug interactions constitutes a very serious hazard to mental and physical health.

Use of Cannabis and Social Erosion

Impairment of man's health also impairs the social structure. Society tends, therefore, more and more to regulate factors which will protect or improve the health of its citizens. The aim of all modern nations today is to provide adequate medical care for all their people.

The state, that is, the administrative body supported by the productive portion of a nation, is more and more involved in the dispensing of health services. In some developed countries, such as Sweden, more than a third of the total budget of the nation is earmarked each year to finance health care to the entire population from conception to death. As a result of this ever-increasing participation of the state in organizing health care, administrative machineries have been established to control all drugs and other factors which will affect the health of citizens.

Danger to society of a physically harmful drug is gauged by the prevalence of its use in different social groups. Because *Cannabis* is preferentially used by the young, its widespread use and abuse potential in this age group represents a major hazard to any structured society.

From a pharmacological viewpoint it is quite obvious that *Cannabis* intoxication may create disruptive social behavior because of the following manifestations which have been described after acute or chronic usage of this drug. 1. Auditory and visual distortions, including illusions and hallucinations, and possibly panic states or acute toxic psychosis. 2. Impairment of psychomotor performance and incoordination. 3. State of mental and physical lethargy. All of these effects may lead the user, especially the adolescent, to an incapacity or to a refusal to assume individual or social responsibility.

Acute Disorders

The usual disorders of perception and disorientation present among people who smoke a weak form of marihuana at congenial gatherings in a friendly setting are not likely to be accompanied by overt antisocial actions. The behavior of this group is much less boisterous and disruptive than that where large amounts of alcohol are consumed. But this smoking of marihuana in a pleasant "salon" is not the only pattern of *Cannabis* consumption. Large doses of potent material may also be consumed by less sophisticated people in less distinguished places. Acute toxic psychoses or panic reaction may develop in certain users who become agitated and feel threatened by everything. In this case reaction to unpleasant stimuli may be violent. Such overt aggressive behavior, which certainly may occur as described by Murphy (1963), requires the absorption of enough active strong material and also an unfavorable setting.

Criminal behavior is the most overt manifestation of social malaise and has multiple causes. Its incidence among *Cannabis* users has been exaggerated by well-meaning antidrug crusaders. The countries where endemic *Cannabis* intoxication prevails are not those where excessive incidence of serious crime (murder, arson, burglary) occurs. On the contrary, Soueif (1971) reports that in Egypt *Cannabis* users have a lower criminal record than non-users (other than pushing or taking narcotics). If it is difficult to relate *Cannabis* use to violent criminal behavior, it is obvious that it will affect performance of any complex task requiring alert psychomotor coordination, such as driving a car or using a typewriter.

Impairment of Psychomotor Performance: Cannabis and Driving

It should be considered axiomatic that *Cannabis* intoxication, which distorts perception and decreases psychomotor performance, will also impair driving ability. Unfortunately, as a result of some widely publicized experiments, which have been analyzed in Chapter 5, serious doubts have been expressed about the real dangers of driving under the influence of *Cannabis*. After J. Kaplan (1971), Grinspoon (1971), Snyder (1971), and the H.E.W. report on *Marihuana and Health* (1971), Schofield (1971) describes what has become a typical but erroneous marihuana stereotype:

"An experimental study from the State of Washington Department of Motor Vehicles (Crancer, 1969) has shown that *Cannabis* has very little effect on driving ability. Weil et al. (1968) found that the performance of novice users of *Cannabis* deteriorated slightly in tests of physical and mental dexterity, but sophisticated pot smokers actually improved their performance in these tests. This is in line with the saying in *Cannabis* circles that inexperienced users find it difficult to drive while high, but regular users have no difficulty. Joe Rogaly, writing in the *Financial Times* about a group of young Americans he met at Cape Kennedy, had surprising confidence in them. 'My wife quickly decided it was safe to let our young children drive in their van with them, even though they were high on marijuana. For the effect of this drug on these young people seemed to give them an all-pervading gentleness.' "

It is apparent that the material used by Crancer, Weil, and by the young friends of Mr. Rogaly contained only subthreshold amounts of psychoactive substances and is not comparable to that used by Moreau (1845) or by Isbell et al. (1967) or Hollister et al. (1969). Not only was this basic point overlooked, but information indicating the hazards of driving when intoxicated with *Cannabis* was ignored by Schofield and his American colleagues. Lambo (1965) states that in three African countries 53% of all driving offenses were committed by *Cannabis* users. Bejerot (1970) suggests that there may be a direct connection between the widespread use of hashish prevailing among pop artists and the very high rate of car accidents they have: seven dead and 70 injured in Sweden in 1967.

It is easy to discard such reports as merely folklore or as fraught with methodological errors. But should a scientist readily espouse a study which concludes "that driving performance is not influenced by *Cannabis* intoxication." After all, how could a drug which produces distortion of time and space perception, decreases reaction time, impairs psychomotor performance, produces hallucinations, has sedative properties, and interacts with drugs as commonly used as amphetamines and barbiturates not impair driving performance? As Hollister says, "sometimes it is better not to be too scientific." A scientific experiment might also be fraught with methodological errors, and "scientific" evidence is no substitute for common sense or good judgment (Fig. 25).

The experiments carried out in Germany by Luff (1972) indicate that driving under the effects of *Cannabis* intoxication induced by active material

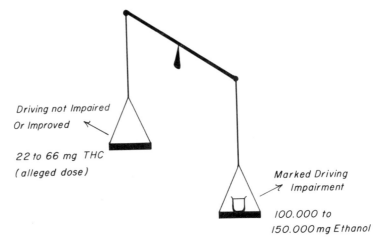

Fig. 25. A schematic illustration of a most widely quoted study comparing the effects of marihuana and alcohol on driving performance. A weighted comparison.

is hazardous. Twelve young volunteers ingested 3.2 gr of a potent preparation, and were tested under actual driving conditions. They passed through 35 stop signs, ignored three red lights, made 233 parking mistakes, ran through 19 pedestrian crossings, demolished a simulated wall of plastic blocks, and ran over a large stuffed lion. The dose of delta-9-THC these volunteers absorbed was certainly elevated (60 to 100 mg). But it was more comparable to the dose of alcohol (100,000 mg) administered in the United States to subjects under simulated driving conditions (Fig. 23), and who presented marked impairment of driving performance.

It is evident that any task requiring immediate memory storage, psychomotor coordination, or hand steadiness will be impaired by *Cannabis* intoxication; this therefore represents a major liability for the adolescent in the classroom or in the stadium. An adolescent smoking marihuana with any regularity is likely to develop serious difficulties in achieving his educational goals. But will he abstain if he knows that his instructor is using the weed?

Many users of *Cannabis* in the Western world are favored with intelligence and opportunity and belong to the student elite from which future leaders are recruited. The possibility that a significant number, as a result of drug use, might desert the mainstream of a productive and progressive society would have important social consequences.

Habitual Cannabis Use and Productivity

Nowhere in the world has *Cannabis* been used more extensively in the past 600 years than in Egypt (See Chapter 1). In spite of the formal ban on possession and sale, the drug is still very popular. The unfavorable influence of the habitual use of the drug by the population at large on the social and political development of the country has been stated many times. A comprehensive survey on the "Consumption of Hashish in Egypt" was carried out between 1958 and 1962 by the National Center for Social Research (Ziwar et al., 1960–1964).

According to this survey *Cannabis* consumption is accompanied by a marked decrease in the productivity of the working classes. Under conditions of hashish intoxication, the percentage of workers who consider their productivity poor or inefficient increases from 14 to 50%, and the percentage of those who consider themselves workers of average productivity falls from 54 to 12%. The percentage of those who believe that their work is satisfactory falls from 80 to 40% after the drug has been consumed. Furthermore, during periods of abstinence from the drug the figures of productivity are still considerably lower. Sami-Ali (1971), who reports this data, concludes, "Such observations brutally emphasize the grave consequences, in the area of productivity, of a habit which is so prevalent among the working class." It is obvious that no modern technologically advanced society could function under such conditions.

It is not difficult to associate social stagnation in under-developed countries to many other factors besides chronic *Cannabis* intoxication. But the association of this widespread habit to a climate of general unproductivity and indifference cannot be discarded.

Miras (1969) also reports that the daily hashish smoker in Greece develops poor working habits and performs unsatisfactorily, especially in any occupation requiring steady physical effort, efficiency, and judgment. "He shows increased talking which substitutes for productive work and physical effort. He is satisfied with himself so makes little effort to improve as a student or an employee. He gradually slips out of his duties and responsibilities but he thinks that he is right and accepts himself as he is. Depending on his personal ability and intelligence, the young hashish smoker will jump from one job to another until he finds the one requiring the minimal effort with more time and freedom for 'thinking.' He can try other drugs too, or increase the quality or quantity of the consumed hashish."

A significant decrease in work efficiency was also observed among Jamaican farmers who were heavy smokers of ganja (Rubin and Comitas, 1972): "Most smokers enact more movements per minute, often with greater variations, and expend more energy (kilocalories per unit of area cultivated) immediately after use." And these same farmers claim that *Cannabis* makes them work more effectively!

This decrease in productivity of Jamaican workers was not even mentioned in the Report of the President's Commission on Marihuana which actually sponsored the study!

A Vicious Circle

The progressive mental and physical deterioration of the young chronic users of *Cannabis* in Sweden and its obvious social consequences have been described by Bejerot (1970). "The more I have seen of the Swedish hashish veterans the more convinced I have become that hashish, in time, leads people away from an ordered form of life. The attitude to life of veteran hashish smokers in many ways is reminiscent of the Orient—with its passivity, unworldliness, tendency to mysticism and fatalism—that one wonders to what degree these old and largely stagnant cultures are marked by the effects of the drug. On the other hand the Asiatic countries which have resisted dangerous drugs or overcome the drug problem, Israel, Japan and China, all present a dynamic development."

Individuals dependent on *Cannabis* not only lose interest in worthwhile goals, but are usually so engrossed in maintaining their dependence and so chronically stupefied by the drug that they are unable to assume their expected roles as individuals or roles compatible with the expectations of society. Indifference and lethargy are incompatible with the democratic form of government which requires, to maintain its free institutions, the mental and physical integrity of its citizens.

The use of *Cannabis* or any other psychotropic drugs can only accelerate the erosion of a free society, already so much apparent around us, by sapping the moral and intellectual fiber of its youth. For this reason the governments of the world decided to control the use of all psychotropic stupefying drugs, including *Cannabis,* many years before the use of these substances became widepsread.

Wide use of marihuana in a society does not seem to be associated with an improvement of the quality of life. The most detrimental effect of this drug is a subtle erosion of man's creative ability and power of growth, which results in social stagnation. Such an erosion is difficult or even impossible to evaluate in quantitative terms which are scientifically or statistically meaningful. There are no methods presently available to measure and quantitate the quality of life which man may achieve or the dedication of a people oriented toward a common goal.

Throughout the ages, drug taking has conferred to man the illusion of reaching the eternal and of communicating with the Universe. In our present society, this habit makes him regress to a level poorly compatible with the demands of a free, ordered society. Nobody can deny that *Cannabis* intoxication impairs the normal brain function of the waking state.

By regressing daily toward inferior forms of mystical experiences, "civilized man" might be unconsciously working towards his own demise. Technological development is no substitute for a certain quality of life, and the consumer society too often accepts or even fosters dullness of the spirit.

A strictly profit-oriented society is quite uninspiring and runs a great risk of becoming drug oriented. If *Cannabis* usage is not the main cause of social erosion, it certainly does contribute to a further erosion of society.

INDIVIDUAL FREEDOM AND DRUG ABUSE

The taking of drugs by young people might be triggered at first by a desire to assert their freedom and independence. As a result, youth tend to interpret the control of drug use as an infringement of individual freedom.

Indeed, writes Schofield (1971), "Inevitably, laws that are concerned with private activities are an interference with our freedom, and they pose a still more serious threat, for there is only a slight difference between the control of moral behavior and thought reform or brain washing."

The Liberal Approach to Drug Taking

By assuming such an attitude, the young people of today are echoing the philosophy of John Stuart Mill as it has been vigorously restated by Lindesmith (1969) to support a liberal drug policy in the United States.

"To put the problem of drug use in a broader setting," writes Lindesmith, "and to indicate the significance it has for our society, I propose to take as a theme a statement made more than a century ago by John Stuart Mill in a famous essay, 'On Liberty.' Mill was concerned with the question of when governments are justified in forcibly intervening in the lives of citizens with the police power and the apparatus of the criminal law. He was worried about what he called 'the tyranny of the majority.' The principle he formulated reads in part as follows:

'. . . The only purpose for which power can be rightfully exercised over any member of a civilized community, against his will, is to prevent harm to others. His own good, either physical or moral, is not a sufficient warrant. He cannot rightfully be compelled to do or forbear because it will make him happier, because, in the opinion of others, to do so would be wise or even right. These are good reasons for remonstrating with him, or reasoning with him, or persuading him, or entreating him, but not for compelling him, or visiting him with any evil in case he do otherwise. To justify that, the conduct from which it is desired to deter him must be calculated to produce evil to someone else. The only part of the conduct of anyone, for which he is amenable to society, is that which concerns others. In the part which merely concerns himself, his independence is of right, absolute. Over himself, over his own body and mind, the individual is sovereign.' "

Lindesmith adds that this principle was intended to apply to normal adults (he could have said mature) and as Mill pointed out, needs to be qualified with respect to the young, the weak, and the helpless. Lindesmith says that this principle of freedom is a fundamental one in our legal system and in our way of life, and he quotes Mill again: "The only freedom which deserves the name is that of pursuing our own good in our own way so long as we do not attempt to deprive others of theirs or impede their efforts to obtain it."

As appealing as this oratory might sound, it considerably simplifies the many aspects which one has to consider in relation to man's freedom. Is man entitled to prevent his fellow man from impairing his brain? This is a question which cannot be answered by the pharmacologist. The physician is more likely to give a positive answer to this query if he subscribes to the aphorism of Hippocrates, "Above all do no harm," or the motto of Dr. Albert Schweitzer, "Reverence for life."

Freedom of Youth and Informed Decision

In the first place, it is questionable to apply the words of John Stuart Mill, a political economist whose theories today are somewhat obsolete, to an area which he had no intention of discussing 100 years ago. The problem of toxicomania among adolescents did not exist in the time of John Stuart Mill, who was very concerned about educating the young with proper guidelines. He was also careful to exclude youth from his lofty admonition on freedom so eloquently quoted by Lindesmith. Mill, who was favored with exceptional parental guidance, accepted the proposition that one of the responsibilties of family and society was to protect and guide adolescents until they are able to make an informed decision.

Some restrictions on the freedom of youth have been applied in all societies as an inherent part of education. We have seen that today adolescence is the age most vulnerable to toxicomania epidemics. In order to protect the young, stupefying drugs should not be made available to them, because drug use impairs their ability to develop into free human beings.

Mind-Altering Drugs and Freedom

Individual freedom is threatened by the use of *Cannabis* or by any other stupefying drug. Psychodysleptic drugs, containing psychoactive ingredients, by disintegrating brain mechanisms and thought processes, impair awareness and judgment which are essential for the exercise of personal freedom.

We have noted that the repetitive use of *Cannabis* leads to a pattern of behavior biochemically conditioned by the drug, to the development of tolerance, to a state of psychological dependence in which man's freedom is abridged. Is a person whose brain has been progressively altered biochemically by drug use able to exert free choice? Is it not spurious to defend the use of psychotropic drugs like *Cannabis* in the name of individual freedom?

Can one speak of a "freely" chosen passive withdrawal to a life of drug-induced fantasy? (McGlothin and West, 1968.) As we have already noted, acceptance of the casual use of mind-altering drugs carries with it the additional danger of thought control. One thing is certain, if man is to remain free in the years ahead, he will have to free his mind from the influence of psychotropic stupefying drugs.

The concept of freedom and its meaning in man's life might also have to be more clearly defined than it was by John Stuart Mill. This definition will require more than an objective analysis of scientific facts; it will also necessitate the awareness, the commitment, and the personal knowledge which led Michael Polanyi (1958) to state: "The freedom of the subjective person to do as he pleases is overruled by the freedom of the responsible person to act as he must."

Free Society, Civic Virtues, and Drug Abuse

It should also be clearly stated here that throughout history individual freedom has been best expressed and exerted through a social and political framework usually referred to as a democratic form of government. Furthermore, again referring to history, the maintenance of free democratic institutions requires on the part of the individual the acceptance of a moral or religious code which implicitly repudiates the use of stupefying drugs.

Montesquieu (1748) was the first sociologist to stress the relationship between individual morality and the democratic form of government known to preserve individual freedom. He summarized this relation in a brief statement: "Democracy is the form of government which requires the most virtue." The civic virtues to which Montesquieu refers are rarely exerted by those who base their "life style" on hedonism and elect to exert their freedom by using mind-altering drugs for pleasure. One might surmise that the widespread use of *Cannabis* in a society will weaken its very structure, because users would tend to detach their attention from the many arduous tasks which confront them in a democratic society. The best illustration of Montesquieu's proposition was afforded after his death by the creation and development of the American democracy.

Alexis de Tocqueville (1843) was the first to define the unique character of American society, as a result of two distinct and apparently incompatible elements: religion and the spirit of freedom. Only in American democracy were these two elements combined to their mutual advantage.

> "Religion perceives that civil liberty affords a noble exercise to the faculties of man, and that the political world is a field prepared by the Creator for the efforts of mind. Free and powerful in its own sphere, satisfied with the place reserved for it, religion never more surely establishes its empire than when it reigns in the hearts of men supported by nothing besides its native strength. Liberty regards religion as its companion in all its battles and its triumphs, as the cradle of its infancy and the divine source of its claims. It considers religion as the safeguard of morality, and morality as the best security of law and the surest pledge of the duration of freedom."

Two human tendencies which had rarely coexisted before came together early in the American ethic and grew side by side. The two seemingly irreconcilable paths of religion, with voluntary obedience, and of freedom, with disregard for authority, did advance together in the United States for several centuries. Winston Churchill summarized the reconciliation of opposite tendencies, which he placed at the base of a democratic government, when he spoke of "freedom under the law." According to Tobin (1972), "much of America's difficulty in recent years has come at least in part from rejection of the Puritan ethic, the traditional American pattern of freedom and strong moral fiber, woven together from the opposite natures in man and discernible everywhere in the manners and laws of America." One must add that the rejection of this ethic, hypocritical and uninspiring as it has become in modern times, has not been replaced by a true mystique underpinned by a personal commitment and a disciplined existence. The definition of such a mystique which could rally and inspire the youth of today is one of our most urgent goals. One fails to see how it will be achieved by a liberal drug policy. Certainly, a portion of any new value system would include an honest scientific approach. Science will not remain a sacred area where only a few initiates may enter. The scientist is not the Western equivalent of the African witch doctor. To ignore basic facts concerning brain metabolism for the sake of developing tribal use of a psychotropic drug seems to be a dangerous step for a developed country.

In any orderly society, patterns of behavior have to be based on certain scales acceptable by all and on which reasonable laws can be based.

One of the clearest lessons of history is that a decadent democracy steps progressively into a tyrannical form of government. This situation will occur when liberty is identified with libertarianism, and when exercise of freedom countenances license of behavior.

The Burden of Proof

The protagonists of the free availability of *Cannabis* who are convinced that this drug does not constitute a serious health hazard will claim that "those who wish to ban *Cannabis* must produce convincing reasons before we restrict the individual's right to choose" (Schofield, 1971).

This view is a transposition of a legal concept regarding man's innocence until proven guilty into the field of medicine, where a different viewpoint prevails in respect to drug usage. Indeed, physicians have to take a guarded view of all drugs, which are considered guilty until proven innocent. The state, which has the mandate to protect the health of the people, must hold a view similar to that of the physician.

On this basis, the onus of proof belongs to those who wish to promote the use of a drug, and the regulatory agencies such as the F.D.A. in charge of regulating drug usage base their policies on this principle: A drug has to be proven innocuous by the promoter before it can be released for general use. We have already seen that the 1971 F.D.A. regulations regarding the use of *Cannabis* for clinical investigation in man curtail the use of smoked total extract to 1 month, and ban altogether prolonged oral doses.

THE EPIDEMIC NATURE OF *CANNABIS* USAGE

In its 1964 report, the World Health Organization stated that "there was an epidemic-like outbreak of abuse of hypnotic drugs in a particular region" and commented, "Sudden changes in the drug of choice for abuse amongst groups within a population in circumscribed areas shows, in the committee's view, the relevance of sociological and environmental factors, as distinct from individual motives, in the etiology of drug abuse."

Bejerot (1970) has described the dynamics of these epidemic toxicomanias, which are characterized by contagion, wide diffusion, and rapid spreading, "attacking many people in many regions at the same time."

There have been epidemics of glue sniffing in the Los Angeles area. The most serious epidemic of intravenous amphetamine administration occurred in Sweden. The number of addicts doubled every thirtieth month from 1948 to 1968 (Bejerot, 1970). In Britain, the number of heroin addicts among youth doubled every sixteenth month from 1959 to 1968. Drug epidemics tend to increase geometrically, says Bejerot, as long as the conditions of development remain stable.

Such epidemics spread rapidly, are limited to certain areas in time and space, have a given age distribution, characteristic sex proportions, and specific routes of entry. All of these characteristics of epidemic drug use apply to the spread of *Cannabis* in the Western world during the past two decades, as illustrated in Fig. 1 of Chapter 1.

Contagious Spread of Cannabis Use

Until 1950 *Cannabis* use was endemic in Asian, African, and South African countries. Its use was limited in other parts of the world within certain well-defined cultural and ethnic boundaries. As a result of the cultural factors described previously, *Cannabis* intoxication spread rapidly to the youth in schools, universities, middle and upper class groups in the Western democracies.

The rapid spread of drug use is due to the intense urge to proselytize by the drug user which combines with the receptive condition of the population primarily interested in the drug. The user spreads the use of the drug to others by praising its wonderful effects to a receptive audience. The very sight of the drug scene is a contagious example for youth.

Historic, Geographical, Ethnic, and Group Boundaries of Epidemic Drug Use

Widespread epidemic use of any given drug, like any epidemic infection, appears at a particular time in history as a result of a combination of factors. It then follows a definite course, growing and subsiding or installing itself and becoming endemic. Given geographical areas also characterize the appearance of drug abuse. In the case of *Cannabis* use in the United States, we have seen its prevalence among the large urban communities of the Eastern and Western seaboards, from which it spread inland.

Epidemic toxicomanias develop within certain ethnic groups. We have seen that the first widespread use of *Cannabis* was limited in the United States to the impoverished, mainly Black and Mexican, populations of the slum areas in large cities. The epidemic of *Cannabis* use developed among white middle and upper class youths of school and college age. Throughout the world, *Cannabis* epidemics in recent decades have tended to develop among the Anglo-Saxon and Scandinavian countries, leaving the Latin ethnic groups of Spain, Italy, and France relatively free.

Epidemic toxicomanias also affect certain cultural groups. Marihuana smoking in the United States occurred for many years among jazz performers from New Orleans, and spread to other performers in entertainment, the theater, and their satellite bohemian circles. Even after the epidemic has broken out of the primary circle and gained wide distribution, drug use will remain ingrained in that primary culture with which it has become closely associated.

Epidemic Drug Use, Adolescence, and Sex Distribution

Cannabis epidemics affect principally the age group from 13 to 20 years, which is the most vulnerable. (*Cannabis* users are observed mostly within this age distribution.) The epidemic use of intravenous amphetamines or heroin has a little older profile, from 16 to 25.

Deniker (1971) states that young people are attracted to the drug culture today as they were to the boy scout and girl scout movements before World War II. Drug use and the drug scene exert, on the minds of young people, a profound attraction and a mysterious fascination—a fascination of the unknown, of the forbidden, which is fanned by the misinformation promulgated for lucrative purposes or mere sensationalism. There is a rage to live, a desire to go beyond the limits of nature, to feel all powerful.

Young people have a profound desire to conform to the fashions promoted by their peers. According to Solursh et al. (1971), young people 12 to 13 years old in the United States who have never used drugs often say that they have used some; they want to conform to the tremendous peer-group pressure prevailing in some sectors of American society. Liebert (1967) even suggests that "these days if a young male goes through four years of college, without having experienced marihuana, some might feel he had a rigidity of character structure and a fear of his impulses that was hardly desirable."

As use of *Cannabis* or any other drug extends over the years, the age distribution tends to become more widespread. Young users become older.

older groups become interested, and younger age groups are drawn in. Such a pattern is already noticeable in the United States.

Males outnumber females in drug use of the epidemic type, in a proportion as high as 8 to 1 at the start of the epidemic. This discrepancy falls to 4 to 1 as the epidemic spreads. (These figures are true for heroin in the United States and England, amphetamines in Sweden and Japan.) There are also more male users and smokers of *Cannabis,* but the differential is not as marked. As a drug epidemic becomes endemic and socially accepted (as for alcohol and tobacco), the proportion of women users increases but rarely approaches the ratio of 1 to 1 (except for alcohol and tobacco in the Western world). A similar ratio is also expected in a society where sex discrimination is anathema.

Cannabis—Endemic or Pandemic Toxicomania?

Endemic toxicomania results from the abuse of drugs which have become socially accepted as pleasurable substances, part of the local culture, and used at social gatherings. In this case, the whole population is exposed to the risk of taking the specific drug, while in an epidemic situation exposure to the drug is limited to a number of selected groups.

A classical example of endemic toxicomania is alcoholism in grape-growing countries. Since the use of wine became a part of Christian ritual, the geographical spread of alcoholism has followed the areas where this religion is prevalent, and spared until recently the Moslem and Buddhist parts of the world.

As pointed out by Bejerot, the endemic use of *Cannabis* preparations in the form of hashish smoking in North Africa may be traced to an epidemic started by the Arab and Moslem conquerors in the twelfth and thirteenth centuries.

But now a pandemic extension of the use of *Cannabis* is becoming a distinct possibility because of the rapid extension of communication and travel and the resulting interactions between cultures. In the Western world the use of *Cannabis* may become endemic before the end of the century, while the Western habit of consuming alcohol is at the same time spreading to the Moslem world. In both cases, an additional form of intoxication is being added to the prevailing one.

Epidemic Toxicomania and Chemical Warfare

J. H. Kaplan, who was commanding officer of a neuropsychiatric team in Vietnam, reports (1971) that toxicomanias (marihuana and abuse of all types of drugs) were the most overwhelming psychiatric problems among troops in Vietnam. As the war dragged on, marihuana was the drug most heavily abused. In the fall of 1969, 50% of the 550,000 soldiers in Vietnam had experimented with *Cannabis* preparations. The use of opium and heroin was associated with that of marihuana in a significant number of cases. According to Kaplan, the standard progression was from marihuana to *Cannabis* dipped in opium and finally to intravenous opiates and methedrine. Increase in psychiatric casuality rate was associated with the rising use of drugs: from 13 per 1000 in 1968 to 24 per 1000 in 1969 (Colbach, 1971). *Cannabis* toxicomania was associated with ineffectiveness, panic states, and psychoses, conditions which are not likely to improve troop morale or combat performance. The widespread self-administration of *Cannabis* and other incapacitating psychotropic drugs appears to be a most effective method of waging chemical warfare.

It must also be added that very powerful political and commercial interests, independently or in association, favor the spread of different forms of toxicomania which were previously localized in small areas. Some political leaders have not concealed that they are willing to take the best advantage of the toxicomanias which are disrupting the social fabric of the Western world. In this respect, the conversations between Chou En Lai and Nasser, reported by Heykal (1972) are quite revealing.

An Epidemiological Approach to Treatment

If one considers the problem of free drug availability from an epidemiological point of view, and the drug is similar to a contaminating noxious agent, the inescapable consequences of making a drug freely available as advocated by many today becomes all too apparent. Drug abuse will become endemic and result in a steady, permanent damage to the health of a significant number of citizens. There is only one major difference, says Cameron (1969), between the classical infectious disease model of illness and drug dependence as a communicable disorder. "With infectious diseases, the host does not seek the agent of infection. At worst, the host may be indifferent to the agents of such diseases as cholera or malaria but with drug dependence, the host wants and seeks out the agent. This surely adds a dimension to the control of the agent which becomes difficult in the extreme." Everyone seems to agree that the infective agents which attack man's body should be controlled by preventive epidemiological measures. Such measures have been quite successful in eliminating large epidemics of infectious diseases.

Similar measures are now advocated for the elimination of toxicomanias; but many disagree, claiming, in the name of individual freedom, that drugs which impair the brain and disrupt the normal thought process should not be controlled or curtailed.

If the *Cannabis* epidemic is to be stopped in the Western countries and prevented from turning into an endemic toxicomania, epidemiological methods
of treatment will have to be urgently established. The measures to be followed have been outlined by Bejerot and successfully applied in Sweden
(1967) and Japan (1968) to stop very serious epidemics of amphetamine
abuse. They include early treatment and concentration on prevention.

1. The responsible infective agent, *Cannabis,* must be as far as possible
eliminated. Since *Cannabis* derivatives have no therapeutic use, there is no
justification for their medical availability (unlike opiates and amphetamines).
Such elimination of *Cannabis* preparations will require international cooperation. Crops of the drug-type hemp plant in Asia, Africa, Central, and South
America will have to be replaced by nontoxic crops. The elimination of the
international commercial interests which favor the spread of *Cannabis* use
will be a major problem—one which has never been solved in the past.

2. Preventive (prophylactic) measures should be organized for the welfare
of that susceptible adolescent population which has not been infected. The
best educational methods should be directed toward a positive approach of
developing in growing man "a healthy mind in a healthy body." This should
result in a spontaneous negative attitude toward all drugs, which should be
administered only by a physician to cure an ailment.

3. Long-term chronic users who have become dependent will require special therapy, including a period of isolation and reeducation. Since no physical dependence develops with *Cannabis* use, the control of this toxicomania
should be relatively easy to achieve from a medical point of view. But such
measures are most unlikely to be taken soon in the United States, where more
and more physicians and educators claim that marihuana is a relatively harmless drug, less toxic than tobacco and alcohol. It is to be expected that the
laws repressing use and possession of *Cannabis* will soon be drastically revised. The social acceptance of marihuana in American society which will
follow the licensing of the sale of this drug will transform an epidemic toxicomania into an endemic one with far-reaching consequences. In the meantime,
the problem of "marihuana legalization" raises a few immediate practical
problems.

THE PROBLEMS OF MARIHUANA "LEGALIZATION"

The Substantive Issues

Any law is based on a substantive issue. In the case of marihuana and
other stupefying drugs, the prohibition of their use is based on the general
philosophy of protecting man, especially adolescent man, from harming him-

self and society. The libertarian outlook is based on the contention that conduct which is harmful only to the user should not be penalized, because the legislation of morality is an unjust and unfair invasion of privacy and an infringement of individual liberty.

The American Civil Liberties Union advocates "a right to use one's own body as one sees fit as a bar to criminal sanctions against drug use."

Many distinguished lawyers, such as Brooks (1969) and Bonnie and Whitebread (1971), believe that new drug legislation should ratify this crucial human right and promulgate a major reform. By major reform, Bonnie and Whitebread mean "the use of persuasion rather than prosecution to protect the individual from his own folly." Such a noble pronouncement would actually put the whole burden of drug abuse measures on educators and psychiatrists and rely upon the spoken word. But these jurists seem to overlook a simple fact: Rational persuasion will only impress the open mind unfettered by drugs or the fantasies of a chemically induced gratification.

One cannot protect the individual from his own folly merely by speaking to him, because in most instances it is futile to try to reason with a mentally ill person. Too many distinguished lawyers and sociologists fail to realize that *Cannabis* preparations selectively alter brain mechanisms and produce what Moreau called in 1845 "a state of mental alienation."

It seems that following John Kaplan (1971), too many lawyers have underestimated the toxicity of *Cannabis* preparations to the central nervous system. It is scientifically incorrect to claim, as did Bonnie and Whitebread (1971) in a review published in *Science,* that marihuana is "scientifically" analogous to tobacco cigarettes. Tobacco is not a psychodysleptic substance which disintegrates mental function, and can be smoked daily without impairment of psychomotor performance.

We have seen that, in the present irrational epidemic of toxicomania, the freedom of adolescents is fundamentally threatened. This, in turn, threatens the free institutions of a democratic society. To make stupefying drugs more freely available cannot be considered today a victory for freedom. And in the case of free availability of such drugs, a fundamental substantive question still remains: How to protect those who are too young to make an informed decision. Lawyers and judges who advocate a freer availability of stupefying drugs should attempt to formulate answers to this question.

Marihuana Legalization: Procedural Matters

In 1971, Dr. Lesse, editor of the *American Journal of Psychotherapy,* wrote, "It should be obvious even to the most blind of health scientists that the legalization of marihuana is for all practical purposes, a 'fait accompli.'

The prime question is no longer whether or not this drug is harmful or whether it is less or more damaging than alcohol, the central issue now is exactly how marihuana should be legalized." Lesse, like many pragmatic educators and scientists, believes that in the United States the substantive question concerning drug availability is no longer relevant and that the best procedural matters should be considered with regard to the legalization of marihuana use. Should scientists start pondering the problems of how marihuana cigarettes should be sold? A manual of instruction detailing the best method of smoking, to obtain the greatest beneficial effect and the least unpleasant side effects, could also be prepared.

The word "legalization" itself is deceptive and misleading. What marihuana legalization means in reality is the substitution for a very simple repressive law modeled after most criminal laws of a much more complex set of regulations which will have to be installed in order to control the sale of a certain kind of *Cannabis* to a certain group of people within certain limitations of age. In reality, what the proponents of marihuana legalization want is to make *Cannabis* "less illegal." Three legal models have been suggested to replace the present "marihuana laws" in the United States.

The Medical Model

The medical model, under which *Cannabis* derivatives would be prescribed by physicians like any other drug, is not possible for strictly medical reasons. We have seen that *Cannabis* derivatives are an obsolete form of therapy, and there is no justification for their medical use. Such derivatives would never pass the stringent regulations of the F.D.A. for all new medications. Furthermore, regulation based on medical utility would not provide enough *Cannabis* to meet the demand of users of *Cannabis* for pleasure.

The Vice Model

The vice model is another possibility; using such a model, *Cannabis* use would be dealt with as are other "victimless crimes" such as gambling, prostitution, or obscenity—the user is not penalized, but the "pusher" or supplier is punished. By treating marihuana dealing and distribution as criminal acts, society demonstrates its steadfast opposition to it, maintains a measure of control over its use, impedes proselytizing, and forbids advertising. By removing the user, and especially the casual user, from criminal prosecution, the cost of enforcing the present marihuana laws, which J. Kaplan claims is outrageously high, would be considerably reduced. However, using the vice model would be a compromise difficult to enforce in practice. It is not always possible to differentiate between sale and possession. Such a vice model was rejected by the delegates to the Single Convention, which obligates the parties (Art. 4C), "to limit exclusively to medical and scientific purposes, the production, manufacture, export, import, distribution, trade, use and possession of drugs covered by the Convention."

Therefore, a modified version of the vice model, reducing the penalties for possession to a misdemeanor, for example, might be more readily formulated. In the spirit of fairness and appeasement, more humane legislation has been drafted in all Western countries. It is far better to try to rehabilitate or reform users of *Cannabis* and other stupefying drugs than to punish them with harsh sentences which result in their association with common criminals. In the United States, the Comprehensive Drug Abuse Prevention and Control Act of 1970 was passed by Congress. Under this law, possession of marihuana is classified as a misdemeanor punishable by not more than 1 year in jail, while it increased the penalties for professional dealers. A person who gives away small amounts of marihuana without exchange of money is treated as a possessor rather than a vendor. More important, the judges have, under the new law, the discretion to declare the first-time offender a noncriminal. This new federal law has been followed by similar more lenient legislation for marihuana users in several states such as California, New York, and New Jersey. However, all of this new legislation lacks a fundamental definition: that is, of the psychotoxicity of marihuana, which is determined by its delta-9-THC content.

The Legal Necessity of a Scientific (Pharmacological) Definition of Marihuana

It is now well established that delta-9-THC is a potentially harmful psychotomimetic substance. Therefore, marihuana or *Cannabis* preparations should be defined in terms of their delta-9-THC content. The law banning or controlling use of marihuana or *Cannabis* as a psychotoxic agent should be based on the properties of this plant to disintegrate mental function. The amount of delta-9-THC contained in a *Cannabis* preparation constitutes the only reliable index of its psychotoxicity and its potential harmfulness. This amount can be readily and accurately measured and should become the yardstick used for legislation. It is obviously unfair to punish an individual for possession of what may amount to lawn grass or powdered rope. Some people may still get euphoria by using *Cannabis* preparations without active psychotropic ingredients and should not be penalized or even prevented from smoking hay. The substitution of delta-9-THC for marihuana in the present international and national legislation would help to dissipate the confusion created by those who have failed to distinguish between the fiber- and drug-types of the marihuana plant.

The Licensing Model

Elimination of penalties for simple possession of *Cannabis* does not satisfy many of the more outspoken critics of the marihuana laws such as John Kaplan. These critics are advocating a third model, the licensing model, which would amount to a total repeal of present legislation.

Under this model, the state would license distribution and sale of marihuana. Neither its use nor possession would be a criminal act. A bill to this effect has been introduced (1971) in the New York State Assembly by delegate Frantz Leichter, who represents the Manhattan District (which includes Columbia University).

> "There shall be established a marijuana control authority which shall license and regulate growers, producers, manufacturers and distributors of marijuana. . . . The authority shall prescribe the strength of marijuana to be sold at retail . . . and shall also prescribe a suitable warning on every package of marijuana regarding possible ill effects on the health of the user. . . . Marijuana may be sold at retail *only* in licensed liquor stores. . . . There are no restrictions on the amount of marijuana a person may buy. It shall however be unlawful to sell (and give) any marijuana to a person under eighteen years years of age. . . . All marijuana will be taxed in an amount similar to cigarettes" (F. S. Leichter, personal communication, to Snyder, 1971).

Proponents of Leichter's bill feel confident that this or similar legislation will be enacted within 2 to 4 years. A similar bill has been introduced in the California legislature. Such schemes would constitute welcome added revenues to the state, and Kaplan suggests that they should be used for research in drug dependence.

The major obstacles to such schemes are both ideological and operational. We have already described the substantive objections to making *Cannabis* preparations widely available to adolescent man. The operational difficulties in drafting and enforcing the licensing model of marihuana usage would be formidable. The state would have to organize a sizeable new bureaucracy to take over the licensing and control of production, manufacture, distribution, and sale of *Cannabis*. One of the major problems of the new "Marihuana Authority" would be to make a preparation of a potency and a quality acceptable to the users, or how best to deliver poison in a small pot. This would be done by mixing marihuana of the fiber type with plant of the drug type, or by using synthetic delta-9-THC to spike the plentiful American fiber-type hemp. But, how much delta-9-THC should the final product contain? Kaplan advocates that marihuana contain 1 to 1.25% delta-9-THC, Grinspoon, 1.5%. A 1-g cigarette of such a preparation would contain 10 to 15 mg of active material, enough, according to Isbell, to produce acute panic states or even psychotic effects. The medical advisory board to the "Marihuana Authority" would probably recommend the manufacture of smaller cigarettes, containing 5 mg of delta-9-THC. But the final amount smoked will have to be left to each individual. And one has to hope that the majority of marihuana smokers will use the drug wisely day in and day out with just the right amount required to produce the desired effect and that such self-titration will be possible regardless of development of tolerance, associated medication, prevailing mood, physiological condition, social setting—all factors which alter, in a variable way, the psychological and emotional response to *Cannabis*. As in all licensing schemes, the price of the licensed product would have to be set high enough to ensure profitable return to the state and also to act as a deterrent to excessive use, especially by the young.

This is precisely the point at which law enforcement will become difficult. The control of illegally manufactured alcohol is still possible though difficult. It is not necessary to guard every field where wheat, corn, or grapes are grown and from which alcohol can be made. It is enough to control distillation equipment. But marihuana fields of the drug type cannot be left unwatched; and how can one control the growing of a plant on a window sill, or even in a closet under a light? A few tiny seeds properly selected may give rise, even as far north as New Hampshire, to a 10-ft plant containing 4% delta-9-THC (Doorenbos et al., 1971). Social acceptance of *Cannabis,* combined with the facilities for growing the plant, the profit motive, and the free-enterprise system prevailing in the United States, would render enforcement of restrictions on price and potency of marihuana exceedingly difficult. Establishing of the licensing system, so eagerly advocated by Kaplan, may well result in a still greater disrespect for an unenforceable law than the one existing today. It is practically impossible to impose sanctions *which are enforceable* on a half-good, half-bad basis, or on the differences in pharmacological effects of small versus large quantities of the same toxic agent, or on weak or strong preparations of the same poisonous substance. For the same reason, one cannot, for all practical purposes, license beer or wine and ban alcohol.

The problem of limiting mild forms of marihuana and eliminating strong preparations such as hashish would be difficult to solve. Legalization of *Cannabis* use through a licensing model would in no way remove the social malaise which entices the young to smoke marihuana. For many social reformers, it would be the first step towards removing present controls over the use of all drugs. These controls, according to Lindesmith, have failed and in a large measure are responsible for many of the ills which have fallen on our society. A more difficult solution, albeit an unpopular one, is to restrain and limit as much as possible the use of *Cannabis* and of all other mind-altering drugs which carry with them the danger of serious impairment to mental health, but which also carry with them a much greater threat—the possible mass manipulation of man's mind by chemical substances. If man wishes to remain free, he will have to free himself from the influences of psychotropic drugs. The easier solution for America today is certainly to let disillusioned youth enjoy a pleasurable drug which they are requesting with such persistence.

Another obstacle to the licensing model is the treaty obligation of the United States, which is a party to the United Nations Single Convention for the Control of Narcotic Drugs (see Chapter 1). The signatories of this Convention have pledged to prohibit use and possession of *Cannabis*. The United States delegates also approved the United Nations Vienna Convention (1971), which added delta-9-THC to the list of stupefying drugs to be banned from general use. However, such treaty obligations are considered to be minimal obstacles by the proponents of the licensing of marihuana sale in the United States. John Kaplan is even willing to dispose summarily of the international treaty standing in the way of this lofty goal. So he seriously considers the possibility that the United States might terminate its adherence to the Single Convention by taking advantage of the escape clause which it contains (Art. 46). He therefore concedes that the United States might unilaterally denounce the Convention, but he does not discuss any of the very serious consequences which would result from such a move. Schofield is somewhat more careful and admits, "The Convention is an agreement accepted by most countries in the world after a great deal of discussion and hard work. The British representatives are surely quite right to be most reluctant to do anything which might weaken an agreement which controls the production and distribution of opium and other dangerous drugs." One might easily imagine what would be the situation today in the United States if no such international treaties existed. Indeed, all of the plants from which the derivatives of opium, coca leaves, and *Cannabis* are manufactured do grow outside of the United States. Since there is a strong demand for such drugs, they still are penetrating the country in significant amounts, in spite of international controls. Should these controls be removed, real flooding could occur. Today, a decade after the Geneva Single Convention, many other substances besides opium, coca leaves, and *Cannabis* derivatives are abused in the world, while the older intoxicants are still widely used. Should this be a sufficient reason to abandon all efforts at international controls—on the basis that they just don't work very effectively?

Just because efforts to control and prevent drug abuse have not been successful, should they be abandoned? Should we curtail our attempts to fight against war and pollution or atomic proliferation or any other global threat to man's survival just because we have been unable so far to achieve success in all these areas? What is the alternative, "liberalization" of the law in order to make drugs more freely available?

A tolerant policy to drug use was tried in Sweden when amphetamine toxicomania swept that country a decade ago. Stupefying drugs were made readily available by medical prescription (Bejerot, 1970). A chaotic situation resulted. After a few years, when thousands of drug addicts had been arrested for criminal behavior, strict control had to be instituted and enforced.

In any event, the licensing of marihuana sale in the United States is contrary to the spirit and the letter of all of the treaties signed by this country over the past 50 years for the control of stupefying drugs.

A Long-Range View

There are many apparently insurmountable obstacles in Western countries to a comprehensive plan to control and eliminate the use of *Cannabis* and other psychotropic drugs leading to toxicomania. Just to mention a few: the individual's right to choose and experiment; social unrest; pressure groups and lobbies; social ennui and disenchantment; political interests; commercial influences and the profit motive. The causes of drug use are so numerous—and how does one get to all of them!

William the Silent, confronted with the rebuilding of his country ruined by years of war, had just this to say: "One need not hope to undertake nor courage to persevere." But he had the faith which gave him a perspective and allowed him to look beyond the ruins.

With such sobering remarks in mind, an overall view of the problem of toxicomania may be better achieved if one tries to encompass more than a decade, more than one generation, more than one local drug subculture. In this perspective, one cannot ignore the fact that a worldwide trend emerged at the turn of the century toward control and elimination of the use of drugs which impede human development. This trend was strong enough to rally the allegiance of the sovereign nations of the world, which have pledged for the past 60 years to cooperate in the task of international drug control. Some have derided these attempts as the futile exercises of "moral entrepreneurs" who seek self-aggrandizement by trying to legislate morality and curtail basic freedoms. But the history of the international regulation of *Cannabis* and other dangerous drugs, in spite of all of its setbacks and shortcomings, is by no means a failure and deserves more than the casual treatment it has so far received from too many intellectuals. The control and elimination of mind-altering drugs represents a challenging goal in itself, which the United States was the first to champion. Theodore Roosevelt was one of the initiators of the Shanghai Conference of 1909, which preceded the First Opium Conference at the Hague in 1912. Many other American statesmen have followed the path on which he began.

Regardless of which road their successors take today, the general trend begun at the turn of the century to eliminate or control the use of stupefying drugs should not be profoundly altered. This trend has already gained too much momentum to be stopped. It might just be slowed down, and its ultimate goal delayed. For international drug control is based on a simple and sound premise, namely, that man's growth toward maturity and freedom, anywhere in the world, is impeded by mind-altering drugs, and that such drugs should be used only by physicians to relieve symptomatic ailments.

The orderly and continued development of a number of very powerful political systems which have emerged in the past 60 years require from their people life styles which are drug free. These systems, especially those in the East, have gained great political and economic power and their influence is more and more felt throughout the world. One should therefore expect that the efforts to achieve the control of stupefying drugs, including *Cannabis,* will continue in the years ahead in some of the most powerful and dynamic countries of the world, with or without America. And it is hard to envision how a drug-consuming, pleasure-oriented society will be able to face the challenge which these countries have thrust upon the Western world.

SUMMARY

1. *Cannabis* intoxication prevails in the world under two completely different sets of social circumstances:

A. Endemically in poor agrarian societies (Middle East, India, Jamaica) or amidst an impoverished proletariat to escape from the daily dreariness of a marginal existence. *Cannabis* is the most available drug and is preferentially used; it is the opium of the poor. These societies are stagnant.

B. Epidemically amidst the educated affluent youth who are disenchanted by the offerings of a technological society and who seek instant pleasure. *Cannabis* is one of the many drugs which are used legally or illegally.

2. All available evidence indicates that regular *Cannabis* consumption is

associated with multiple drug use, including opiate derivatives (when these are available).

3. When under the influence of the drug the chronic users present a significant decrease in their productivity, efficiency and dependability.

4. There are today two diametrically opposed attitudes in the world toward *Cannabis* use. The first, supported by the World Health Organization and the United Nations, considers *Cannabis* to be a stupefying drug, harmful to man and society. As a result, *Cannabis* must fall under national and international legislation aimed at eliminating its usage. The second attitude, assumed in England and the United States during the past decade, claims that *Cannabis* is a mild intoxicant which should be made freely available to anyone who wishes to enjoy it.

5. The licensing of marihuana sale, as increasingly advocated in the United States, can only increase this major cleavage between the nations of the world. One fails to see how such a measure will . . .

—remove the social malaise which has befallen American society
—orient members of society away from the unhealthy habit of drug taking.

6. It is doubtful that this American example, if it came to pass, would be followed by the countries which have challenged the perenniality of American democracy.

REFERENCES

Andrews, G., and Vinkenoog, S. (eds.) (1967). *The Book of Grass—An Anthology of Indian Hemp.* Grove Press, New York.

Ball, J. C., Chambers, C. D., and Ball, M. J. (1968). The association of marihuana smoking with opiate addiction in the United States. *J. Crim. Law Criminol. Pol. Sci.,* 59:171–182.

Becker, H. (1963). *Outsiders: Studies in the Sociology of Deviance.* The Macmillan Company, New York.

Bejerot, N. (1970). *Addiction and Society.* Charles C. Thomas, Springfield, Ill.

Benson, V. M. (1971). Marihuana study, Critique. *J. Amer. Med. Ass.,* 217:1391.

Bewley, T. H. (1966). Recent changes in the pattern of drug abuse in the United Kingdom. *Bull. Narcotics,* 18:1.

Bey, D. R., and Zecchinelli, V. A. (1971). Marijuana as a coping device in Vietnam. *Milit. Med.,* 136:448–450.

Black, S., Owens, K., and Wolff, R. P. (1970). Patterns of drug use: A study of 5,482 subjects. *Amer. J. Psychiat.,* 127:420–423.

Blum, R. H. (1969). *Students and Drugs.* Jossey-Bass, Inc., San Francisco.

Bogg, R., Smith, R., and Russell, S. (1968). *Drugs and Michigan High School Students.* Final report of a study conducted for the Special Committee on Narcotics, Michigan Legislature.

Bonnie, R. J., and Whitebread, C. H. (1971). Laws and morals. *Science,* 172:703–705.

Bouquet, J. R. (1951). Cannabis, Part III–V. *Bull. Narcotics,* 3:22–43.

Brooks, A. D. (1969). Marijuana and the Constitution: Individual liberties and puritan virtues. In *Drugs and Youth,* J. R. Wittenborn, H. Brill, J. P. Smith, and S. A. Wittenborn (eds.). Charles C. Thomas, Springfield, Ill., pp. 280–298.

Cameron, D. C. (1969). Drug dependence and the law: A medical view. In *Drugs and Youth,* J. R. Wittenborn, H. Brill, J. P. Smith, and S. A. Wittenborn (eds.). Charles C. Thomas, Springfield, Ill., pp. 219–228.

Canadian Commission of Inquiry into the Non-Medical Use of Drugs (1970). G. LeDain, Chairman. Queen's Printer for Canada, Ottawa.

Carlin, A. S., and Post, R. D. (1971). Patterns of drug use among marihuana smokers. *J. Amer. Med. Ass.,* 218:867–868.

Carstairs, G. M. (1954). Daru and bhang: Cultural factors in choice of intoxicant. *Quart. J. Studies Alcohol,* 15:220–237.

Chapple, P. A. (1966). *Cannabis*—A toxic and dangerous substance—a study of eight takers. *Brit. J. Addictions,* 61:269–282.

Christozov, C. (1965). L'aspect marocain de l'intoxication cannabique d'áprès des études sur des malades mentaux chroniques: 1ere partie et 2eme partie. *Maroc. Med.,* 44:630–642, 866–899.

Churchill, W. (1956). *History of the English Speaking Peoples.* Dodd Publishing, London.

Colbach, E. (1971). Marijuana use by GIs in Vietnam. *Amer. J. Psychiat.,* 128:96–99.

Crancer, A. (1969). Marihuana and simulated driving. *Science,* 166:640.

Crompton, E., and Brill, N. Q. (1970). The marihuana problem. *Ann. Intern. Med.,* 78:449–465.

Crompton, E., and Brill, N. Q. (1971). Personality factors associated with frequency of marihuana use. *Calif. Med.,* 115:11–15.

de Felice, P. (1936). *Poisons Sucres, Ivresses Divines.* Editions Albin Michel, Paris.

Deniker, P. (1971). Personal Communication.

Deniker, P., and Ginestet, B. (1969). Pharmacologie humaine de l'usage incontrole des drogues psychodysleptiques. *Laval Med.,* 40:25–36.

Doorenbos, N. J., Fetterman, P. S., Quimby, M. W., and Turner, C. E. (1971). Cultivation, extraction and analysis of *Cannabis sativa* L. *Ann. N.Y. Acad. Sci.,* 191:3–14.

Elinson, J. (1970). *A Study of Teen-age Drug Behavior* (N.I.M.H. grant 17589. Columbia University, New York.

El-Maghrabi, Saad (1962). *Zaherat taati el-haschisch* (*Phénomène de consommation du haschisch*). Daar-El-Maaref, Cairo.

Farnsworth, D. L. (1970). Drug dependence among physicians. *N. Eng. J. Med.,* 282:392–393.

F.D.A. Announcement (1971). Clinical studies with marihuana and tetra-hydrocannabinol currently being allowed by the Food and Drug Administration. *Clin. Pharmacol. Therap.,* 12:1019.

Francis, J. B., and Patch, D. J. (1969). *Student Attitudes Toward Drug Programs of the University of Michigan.* University Committee on Drug Education, Ann Arbor, Mich.

Freedman, I., and Peer, I. (1968). Drug addiction among pimps and prostitutes in Israel. *Int. J. Addictions,* 3:271–300.

Gautier, T. (1846). Le club des hachischins. In: *La Revue des Deux Mondes.* Paris.

Glatt, M. M. (1969). Is it all right to smoke pot? *Brit. J. Addictions,* 64:109–114.

Goldstein, J. (1970). *The Social Psychology of Student Drug Use.* Dept. of Psychology, Carnegie-Mellon University, Pittsburgh, Pa.

Goode, E. (1970). *The Marihuana Smokers.* Basic Books, New York.

Goodman, L. S., and Gilman, A. (1965). *The Pharmacological Basis of Therapeutics.* The Macmillan Company, New York, p. 44.

Governor's Citizens Advisory Committee on Drugs (1969). Drug use among high school students in the state of Utah. In *Advisory Committee Report on Drug Abuse.* State Capitol Building, Salt Lake City, Utah.

Greenwald, L. (1968). Marihuana goes to college. *The Sciences,* 7:137–146.

Grinspoon, L. (1971). *Marihuana Reconsidered.* Harvard University Press, Cambridge, Mass.

Grosse Point [Michigan] Public School System (1970). *PSC Communicator,* Jan. 13.

H.E.W. Report to Congress (1971). *Marihuana and Health.* U.S. Government Printing Office, Washington, D.C.

Heykal, M. (1972). Conversations with Gamal Abdel Nasser.

Hochman, J. S., and Brill, N. Q. (1971). Chronic marihuana usage and liver function. *Lancet,* 2:818–819.

Hollister, L. E., Richards, R. K., and Gillespie, H. K. (1969). Comparison of tetrahydrocannabinol and synhexyl in man. *Clin. Pharmacol. Therap.,* 9:783–791.

Hospital Tribune Report (1971a): Use of peyotyl in Indian rite believed safe. *Hospital Tribune,* July 12.

Hospital Tribune Report (1971b): 15% of young Americans have smoked marijuana. *Hospital Tribune,* October 18.

Huxley, A. (1946). *Brave New World.* Harper and Row, New York.

Idanpaan-Heikkila, P., and Schoolar, J. C. (1971). Characteristics in a young drug user turning from hallucinogen usage to heroin. *Scand. J. Clin. Lab. Invest.,* 27:80.

Indian Hemp Drug Commission (1969). *Report on Marihuana of the Indian Hemp Drug Commission, 1893–1894.* Thomas Jefferson Publishing Company, Silver Springs, Md.

Isbell, H., and Chrusciel, T. L. (1970). *Dependence Liability of "Non-Narcotic Drugs.* World Health Organization, Geneva.

Isbell, H., Gorodetsky, G. W., Jasinski, D., Claussen, U., Spulak, F., and Korte, F. (1967). Effects of (−) delta-9-*trans*tetrahydrocannabinol in man. *Psychopharmacologia,* 11:184–188.

Joachimoglu, G. (1965). Natural and smoked hashish. In *Hashish: Its Chemistry and Pharmacology,* G. E. W. Wolstenholme and J. Knight (eds.). Little, Brown and Company, Boston.

Kaplan, H. S. (1971). Psychoses associated with marijuana. *N.Y. State J. Med.,* 71:433–435.

Kaplan, J. (1971). *Marihuana—The New Prohibition.* World Press, New York.

Kaplan, J. H. (1971). Marihuana and drug abuse in Vietnam. *Ann. N.Y. Acad. Sci.,* 191:261–269.

Kolansky, H., and Moore, W. T. (1968). Marihuana and society. *J. Amer. Med. Ass.,* 204:1181–1182.

Kolansky, H., and Moore, W. T. (1971). Effects of marihuana on adolescent and young adults. *J. Amer. Med. Ass.,* 216:486–492.

Lambo, T. A. (1965). The use of cannabis in Nigeria. *Bull. Narcotics,* 17:3–13.

Leary, T. (1966). The politics, ethics and meaning of marihuana. In *The Marihuana Papers,* D. Solomon (ed.). The Bobbs-Merrill Co., Inc., Indianapolis, Ind.

Leonard, B. E. (1969). Cannabis, a short review of its effects and the possible dangers of its use. *Brit. J. Addictions,* 64:121–130.

Lesse, S. (1971). Surprise doctor! Pot is here to stay! Where were you when the grass was cut? *Amer. J. Psychother.,* 25:1–3.

Levy, M. R. (1971). Drug abuse education: A pedagogical schizophrenia. *Amer. J. Pharm.,* 143:51–57.

Liebert, R. S. (1967). Symptoms, disease or adolescent experimentation. *J. Amer. Coll. Health Ass.,* 16:25.

Lindesmith, A. R. (1965). *The Addict and the Law.* Indiana University Press, Bloomington, Indiana.

Lindesmith, A. R. (1969). Assessment of the current situation by a sociologist. In *Drugs and Youth,* J. R. Wittenborn, H. Brill, J. P. Smith, and S. A. Wittenborn (eds.). Charles C. Thomas, Springfield, Ill., pp. 320–331.

Lipp, M. R., Benson, S. G., and Taintor, Z. (1971). Marijuana use by medical students. *Amer. J. Psychiat.,* 128:99–104.

Luff, K. (1972). *Personal communication.*

Mabileau, M. (1970). *Ivresse Chimique et Crise de Civilisation.* Sandoz Symposium, Paris.

McGlothin, W. G., and West, L. J. (1968). The marihuana problem: An overview. *Amer. J. Psychiat.,* 125:126–134.

McKenzie, J. D. (1970). *Trends in Marihuana Use Among Undergraduate Students at the University of Maryland.* Research Report No. 3, University of Maryland, College Park.

Manheimer, D. I., Mellinger, G. B., and Balter, M. B. (1969). Marihuana use among urban adults. *Science,* 166:1544–1545.

Manheimer, D. I., Mellinger, G. B., and Balter, M. B. (1970). Use of marihuana in an urban cross-section of adults. In *Communication and Drug Use,* J. R. Wittenborn, J. P. Smith and S. A. Wittenborn (eds.). Charles C. Thomas, Springfield, Ill.

Marshman, J. A., and Gibbons, R. J. (1969). The credibility gap in the illicit drug market. *Addiction,* 16:4.

Mauss, Armand L. (1969). Anticipatory socialization toward college as a factor in adolescent marihuana use. *Soc. Probl.,* 16:357–364.

Mello, N. K. (1972). The effect of alcohol on short-term memory in rhesus monkey. *Psychopharmacologia,* 8:20–22.

Mikuriya, T. H. (1969). Marihuana in medicine, past, present and future. *Calif. Med.,* 110:34–40.

Mill, J. S. (1957). On liberty. In *Philosophic Problems: An Introductory Book of Readings,* M. Mandelbaum, F. W. Gramlich, and A. R. Anderson (eds.). The Macmillan Company, New York.

Miras, C. J. (1969). Experience with chronic hashish smokers. In *Drugs and Youth,* J. R. Wittenborn, H. Brill, J. P. Smith, and S. A. Wittenborn, (eds.). Charles C. Thomas, Springfield, Ill., pp. 191–198.

Mirin, S. M., Shapiro, L. M., and Meyer, R. E. (1971). Casual versus heavy use of marijuana: A redefinition of the marijuana problem. *Amer. J. Psychiat.,* 127:1134–1140.

Mizner, G. L., Barter, J. T., and Werme, P. H. (1970). Patterns of drug use among college students: A preliminary report. *Amer. J. Psychiat.,* 127:15–24.

Montesquieu, C. L. (1955). The Spirit of Laws, G. D. H. Cole (trans.). *Encyclopedia Brittanica.*

Montgomery County Joint Advisory Committee on Drug Abuse (1969). *Final Report,* vol. 2, Montgomery Co. Public Schools, Rockville, Md.

Moreau, J. J. (1845). *Du Hachish et de l'Alienation Mentale: Etudes Psychologiques 34.* Libraire de Fortin, Masson, Paris (English edition: Raven Press, New York, 1972).

Multi-Lingual List of Narcotic Drugs Under International Control (1968). United Nations, New York.

Murphy, H. B. M. (1963). The cannabis habit—A review of recent psychiatric literature. *Bull. Narcotics,* 15:15–23.

Newsweek Staff (1969). Report of a national college student survey. *Newsweek Magazine,* Dec. 29.

Olds, J., and Milner, P. (1954). Positive reinforcement produced by electrical stimulation of septal area and other regions of rat brain. *J. Comp. Physiol. Psychol.,* 47:419.

Olivenstein, J. (1970). Aspects actuels de l'ivresse chimique. In *Ivresse Chimique et Crise de Civilisation.* Laboratoires Sandoz, Rueil, France, pp. 13–27.

Orwell, G. (1949). *1984.* Harcourt Brace Jovanovich, Inc., New York.

Paton, W. D. M. (1968). Drug dependence—A socio-pharmacological assessment. *Advancement of Science,* December:200–212.

Pescor, M. J. (1943). A statistical analysis of the clinical records of hospitalized drug addicts. *Supplement to Public Health Reports,* No. 143.

Pillard, R. C. (1970). Marihuana. *New Eng. J. Med.,* 283:294–303.

Pillard, R. C. (1971). Book review: *Marihuana Reconsidered* by L. Grinspoon. *New Eng. J. Med.,* 285:416–417.

Pohl, F. (1970). *What Shall We Do Til the Analyst Comes?* Walker & Company, New York.

Pohl, F., and Kornbluth, C. M. (1969). *Space Merchants.* Walker & Company, New York.

Polanyi, M. (1958). *Personal Knowledge.* University of Chicago Press, Chicago, p. 309.

Proceedings of the White House Conference on Narcotics and Drug Abuse (1962). U.S. Government Printing Office, Washington, D.C.

Rabelais (1944). *The Five Books of Gargantua and Pantagruel,* Jacques LeClerq (transl.). The Modern Library, Random House, New York. Book 11, Chap. 8, p. 194.

Robbins, E. S., Robbins, L., and Frosch, W. A. (1970). College student drug use. *Amer. J. Psychiat.,* 126:1743.

Robins, L. N., Darvish, H. S., and Murphy, G. E. (1970). The long term outcome for adolescent drug users: A follow-up study of 76 users and 146 non-users. In *Psychopathology and Adolescence,* J. Zubin (ed.). Grune & Stratton, New York.

Robins, L., and Murphy, G. (1967). Drug use in a normal population of young Negro men. *Amer. J. Public Health,* 57:1580–1596.

Romitscher, J. (1969). The right of society to protect its members. In *Drugs and Youth,* J. R. Wittenborn, H. Brill, J. P. Smith, and S. A. Wittenborn (eds.). Charles C. Thomas, Springfield, Ill., pp. 229–306.

Roffman, R. A., and Sapol, E. (1969). Marihuana in Vietnam. *J. Amer. Pharm. Ass.,* 9:615–618.

Rubin, V., and Comitas, L. (1972). Effects of chronic smoking of *Cannabis* in Jamaica. Research Institute for the Study of Man, New York, and the Center for Studies of Narcotic and Drug Abuse, National Institute of Mental Health, Contract No. HSM–42–70–97.

Sami-Ali (1971). *Le Haschisch en Egypte.* Payot, Paris.

San Mateo Dept. of Public Health and Welfare (1969). *The Use of Alcoholic Beverages, Amphetamines, LSD, Marihuana and Tobacco Reported by High School and Junior High School Students.* Research and Statistics Section, San Mateo, Calif.

Schofield, M. (1971). *The Strange Case of Pot.* Penguin Books, Middlesex, England.

Schweitzer, A. (1916). *Out of My Life and Thoughts.* The Macmillan Company, New York.

Seevers, M. H. (1970). Drug dependence and drug abuse, A world problem. *Pharmacologist,* 12:172–181.

Silberman, P., and Levy, J. (1969). A preliminary survey of 24 Victorian marihuana users. *Med. J. Aust.,* 2:286–289.

Smart, R. G., and Fejer, D. (1971). Recent trends in illicit drug use among adolescents. *Can. Ment. Health,* 68:1–13.

Smith, D. (1968). Acute and chronic toxicity of marihuana. *J. Psychedelic Drugs,* 2:37–47.

Snyder, S. H. (1971). *Uses of Marijuana.* Oxford University Press, New York.

Solomon, D. (ed.) (1966). *The Marihuana Papers.* The Bobbs-Merrill Co., Inc., Indianapolis, Ind.

Solursh, L. P., Weinstock, S. J., Saunders, C. S., and Ungerleider, J. T. (1971). Attitudes of medical students toward cannabis. *J. Amer. Med. Ass.,* 217:1371–1372.

Soueif, M. (1967). Hashish consumption in Egypt with special reference to psychosocial aspects. *Bull. Narcotics,* 19:1–12.

Soueif, M. I. (1971). The use of cannabis in Egypt: A behavioural study. *Bull. Narcotics,* 33:17–28.

Speck, Ross V. (1970). *Psychosocial Networks on Young Drug Users* (N.I.M.H. grant 14943). Hahnemann Medical College, Philadelphia, Pa.

Staff Report (1971). Harvard's dropouts attributed largely to mental illness. *World Med. News,* 5:11.

Study of Life Styles and Campus Communities (1970). Department of Social Relations, Johns Hopkins University, Baltimore, Md.

Suchman, Edward A. (1968). The "hang loose" ethic and the spirit of drug use. *J. Health Soc. Behav.,* 9:146–154.

Talbott, J., and Teague, J. (1969a). Marihuana psychosis. *J. Amer. Med. Ass.,* 210:299–303.

Talbott, J., and Teague, J. (1969b). *Time Magazine,* 26:78.

Teste, M. (1972). *Personal Communication.*

Tinklenberg, J. R. (1972). Marihuana and alcohol. *Psychopharm. Bull.,* 8:9–10.

Tobin, R. L. (1972). The Puritan ethic today. *Saturday Review,* Jan. 1.

Tocqueville, Alexis de (1843). *Democracy in America,* H. Reeve (transl.). Langley Press, New York.

Udell, Jon G., and Smith, R. S. (1969). *Attitudes, Usages and Availability of Drugs Among Madison High School Students.* University of Wisconsin, Bureau of Business Research and Service, Madison, Wisc.

United Nations Conference for the Adoption of a Single Convention on Narcotic Drugs (1961). Vols. I and II. United Nations, New York.

Vaillant, G. E., Brighton, J. R., and McArthur, C. (1970). Physicians' use of mood altering drugs. *N. Eng. J. Med.,* 282:365–370.

Weil, A. T., Zinberg, N. E., and Nelsen, J. M. (1968). Clinical and psychological effects of marihuana in man. *Science,* 162:1234–1242.

West, L. (1970). General discussion. In *Psychotomimetic Drugs,* D. Efron (ed.). Raven Press, New York.

W.H.O. Expert Committee on Addiction-Producing Drugs (1964). *Thirteenth Report.* World Health Organization Technical Report Series No. 273. Geneva.

W.H.O. Expert Committee on Drug Dependence (1970). *Seventeenth Report.* World Health Organization Technical Report Series No. 437. Geneva.

W.H.O. Scientific Group (1971). *The Use of Cannabis.* World Health Organization Technical Report Series No. 478. Geneva.

Williams, E. G., Himmelsbach, C. K., and Wikler, A. (1946). Studies of marihuana and pyrahexyl compounds. *Public Health Reports,* 61:1059–1083.

Wilson, C. (1969). Cannabis and alcohol: Is there a scientific basis for comparison? In *Scientific Basis of Drug Dependence,* H. Steinber (ed.). J. A. Churchill, London.

Wilson, C., and Linken, A. (1968). *The Use of Cannabis in Adolescent Drug Dependence.* Pergamon Press, Oxford.

Wolff, P. O. (1949). *Marihuana in Latin America, The Threat It Constitutes.* Linacre Press, Greens Farms, Conn.

Ziwar, M. (1963). La consommation du hachisch en tant que problème psychologique. Publication of the National Center of Social and Criminal Research, Cairo.

Ziwar, M., Soueif, M., and Kheyri, S. (1960–1964). *La Consommation du Hachisch,* Vols. I and II. Publication of the National Center of Social and Criminal Research, Cairo.

8

General Summary and Conclusion

The derivatives of *Cannabis sativa* (Marihuana Hashish) owe their intoxicating properties to a psychoactive substance, delta-9-THC. The concentration of this toxic in different parts of the plant and different preparations varies from 0.2 to 6%. Concentration of preparations used until now in the United States varies from 0 to 1%. This explains the wide variety of effects which have been reported.

Delta-9-THC is insoluble in water, has a very high fat solubility, and is irregularly absorbed by the gut. It induces enzymes in lung and liver and is converted into active and inactive metabolites. These metabolites persist in the plasma for more than 3 days and require 8 days to be eliminated from the body. Administration of *Cannabis* derivatives at less than 1-week intervals results in the accumulation of its metabolites in tissues and body fluids. It produces ambivalent action in the central nervous system, with stimulatory sensory effects combined or followed by depressant ones. It interferes with other centrally acting drugs such as amphetamines, ethanol, and barbiturates. It does not present any pharmacological property which could justify its use as a therapeutic agent more effective than any presently in use. Delta-9-THC is three to four times more active when smoked than when ingested. Increased heart rate, which is dose related, is the most consistent physical symptom observed during *Cannabis* intoxication. Delta-9-THC in doses of 15 mg smoked or 40 mg ingested can produce hallucinations and a psychotic-like episode. Such a dose is within the range which may be consumed by occasional *Cannabis* users. *Cannabis* extracts containing 5 to 10 mg of delta-9-THC smoked or 15 to 25 mg ingested significantly impair motor and mental performance. With similar dosages panic reactions and acute toxic psychoses, especially in unfavorable settings, do occur, infrequently but also unpredictably. But euphoria usually predominates over dysphoria, and the pleasant feelings experienced by the users tend to create a positive reinforcement. *Cannabis* use can also precipitate an underlying psychosis. Prolonged daily use of *Cannabis* preparations (1 to 5% of delta-9-THC) is associated with mental and physical deterioration. *Cannabis* intoxication may have most serious adverse effects in adolescents (13 to 18 years old) who are attempting to structure their personalities while their vulnerable brains are in the process of integration.

The first widely publicized studies claimed that smoked marihuana containing 5 to 66 mg of delta-9-THC was a mild "intoxicant." It appears that these studies were performed with extracted material containing, in reality, subthreshold amounts of delta-9-THC. *Cannabis* effects depend upon amount of delta-9-THC, frequency of administration, individual characteristics, psychological conditioning, use of other common drugs (amphetamines, alcohol), environmental factors, and development of tolerance. A marked tolerance develops to the physiological and psychological effects of delta-9-THC, requiring increased dosage to obtain the desired effects. As a result of this tolerance, frequent (daily) users of *Cannabis* may require larger doses or may be led to use more potent hallucinogens (LSD, mescaline) or opiate derivatives. Frequent users of *Cannabis* extracts in the United States are multiple drug users; although they do not develop the physical dependence identifiable by a specific withdrawal symptom, they present a psychological dependence on the drug.

In the countries of endemic *Cannabis* intoxication the widespread use of this drug by the working class is associated with inefficiency and social stagnation. These countries, where *Cannabis* has been used for centuries and which are afflicted with underdevelopment in all areas, are exerting today concerted efforts to ban the use of the drug through national and international legislation fully endorsed by the U.N. Division on Drug Dependence and by the World Health Organization. Repeal of present legislation, and unilateral abrogation by the United States of the international convention which outlaws the use of this compound, lacks medical and social justification. The "legalization" of the use of *Cannabis* would further compound the major drug abuse problem which presently besets American society. This does not preclude the introduction in the United States of more humane legislation for the control of *Cannabis* abuse.

It is deceptive to consider marihuana intoxication as a youthful fad, similar to many which have occurred in the past. Marihuana intoxication among the affluent youth of today is part of the pandemic toxicomania which has developed in the second half of this century in the Western world dominated by Anglo-Saxon technology.

Drug taking is symptomatic of the dissatisfaction and the craving for fulfillment of disillusioned youth seeking new values. Such fulfillment cannot be found in any lasting way through any type of intoxication. To make marihuana, or any other hallucinogenic drug, available will in no way solve the social malaise which has beset the youth of America and its Western allies.

One may also wonder how long a political system can endure when drug taking becomes one of the prerequisites of happiness. If the American dream has lost its attraction, it will not be retrieved through the use of stupefying drugs. Their use only delays the young in their quest to understand the world they now live in and their desire to foster a better world for tomorrow.

Selected Bibliography

BOOKS

Bejerot, N. (1970). *Addiction and Society*. Charles C. Thomas, Springfield, Ill.

de Felice, P. (1936). *Poisons Sacrés, Ivresses Divines*. Editions Albin Michel, Paris.

Joyce, C. R. B., and Curry, S. H. (1970). *The Botany and Chemistry of Cannabis*. J. & A. Churchill, London.

Kaplan, J. (1971). *Marihuana—The New Prohibition,* World Publishing Company, New York.

Marihuana: Chemistry, Pharmacology and Patterns of Social Use (1971). Ann. N.Y. Acad. Sci., Vol. 191, pp. 1–269.

Marihuana and Its Surrogates (1971). Pharmacological Reviews, Vol. 23, pp. 263–389.

Moreau, J. J. (1845). *Du Hachish et de l'Alienation Mentale, Etudes Psychologiques 34*. Libraire de Fortin, Masson, Paris (English edition: Raven Press, New York, 1972).

Wilson, C. W. M. (1968). *Adolescent Drug Dependence*. Pergamon Press, Oxford.

Wittenborn, J. R., Brill, H., Smith, J. P., and Wittenborn, S. A. (1969). *Drugs and Youth*. Charles C. Thomas, Springfield, Ill.

PAPERS

Agurell, S. (1970). Chemical and pharmacological studies of cannabis. In *The Botany and Chemistry of Cannabis,* C. R. B. Joyce and S. H. Curry (eds.). J. & A. Churchill, London, pp. 175–191.

Asuni, T. (1964). Socio-psychiatric problems of *Cannabis* in Nigeria. *Bull. Narcotics,* 16:17–28.

Ball, J. C., Chambers, C. D., and Ball, M. J. (1968). The association of marihuana smoking with opiate addiction in the United States. *J. Crim. Law Criminol. Pol. Sci.,* 59:171–182.

Boyd, E. S., Boyd, E. H., Muchmore, J. S., and Brown, L. E. (1971). Effects of two tetrahydrocannabinols and of pentobarbital on cortico-cortical evoked responses in the squirrel monkey. *J. Pharmacol. Exp. Ther.,* 176:480–488.

Cameron, D. C. (1969). Drug dependence and the law: A medical view. In *Drugs and Youth,* J. R. Wittenborn, H. Brill, J. P. Smith, and S. A. Wittenborn (eds.). Charles C. Thomas, Springfield, Ill., pp. 219–228.

Campbell, A. M. G., Evans, M., Thompson, J. L. G., and Williams, M. J. (1971). Cerebral atrophy in young *Cannabis* smokers. *Lancet,* 7736:1219–1224.

Carlin, A. S., and Post, R. D. (1971). Patterns of drug use among marihuana smokers. *J. Amer. Med. Ass.,* 218:867–868.

Carlini, E. A. (1968). Tolerance to chronic administration of *Cannabis sativa* (marihuana) in rats. *Pharmacology,* 1:135–142.

Carstairs, G. M. (1954). Daru and bhang: Cultural factors in choice of intoxicant. *Quart. J. Studies Alcohol,* 15:220–237.

Chopra, G. S. (1969). Man and marihuana. *Int. J. Addictions,* 4:215–247.

Chopra, G. S. (1971). Marihuana and adverse psychotic reactions. *Bull. Narcotics,* 28:15–22.

Christozov, C. (1965). L'aspect marocian de l'intoxication cannabique d'après des études sur des malades mentaux chroniques: 1ere partie et 2eme partie. *Maroc. Med.,* 44:630–642; 866–899.

Clark, L. D., Hughes, R., and Nakashima, E. N. (1970). Behavioral effects of marihuana: Experimental studies. *Arch. Gen. Psychiat. (Chicago),* 23:193–198.

Colbach, E. (1971). Marijuana use by GI's in Viet Nam. *Amer. J. Psychiat.,* 128:96–99.

DeFarias, C. (1955). Use of maconha (*Cannabis sativa* L.) in Brazil. *Bull. Narcotics,* 7:5–19.

Delay, J. (1965). Psychotropic drugs and experimental psychiatry. *Int. J. Neuropsychiat.,* 1:104–117.

Dhunjibhoy, J. E. (1930). A brief résumé of the types of insanity commonly met with in India with a full description of "Indian hemp insanity" peculiar to the country. *J. Ment. Sci.,* 76:254–264.

Doorenbos, N. J., Fetterman, P. S., Quimby, M. W., and Turner, C. E.

(1971). Cultivation, extraction and analysis of *Cannabis sativa* L. *Ann. N.Y. Acad. Sci.,* 191:3–15.

Dornbush, R. L., Fink, M., and Freedman, A. M. (1971). Marijuana, memory and perception. *Amer. J. Psychiat.,* 128:194–197.

Ferraro, D. P., Grilly, D. M., and Lynch, W. C. (1971). Effects of marihuana extract on the operant behavior of chimpanzees. *Psychopharmacologia,* 22:333–351.

Foltz, R. L., Fentiman, A. F., Jr., Leighty, E. G., Walter, J. L., Drewes, H. R., Schwartz, W. E., Page, T. F., Jr., and Truitt, E. B., Jr. (1970). Metabolite of (−)-*trans*-Δ⁸-tetrahydrocannabinol: Identification and synthesis. *Science,* 168:844–845.

Forney, R. B., (1971). Toxicology of marihuana. *Pharmacol. Rev.,* 23:279–284.

Frankenheim, J., McMillan, D., and Harris, L. (1971). Effects of 1-Δ⁹- and 1-Δ⁸-*trans*-tetrahydrocannabinol on schedule-controlled behavior of pigeons and rats. *J. Pharmacol. Exp. Ther.,* 178:241–252.

Freedman, I., and Peer, I., (1968). Drug addiction among pimps and prostitutes in Israel. *Int. J. Addictions,* 3:271–300.

Gourves, J., Viallard, C., LeLuan, D., Girard, J. P., and Aury, R. (1971). Case of coma due to *Cannabis sativa. Presse Med.,* 79:1389.

Halikas, J. A., Goodwin, D. W., and Guze, S. B. (1971). Marihuana effects, A survey of regular users. *J. Amer. Med. Ass.,* 217:692–694.

Haney, A., and Bazzaz, F. A. (1970). Some ecological implications of the distribution of hemp (*Cannabis sativa* L.) in the United States of America. In *The Botany and Chemistry of Cannabis,* C. R. B. Joyce and S. H. Curry (eds.). J. & A. Churchill, London, pp. 38–48.

Hardman, H. F., Domino, E. F., and Seevers, M. H. (1971). General pharmacological actions of some synthetic tetrahydrocannabinol derivatives. *Pharmacol. Rev.,* 23:295–315.

Harris, L. S. (1971). General and behavioral pharmacology of Δ⁹-THC. *Pharmacol. Rev.,* 23:285–294.

Hollister, L. E. (1970). Tetrahydrocannabinol isomers and homologues: Contrasted effects of smoking. *Nature,* 227:968–969.

Hollister, L. E. (1971a). Marihuana in man: Three years later. *Science,* 172:21–24.

Hollister, L. E. (1971b). Action of various marihuana derivatives. *Pharmacol. Rev.,* 23:349–358.

Isbell, H., Gorodetsky, G. W., Jasinski, D., Claussen, U., Spulak, F., and Korte, F. (1967). Effects of (−) delta-9-*trans*tetrahydrocannabinol in man. *Psychopharmacologia,* 11:184–188.

Isbell, H., and Jasinski, D. (1969). A comparison of LSD-25 with (−)

delta-9-*trans*tetrahydrocannabinol (THC) and attempted cross tolerance between LSD and THC. *Psychopharmacologia,* 14:115–123.

Jones, R. T. (1971). Marihuana-induced "high": Influence of expectation, setting and previous drug experience. *Pharmacol. Rev.,* 23:359–370.

Kaplan, H. S. (1971). Psychosis associated with marijuana. *N.Y. State J. Med.,* 71:433–435.

Kaplan, J. H. (1971). Marihuana and drug abuse in Vietnam. Ann. N.Y. Acad. Sci., 191:261–269.

Keeler, M. H., Ewing, J. A., and Rouse, B. A. (1971). Hallucinogenic effects of marijuana as currently used. *Amer. J. Psychiat.,* 128:105–108.

Keup, W. (1970). Psychotic symptoms due to *Cannabis* abuse. *Dis. Nerv. Syst.,* 31:119–126.

Klausner, H. A., and Dingell, J. V. (1971). The metabolism and excretion of Δ^9-tetrahydrocannabinol in the rat. *Life Sci., Pt. I,* 10:49–59.

Kolansky, H., and Moore, W. T. (1971). Effects of marihuana on adolescents and young adults. *J. Amer. Med. Ass.,* 216:486–492.

Kornhaber, A. (1971). Marihuana in an adolescent psychiatric outpatient population. *J. Amer. Med. Ass.,* 215:1000.

Kubena, R. K., and Barry, H., III. (1970). Interactions of delta-9-tetrahydrocannabinol with barbiturates and methamphetamine. *J. Pharm. Exp. Ther.,* 173:94–100.

Lambo, T A. (1965). Medical and social problems of drug addiction in West Africa. *Bull. Narcotics,* 17:3–14.

Lemberger, L., Axelrod, J., and Kopin, I. J. (1971). Metabolism and disposition of delta-9-tetrahydrocannabinol in man. *Pharmacol. Rev.,* 23:371–380.

McIsaac, W. M., Fritchie, G. W., Idanpaan-Heikkila, J. E., Ho, B. T., and Englert, L. F. (1971). Distribution of marihuana in monkey brain and concomitant behavioral effects. *Nature,* 230:593–594.

McMillan, D. E., Dewey, W. L., and Harris, L. S. (1971). Characteristics of tetrahydrocannabinol tolerance. *Ann. N.Y. Acad. Sci.,* 191:83–99.

Magus, R. D., and Harris, L. S. (1971). Carcinogenic potential of marihuana smoke condensate. *Fed. Proc.,* 30:279.

Mann, P. E., Cohen, A. B., Finley, T. N., and Ladman, A. J. (1971). Alveolar macrophages. Structural and functional differences between nonsmokers and smokers of marijuana and tobacco. *Lab. Invest.,* 25:111–120.

Manning, F. J., McDonough, J. A., Jr., et al. (1971). Inhibition of normal growth by chronic administration of delta-9-THC. *Science,* 74:424–426.

Manno, J. E., Kiplinger, G. F,, Haine, S. E., Bennett, I. F., and Forney, R. B. (1970). Comparative effects of smoking marihuana or placebo on human motor and mental performance. *Clin. Pharmacol. Ther.,* 11:808–815.

Manno, J. E., Kiplinger, G. F., Scholtz, N., and Forney, R. B. (1971). The influence of alcohol and marihuana on motor and mental performance. *Clin. Pharmacol. Ther.,* 12:202–211.

Mechoulam, R., Shani, A., Edery, H., and Grunfeld, Y. (1970). Chemical basis of hashish activity. *Science,* 169:611–612.

Melges, F. T., Tinkelberg, J. R., Hollister, L. E., and Gillespie, H. K. (1970). Marihuana and temporal disintegration. *Science,* 168:1118–1120.

Miras, C. J. (1969). Experience with chronic hashish smokers. In *Drugs and Youth,* J. R. Wittenborn, H. Brill, J. P. Smith, and S. A. Wittenborn (eds.) Charles C. Thomas, Springfield, Ill., pp. 191–198.

Mirin, S. M., Shapiro, L. M., Meyer, R. E., Pillard, R. C., and Fisher, S. (1971). Casual vs. heavy use of marihuana, a redefinition of the marihuana problem. *Amer. J. Psychiat.,* 127:1134–1140.

Nahas, G. G. (1972). *Cannabis sativa,* the deceptive weed. *N.Y. State J. Med.* 72:856–868.

Nakazawa, K., and Costa, E. (1971). Metabolism of D9 tetrahydrocannabinol by lung and liver homogenates of rats treated with methylcholanthrene. *Nature,* 234:48–49.

Petrzilka, T. (1970). Synthesis of (−)-tetrahydrocannabinol and analogous compounds. In *The Botany and Chemistry of Cannabis,* C. R. B. Joyce and S. H. Curry (eds.). J. & A. Churchill, London, pp. 79–92.

Podolsky, S., Pattavina, C. G., and Amaral, M. A. (1971). Effect of marihuana on glucose tolerance test. *Ann. N.Y. Acad. Sci.,* 191:54–60.

Renault, P. F., Schuster, C. R., Heinrich, R., and Freeman, D. X. (1971). Marihuana: Standardized smoke administration and dose effect curves on heart rate in humans. *Science,* 174:589–591.

Rolland, J. L., and Teste, M. (1957). Le cannabisme au Maroc. *Maroc. Med.,* 387:694–703.

Scher, J. M. (1970). The marihuana habit. *J. Amer. Med. Ass.,* 214:1120.

Schultes, R. E. (1970). Random thoughts and queries on the botany of *Cannabis.* In *The Botany and Chemistry of Cannabis,* C. R. B. Joyce and S. H. Curry (eds.). J. & A. Churchill, London, pp. 11–38.

Seevers, M. H. (1970). Drug dependence and drug abuse, A world problem. *Pharmacologist,* 12:172–181.

Solursh, L. P., Weinstock, S. J., Saunders, C. S., and Ungerleider, J. T. (1971). Attitudes of medical students toward cannabis. *J. Amer. Med. Ass.,* 217:1371–1372.

Soueif, M. I. (1967). Hashish consumption in Egypt with special reference to psychological aspects. *Bull. Narcotics,* 19:1–12.

Soueif, M. I. (1971). The use of *Cannabis* in Egypt: A behavioural study. *Bull. Narcotics,* 33:17–28.

Stearn, W. T. (1970). The *Cannabis* plant: Botanical characteristics. In *The Botany and Chemistry of Cannabis,* C. R. B. Joyce and S. H. Curry (eds.). J. & A. Churchill, London, pp. 1–10.

Talbott, J., and Teague, J. (1969). Marihuana psychosis. *J. Amer. Med. Ass.,* 210:299–303.

Tennant, F. S., Jr., Preble, M., Prendergast, T. J., and Ventry, P. (1971). Medical manifestations associated with hashish. *J. Amer. Med. Ass.,* 216:1965–1969.

United Nations Conference for the Adoption of a Single Convention on Narcotic Drugs (1961). Vols. I and II. United Nations, New York.

W.H.O. Scientific Group (1971). *The Use of Cannabis.* World Health Organization Technical Report Series No. 478. Geneva.

Williams, E. G., Himmelsbach, C. K., Wikler, A., Ruble, D. C., and Lloyd, B. J., Jr. (1946). Studies on marihuana and pyrahexl compound. *Public Health Rep.,* 61:1059–1083.

Index

327